Sociological studies

Statement of sponsorship

The Jean Piaget Society (USA) and the Fondation Archives Jean Piaget (Geneva) encourage translations of important works not yet translated, support translations of inadequately translated texts, foster consistent translations of technical terms and provide translators with expert consultation. Their goal is to promote easier access to and better understanding of ideas in both French- and English-speaking worlds. This translation of Jean Piaget's *Sociological studies* reflects the efforts of these scholarly organizations.

Sociological studies

Jean Piaget

Edited by Leslie Smith

*Translated by Terrance Brown, Robert Campbell,
Nick Emler, Michel Ferrari, Michael Gribetz,
Richard Kitchener, Wolfe Mays, Angela Notari,
Carol Sherrard and Leslie Smith*

London and New York

First published as *Études sociologiques* in 1965
by Librairie Droz, Switzerland

First published in English 1995
by Routledge
11 New Fetter Lane, London EC4P 4EE

Simultaneously published in the USA and Canada
by Routledge
29 West 35th Street, New York, NY 10001

© 1965, 1977 Librairie Droz
Editorial selection and introduction © 1995 Leslie Smith
English language translation © 1995 Terrance Brown, Robert Campbell, Nick Emler,
Michel Ferrari, Michael Gribetz, Richard Kitchener, Wolfe Mays, Angela Notari, Carol
Sherrard and Leslie Smith

The right of the translation team to be identified as the translators of this work has been
asserted in accordance with the Copyright, Designs and Patents Act 1988.

The right of Leslie Smith to be identified as the author of the Introduction to this work has
been asserted in accordance with the Copyright, Designs and Patents Act 1988.

Typeset in Times by Solidus (Bristol) Limited
Printed and bound in Great Britain by
Mackays of Chatham PLC, Chatham, Kent

British Library Cataloguing in Publication Data
A catalogue record for this book is available from the British Library

Library of Congress Cataloguing in Publication Data
A catalogue record for this book has been requested

ISBN 0–415–10780–6

Contents

Notes on the source publication

Chapters 1–4 and the Preface were published in the first edition of *Études sociologiques* (Geneva: Droz, 1965) with chapters 5–9 appearing in the second edition (1977). The original publication details shown below correspond to those given in *Bibliographie Jean Piaget* (Geneva, 1989).

Original publication
Preface   Preface to the first edition
            Études sociologiques. Geneva: Droz, 1965.
            Preface to the second edition
            Études sociologiques. Geneva: Droz, 1977.
Chapter 1   Explanation in sociology
            Introduction à l'épistémologie génétique. vol. 3. Paris: Presses Universitaires de France, 1950.
Chapter 2   Essay on the theory of qualitative values in static sociology
            Études économiques et sociales. Genève: Georg, pp. 100–142, 1941. Publication à l'occasion du XXV anniversaire de la fondation de la Faculté des sciences économiques et sociales de l'Université de Genève, 1941.
Chapter 3   Logical operations and social life
            Mélange d'études économiques et sociales offerts à Edouard Folliet et Liebermann Hersch. Genève: Georg, pp. 143–171, 1945.
Chapter 4   The relationship between morality and law
            Mélanges d'études économiques et sociales offerts à William E Rappard. Genève: Georg, pp. 19–54, 1944.
Chapter 5   Genetic logic and sociology
            Revue philosophique de la France et de l'Etranger, vol. 105, no. 1–2, 168–205, 1928.
Chapter 6   Individuality in history: the individual and the education of reason
            L'individualité. Troisième semaine internationale de synthèse, Centre international de synthèse. Exposés par M. Caullery, *et al.* Paris: Alcan, pp. 67–121, 1933.

Notes on the translators

Terrance Brown, Chicago, USA.

Robert Campbell, Department of Psychology, Clemson University, Clemson, SC 29634-1511, USA

Nick Emler, Department of Experimental Psychology, Oxford University, Oxford, OX1 3UD, GB.

Michel Ferrari, Department of Psychology, Yale University, New Haven, Connecticut, 06520-8205, USA.

Michael Gribetz, Chicago, USA.

Richard Kitchener, Department of Philosophy, Colorado State University, Fort Collins, CO 80523, USA.

Wolfe Mays, Institute of Advanced Studies, Manchester Metropolitan University, Manchester, M15 6BH, GB.

Angela Notari, Experimental Education Unit, University of Washington, Seattle, Washington, 98195, USA.

Carol Sherrard, Department of Psychology, University of Leeds, Leeds, LS2 9JT, GB.

Leslie Smith, Department of Educational Research, Lancaster University, Lancaster, LA1 4YL, GB.

Acknowledgements

My sincere thanks to Silvia Parrat-Dayan and Anastasia Tryphon (both at the Fondation Archives Jean Piaget, Geneva) for their valuable advice, especially with regard to references, textual omissions and obscure French constructions, and to Jenny Hills (Lancaster University Library) for her welcome help in compiling the References. My thanks also to Richard Kitchener and Wolfe Mays for their commentary on an earlier draft of the Introduction, to which neither is of course committed.

Leslie Smith
May 1994

Introduction to the translation

Leslie Smith

The primary aim of this translation has been to preserve for the English reader Piaget's original ideas. This is no easy task since these ideas are distinctive and their multiple demands on the French reader are substantially increased for the English reader, as Piaget noticed in an early allusion to these difficulties: 'I wrote my first books for readers of the French language without foreseeing the possibility of translation. Moreover I did not over-state what is familiar in French psychology and in consequence I would have spoken quite differently in English contexts' (Piaget, 1931, p. 146). But conservation is essential to translation and *Sociological studies* aspires to present an accurate version of Piaget's original text.

The translation has been collaborative throughout. A three-step procedure was followed for each of the nine chapters as well as the Preface. The first step was for each chapter to be individually translated as follows:

Preface: Leslie Smith
Chapter 1: Carol Sherrard
Chapter 2: Wolfe Mays
Chapter 3: Terrance Brown and Michael Gribetz
Chapter 4: Robert Campbell
Chapter 5: Richard Kitchener
Chapter 6: Michel Ferrari
Chapter 7: Angela Notari
Chapter 8: Nick Emler
Chapter 9: Terrance Brown

The second step was for each draft to be checked for accuracy and consistency by Leslie Smith who commented on the whole text making suggested amendments for a jointly agreed translation and notes. Wolfe Mays assumed this same role for the Preface. The third step was a repetition of the two previous steps whereby the revised version was checked again, leading to the final and mutually agreed version.

The translation uses masculine nouns, pronouns and adjectives where it is evident from the text that children and adults of both sexes are to be understood (though see the Translation Notes to Chapter 7). The central issue concerns knowledge of universals. Such knowledge is accessible to all people. It is in this traditional and well-understood sense that masculine expressions are used in *Sociological studies*.

The French text has been supplemented in several ways for this English translation:

- where errors and omissions have been found in the French text, they have been corrected on the basis of the text found in Piaget's original papers.
- the original pagination has been included to indicate the start of a new page of the French text, for example [p. 7].
- *Bibliographie Jean Piaget* (Fondation Archives Jean Piaget, Geneva, 1989) has been used to identify the source references of the original publication of Piaget's papers which comprise the nine chapters of *Sociological studies*.
- Piaget makes frequent mention of authors in the absence of supporting references. An attempt has been made to remedy this omission in the References which indicate possible texts that Piaget had in mind. These references were typically provided by Leslie Smith (with the help already noted of Silvia Parrat-Dayan, Anastasia Tryphon and Jenny Hills).
- author's footnotes are all due to Piaget and are shown in square brackets, for example [1].
- translation and editorial notes have also been included to supplement the French text and appear as unbracketed superscript numbers, for example[2]. Leslie Smith provided many – though not all – of these notes except for many of those in Chapter 2, due to Wolfe Mays, in Chapter 4, due to Robert Campbell, and in Chapter 5, due to Richard Kitchener.

Introduction to Piaget's
Sociological studies[1]

When we ask someone what the number one is ... we shall very likely be invited to select something for ourselves – anything we please – to call one. Yet if everyone had the right to understand by this name whatever he pleased, then the same proposition about one would mean different things for different people – such propositions would have no common content.

G. Frege (1888)

Eadem sunt quorum unum alteri substitui potest salva veritate.
(Those concepts are identical if either can be substituted for the other without change in truth-value.)

G. W. Leibniz, in Ishiguro (1972)

Sociological studies is a collection of nine papers written by Jean Piaget during the period 1928–1960 and published together in a French edition (Piaget, 1977). Although there are commentaries (Chapman, 1986; Kitchener, 1981; Mays, 1982; Smith, 1982; Moessinger, 1978, 1991) on some of these papers, none has been translated into English, nor subject to systematic interpretation and evaluation.

The central question addressed by Piaget in *Sociological studies* appears at the beginning of Chapter 5: how does a rational mind attain truth? The apparent simplicity of this question masks fundamental complexity. Piaget's question concerns the developmental mechanism which makes possible both the acquisition of available knowledge and the creation of novel knowledge. It thus presupposes that there are laws of truth which govern the operation of this developmental mechanism. Now there is an obvious answer to this question. Children are born into a social world where communication occurs between people through their joint use of language based on familiar social practices. The adults of any one generation are thus in a position to share their understanding of truth, contextualized in terms of accepted social practices, so as to allow children in the next generation to acquire this antecedently available understanding. But this answer will not do at all. First, it is circular and presupposes that children already understand both what truth is and how it differs from falsity. Not all adult beliefs are true (compare the account of biological creation in Genesis and Darwin's account: are they both true, or is only one of them true, or are they both false?), nor do all social practices lead to truth (television advertising and children's birthday parties: does each of these contribute directly to knowledge, or does only one of them, or do neither?). Second, acceptance and acceptability are treated as equivalent in this answer. But if common acceptance was equivalent to rational accept-ability, the formation of new beliefs which are incompatible with accepted beliefs could not take place. Children in the next generation would have beliefs which were clone-copies of the beliefs shared by adults of the previous generation. Novel beliefs due to critical rejection of currently available beliefs could not be formed at all. Third, thought and action can be in conformity with the truth in the absence of an understanding of truth. Animals can display complex behaviour patterns which are in conformity with the truth, as when one bee correctly locates a source of food on the basis of the dance-language of another bee. Children can be taught to think and act in conformity with the truth, as when pre-schoolers on a seesaw interact in a manner fully compatible with Newtonian mechanics. But behavioural conformity is not rational understanding. Thus Piaget's question poses a major problem since adults evidently do understand how truth differs from falsity. At the beginning of the film *Goodfellas*, there appear the words 'This film is based on a true story'. At the beginning of Beatrix Potter's *The tale of Peter Rabbit*, there appear the words 'Once upon a time there were four little rabbits and their names were Flopsy, Mopsy, Cotton-tail and Peter'. How is it that, from our earliest years, we are in a position to draw the distinction between truth and falsity?

Truth bears upon what reality is like and so upon our knowledge of reality. Yet false belief has also to be reckoned with. Although minds are full of multiple beliefs, not all beliefs are true. There is a human propensity for distorting subjectivity on the basis of which reality is assimilated to individually held or socially shared beliefs, whereas all such beliefs should as well be accommodated to reality (p. 45). Wishful thinking, the allure of fantasy, fertile imagination and conviction expressed in terms of personally meaningful symbols are pervasive mental phenomena. But they are not rational thinking. Social orthodoxy, the rigid conformity of closed societies, ideological fervour and the power of tradition are familiar social phenomena. But none provide a guarantee of truth. Piaget's question, then, concerns how the developing mind comes to understand that some available beliefs are true rather than false, how one generation comes to replace false values by true values. Quite simply, how does anyone escape from the confines of an available single point of view by the development of a reciprocally available system which is open to any possible point of view (p. 71)?

Some philosophers have argued that questions about the laws of truth are not empirical questions at all. This position has its basis in the premise that psycho-social processes can result in error and is used as an argument against psychologism. Even though 'to discover truths is the task of all sciences' (Frege, 1956, p. 18), an account of logical laws which is exclusively, or even partially psychological, could not remove the possibility of error and so could not – in principle – provide the laws of truth. If Frege's view is accepted, psycho-social processes would have no place at all in an answer to Piaget's question. Piaget readily accepts that psychologism (the laws of truth are psycho-social) is inadequate. But he also rejects Frege's logicism (the laws of truth are logical, and not psychological at all). It is in this sense that his position is a *tertium quid* (Smith, 1993, §7). Piaget addresses the question of how psychological and logical factors are inter-related in the development of *true concepts* (p. 238), *true obligations* (p. 177), and *true rules* (p. 303). Although the initial transmission of all concepts is psycho-social, their rational legitimation requires the intervention of logical factors as well. A special case of this problem is the development of necessary knowledge – 'the transition from action to conscious necessity' (p. 53) – in that necessary knowledge is true throughout time, but has a temporal origin in the human mind (Piaget, 1950, p. 23; Smith, 1993, p. 1). Such fundamental concepts as *truth* and *necessity* are essential for the development of culturally specific concepts, and indeed for human communication to occur successfully at all. Thus, Piaget addresses questions about the inter-relations of the individual, society and rational knowledge. These questions concern whether the logic of human rationality is individual or social, how the transmission of available knowledge from one generation to the next makes possible the growth of new knowledge, and how children acquire systems of thinking which preserve the constitutive features of the systems used by their parents, teachers and peers.

The strategy adopted by Piaget has both a negative and positive element. The negative element is to identify two distinct, but parallel, factors that preclude the mechanical transmission of a rational understanding of truth. One set of factors lies in the human mind. According to Freud (1922), there is an affective unconscious with considerable potency over mind and behaviour. Piaget set out to show that there is an intellectual unconscious which has a comparable but distorting effect. Piaget styled this factor egocentrism. The second set of factors lies in society. According to sociologists such as Marx (1867/1970) and Pareto (1923/1963), human society is marked by the admixture of reason and sentiment, by the corruption of true values by false values. Piaget set out to show that there are social forces which lead to the rigidity of human knowledge rather than human creativity. Piaget styled this factor sociocentrism. The two factors work together to constrain the growth of rational understanding. The positive element of Piaget's strategy is to identify some of the conditions which would have to be satisfied by any account of the development of rationality. His claim is that these conditions bear upon the mutuality of human communication and whether the partners in an exchange of ideas have the capacity to act as equals in a reasoned exchange of views, including rational disagreement and the construction of novelty. This strategy can now be elaborated in more detail.

Piaget accepts as a given that human experience is, and has to be, both psychological and social. Recognition of their joint importance is apparent in the first paragraph of the first chapter of his first book (Piaget, 1923/1959) in that children have needs. Central to Piaget's concern is the specific question of whether some of children's needs are rational, whether they base what they say and think on reasons, rules, and values which are truth-preserving. Yet not all needs are completely, or even ever, rational. Do needs have their basis in the affective psyche (Freud, 1922) or are needs intellectual by virtue of their correspondence with the laws of thought (Boole, 1854/1958)? Do human needs have their origin in the collectives of human society in as much as if the Kantian categories of 'time, space, class, cause, or personality are constructed out of social elements ... their social origin rather leads to the belief that they are not without foundation in the nature of things' (Durkheim, 1915, p. 19)? Or are human needs a mixture of sentiment and rationalization?:

> the demand for logic is satisfied by pseudo-logic as well as by rigorous logic. At bottom what people want is to think – it matters little whether the thinking be sound or fallacious. We need only reflect on the tangle-wood of fantastic discussion that has flourished and still flourishes ... to gain some conception of the imperiousness of the need that is satisfied by such lucubrations.
>
> (Pareto, 1963, §972)

Indeed, Marx (1867/1970) pointed out with some vigour that some false values, manifest as the fetishism of commodities, are more prevalent in human societies than real values. So although human intelligence always has a psycho-social basis, that is not in itself adequate to ensure the growth of rational intelligence which is deductive and based on proof rather than on personal preference and false beliefs (cf. Piaget, 1923/1959, p. 47). It is Piaget's claim that a common barrier precludes the mechanical replacement of behavioural mastery (in infancy) or practices and techniques (in society) by rational operations of the mind or by science. This barrier is partly psychological (symbolic thinking due to fertile imagination) and partly social (orthodoxy and ideology). Their conspiracy can be especially acute in education: it is, of course, a delusion to regard everything that a parent or teacher says as true (p. 289). The problem is that neither rational operations nor science ever appear in completely pure forms since they are instead always mixed together with symbolic thinking and ideology. So much is clear from Piaget's early statement that children differ from adults comparatively rather than absolutely: adult thinking is merely less liable to be egocentric than children's thinking (Piaget, 1923/1959, p. 38). An analogous claim applies to social beliefs and practices: the rational acceptance of the Pythagorean theorem in a school mathematics class is patently different from an induction into one of the dogmas of the Hitler Youth (pp. 25, 243). Well, it is patently different to anyone who understands the difference between proof and conviction. But how is the difference drawn by anyone whose early experience is exclusively based on conviction rather than proof? The principle which underlies the example has universal applicability for all developing individuals in all societies. It is for this reason that differentiation is central to development aimed at conservation (truth-preservation) and novelty.

A similar interest was evident in Piaget's subsequent texts, which included the claim that 'the social need to share the thought of others and to communicate our own and to convince is at the basis of our need for verification. Proof is born through discussion' (Piaget, 1924/1928, p. 204; my amended translation) or the claim that 'logic is a morality of thought, just as morality is a logic of action' (Piaget, 1932/1932, p. 404). Furthermore, Piaget continued to make the explicit claim that psycho-social experience is a *sine qua non* of intellectual development (Piaget, 1947/1950; 1969/1970). The issue is not whether children have psycho-social experience, because of course they do, but is rather about the respects in which such experience is rationally successful. It is Piaget's main aim in *Sociological studies* to address this problem by formulating some of the success-conditions of social experience as a contributory aspect of rationality.

Prior to the identification of Piaget's specific proposals, it is well known that criticism has been directed during the last decade at the adequacy of Piaget's general position which has been taken to be incomplete, and even inadequate, in its treatment of the social basis of the formation of knowledge. Typically, this social criticism of Piaget's position has not been based on *Sociological studies*. It will, therefore, be instructive to review some of the salient instances of these criticisms to see how they fare. After all, Piaget's work is a social phenomenon and is well known in the public domain. We need to check the extent to which Piaget's general position stands up to collective scrutiny.

THE SOCIAL CRITIQUE OF PIAGET'S ACCOUNT

The criticism that insufficient attention has been given in Piaget's account to the social aspects of children's experience was well expressed by his contemporaries. Lev Vygotsky died in 1934, and so his well-known (Vygotsky, 1978; 1986), and more recently translated (Vygotsky, 1994), papers are exclusively restricted to commentary on Piaget's first two books, originally published in the 1920s. A comparable preoccupation with Piaget's first quartet of books is evident in the work of Susan Isaacs (1930). Note that Piaget explicitly responded to both of these critics (Piaget, 1962 and 1931 respectively), denying that his position was vulnerable to these early criticisms (for a review, see Parrat-Dayan, 1993, a, b). Note also that Piaget (1952) was himself critical of what he took to be deficiencies in his early studies and so there is an expectation that *Sociological studies* will be sensitive to the issues raised in this early social critique (see Montangero and Maurice-Naville, 1994 for a general guide to Piagetian constructs.)

In recent times, several versions of this social criticism have been widely stated. Four such criticisms are now reviewed, including:

1   The solitary knower in a physical world.
2   Empirical under-determination of social experience.
3   Flawed epistemic norms.
4   Available alternatives to Piagetian theory.

This is a formidable list of criticisms. First, they include criticisms on both empirical and rational grounds. Second, these criticisms apply to central features of Piaget's account, namely that its phenomena are too narrowly conceived, that it is empirically under-elaborated, and that its interpretation is flawed. Third, these criticisms are comprehensive since Piaget's account of intellectual development – and not merely Piaget's account of the social basis of intellectual development – is taken to be inadequate. In fact, each of the previous criticisms is open to direct reply using positions taken from *Sociological studies*. Showing that these criticisms do not arise is important on two counts. First, the criticisms are stringent and so their presence can impair, and even destroy, the intelligibility of Piaget's account. Second, these criticisms apply to all accounts of intellectual development which make intra-individualistic commitments (Case, 1991; Demetriou *et al.*, 1992; Karmiloff-Smith, 1992), so their appraisal has a general relevance to contemporary accounts.

1. The solitary knower in a physical world

> Too often, human learning has been depicted in the paradigm of a lone organism pitted against nature . . . in the Piagetian model where a lone child struggles single-handed to strike some equilibrium between assimilating the world to himself or himself to the world.
>
> (Bruner, 1985, p. 25)

The criticism is that Piaget's commitment to some version of Cartesian individualism has resulted in radical omission, marked by exclusion of the social, and thus inter-subjective and societal, aspects of intellectual development. The related criticism is that Piaget's commitment has resulted in an exclusion of the social, and thus contextual and cultural, aspects of intellectual development. This commitment is evident in the concern with physico-mathematical concepts rather than with psycho-social concepts. The charge is that Piaget is committed to the assumption of the solitary knower in the physical world.

This charge has to face the fact that Piaget's stated position is completely different. Social experience is stated to be necessary – but not sufficient – for intellectual development; social experience is stated to be present and potent from the cradle to the grave (p. 278). And social adaptation is stated to be as important as other any other form of adaptation, including physical adaptation (pp. 185, 217, 240). Many examples are provided in Piaget's text: rules of eating, dress and hygiene imparted to infants by adults; school education and intellectual growth; cultural tradition and the conforming tendencies in gerontocratic societies; the mystical beliefs of primitive societies and contemporary ideology; the clash of theories in the search for scientific truth. It is Piaget's explicit claim that the individual and society *per se* are severally and jointly insufficient in the formation of rationality (pp. 143, 227).

But this last claim goes to the heart of the matter: an individual can only know what is true. That is, a rational consciousness is concerned to search for truth, where truth is in principle open to all members of a society even though it is not to be identified with social conformity within that society. Neither consensus nor conviction are guarantors of truth which is in all cases accessible to all. This is an important distinction, which has been well known since Plato (nd/1935). In no way does Piaget state or imply that an individual alone in a physical world can acquire true knowledge. Rather, his question is about the inter-relation between social and individual contributions in the search for true knowledge, which is accepted autonomously and which assumes multiple and indefinite forms due to its expansion in novel creation. Adapting Piaget's Hitlerian allusion (p. 25), there is all the difference in the world between an ideological conviction such as 'Ein Volk, ein Reich, Ein Führer' and von Neumann's (Korner, 1969) proof that '1 + 1 = 2'. Further, to see this difference as merely a social difference, or as an individual difference, is to miss the point about one of the intrinsic features of knowledge. Piaget's aim is not to ignore the social basis of knowledge but rather to focus on the acquisition of knowledge with due attention to its rational legitimation. Piaget commended the Kantian element in his work and, by implication, the Kantian claim (see Korner, 1969) that human communication and rational agreement strictly depend on the use of knowledge of universals which provide the epistemological architecture of the mind.

2. Empirical under-determination of social experience

This criticism states that although Piaget paid some attention to social and contextual factors, such attention is too general and insufficiently specific. In any case, such factors are bypassed in Piaget's empirical studies. This is shown by the practice adopted in typical studies in which children are individually interviewed about their understanding of physico-mathematical concepts. In consequence, the social and contextual aspects of human understanding are largely ignored since there is inadequate mapping from specific claims about internalized intellectual processes to social context and conversely (Doise and Mugny, 1984; Donaldson, 1992; Edwards and Mercer, 1986; Light and Butterworth, 1992; Perret-Clermont, 1988). This criticism leads to two replies, one specific and the other general.

The specific reply is that evidence is reported by Piaget about children's thinking about the social world. *Sociological studies* includes one empirical study (see Chapter 7) concerning children's ideas about the homeland and foreign relationships. Further, there are anticipations of this study in early studies (Piaget, 1924/1928, chapter 3, section 6; 1945/1951, Obs. 108). Moreover, Piaget (1954/1980) has explicitly contrasted affective and social relationships, on the one hand, and intellectual relationships, on the other, stating that the former reflect the latter but not conversely. The findings offered in Chapter 7 are confirmatory. At one pole were the Swiss children who denied, and justified their denial, that anyone could be both Genevan and Swiss, despite accepting, and justifying their belief, that Geneva is in Switzerland. They regarded these alternatives as exclusive, even though their own drawings revealed them to be inclusive. A similar response was evident about affective issues: Denise liked Switzerland because it has pretty houses and mountain chalets. Herbert thought that Americans are stupid because they do not know where the rue du Mont-Blanc is in central Geneva. At the other pole are children whose responses were based on rational considerations: of course you can be both Swiss and Genevan since one includes the other; Switzerland is admirable because it is a free country; there are similarities and differences between people in all countries. Obviously, one study is not enough and the range of social phenomena is vast. Even so, it does make the point that social experience has been investigated in Piagetian studies where it is claimed that children's affective thinking parallels, and is an epiphenomenon in relation to, their logical thinking. Cosmopolitan experience in an international city such as Geneva counts for nothing if children display irrationality in their thinking about their own social experience.

There is also a general reply to the assumption behind the second criticism, namely that empirical evidence relevant to social phenomena must be evidence about social phenomena. But this assumption raises the question as to exactly what counts as a social phenomenon. Adapting the argument stated by Piaget about 'intellectual mutations' (p. 37), the creation of new knowledge on the part of an intellectual giant can be standardly acquired by school children. Note in this regard the comment made by Einstein that Western science is underpinned by the twin achievements of logical thinking and methodology: 'the development of Western science has been based on [these] two great achievements .... In my opinion one need not be astonished that the Chinese sages did not make these steps. The astonishing thing is that these discoveries were made at all' (in Wolpert, 1992, p. 48). Science is an integral part of culture and tracking the course of 'intellectual mutations' as they occur in children's re-discovery of logic and scientific method is a legitimate form of social investigation. Thus it could be said that all of the phenomena investigated in Piaget's empirical studies are social phenomena, even if the converse is not true. Logical thinking and experimental methodology are central to contemporary physics (Gleick, 1992, p. 333) as much as they are to naturalistic studies of conservation (*nota bene* the social practice which is central to the procedure outlined in Bon's protocol by Piaget and Szeminska, 1941/1952, p. 43) and of problems in school physics (Inhelder and Piaget, 1955/1958).

3. Flawed epistemic norms

This criticism states that social elements are constitutive features of knowledge, which is viewed individualistically in Piaget's account. The grounds on which it is based may vary and include Vygotskian (Cole and Cole, 1989) and Wittgensteinian arguments (Harré, 1986). A clear formulation of this criticism is that

> the acquisition of knowledge, however, is in effect the initiation into a body of knowledge that others either share or might in principle share .... The concepts of knowledge, truth and objectivity are social in the sense that they imply a framework of agreement on what counts as known, true and objective ... (and Piaget's biological model) must prove inadequate for the task in hand.
>
> (Hamlyn, 1978; see also Hamlyn, 1982; Haroutunian, 1983)

The criticism is that some of the constitutive elements of epistemic concepts are social and that Piaget's account could not accommodate them. Yet this is not so. Piaget explicitly commits himself to the very position on which this criticism rests in the first paragraph of Chapter 1 (p. 30). Evidently Piaget's own position states that social elements are indeed essential to the formation of knowledge, whether pre-scientific or scientific and, as such, are constitutive or defining elements of the growth of knowledge. In short, the position outlined in the criticism is actually embodied in Piaget's own position, which predates the putative criticism of his work.

The argument which underpins Piaget's position has two separable, but inter-dependent, components. One component is psycho-social: what is the contribution of experience to the initial origins of knowledge? The other component is epistemological: how does experience contribute to the legitimation of knowledge by making it rationally successful? In Piaget's (1950) genetic epistemology – that is, cognitive science with an explicitly developmental focus (Campbell and Bickhard, 1986; Inhelder and Cellérier, 1992; Kitchener, 1986; Leiser and Gillièron, 1990) – both questions are taken to be empirical and to require joint consideration in an account which is neither reducible to empirical psychology alone (for the former question) nor to philosophical epistemology alone (for the second question). Thus in Piaget's view, genetic epistemology is a *tertium quid* (see Smith, 1993, §7). It is a strict requirement of this position that rationally acceptable knowledge is knowledge which is, in principle, open to all individuals due to a common mode of construction. Agreement is rational not because it is generally accepted and marked by consensus in some collective group but because it is valid in relation to universally accessible norms which are accepted even in cases of disagreement as to their application to specific cases.

4. Available alternatives to Piagetian theory

The final criticism is that alternatives to Piaget's theory are to hand. A notable alternative is afforded in the work of Vygotsky which stands in need of worthwhile elaboration. This is indeed so. Yet Vygotsky's work is as suggestive as it is under-elaborated, leading to differential interpretation and application (Adey and Shayer, 1994; Brown *et al.*, 1983; Cole and Cole, 1989; Daniels, 1993; Light and Butterworth, 1992; Newman *et al.*, 1989; van der Veer and Valsiner, 1991; Wertsch, 1985). Consider, for example, an oft-quoted claim that 'every function in the child's cultural development appears twice: first, on the social level and, later, on the individual level .... All the higher functions originate as actual relations between human individuals' (Vygotsky, 1934/1978, p. 57). This insightful claim does not stand alone in Vygotsky's writings since two related claims must also be reckoned with. One is the additional claim about 'the unity, but not the identity, of higher and lower psychological functions' (Vygotsky, 1994, p. 163). In a shared activity, a child may contribute to a successful outcome with an adult (functional unity) but not through their use of the same abilities and understanding (functional non-identity). This is because Vygotsky makes developmental commitments in that 'one and the same event occurring at different ages of the child is reflected in his consciousness in a completely different manner and has an entirely different meaning for the child' (Vygotsky, 1994, p. 344). If there is unity in functioning, this is a suggestive and interesting claim. But if there is non-identity in functioning, there is a clear difference which merits attention and interpretation. Children may successfully contribute to a shared practice without possessing an adult's understanding. This non-identity is not important if the sole concern is to ensure that the practice is successful (for example, in visiting a supermarket to do the family shopping). But it is important if there is a concern to ensure the independence of each member of the family (for example, when a child carries out alone the same family shopping). There is also a second claim. This is a qualification relevant to the process by which inter-individual functioning becomes intra-individual functioning. This process is characterized as internalization by Vygotsky – who then honestly declares that although internalization is 'socially rooted ... as yet, the barest outline of this process is known' (Vygotsky, 1934/1978, p. 57). This admission is clear: Vygotsky denies that his account is explanatory of one of its own central processes. In short, Vygotsky's work is suggestive but it does stand in need of interpretation.

Alternative theories are as welcome as they are necessary. Piaget's own commitment to the joint use of multiple theories in the evaluation of his own work was regularly stated up to 1987 (quoted in Smith, 1992, pp. 423–424) and evident in the re-analysis of his own studies (cf. Piaget, 1924/1928, chapter 3 with Piaget *et al.*, 1990/1992, chapter 9). Effectively, this means that the global comparison of a Vygotskian perspective with a Piagetian perspective has much less to offer than the comparative scrutiny of their specific positions.

But there are at least two respects in which Piaget's account is an advance over that of Vygotsky. One advance is that Piaget's account does address the question as to when social experience is successful. A central feature of social experience is human communication leading to an exchange of thought. Yet not all communication is successful. In consequence, criteria are necessary to identify the minimum conditions which must be satisfied for attempted, or intended, communication actually to succeed. But, first, it was previously noted that Vygotsky does not in the passage already cited above offer a criterion as to when an exchange of thought leads to successful internalization. Second, Piaget does state conditions which have to be satisfied for an exchange of thought to occur. These conditions are elaborated in more detail in the next section.

The second advance of Piaget's work over that of Vygotsky is that it does squarely address the 'learning paradox' (Bereiter, 1985) in that, according to constructivism, better knowledge is a development from available knowledge inferior to it. Note that Vygotskian theories make constructivist commitments. Even so, avoidance of the 'learning paradox', rather than its resolution, is the strategy which follows from a Vygotskian position. To see why, consider the argument used by Newman *et al.* (1989, p. 66), who remind us that new knowledge can always be introduced at the social level by the more advanced individual – in their example, by the experimenter! But this is inadequate since it pushes the problem one step back: just how did the experimenter gain that novel knowledge in the first place? Isaac Newton said that he achieved so much because he stood on the shoulders of giants. True enough; but it is not an accident that 'Newton's theory' is called thus rather than 'the theory due to the contribution of giants'. Note here the telling claim made by Gleick (1992, p. 130; my emphasis) about how Richard Feynman, in the oral examination for his doctorate, replied to a question based on an accepted textbook theory: 'Feynman saw that this was a trick. He replied that the textbook *must* be wrong.... So he worked the problem out for himself', inventing a novel solution as an improvement over an available solution. There are two points here. One is Feynman's own challenge of socially accepted belief, manifest in textbooks. The other is that his challenge has a modal character: the textbook is not merely wrong, but must be so. Even though all knowledge has its origins in a social world (for example, in a publicly available textbook), novelty and originality may still be due to one individual mind (for example, because of rational thinking). The interpretation offered by Newman *et al.* does not account for genuinely novel knowledge due to the genius. Nor for that matter does that position account for the legion of cases of reconstruction where human minds simply reinvent the wheel, or fail to match reality, whether physical, social or abstract, in the generation of novel intellectual creations which are idiosyncratic and even wrong.

Piaget's work does at least address this issue squarely. An educational advance or even a modest exchange of thought require individuals to think initially in terms of the culturally transmitted values, rules, concepts and signs at their disposal and then to re-think them using their own intellectual resources (pp. 76, 138). It is this point which is central to Piaget's *Sociological studies*. What now follows is a review of some of the specific features of Piaget's account.

SOCIAL PERSPECTIVE IN PIAGET'S ACCOUNT

There are several overlapping themes which run through *Sociological studies*, including the following:

1   Action as the unit of analysis.
2   Problems of the match.
3   Intellectual autonomy.
4   Developmental levels in the knowledge of universals.
5   Exchange model.
6   Normative intervention.

1. Action as the unit of analysis

The unit of analysis used by Piaget is neither representation (as in cognitive science) nor practice (as in sociology) but action. To know an object is to act on that object by its assimilation to action-schemes (Piaget, 1967/1971, pp. 6–8). Further, there is a logic of action coordination and one-and-the-same logic coordinates actions at both psychological and social levels (p. 145). This definition holds not just for physical objects but also for social objects, such as groups and society, and for abstract objects, such as number and necessity. An action may be the action of a person (pp. 109, 169) or a social group (p. 146) or a generation (p. 134). Work is a paradigm example of shared action in much the way that logical contradiction can inform operations of the mind (cf. the examples used on pp. 55–6, 190–1). If knowledge is action on objects, where those objects extend to both actual and abstract objects, the theoretical task is to identify the characteristics of those objects in their mental construction with due allowance both for psycho-social origins and for rational legitimation. The empirical task is to gain evidence as to which properties of actual and abstract objects are, and which are not, embodied in the developing mind of the individual, or embedded in socially held beliefs and practices. The central reason why both tasks are difficult is because objects may have intrinsic properties, which are logically necessary and intellectually universal. It is for this reason that Piaget commits himself to a structuralist and dispositional account. Rational understanding requires a child to understand not just one instance of a property which is contexualized in some particular way but rather that property *qua* class of instances with universal application. Further, this understanding should be such that it can be shown in an indefinite range of actions which that individual has the power or capacity to perform. Since rational understanding is an ideal form of understanding, it is not present at the outset of development but is instead open to construction (it constitutes a term *ad quem*, not a term *a quo*). In short, although society does act on individuals and although individuals do interact with each other, not all actions are the source of rationality (p. 136).

2. Problems of the match

If there is a logic of action coordination, two problems arise about the match of this logic. One problem is the match between subject and object (S–O match). Which system of logic matches the logic used in the actions of any one individual in relation to physical, social and abstract objects? Constructivism leads to the claim that the objects arising from Platonist commitments (cf. p. 196) – for example, Popper's (1979) 'third world' or the 'possible worlds' of modal realism (Lewis, 1986) – must in all cases be constructed with consequential variation in the extent of the subject–object circuit (Piaget, 1947/1950; for a discussion of Platonism, see Smith, 1993, §20). Central to this problem is the reconciliation between self and law (*son moi avec la loi*), between the stock of human aspirations, affections and affirmations and the discipline imposed by normative systems (p. 241). Note that there are many logical systems and so the question of which ones fit the logic of action coordination is unresolved since systematic comparison has not been carried through (Vonèche and Vidal, 1985; for a survey of logical systems, see Apostel, 1982). A second problem is the match between two or more subjects (S–S match). To what extent does the logic used in action by any one individual match that used by any other? Note that this matching problem is applicable to education by virtue of the action of cultural transmission across generations on individual persons (socialization) and conversely (creativity). The match has to be mutual just because the perspective adopted by either can be related to an indefinite and open series of alternative points of view [pp. 209, 219, 315]. The extent to which any specified logic is used consistently and reciprocally by both partners to an exchange is in part an empirical issue. In Piaget's account, S–S matching is an identity or non-identity, either of which can be intensively, and not merely metrically, understood [p. 102]; (cf. Smith, 1993, p. 166). This is shown by the formal identities arising from equations I and II of Piaget's exchange model. However, there is also scope for an indefinite series of inequalities. But his conceptual analysis is admitted not to be exhaustive (p. 23), still less subjected to an operational analysis. Piaget (1941, §5) specifically noted that there are 'practical operations' coordinating means-end relationships which are a development from their precursors in infancy due to their *groupement* structure (see also Brown and Weiss, 1987; Inhelder and Cellérier, 1992; Leiser and Gillièron, 1990).

3. Intellectual autonomy

A real exchange has two features. The negative feature is that it is not coercive. Piaget cites several examples of (potentially or actually) coercive processes, including the Freudian unconscious [p. 298], affective pressures [p. 164], the family and schooling [p. 295], undue respect for tradition and authority [pp. 203, 260], ideology [p. 282]. Coercion may be morally difficult to resist through limitation on freedom of the will (Aristotle, nd/1953). Coercion will be psychologically impossible to resist if its presence is unconscious and non-detected, resulting in heteronomy rather than autonomy of the will. Thus a prohibition on suicide may be psychologically efficacious as a taboo (Freud, 1938) in much the way that rates of suicide may be due to a social cause such as anomie (Durkheim, 1915). On Piaget's view [p. 92], suicide so conceived is importantly different from suicide conceived as a reasoned rejection of the categorical imperative (Kant, 1791). Compulsion which is manifest as a psycho-social cause is different from a moral obligation laid upon conscience (Wright, 1981). Aristotle's (nd/1953, Book 6, chapter 13) remark that 'virtue is not merely a disposition in *conformity* with the right principle but a disposition *in collaboration* with the principle' generalizes from the moral to the intellectual domain. It is one thing to form beliefs which issue in true judgments (beliefs in conformity with the truth) and quite something else to accept these beliefs on rational grounds (beliefs in collaboration with epistemic principles). Piaget's general characterization of heteronomous processes of understanding is that they are egocentric, when based within the individual's mind (p. 249), and sociocentric, when based in social interactions (p. 280). A child who accepts as true what a parent says (p. 289) or who accepts as true whatever is stated in a school textbook (p. 295) – merely on that account – are victims of heteronomous belief. A real exchange of thought is liberating, permitting the individual to re-cast available knowledge into valid forms of new knowledge (pp. 76, 138, 169) which is manifest both in the continual adaptation to new circumstances which are never identical (p. 174) and in the growth of the human powers required in their coordination (p. 306). We all have access to some system of collective notions, rules and signs but each individual has variable powers to think through them (pp. 218–19). But transmission is not reconstruction, replication is not re-evaluation. Piaget (1969/1970) views education as a two-termed relation which links, on the one hand, the values (intellectual, moral, social) under the charge of an educator and, on the other hand, the individual mind of the child or learner. Thus at one pole is the educator who has access to the available knowledge in some society, where this knowledge is set in over-arching systems, the connections within which produce intellectual and pedagogical difficulties. This knowledge is also enmeshed in systems of belief and ideology. At the other pole is the individual learner, who is a bundle of intellectual and affective propensities and powers. A rationally successful exchange should lead to truth rather than to conformity and gerontocratic tradition. Intellectual activity requires the individual to think through, and to re-think with, collectively transmitted concepts rather than to be the passive recipient of the legacies of past generations. But this is possible only if the human mind has the capacity to think autonomously, that is, to act on the basis of reasons rather than through the occurrence of causes and to engage in reasoning on the basis of formal rather than merely functional factors. If childhood is 'the sleep of reason' (Rousseau, 1762/1974, pp. 71–72), there are multiple intermediate waking states. Rational consciousness is the term of a developmental process that occurs as the restructuring of the mental powers of the mind through its functioning in a psycho-social world.

4. Developmental levels in the knowledge of universals

Piaget takes there to be three levels of development in the psycho-social genesis of knowledge (pp. 56, 280). These levels are hierarchically related, even though there is overlap in their actual manifestation at different ages. Note that in stating his defining criteria of developmental stages, Piaget (1960, pp. 13–14) did not include generality as a criterion (*pace* the English translation) but rather *structure d'ensemble* or over-arching structure. Such a structure is universal, whether or not it generalizes across a population. To see why, note that Piaget contrasts two senses of individuality (pp. 218–19). One is the self which is a set of intellectual and affective propensities. The other is the personality due to powers which are productive of an original and conserving synthesis of collective norms and concepts [p. 245]. Each and any person, group or society is an individual in both senses with all possible permutations of these propensities and powers at different ages. According to this view, there is a parallelism in the logical structure of the egocentric thought of children and tribal mentality in primitive societies to the extent that each is marked by rigidity and conformism of thought (p. 137). Note that intellectual constraint occurs at all ages in all cultures: what varies – and this is in part an empirical issue – is the proportion of both ego- and sociocentric thought (pp. 119, 148). The epistemic subject at any developmental level is a universal, but not thereby a general, feature of thought (pp. 38, 80, 178). The theoretical question as to what counts as an epistemic universal should be kept distinct from the empirical question of generality across individuals and populations. Piaget's account addresses the problem of the developmental mechanism which makes it possible to acquire universal knowledge rather than the problem of the conditions under which such knowledge can be generalized.

Universal knowledge is knowledge of a universal. The question of whether human knowledge of a universal is possible has been central to philosophical discussion from Plato (nd/1935) to Popper (1979). In fact, Piaget (1918, p. 46) did specifically pose the question 'Can there be universal knowledge?' and it is arguable that his genetic (empirical) epistemology is a systematic attempt to transpose questions in philosophical epistemology into empirical counterparts (Piaget, 1950; cf. Smith, 1993, §7). Thus in Piaget's account, a cognitive structure, such as a *structure d'ensemble*, is universal in the specific sense that its use in a subject's actions makes possible some knowledge of a universal. One example of a universal is logical validity; another is the modal concept of necessity. Both are defined across all possible worlds and not merely in terms of truth in the actual world. There are multiple degrees of universality (subsumption of weaker in stronger normative systems) and there are many types of universals (proliferation of geometrical systems). The question of whether universal knowledge, in this sense, generalizes and transfers across contexts, individuals, domains and cultures is a legitimate question in psychology (Case, 1991; Fischer *et al.*, 1993; Karmiloff-Smith, 1992; Resnick, 1990). But it is otherwise quite distinct from the question of how individuals develop such knowledge at all on the basis of the particular knowledge available in the actual world. It is for this reason that Piaget sharply notes that claims about *universality* and *generality* do not mean the same thing (p. 178).

5. Exchange model

Piaget claims that successful interaction depends upon the exchange of values (rules, signs, concepts). A rational exchange requires certain conditions to be met. The conditions are stated by Piaget to be at least necessary (p. 146) – though they are sometimes stated to be sufficient as well (p. 91) – for successful exchange. Note that Piaget's conditions apply to rationally successful exchange as well as to psycho-social encounters which are independently interesting, perhaps because they are indicative of 'first in' rather than 'fully in' competences (Flavell *et al.*, 1993) or of functional rather than optimal levels of ability (Fischer *et al.*, 1993). The central claim made by Piaget is that rationally successful exchange requires that each partner to the exchange should have the intellectual powers to carry out the same operation as the other (p. 152). Rationally successful exchange can occur only if there is a common scale of values, where the scale is used by each partner with due respect for both conservation and novelty. That is, two partners to an interaction should use one and the same system of signs and meanings, which system is conserved and used – and reciprocally so by both partners – in a self-identical way through a train of thought (pp. 91, 146). It is in this sense that Piaget's notion *structure d'ensemble* (over-arching structure) is to be understood (Smith, 1993, §8.6). Note that analogous claims are made in *Sociological studies*, for example to the sets or systems of operations available in a society (p. 114) and to objectively valid over-arching systems in science (p. 235). This condition does not imply that there is one and only one set of norms by which that proposition is judged since either partner may have access to alternative normative systems. The presence of such alternatives makes rational dispute possible, for example in science (p. 230). Nor does this condition imply consensus. The universalizability that Piaget has in mind is methodological rather than substantive. Unlike those moral philosophers (Kant, 1791) who use universalizability as a criterion of moral obligation, Piaget's epistemological claim is methodological: use whatever value systems you want provided each partner has the capacity to use the same system.

One interpretation of these conditions has its basis in the principle due to Leibniz: '*eadem sunt quorum unum alteri substitui potest salva veritate*' (those concepts are identical if either can be substituted for the other without change in truth-value), where this principle is taken to provide 'the link between concept-identity and truth-conditions' (Ishiguro, 1972, p. 17). The proposal is that even though two non-synonymous expressions, such as *trilateral* and *triangle*, are different in meaning, they may express the same concept and, indeed, are identical just in case they satisfy the *salva veritate* principle. This principle requires that the propositions expressing these concepts are both extensionally equivalent (true and false together in the actual world) and intensionally coincident as well (true and false together across possible worlds). According to Leibniz (1765/1981), a necessary truth is true in all possible worlds. It is for this reason that modality and conceptual identity are inter-linked. Although Piaget rejects the nativism and the platonism of Leibniz (see Smith, 1993, §3), his commitment to intensional logic is evident (Piaget and Garcia, 1987/1991) and his account is compatible with with the Leibnizean claims about modality and concept-identity. Two displays – either in one and the same mind or in the minds of distinct individuals – are displays of the same concept just in case they are extensionally equivalent, and so are used to generate knowledge true of the actual world, and also intensionally coincident across possible worlds, since the individual possessor has the human powers to coordinate any one perspective with any other perspective (pp. 236–7). Heteronomous thinking fails to meet this requirement due to ego- and sociocentrism, which sets a modal limit on the epistemic search for coherence (pp. 144, 189). Commu-nication in such cases may not be rationally successful since the underlying concepts of the partners correspond to systematically divergent human capacities (pp. 314–15). Note that Piaget claims that no two situations – no two communicative contexts – are ever identical (p. 174). It follows that the use of a self-identical concept in two situations requires the possessor to have the capacity to cope with irrelevant transformations which have a bearing on neither the correctness nor the logical modality of a conceptual display. It is for this reason that conservation has a fundamental role to play in Piaget's account where it appears as the ability to use one and the same proposition in which a concept is expressed through irrelevant transformation – that is, in rational conservation (pp. 147, 153, 175, 236).

6. Normative intervention

Piaget's genetic epistemology makes the claim that norms have a history which includes both social and rational elements. This history includes their origin in society or in the human mind. A norm such as truth is not taken on 'ready made' but is instead revealed by its construction in actions. Reason is not a given even if rational forms of understanding can successfully be constructed, manifest as over-arching systems with modal characteristics that match onto the dispositional powers of the human mind. Taking modality as an example of an abstract object, necessity is defined through the impossibility of a relevant negation (Piaget, 1977/1986) and thus is different from a truth-functional negation: if something is necessary, it could not be false, whereas if something is true, it is not false. This is a fundamental, and universal, difference which has to be respected. But this difference is independent of both society and the individual. Necessity is defined in this way not because some social group has conventionally defined it thus, nor because some logician has offered this definition. Rather, this is the definition of necessity. And it is for this reason that social factors could no more be responsible for the development of reason than could individual factors. Piaget's concern in *Sociological studies* is with the acquisition and legitimation of norms such as truth and necessity. Central to normative intervention is both the capacity to use the same operation as any other individual on one's own account and also the capacity to substitute any one operation for any other in any possible system. It is significant that the modal understanding of possibility and necessity is both an intrinsic feature of rationality and central to Piaget's account (Smith, 1993). Rationally acceptable knowledge must be legitimated by its match with this fundamental category since – in this sense – necessity is an abstract object which human thought must match. Further, the thought of any one individual must also match that of any other in precisely this respect, if there is to be a genuine meeting of minds. Conservation and novelty are two manifestations of this match. Conservation has its basis in identity, which is a paradigm case of necessity in that anything is necessarily self-identical. Novelty has its basis in transformation, which is a paradigm case of possibility. The link between these two pervasive modal forms is made by a human mind which can isolate and integrate these separate modal forms in a unified system of knowledge.

CONCLUSION

Piaget's work does have an account of the psycho-social origins of intellectual development but his constructivist commitments require all specific forms of experience to be legitimated in relation to norms of rationality. In particular, Piaget's account is concerned less with questions about the initial origins of knowledge – important though these are – than with the intervention of rational norms, that is, with their acquisition, construction and integration. Rational norms concern the universal aspects of knowledge. This is a distinct question which is separate from issues about the generality of knowledge. The question of whether the universal is knowable was specifically raised by Piaget (1918, p. 46) in *Recherche*, where a programmatic answer was outlined by reference to psychological equilibration, and an answer outlined in an account which was published some sixty years later:

> Fact is a form of equilibrium – or disequilibrium – whilst the ideal is another equilibrium, as real in a sense as the first, but often sketched rather than realised: the ideal is a limiting case, as the mathematicians say, or even the full equilibrium towards which the false or unstable equilibria of the actual world tend . . . . Ideal psychological equilibrium occurs when whole and parts are in a state of harmony, of reciprocal conservation.
>
> (Piaget, 1918, pp. 46, 178)

> The subject searches to avoid incoherence and for that reason always tends towards certain forms of equilibrium without ever attaining them, unless sometimes at provisional levels . . . (the latter attainment) always opens onto new problems owing to virtual operations which it remains possible to construct using available operations. The most elaborated scientific knowledge thus remains in a continual state of development.
>
> (Piaget, 1975/1985, p. 139; my amended translation)

Piaget's account makes the positive and optimistic assumption that objectively true knowledge is possible through the search for coherence, even though there are fallibilist constraints on the identification of the full system of true knowledge (for a discussion of fallibilism, see Haack, 1978). Piaget's account of equilibration has a social component because the search for coherence requires two types of matching, both within one mind and between the minds of partners to a communicative exchange. Matching does occur to the extent that the *salva veritate* principle is satisfied, whereby the propositions expressing different concepts can be shown to be extensionally equivalent and intensionally coincident through a display of human powers and capacities across an indefinite series of contexts and transformations. Although developmentalists continue to address independently interesting questions about the extent to which intellectual processes are domain-independent, or to which they generalize across all individuals, or to which they transfer across all contexts, such questions are not central to Piaget's main concern.

In short, *Sociological studies* was written over the first part of one century but arguably has a relevance for the next one. That account has distinctive features and these merit both rational and empirical scrutiny.

REFERENCES

ADEY, P. and SHAYER, M. (1994) *Really raising standards: cognitive intervention and science achievement*, London: Routledge.

APOSTEL, L. (1982) 'The future of Piagetian logic', *Revue internationale de philosophie*, 142–3, 567–611. Reprinted in L. Smith (1992) *Jean Piaget: critical assessments*, vol. 4, London: Routledge.

ARISTOTLE (nd/1953) *The ethics of Aristotle*, London: Allen & Unwin.

BEREITER, C. (1985) 'Toward a solution of the learning paradox', *Review of educational research*, 55, 201–226.

BOOLE, G. (1854/1958) *The laws of thought*, New York: Dover.

BROWN, A., BRANSFORD, J., FERRARA, R. and CAMPIONE, J. (1983) 'Learning, remembering and understanding', in P. Mussen (ed.) *Handbook of child psychology*, vol. 3, New York: Wiley.

BROWN, T. and WEISS, L. (1987) 'Structures, procedures, heuristics and affectivity', *Archives de psychologie*, 55, 59–94. Reprinted in L. Smith (1992) *Jean Piaget: critical assessments*, vol. 4, London: Routledge.

BRUNER, J. (1985) 'Vygotsky: a historical and conceptual perspective', in J.V. Wertsch (ed.) *Culture, communication and cognition: Vygotskian perspectives*, Cambridge: Cambridge University Press.

CAMPBELL, R. and BICKHARD, M. (1986) *Knowing levels and developmental stages*, Basel: Karger.

CASE, R. (1991) *The mind's stair-case*, Hillsdale, NJ: Erlbaum.

CHAPMAN, M. (1986) 'The structure of exchange: Piaget's sociological theory', *Human development*, 29, 181–194.

COLE, M. and COLE, S. (1989) *The development of children*, New York: Freeman.

DANIELS, H. (1993) *Charting the agenda*, London: Routledge.

DEMETRIOU, A., SHAYER, M. and EFKLIDES, A. (1992) *Neo-Piagetian theories of cognitive development*, London: Routledge.

DOISE, W. and MUGNY, G. (1984) *The social development of the intellect*, Oxford: Pergamon Press.

DONALDSON, M. (1992) *Human minds*, London: Allen Lane Press.

DURKHEIM, E. (1915) *Suicide: a study in sociology*, New York: The Free Press.

EDWARDS, D. and MERCER, N. (1986) *Common knowledge*, London: Methuen.

FISCHER, K., BULLOCK, D., ROTENBERG, E. and RAYA, P. (1993) 'The diagnosis of competence: how context contributes directly to skill', in R. Wozniak and K. Fischer (eds) *Development in context*, Hillsdale, NJ: Erlbaum.

FLAVELL, J., MILLER, P. and MILLER, S. (1993) *Cognitive development*, Third edition, Engelwood Cliffs, NJ: Prentice Hall.

FREGE, G. (1888/1980) *The foundations of arithmetic*, Oxford: Blackwell.

FREGE, G. (1956) 'The thought: a logical inquiry', in P. Strawson (ed.) *Philosophical logic*, Oxford: Oxford University Press.

FREUD, S. (1922) *Introductory lectures on psycho-analysis*, London: George Allen & Unwin.

FREUD, S. (1938) *Totem and taboo*, Harmondsworth: Penguin Books.

GLEICK, J. (1992) *Genius: Richard Feynman and modern physics*, New York: Little, Brown & Co.

HAACK, S. (1978) *Philosophy of logics*, Cambridge: Cambridge University Press.

HAMLYN, D.W. (1978) *Experience and the growth of understanding*, London: Routledge & Kegan Paul.

HAMLYN, D.W. (1982) 'What exactly is social about the origin of understanding?' in P. Light and G. Butterworth (eds) *Social cognition*, Brighton: Harvester Press.

HAROUTUNIAN, S. (1983) *Equilibrium in the balance*, New York: Springer.

HARRE, R. (1986) 'The step to social constructionism', in M. Richards and P. Light (eds) *Children of social worlds*, Cambridge: Polity Press.

INHELDER, B. and CELLERIER, G. (1992) *Le cheminement des découvertes de l'enfant*, Lausanne: Delachaux et Niestlé.

INHELDER, B. and PIAGET, J. (1955/1958) *Growth of logical thinking*, London: Routledge & Kegan Paul.

ISAACS, S. (1930) *Intellectual growth in young children*, London: George Routledge & Sons.

ISHIGURO, I. (1972) *Leibniz's philosophy of logic and language*, London: Duckworth.

KANT, I. (1791) in H. Paton (1948) *The moral law*, London: Hutchinson.

KARMILOFF-SMITH, A. (1992) *Beyond modularity*, Cambridge, MA: MIT Press.

KITCHENER, R.F. (1986) *Piaget's theory of knowledge*, New Haven: Yale University Press.

KITCHENER, R.F. (1981) 'Piaget's social psychology', *Journal for the theory of social behaviour*, 11, 258–277.

KORNER, S. (1969) *Fundamental questions in philosophy*, Harmondsworth: Penguin Books.

LEIBNIZ, G.W. (1765/1981) *New essays on human understanding*, Cambridge: Cambridge University Press.

LEISER, D. and GILLIERON, C. (1990) *Cognitive science and genetic epistemology*, New York: Plenum Press.

LEWIS, D.K. (1986) *On the plurality of possible worlds*, Oxford: Blackwell.

LIGHT, P. and BUTTERWORTH, G. (1992) *Context and cognition*, New York; Harvester.

MARX, K. (1867/1970) *Capital: a critique of political economy*, London: Lawrence & Wishart.

MAYS, W. (1982) 'Piaget's sociological theory', in S. Modgil and C. Modgil (eds) *Jean Piaget: consensus and controversy*, London: Holt, Rinehart & Winston. Reprinted in L. Smith (1992) *Jean Piaget: critical assessments*, vol. 3, London: Routledge.

MOESSINGER, P. (1978) 'Piaget et Homans, même balance?', *Canadian Psychological Review*, 19, 291–295.

MOESSINGER, P. (1991) *Les Fondements de l'organisation*, Paris: Presses Universitaires de France.

MONTANGERO, J. and MAURICE-NAVILLE, D. (1994) *Piaget ou l'intelligence en marche*, Liège: Mardaga.

NEWMAN, D., GRIFFIN, P. and COLE, M. (1989) *The construction zone: working for cognitive change in school*, Cambridge: Cambridge University Press.

PARETO, V. (1923/1963) *A treatise on general sociology*, 4 vols, New York: Dover.

PARRAT-DAYAN, S. (1993a) 'Le Texte et ses voix: Piaget lu par ses pairs dans le milieu psychologique des années 1920–30', *Archives de psychologie*, 61, 127–152.

PARRAT-DAYAN, S. (1993b) 'La Réception de l'œuvre de Piaget dans le milieu pédagogique dans les années 1920–30', *Revue française de pédagogie*, 104, 73–83.

PERRET-CLERMONT, A-N. (1988) 'Introduction pour l'édition en langue russe', *La Construction de l'intelligence dans l'interaction sociale*, Berne: Peter Lang.

PIAGET, J. (1918) *Recherche*, Lausanne: La Concorde.

PIAGET, J. (1923/1959) *Language and thought of the child*, third edition. London: Routledge & Kegan Paul.

PIAGET, J. (1924/1928) *Judgment and reasoning in the child*, London: Routledge & Kegan Paul.

PIAGET, J. (1931) 'Le Développement intellectuel chez les jeunes enfants', *Mind*, 40, 137–160.

PIAGET, J. (1932/1932) *The moral judgment of the child*, London: Routledge & Kegan Paul.

PIAGET, J. (1941) 'Le Mécanisme du développement mental et les lois du groupement des opérations: esquisse d'une théorie opératoire de l'intelligence', *Archives de psychologie*, 28, 215–285.

PIAGET, J. (1945/1951) *Play, dreams and imitation in children*, London: Routledge & Kegan Paul.

PIAGET, J. (1947/1950) *The psychology of intelligence*, London: Routledge & Kegan Paul.

PIAGET, J. (1950) *Introduction à l'épistémologie génétique*, 3 vols. Paris: Presses Universitaires de France.

PIAGET, J. (1952) 'Autobiography', in E. Boring (ed.) *A history of psychology in autobiography*, vol. 4, Worcester, MA: Clark University Press/Autobiographie. (Extended to 1976.) *Cahiers Vilfredo Pareto: revue européenne d'histoire des sciences sociales*, 14, 1–43.

PIAGET, J. (1954/1980) *Intelligence and affectivity*, Palo Alto, CA: Annual Reviews.

PIAGET, J. (1960) 'The general problems of the psychobiological development of the child', in J. Tanner and B. Inhelder (eds) *Discussions on child development*, vol. 4. London: Tavistock.

PIAGET, J. (1962) Comments on Vygotsky's critical remarks concerning *The language and thought of the child* and *Judgment and reasoning in the child*, Cambridge, MA: MIT Press.

PIAGET, J. (1967/1971) *Biology and knowledge*, Edinburgh: Edinburgh University Press.

PIAGET, J. (1969/1970) *Science of education and psychology of the child*, London: Longman.

PIAGET, J. (1975/1985) *Equilibration of cognitive structures*, Chicago: University of Chicago Press.

PIAGET, J. (1977) *Etudes sociologiques*, Second edition, Geneva: Droz.

PIAGET, J. (1977/1986) 'Essay on necessity', *Human development*, 29, 301–314.

PIAGET, J. and GARCIA, R. (1987/1991) *Toward a logic of meanings*, Hillsdale, NJ: Erlbaum.

PIAGET, J., HENRIQUES, G. and ASCHER, E. (1990/1992) *Morphisms and categories*, Hillsdale, NJ: Erlbaum.

PIAGET, J. and SZEMINSKA, A. (1941/1952) *The child's conception of number*, London: Routledge & Kegan Paul.

PLATO (nd/1935) 'Theaetetus', in F. Cornford (ed.) *Plato's theory of knowledge*, London: Routledge & Kegan Paul.

POPPER, K. (1979) *Objective knowledge*, Second edition, Oxford: Oxford University Press.

RESNICK, L. (1990) *Perspectives on socially shared cognition*, New York: American Psychological Association.

ROUSSEAU, J-J. (1762/1974) *Emile*, London: Dent.

SMITH, L. (1982) 'Piaget and the solitary knower', *Philosophy of the social sciences*, 12, 173–182.

SMITH, L. (1992) *Jean Piaget: critical assessments*, vol. 4, London: Routledge.

SMITH, L. (1993) *Necessary knowledge: Piagetian perspectives on constructivism*, Hove: Erlbaum.

van der VEER, R. and VALSINER, J. (1991) *Understanding Vygotsky*, Oxford: Blackwell.

VONECHE, J-J. and VIDAL, F. (1985) 'Jean Piaget and the child psychologist', *Synthèse*, 65, 121–138.

VYGOTSKY, L. (1934/1978) *Mind in society*, Cambridge, MA: Harvard University Press.

VYGOTSKY, L. (1934/1986) *Thought and language*, Second edition, Cambridge, MA: MIT Press.

VYGOTSKY, L. (1994) in R. van der Veer and J. Valsiner (eds) *The Vygotsky reader*, Oxford: Blackwell.

WERTSCH, J. (1985) *Culture, communication and cognition*, Cambridge: Cambridge University Press.

WOLPERT, L. (1992) *The unnatural nature of science*, London: Faber & Faber.

WRIGHT, D. (1981) 'The psychology of moral obligation', reprinted in L. Smith (1992) *Jean Piaget: critical assessments*, vol. 1, London: Routledge.

Preface

[p. 7] The dynamic character of the sociological publications of Editions Droz and the loyalty of my colleagues Busino and Girod[1][1] were the two factors which finally led me to agree (as often happens in such cases) to bring together in one volume three disparate papers in sociology, which appeared in 'Publications of the Faculty of Economic and Social Sciences, University of Geneva', together with the chapter 'Explanation in sociology' from my *Introduction à l'épistémologie génétique*. (I wish to thank the Presses Universitaires de France who have agreed to the reproduction of this chapter from volume III, which is currently out of print.)

These writings date from 1941 to 1950. It suffices to say that, with respect to their content, reference ought to have been made to many other facts and works. The very brief remarks on 'regulations' in the field of economics could be extensively supplemented. The transition from regulations to 'operations' *qua* 'groupings' could today be justified in terms of cybernetics, which would carry more conviction.[2] The essential identity of the operations distinctive of the intellectual work of individuals and those which intervene[3] in an interindividual exchange (or 'cooperation') is based, according to my present point of view, on the laws of the general coordination of actions (which are as much collective as they are tied to nervous coordinations).[4] The passages relating to Lévy-Bruhl[5] should be revised in the light of the important work of Lévi-Strauss.[6] However, with respect to the problem under consideration, the latter is not a substitute for the experiments still needing to be done and which alone can inform us about the precise operational level of children and adults in different societies of tribal civilization. Etc.

Such as they are, however, the following pages still seem to preserve[7] some utility with respect to the relations between [p. 8] sociology and psychology on the subject of mechanisms that underlie diverse domains covered by the many human sciences. The rules, values and signs which appear to us to characterize social facts are the subject matter of numerous special sciences, and reflection on the epistemological problems which they engender remains as necessary today as fifteen or twenty years ago.

Among the reactions which these essays have generated, there is first of all one to which we would like to reply, because its phenomenological inspiration appears to us to lead to the same difficulties in sociology as in psychology. Phenomenology was indeed right to emphasize the importance of meanings and intentions, as well as the differences between causal 'explanation' and the 'understanding' of implicatory relationships. But there is no need to be committed to such a philosophical doctrine to recognize that these notions are well founded and, due to our strong 'naturalism', we have not hesitated, in psychology and in sociology, to make evident their role in the analysis of phenomena. This will be seen clearly in this text.

On the other hand, phenomenology often invites us as well, and it is at this point that we part company with it, to substitute 'lived experience' for structuring reality, as if a genetic or historical evolution conditioned consciousnesses only to the extent of their having the 'Erlebnis'[8] of it. Now this already appears to us impossible to accept from an epistemological point of view and seems to constitute a method all the more inadmissible in disciplines which like psychology and sociology are concerned with the real man, in his ontogenesis and his historical filiations. In psychology, we are asked to speak of the body only to the extent that there is consciousness of 'my body': I would like to know if my brain contributes to these written lines only to the extent that I know its mechanism – and this by direct intuition, a condition which is so rarely satisfied that it would be prudent to stop here. In sociology, the temptation is admittedly greater, since everything which transcends the individual appears to constitute an 'Erlebnis' worthy of consideration. But to put everything on the same plane, as we are then fatally led to do, and to 'understand' everything without there being anything else left to 'explain', is simply to renounce the essential mission of science which is both to understand and to explain. That a philosophical movement, whose initial aim for [p. 9] Husserl was to restore the normative in opposition to the prevalent empiricist psychology, has arrived through successive debasements at the subjective cult of ambiguity or the irrational, which Merleau-Ponty[9] or Sartre[10] wished with some candour to substitute for scientific psychology, is an epistemological problem which does not concern us here: its resolution depends on, as we try to show elsewhere[2], the contradictory nature of phenomenological 'intuition' whose aim is to found facts and norms in a unitary whole. This constitutes an astonishing and supreme example of the very 'psychologism' (or transition from fact to norm) that it set out to combat![3] But to wish to generalize the method to sociology itself – that will be the triumph of all forms of idealist and even political sociocentrism.

Yet one of the principal problems of sociology is to explain how social life can be the origin both of rational structures and of the most inconsistent ideologies (this will rightly be one of the major preoccupations of the text which follows). This problem is not to be resolved by fitting all social products on one and the same plane, as we would be led to do by a method which regards them as merely varieties of 'Erlebnis'. To this, the reply will be that the sociologist has no criterion available and that in principle the 'rational' is disregarded in order to know only lived experiences, that [p. 10] it is a question of mass movements or the community of scientists. We have two replies to this.

The first is that, without in any way asking the sociologist to stand in for the epistemologist, all methods of verification are nevertheless available as soon as a genetic, and not only a historical or especially synchronic, point of view is adopted. One must not forget that the education of new generations and their integration into society is the major social phenomenon and that the first concern of every revolutionary movement (there are still plenty of others!) is to act on the rising generations and to reorganize teaching. This being so, it suffices to analyse the facts to observe that social initiation in mathematics[11] is not undertaken in exactly the same manner as, for example, the initiation of Hitlerian youth into the dogma of the supremacy of the 'Aryan race'. Without having to pronounce on the rationality of the doctrines, we are in this respect already able to distinguish between structures A and B. If this method is followed through so that one can find, as did Lévi-Strauss, traces of structure A (or logico-mathematical structure) at ethnographic levels quite different from ours, we will nevertheless end by being obliged to introduce a certain hierarchy in the observed structures, from the dual point of view of their generality and especially from their depth or mode of genetic construction.

In the second place and more importantly, the sociologist is not alone in the world and sooner or later has to take account of the results of related disciplines. The great misfortune of the human sciences, as compared with the exact and natural sciences, is the poverty of their interdisciplinary relations. It is, for example, impossible to do serious biology today without an adequate cultural background, not only in chemistry and physics (from quantum microphysics to thermodynamics) but even in cybernetics (information and regulation) and in the theory of general, algebraic structures. On the other hand, nothing in fact prevents a linguist, except at great personal cost, from being ignorant of economics and conversely, or even a sociologist from ignoring experimental psychology and genetic psychology, where the latter is in reality as sociological as psychological. Yet there exist common mechanisms which are found in all domains of the human sciences. And the rules, values and signs [p. 11] which we take in this text to be essential social facts presuppose exactly such operational, regulatory and semiotic mechanisms, according to which questions arise about one or the other of these categories or of their unions and intersections. It seems to us impossible to deal with such questions sociologically without sufficient data from psychology and neurology, linguistics and economics, etc., but equally from logic or its related, contemporary branches such as the logic of law (Perelman[12] and his group), and especially without knowing the essential connections between logic *qua* pure theory of rules and cybernetics *qua* theory of regulations.

But if such connections are established, and increasingly more of them will be, between sociology and the set of disciplines on which the understanding of man depends, it is evident that the summary views due to a relatively superficial philosophical education (by comparison with the scientific training of those philosophers who have distinguished themselves in the great periods of the history of philosophy) will no longer prevent us, in the name of phenomenological subjectivity, from distinguishing hierarchical levels in the structures of the individual and group mind.

Another kind of reflection appears useful to us. We have just replied to critical remarks which have been made against us by the phenomenologists, but critical remarks of the opposite kind have been presented by the dialecticians, since these are the two major philosophical tendencies of contemporary thought. Now we have sometimes been reproached in this regard, given the evident convergence which exists between genetic constructivism from which we draw our inspiration and dialectical movements, for not having advanced further the convergences in the direction, it has sometimes been said to us, of a return to the most direct origins in contrast to derivative movements. But here again it is necessary to be clear. Either dialectic is a philosophy just like any other, claiming like many others to direct scientific thought and to deal with factual problems and formalization. Or, on the contrary, dialectic – and it is for us just this which confers its power – is the result of a conscious realization of the effective methods used by all disciplines concerned with genetic and historical development, leading us consequently to see in this evolution nothing other than the result [p. 12] of a pre-established programming or a sequence of chance events lacking both structuration and equilibration. But if dialectic, in this second sense of the term, wishes to preserve[7] that which contributes to its raison d'être and success, its cause will not be strengthened by hastening or forcing convergences but rather through patient scientific research taking note of common mechanisms which have been discovered quite independently in different areas of research.

In this respect, two fundamental facts appear to us, in all the biological and human domains as well as in sociology, to direct research in a dialectical direction. The first is that all causal explanation tends towards forms of causality which cease to be linear or unidirectional in favour of interactions and interdependencies whose 'circles' and 'spirals' are impossible to master without the intervention of regulatory and equilibratory systems. But the old notion of 'equilibrium' has meaning in the biological and human sciences only in a perspective of self-regulation.[13] This latter evokes by and large dialectical processes, because in a sequence of multiple disequilibria or crises and re-equilibrations in which there is progress over past events, there necessarily intervene conflicts between tendencies which are initially antagonistic and eventually 'transcended' not by a physical balance of their forces but by a reorganization constituting the equilibrated synthesis. If we could have rewritten today the pages which follow, we would have placed much more emphasis on the self-regulating processes of equilibration, especially in the transition from regulations to the operational structures of 'grouping', 'lattice' and 'group', etc.[14]

The second fundamental fact is that everywhere where subject-to-object relations are present, and this is so in sociology as elsewhere, even and especially if the subject is a 'we' and the object is several subjects at the same time, knowledge arises neither from the subject nor the object but from the inter-dependent interaction between them, so as to advance from there in the dual direction of an objectified exteriorization and a reflexive interiorization. It might be said that this interdependence of the subject and object is the central thesis of phenomenology: true, but in a static sense as the mere presentation or intuition of the 'phenomenon'. It is equally the central thesis of dialectic, but in the dynamic and constructivist sense of [p. 13] continual transcendence. Marx[15] already assigned importance to the fundamental role of the action of the subject on the object and if, in the sequel, the theory of 'reflection' could make us think of neglecting this central role of action, all contemporary adherents of 'reflection' endeavour by every means to make us understand that this reflection is not pure reflection, and, to speak in all innocence, that it is not reflection! For our part in that we set out not to be a philosopher and to accept only facts and demonstrated algorithms, it is impossible not to find in every studied domain of biological and human life that questions arise concerning the relations between the organism and its environment, the child's intelligence in its dual conquest of external objects and logico-mathematical structures, or in the social transition from technique to science, the perpetual dialectical relation of the subject and object whose analysis frees us simultaneously from idealism and empiricism in favour of a constructivism which is both objectifying and reflexive. That is why we do not believe it necessary for the sociologist to belong to a school, nor to strive to place on the same plane all lived experiences, from whatever level they be, nor to accept the constraint of structurations imposed *a priori*. We believe, on the contrary, that the analysis of specific facts of sociology or the common mechanisms studied by each is quite sufficiently enriching to be at the same time liberating and directive, but only on condition of not neglecting neighbouring sciences.[4]

Geneva, April 1965.   J.P.

This second edition has an Appendix with the writings which Giovanni Busino had collected together as *Les Sciences sociales avant et après Jean Piaget* in *Revue européenne des sciences sociales*, vol. 14, n. 38–39 (Geneva, Droz, 1976).

February 1977.

AUTHOR'S NOTES

[1] The latter was my pupil in sociology and succeeded me at Geneva in teaching this subject: the circumstances under which I took on this teaching for several years do not appear to me to excuse entirely the fact that I did so.
[2] J. Piaget, *Sagesse et illusions de la philosophie* (Paris: P.U.F., 1965)/*Insight and*

illusions in philosophy (London: Routledge & Kegan Paul, 1972).

[3] In an interesting paper which has recently appeared in *Critique* (March, 1965, pp. 249–261) and which he takes as supporting our point of view, G.G. Granger writes: 'Phenomenology does not at all require us to believe that that this systematization of objectivity – though *a priori* ["the *a priori* determination of our experience as directed towards objects"] – is unique and immutable, nor does it preclude us from trying to see if and how it is in fact constituted in the course of its genesis. Its *a priori* character simply means here that *once constituted* it is given as a framework and as a norm, and not as a product .... In these conditions, there is no irremediable opposition between Piaget's point of view and that of phenomenology, even if the former is incompatible with that of certain phenomenologists' (pp. 251–252). Of course if the phenomenology of Granger is that of Husserl, I am a phenomenologist, since I have always maintained that a structure can become normative *qua* 'necessary', and only becomes so at the *end* of its development, once its closure has been achieved through its final equilibrium. But this does not remain any the less so when the value of the atemporal terminal norm depends on its mode of construction. It is only by examining the latter that one understands, for example, why the notion of number acquires an intrinsic necessity (and thus transcends the spatio-temporal), whilst that of 'final cause', born of the confusion of the subjective and the physiological, is a weak form of explanation. The evolution of the notion of what is 'self-evident' in mathematics bears eloquent testimony to the role played by the former mode of construction.

Let us point out in passing that the isomorphism between implication and causality through which we interpret psycho-physiological parallelism is therefore more profound than Granger assumes and explains, amongst other things, the fit[16] between mathematics and the real world. Granger claims to find this approach in Merleau-Ponty: the latter would then have borrowed this from Gestalt theory, which brings us back to scientific psychology.

[4] In re-reading these studies, I have had the disquieting experience of repeating myself from one chapter to the next, because Chapter 1 of the present text in fact is a synthesis of the next three Chapters, which have been previously published. It will therefore be seen that I have kept too much to the letter of the famous advice of an old professor: to make yourself understood, it is necessary first of all to say what you are going to say, then it is necessary to say it and finally it is necessary to repeat it by way of a summary. My publisher does not share this disquiet. Readers fortunately have available the means of avoiding this danger by selecting only those parts which interest them (this is the great advantage of books over lectures).

TRANSLATION NOTES

1 For the work of Giovanni Busino, see the reference given by Piaget in his Preface to the second edition of this text. See also Roger Girod, *Attitudes collectives et relations humaines: tendances actuelles des sciences sociales américaines* (Paris: Presses Universitaires de France, 1953).
2 See Jean Piaget, 'Structures opérationelles et cybernétique', *L'Année psychologique* (1953) 53, 379–388.
3 French, *interviennent*. Piaget uses the term *intervention* to refer to an individual's specific use of a norm (rule, value, concept, sign) in the development of knowledge. Central to Piaget's discussion in *Sociological studies* is the question of the origin of these interventions in children's minds or in the history of science.
4 See Jean Piaget, 'Le problème neurologique de l'intériorisation des actions en opérations réversibles', *Archives de psychologie* (1949) 32, 241–258. See also Jean Piaget, 'Operational structures of the intelligence and organic control', in A.

Karczmar and J. Eccles (eds) *Brain and human behaviour* (New York: Springer Verlag, 1972).

5　See L. Lévy-Bruhl, *Ethics and moral science* (London: Constable, 1905) [originally published in 1903]. See also L. Lévy-Bruhl, *Primitive mentality* (New York; Macmillan, 1923) [originally published in 1922].

6　See Claude Lévi-Strauss *Introduction to a science of mythology*, 4 vols. (London: Cape, 1970) [originally published in 1964–1968].

7　French, *conserver*. This term is frequently used in everyday contexts. For example, a motorway sign reads '*Conservez votre distance de sécurité*' (For safety, keep your distance) or a newspaper reports that the current leader in the Tour de France cycle race '*a conservé son maillot jaune*' (has retained the yellow jersey i.e. he is still race leader and so wears the leader's yellow jersey). This same notion is well known in logic where valid inferences are truth-preserving (*salva veritate*, to use a Leibnizean expression), in physics where (compare the recent biography of Richard Feynman) there is concern to establish which values of which particles are conserved, or in political economics in which the Marxist analysis of value is at issue. The centrality of conservation to knowledge is well stated by Piaget and Szeminska (1941/1952, p16/3; my amended translation: 'all knowledge, whether of a scientific nature or arising from plain common sense, presupposes, explicitly or implicitly, a system of conservation principles'.

8　See Edmund Husserl, *Logical investigations*, 2 vols (London: Routledge & Kegan Paul, 1970) [second edition originally published 1913].

9　See Maurice Merleau-Ponty, *Phenomenology of perception* (London: Routledge & Kegan Paul, 1962).

10　See Jean-Paul Sartre, *Being and nothingness* (London: Methuen, 1958) [originally published in 1943]. See also J-P. Sartre, *Critique of dialectical reason*, vol. 1. (London: New Left Books, 1976) [originally published in 1960].

11　See Jean Piaget, 'Comments on mathematical education', in G. Howson (ed.) *Developments in mathematical education* (Cambridge: Cambridge University Press, 1973).

12　See Ch. Perelman, *Cours de logique* (Bruxelles: Presses Universitaires de Bruxelles, 1963).

13　See Jean Piaget, *Recherche* (Lausanne: La Concorde, 1918).

14　See Jean Piaget, *The equilibration of cognitive structures* (Chicago: University of Chicago Press, 1985); Jean Piaget, *Essai de logique opératoire* (Paris: Dunod, 1972).

15　The reference may be to Karl Marx, *Theses on Feuerbach*. Reprinted in *Karl Marx: Collected works*. vol. 5 (London: Lawrence & Wishart, 1970) [original publication in 1845]. See also Karl Marx, *Capital: a critique of political economy*. 3 vols. (London: Lawrence & Wishart, 1970) [original publication in 1867–79].

16　French, *adéquation*, could also be translated as 'match'.

1 Explanation in sociology

[p. 15] Like biology and psychology, sociology is interesting, epistemologically, from two distinct but complementary viewpoints. First, sociology is a type of knowledge worthy of study in its own right, especially with regard to its relations (of difference as well as similarity) with psychological knowledge. Second, the very object of sociological knowledge is of vital interest to epistemology, since human knowledge is essentially collective, and social life constitutes an essential factor in the creation and growth of knowledge, both pre-scientific and scientific.

1. INTRODUCTION. SOCIOLOGICAL EXPLANATION, BIOLOGICAL EXPLANATION AND PSYCHOLOGICAL EXPLANATION

From the first viewpoint, sociological knowledge has obvious interest, and genetic or comparative epistemology should undertake the task of analysing the relations of this type of knowledge with biological, and especially psychological, knowledge.

The complexity of the relations between sociology and biology gives some indication of the degree of complexity to be expected in the relations between sociology and psychology. In the first place, there is an animal sociology, in parallel with animal psychology (the two disciplines being very closely related, since the mental functions of animals living in societies are naturally conditioned by that social life). Animal sociology demonstrates the close interaction which exists between biological organization and elementary social organization: it is well known that, in the case of certain lower organisms (coelenterates etc.) it is impossible to give exact criteria which will distinguish among individuals, 'colonies' (assemblages of semi-individual, interdependent elements), and societies proper. But, since the inception of animal sociology, sociology proper as a type of explanation has begun to separate itself from biological analysis; facts about social organization are already [p. 16] differentiated from facts about organisms, and therefore call for a special type of interpretation. In addition to properly instinctive behaviours (i.e. hereditary behaviour patterns linked to organic structures) which are the defining characteristic of animal behaviours, there exist in social animals 'external' interactions ('external' in contrast to innate displays) among individuals belonging to the same family or social group, which modify their behaviour to a greater or lesser degree. These interactions include the language of gesture (dance) in bees, discovered by von Frisch; the language of cries in higher vertebrates (chimpanzees, etc.), education through imitation (bird song) and through dressage (predatory behaviour of cats, studied by Kuo), etc. These truly social facts, constituted by external transmission and interaction, modifying individual behaviour, call for a new method of analysis at the level of the group (seen as a system of constructive interdependencies) which should supplement biological explanations of organic or instinctual structures.

In the second place, human sociology itself has links with physical anthropology, a branch of biology consisting in the study of the physical structure of the human being, human genotypes (races) and phenotypic populations. Although the concept of race has been used by certain political ideologies in senses very far removed from the biological, and it has thereby sometimes become a simple affective symbol rather than an objective notion, there is still a question remaining as to the relations between human genotypes and collective mentalities, even if the most active societies are those which contain the greatest mixture of genes.

Moreover, statistical anthropology relates quite naturally to demography, or at least to that part of demography which is concerned with the biological aspects of population. But, still more than in the case of animal sociology, the links between human sociology and anthropology or demography highlight the difference between sociological explanation and biological explanation. While the latter is concerned with internal transmission (heredity) and the characters thereby determined, sociological explanation is concerned with external transmission, or the external interactions among individuals and constructs a set of notions designed to account for this distinctive type of transmission. It is in this way that sociological explanation will show why the mentality of a people depends much less on its race than on its economic history, the historical development [p. 17] of its technology and of its collective representations, where this 'history' amounts to an inherited patrimony, indeed a cultural patrimony, i.e. a set of behaviour patterns which are transmitted externally through the generations, but with modifications due to the totality which is the social group. It is in this way, moreover, that the biological aspects of demographic phenomena (birth-rate, death-rate, longevity, mortality related to type of illness, etc.) are strictly subordinate to systems of (especially economic) values and rules, which are the outcome of the external interactions of individuals. A third meeting point between biology and sociology is the analysis of relations between physiological maturation and the pressures of education in the socialization of the individual. Child development offers an area for experimentation of the greatest interest concerning the zone of overlap between internal, or heredity transmission, and external, i.e. social and educational, transmission. For example, language acquisition presupposes, in addition to the assimilation of an already organized language, or collective system of signs transmitted from generation to generation via the pathway of education, a pre-existing biological state (unique to the human species, as far as we know), which is the capacity to learn an articulated language. Now, this capacity is linked to a certain level of development of the nervous system, precocious or delayed depending on individual differences, and determined by a pattern of hereditary maturation. The same is true for the acquisition of intellectual operations, for which both certain collective interactions and a certain level of organic maturation are necessary to their development. In such cases, the link, on the one hand, and the difference, on the other hand, between biological explanation and sociological explanation are so evident that many authors renounce psychological explanation altogether and assimilate psychology to neurology and the social, combined yet distinct.

But when they are sufficiently analysed, and not treated in a global and theoretical manner, such facts raise in a particularly acute manner the problem of the relations between sociological and psychological explanation. In fact, the remarkable nature of all these processes, depending at the same time on maturation and an external or educational transmission, is that they obey an invariant sequence of development (regardless of its rate). Thus, language is not acquired as a totality, but in a sequence which has often been noted: the [p. 18] comprehension of substantives (holophrases) precedes that of verbs, and the understanding of verbs precedes by a long period that of adverbs and conjunctions signalling relationships, ideas, etc. The acquisition of a system of questions does not take place, either, in a single step, but always proceeds in remarkably regular organized phases. It is understandable that clinicians or psychologists concerned with applied studies should ignore such facts in favour of their outcome, especially the stage in which the development culminates. But these developmental processes are highly instructive regarding the relationship between maturation and social transmission. Are the phases of learning regulated by the levels of maturation? Not entirely, since the characteristics of these phases are relative to the collective realities 'external' to the individual: these are the semantic or syntactic categories of language, or the systems of conceptual representations or pre-operations which are their defining criteria. If such a sequence were the outcome solely of maturation, we would have to admit a preformation, or hereditary anticipation of social categories in the nervous system, and this would be a cumbersome, and moreover useless, hypothesis. Is the sequence of these phases of acquisition regulated, then, by social interactions themselves? This is also unlikely, since, even if schooling inculcates the child effectively with the content of collective representations according to a chronological programme, the language and habitual modes of reasoning are transmitted indiscriminately by the environment. If at each stage the child selects certain elements and assimilates them in a particular sequence according to his mentality, this does not mean that the child submits more passively to the pressure of 'social life' than to 'physical reality', considered as totalities, but that he actively selects among available possibilities, and reconstructs them and assimilates them in his own manner.

The mental therefore exists between the biological and the social, and we must now try to distinguish, in a preliminary and introductory fashion, the relations between sociological and psychological explanation. Now, the great difference between the relations of sociology with biology and sociology with psychology is that the second set of relations does not constitute links of superposition or hierarchy, like the first, but rather links of coordination or even interpenetration. In other words, there is no series of three successive terms: biology → psychology → sociology, but rather a simultaneous link from biology to psychology and sociology together, these two disciplines having the same object, [p. 19] but treating it from distinct and complementary viewpoints. The reason for this is that there are not three human natures, the physical person, the mental person, and the social person, superimposed or succeeding one another like the foetus, the child and the adult, but there is on the one hand the organism, determined by hereditary characteristics as well as by ontogenetic mechanisms, and on the other hand the set of human behaviours, each of which has, from birth and in differing degrees, a mental aspect and a social aspect. Psychology and sociology are therefore comparable, in their interdependence, to two closely related biological sciences, such as descriptive embryology and comparative anatomy, or causal embryology and the theory of heredity (including the theory of variations or evolution), but not to physics and chemistry before they began to converge. Yet the image is still deceptive, because ontogenesis and phylogenesis are easier to separate than the individual and the social aspect of human behaviour: we almost need to compare the relations between psychology and sociology to those between number and space, the intervention of neighbourhood sufficing to make spatial any 'set', or any algebraic or analytic relation.

All the problems raised by psychological explanation are therefore also found in sociological explanation, with virtually the sole difference that the 'I' is replaced by the 'we', and that actions and 'operations' become, when a collective dimension is added, interactions, which is to say they become behaviour patterns which are capable of reciprocal modification (in all the intermediate grades between conflict and synergy), or forms of 'cooperation', i.e. operations carried out collectively or in reciprocal correspondence. It is true that this emergence of the 'we' creates a new epistemological problem: while in psychology the observer simply studies the behaviour patterns of others without thereby necessarily being affected as observer (except in certain special situations such as those of psychoanalysis), in sociology the observer is generally part of the totality studied, or of an analogous or opposed totality. The consequence of this is that a large set of 'preconceived notions', feelings, implicit postulates (moral, legal, political, etc.) and social [p. 20] prejudices intervene between the observer and the object of study, and that the decentration of the observer, essential for objectivity, is infinitely more difficult than in other situations. But while the 'we' is a notion specific to sociology, the difficulties raised by it in relation to impartiality and the intellectual courage necessary for research also exist to some extent in psychology, precisely because the human being is a unity, and all mental functions are equally social.

It is also the case that of all of the wide range of questions we shall be treating later in relation to sociological explanation, each has an analogue in psychology. This is particularly true of the central notion by means of which Durkheimian sociologists have wished to sever all relations between sociology and psychology, and this is the notion of totality. A society is a whole irreducible to the sum of its parts, according to Durkheim, and therefore has novel properties vis-à-vis its parts, in the same way in which the molecule possesses, by virtue of its synthesis, properties unknown in the atoms which make it up. There is a very curious passage (one of the few in which he expressed any opinion about psychology) in which Durkheim compares, by a sort of analogical proportion, the collective consciousness in relation to its individual elements with an individual state of consciousness (also envisaged as a whole) in relation to the organic elements on which it depends. Just as an individual representation (perception, image, etc.) is not the product of simple association between organic elements considered in isolation, but rather a unity from the outset, characterized by over-arching properties, so collective representations are not reducible to the individual representations whose synthesis they constitute. This comparison of Durkheim's is more far-reaching than he could have imagined in 1898:[1] not only is it perfectly true that the notion of a totality is common to both sociology and psychology, but the notion is also open to varying interpretations in a parallel manner in both disciplines. The totality via 'emergence', as Durkheim conceived it, corresponds closely to the notion of total form or 'Gestalt' in psychology, while the objections applicable to this latter conception are also applicable to the [p. 21] Durkheimian totality, and more relativistic conceptions of totality can be developed in both domains.

On the other hand, just as in psychology a distinction is made between genetic explanations, concerned with the mechanisms of development, and the analysis of states of equilibrium as such, so there are diachronic or dynamic explanations (about the historical evolution of societies) and synchronic or static explanations (about social equilibrium) in sociology. Similarly, in both psychology and sociology we find three major types of structure, invoked by authors under varying names, but which can be reduced to notions of rhythm, regulation and grouping. In both domains, there is recourse to axiomatized analyses alongside real or concrete explanations, and their use of such analyses reveals especially well the duality of relations of implication (peculiar to systems of norms, e.g. the nesting of legal norms) and of causal relations proper.

This duality of implication inherent in collective representations and of

causality in social behaviour patterns as behaviour patterns raises a fundamental problem of explanation, one which has been posed by Marxist
sociology and taken up in different forms by authors of a very different
persuasion, such as Pareto. This is the question of the relations between
'infrastructure' and the 'superstructure'. Just as psychology has come to the
realization that the contents of consciousness alone explain nothing causally,
and that the only possible causal explanation must move back from
consciousness to behaviour patterns, i.e. action, so sociology in discovering
the relativity of superstructures in relation to infrastructures appeals against
explanations from ideology, in favour of explanations through action (action
carried out in common to preserve the life of the social group in a particular
material environment; concrete and technical actions which become perpetuated in collective representations, rather than deriving from them in the first
place, as 'applications'). The problem of relations between infrastructure and
superstructure is, therefore, closely linked to that of relations between the
causality of behaviour patterns and the implications within representation,
whether these implications are prelogical or even almost symbolic, as in
various ideologies, or [p. 22] whether they are logically coordinated as in
rational collective representations, of which scientific thought is the most
authentic product.

This leads us to the second essential interest which sociological knowledge
holds for genetic epistemology. It is not merely because it is a particular mode
of knowledge, to be analysed like any other, that sociological knowledge is
important for epistemology: it is also because the very object of sociological
research subsumes the whole development of collective knowledge, in
particular the whole history of scientific thought. For this reason, genetic
epistemology, which studies the growth of knowledge from the dual
viewpoint both of its psychological formation and of its historical evolution,
depends as much on sociology as on psychology – the sociogenesis of the
different forms of knowledge being neither more nor less important than its
psychogenesis, since these are two inseparable aspects of any existing
formation. There are two questions of particular significance here because
the answers to them are crucial for the definition of genetic epistemology: the
question of the relationship between sociogenesis and psychogenesis in the
formation of the child's notions during the course of socialization, and the
question of the nature of these same notions in the elaboration of scientific and
philosophical notions as these succeed each other historically.

The interdependence of sociogenesis and psychogenesis[1] is particularly
marked in the field of child psychology, to which I have frequently appealed
in explaining the construction of notions. Such a recourse to the intellectual
development of the child, conceived as a kind of mental embryogenesis,
which is one I have already defended as a principle by indicating the
usefulness of biological embryology to comparative anatomy,[2] could
nevertheless create unease in some readers. The psychology of the child
would no doubt explain the mode of formation of notions and operations,

(some readers will object) if the child could be studied as a self-contained entity, insulated from all adult influences, and if the child's thought were constructed without having to derive its essential elements from the social environment. But what is the child 'in itself', and do not children only exist in relation to certain well-defined collective environments? This is perfectly reasonable, and, if the study of individual mental development has to be called 'child psychology', this is only with reference to the experimental methods used in this discipline. In reality, and as much because of the explanatory notions [p. 23] used as because of the object of study, child psychology is a branch of sociology, concerned with the study of the socialization of the individual, at the same time as a branch of psychology itself. Before developing this point, it should be noted that, far from constituting an objection to the use of psychogenetic results in comparative epistemology, this interdependence between social, mental and organic factors in the individual genesis of notions rather highlights the significance of individual development, especially its regular stages.[2] It is in fact very striking that, in order to be able to construct logical and numerical operations, the representation of Euclidean space, of time, of speed, etc., etc., the child must, in spite of social pressures of all kinds which attempt to impose these notions ready-made and communicable, pass through all the phases of a reconstruction, from the intuitive to the operatory. The construction of the operations of logical addition and seriation, etc., which are necessary for the establishment of a concrete logic; the construction of operations of one-to-one correspondence in the conservation of sets, necessary for the genesis of number; the construction of topological intuitions and operations of ordering, etc., necessary for the concept of space; the seriation of events, the nesting of durations, and the intuition of overtaking, constitutive of time and speed; etc., etc. Each of these thus acquires an epistemological significance all the greater, since the child is immersed in a collective milieu where these notions are available ready-made. Yet, instead of accepting these at face value, the child only selects (as we have just seen in Section 1 above) from the available representations those elements which are assimilable according to the precise laws of operatory development!

Seen in this light, and still being careful to avoid misusing a certain type of comparative explanation, mental embryology does not lose its significance for comparative or genetic epistemology just because individual development is in part conditioned by the social environment, and because psychogenesis is in part also sociogenesis, any more than organic embryology would lose its significance for comparative anatomy because embryogenesis is largely determined by genes or hereditary factors. Just as individual organic development is partially dependent on hereditary transmission, so individual mental development is partially conditioned (over and above factors of organic maturation and mental formation in the strict sense) by social or educational transmission. One process is particularly interesting in this respect, as much for genetic epistemology itself as from the point of view of the relations between sociology and psychology, and [p. 24] this is the process which Bachelard and Koyré have called, metaphorically, 'intellectual mutations'. The history of scientific ideas, as Koyré says 'shows us the human mind at grips with reality; reveals its victories and its defeats; shows us what superhuman effort has been the cost of each step on the road to understanding of the real, an effect which leads, sometimes, to a veritable 'mutation' of the human intellect: a transformation which allows ideas which have been painfully 'invented' by the greatest geniuses to become, not merely accessible, but even easy and obvious, to schoolchildren'.[3] This amounts to saying that a child of 7, 9 or 12 years etc., will have in the twentieth century quite different ideas about movement, speed, time space, etc., from children of the same age in the sixteenth century (i.e. before Galileo and Descartes), or in the tenth century, etc. This is obvious, and shows very clearly the role of social or educational transmission; but its significance is much greater when we realize that the mind of the child is not passive: if the twelve-year-old schoolchild living in the twentieth century comes to think of movement in the Cartesian mode, this level is not reached in a single step; instead a series of preceding levels is passed through, in the course of which the child even resuscitates, without feeling any doubts about it, the Peripatetic 'anti-peristasis'[3] – of which there is no longer any trace in contemporary collective representations. In other words, (and, of course, without needing to invoke an exact parallelism between ontogenesis, phylogenesis and historical sociogenesis) 'intellectual mutation' is not manifested in the form purely and simply of the replacement of old ideas by new ones: rather, it takes the form of an acceleration of the psychogenetic process, the levels of which remain relatively constant in their order of succession, but proceed more or less rapidly according to the social milieu. The necessary appeal to specifically mental factors is, incidentally, justified by the existence of these accelerations and delays in development as a function of collective environments: 'intellectual mutation' as an accelerating factor could never, in fact, be explained by organic maturation alone (without recourse to acquired characteristics or anticipatory preformation), nor by social transmission alone [p. 25] (since this is a matter of acceleration, not replacement), and not, either, by any combination of these two processes (since one of them is invariant, while only the other varies). If social transmission accelerates individual mental development, it must take place in the following manner (as we saw earlier): between organic maturation which furnishes mental potentialities, but without ready-made psychological structuring, and social transmission which furnishes the elements and the model for a possible construction, though without imposing this in a completed state, there occurs an operatory construction which transforms the potentialities furnished by the nervous system into mental structures. But this translation only takes place as a function of the interaction between individuals, and therefore under the accelerating or delaying influence of differing actual modes of social interaction. Thus the invariant biological (in the form of heredity) is continued simultaneously into the mental and the social, and it is the interdependence of these two latter factors which alone can explain the accelerations or delays in development in varying collective environments.

But while the sociogenesis of notions is occurring at the core of psychogenesis from the earliest stages of development, it is obvious that the influence of sociogenesis will increase progressively, even geometrically, in the later stages. The social intervenes before language through sensory-motor training, imitation, etc., though without essentially modifying pre-verbal intelligence. With language, the role of the social augments considerably, since it allows exchange of thought as soon as thought is developed. The progressive construction of intellectual operations presupposes a growing interdependence between mental factors and inter-individual interactions, as we shall see in Section 7. Once the operations are established, an equilibrium is attained between the mental and the social, in the sense that the individual who has become an adult member of a society could no longer think apart from that completed socialization. This leads us to the second essential question which genetic epistemology raises for sociology: that of the role of society in the elaboration of notions, through history, in philosophy and in the various types of scientific knowledge.

Sociological analysis has a critical part to play here, and its importance cannot be [p. 26] underestimated. Since it links thought and action in the closest possible manner, like psychology but with the single difference that sociology is concerned with the relations between collective representations and collective behaviour patterns, sociology sooner or later introduces into the modes of thought that it seeks to explain a distinction analogous to one that is made, in the sphere of individual psychology, between egocentric or subjective thought and decentred or objective thought. Sociology recognizes in certain forms of thought the reflections of the preoccupations of the narrow group to which the individual belongs, whether this be the sociomorphism described in the collective representations of primitive societies, or the national or class sociocentrism, more refined and disguised, that are seen in ideologies and systems of metaphysics. Sociology also recognizes, in contrast, other forms of thought, the possibility of true universalization of the operations of thought, as in the case of scientific thought.

In the sociological analysis of philosophical thought, Lukács has taken a decisive step with his analysis of literary symbols, as has Goldmann with his analysis of such significant philosophical systems as those of Kant and Pascal. It is already possible to conceive of an interpretation of the history of philosophy as a function of the different types of social differentiation in nations and in social classes. We will return to this point when we consider the relations between infrastructure and superstructure (Section 6). The sociological analysis of intellectual operations themselves, which is clearly possible given the history of technology and science, is a question we shall return to at the conclusion of this chapter (Section 7).

2. THE DIFFERENT MEANINGS OF THE CONCEPT OF SOCIAL TOTALITY

Nothing can better demonstrate the impact of the shift of perspective in sociology in the nineteenth and twentieth centuries than to contrast the social philosophies which held places of honour in the seventeenth and eighteenth centuries. How, for example, did Rousseau set about substituting for the theological explanations of the 'Discours sur l'histoire universelle'[4] an interpretation of society based on nature and natural human aptitudes? He imagined a noble savage, gifted in advance with all the moral virtues, and a capacity for intellectual representation such that this isolated individual, having never known society, was able to anticipate mentally all the legal and economic advantages of a 'social contract' binding him to [p. 27] others. A thesis like this rests on two basic postulates, which illustrate very clearly the perpetual prejudices of common sense which scientific sociology has had to, and must continue to, combat. The first postulate is: there exists a 'human nature' prior to social interaction; it is innate in the individual, and possesses in advance all the intellectual, moral, legal, economic, etc. faculties which sociology, in contrast, considers as the most characteristic products of collective life. The second postulate is its correlative: social institutions constitute the derived result, deliberate and therefore artificial, of individual wills motivated by this human nature, and it is only the individual who is in possession of genuinely 'natural' qualities (cf. 'natural' right, etc.).

The reversal of perspective which marked the discovery of the sociological problem leads, instead, to taking as the starting point the only concrete reality present to observation and experience, which is society as a totality, and to seeing individuals with their behaviour patterns and mental activities as a function of this totality, and not as pre-existing entities in an isolable state, provided in advance with the qualities necessary to realize the social totality. 'Man must be explained by society, not society by man', wrote Comte, but his law of the three stages,[5] which furnished at the outset of sociology a general scheme of explanation, placed exclusive emphasis on 'collective representations' as opposed to various types of behaviour patterns, and in so doing he inaugurated a highly abstract sociological tradition which found its fullest expression in Durkheim. 'It is not man's consciousness that determines his way of being, it is his social being that determines his consciousness' said Marx,[6] in contrast, giving rise to a sociology of behaviour which would from the outset be more easily related to the future psychology of behaviour patterns.

The problem raised by sociological explanation, is, therefore, first and foremost, that of the use made of the notion of totality. If the individual is the element and the society is the whole, how is it possible to conceive a totality which modifies the elements which make it up, without making use of other material than these elements themselves? Simply stating this question is sufficient to reveal its close analogy with all the problems of genetic construction, which is merely a special case of the problem of sociological explanation, but a case of exceptional [p. 28] importance, and it is therefore essential for epistemology to know how sociological thought has answered the question.

In this case, as in all similar ones, the history of ideas shows that there are, not two, but at least three possible solutions, and the third itself has several varieties. First of all, there is the atomistic analysis, in which the whole is constituted by the addition of the properties of the elements. In fact no sociologist has ever adopted this point of view; it is a construction of common sense and of pre-sociological social philosophies, which explained the characteristics of all collectivities in terms of the attributes of innate human nature in individuals, without seeing that this reverses the order of cause and effect, accounting for society in terms of the results of the socialization of individuals. The unfortunate debate which opposed Tarde and Durkheim in their solutions to an essentially incoherent question has led to the belief that Tarde did explain society in terms of the individual. By appealing to imitation, opposition, etc., Tarde was in fact invoking the relations among individuals, but without seeing that these relations themselves modify the mental structures of individuals; while Durkheim's appeal to social constraint rightly insisted on the transformations in individual consciousness produced by this constraint, but without understanding the necessity for analysis of this process of the totality to begin by looking at the concrete relations among individuals.

The second solution is Durkheim's, which can be characterized as the notion of 'emergence', developed also in biology and in Gestalt psychology: the whole is not the result of the composition of 'structuring' elements, but adds a set of new properties to the elements, which are 'structured' by it. The additional properties emerge spontaneously from the union of elements, and cannot be reduced to any additive composition since they essentially consist in forms of organization or equilibrium. This is why Durkheim rejected any psychogenetic explanation of social characteristics, genetic explanation in sociology being possible only on the basis of the history of the social totality itself, seen in each of its phases as an indissoluble entity.

[p. 29] Although atomistic explanation of the social totality leads to the attribution to individual consciousness of a set of ready-made faculties, in the form of a 'given' mind untouched by sociogenesis, the simple transfer of this human mind to the core of the 'collective consciousness' is also a rather facile solution, in spite of its positive advantages such as the possibility of reconstructing the history of this new reality, no longer innate and immutable, and open to change over time. The collective consciousness, the heir of mental powers up to then thought to be innate or *a priori*, has the disadvantage that it is still a consciousness, or the unconscious source of conscious products, i.e. it inherits all the substantialism and the spiritual causality left over after psychology has been dismissed as redundant, and sociology instead has to assume that particular burden. This reversal of positions, is, however, only apparent, and is simply a displacement of genetic problems without offering any actual solution.

The third solution arises directly from this difficulty, proposing relativism and concrete sociology: the social totality is neither a combination of pre-existing elements, nor a novel entity, but a system of relationships each of which in its own right brings about a transformation of the elements thus related. This appeal to a set of interactions is no more, in fact, than an appeal to individual characteristics once more, and the individualist cast of many 'interactionist' sociologies stems more from an inadequate psychology than from gaps due to insufficient elaboration of the notion of interaction. When Tarde or Pareto explained social life by imitation, or by composition of 'residues', they were making use of a rudimentary psychology in attributing to the individual a ready-made logic or a permanent array of instincts, without realizing that these entities that they took as given depend, themselves, on more fundamental interactions. In contrast, Baldwin, who was both sociologist and psychologist, saw very clearly the close connection between consciousness of the self and consciousness of the interaction in imitation, and he was the first to pose the basic problem of 'genetic logic'. But the common fault of the great majority of sociological explanations is to try to give at the outset a sociology of consciousness or even of language, when the truth is that in social life, as in the life of individuals, thought is the result of action, and society is essentially a system of activities, in which elementary interactions consist, literally, in actions [p. 30] reciprocally modifying each other according to certain laws of organization or equilibrium: technical actions of manufacture and use of tools, economic actions of production and distribution, moral and legal actions of cooperation or constraint and oppression, intellectual actions of communication, team research, or reciprocal criticism – in short, collective construction and the coordination of operations. The analysis of these interactions, embedded in behaviour, must be the starting point in the exploration of collective representations, or interactions which modify the consciousness of individuals.

It is clear that this third solution could not entail a conflict between sociological and psychological explanation: rather, the two complement each other in revealing the dual aspect, individual and inter-individual, of all behaviour patterns in human society, whether this be conflict, cooperation, or any of the intermediate varieties of social behaviour. Apart from organic factors, which influence the mechanisms of action interiorly, all behaviour in fact presupposes two sorts of interaction which modify it exteriorly, and are inseparable from each other: the interaction between subject and object, and the interaction between subject and other subjects. Thus, the relation between the subject and the material object modifies both subject and object at the same time through assimilation of the object to the subject and accommodation of the subject to the object. The same is true of all collective work by human beings on nature: 'Work is above all a process which takes place between man and nature, a process in which man, by his own activity, realizes, regulates, and controls his exchanges with nature. He therefore appears to himself as a natural force in the face of material nature. He makes use of the natural forces inherent in his bodily nature, arms and legs, head and hands, to appropriate natural substances in a form he can use to ensure his own survival. As he works on external nature and transforms it at the same time he transforms his own nature'.[4] But, if the interaction between subject and object modifies both of them in this way, it is obvious *a fortiori* that each interaction between individual subjects will modify each subject in relation to the [p. 31] other. Therefore every social relation constitutes a totality in itself, with a novel character and the capability of transforming the mental structure of the individual. There exists, then, a continuity from the interaction between two individuals up to the totality constituted by the set of relations among individuals in one and the same society, and, more definitively, the totality conceived in this way is seen to consist, not in a sum of individuals, nor in a reality imposed upon individuals from above, but in a system of interactions which modify the very structure of individuals.

Defined thus as interactions between individuals, with external transmission of acquired characters (as opposed to internal transmission of innate characters), social facts are exactly parallel with mental facts, with the sole difference that the 'we' is always replaced by the 'I', and cooperations by plain operations. Mental facts can be classified according to three distinct, but inseparable, aspects of any behaviour pattern: the structure of the behaviour pattern, which constitutes its cognitive aspect (operations or pre-operations), its energy or economy, which constitutes the affective aspect (values), and the system of indices or symbols which serve as signifiers of these operatory structures and values. Similarly, social facts can be reduced to three types of inter-individual interaction, or rather to three aspects, always present to different degrees, of possible inter-individual interactions. First of all, the structuration of interactions adds to the simple regularity which is a property of mental structuration an element of obligation, which stems from the inter-individual character of interactions: this is expressed in the existence of rules. Second, collective values differ from the values attached to the simple relationship between subject and object, in so far as they imply an element of inter-individual exchange. Finally, the signifiers of collective interactions are constituted by conventional signs, as opposed to the pure indices or symbols available to the individual independently of social life. Rules, exchange values and signs are the three aspects which together constitute social facts, since any behaviours carried out in common are necessarily expressed by norms, values, and conventional signifiers. This is as true of behaviour patterns in conflict or oppression as of the various forms of cooperation, because even in war or in class struggle certain values are defended, certain rules are invoked, and certain signs are [p. 32] used, whatever the objective or subjective meaning of these elements, and whatever level they may occupy in the superstructure or infrastructure of the behaviours at the time.

The existence of rules, found in all societies, raises an interesting problem concerning the nature of norms in general. Individual action already has, in one sense, a normative aspect, to do with its efficacity and its adaptive equilibrium. But nothing obliges individuals to succeed in what they do, and neither the efficacity of actions nor their balanced regularity constitute obligatory norms. On the other hand, the study of mental facts in the child shows that the consciousness of obligation presupposes a relationship of at least two individuals, one who imposes an obligation by giving commands or instructions, and one who is obligated (unilateral respect), or two individuals who reciprocally obligate each other (reciprocal respect). Furthermore it is obvious that the individual who obligates can in turn be obligated by the rules, stretching back in a stepwise fashion to the most remote generations, as a social legacy. These rules apply in all spheres, and therefore structure also the signs themselves (grammatical rules, etc.) and values (moral and legal rules) as well as concepts and collective representations in general (logic). The rules of thought themselves have a dual nature: they are forms of equilibrium in individual actions, in so far as these result in a reversible composition, and they are also imposed as norms by the system of interindividual interactions (we shall see why in Section 7). This amounts to saying, in concrete terms, that if individuals are forced to introduce a certain coherence into their actions for them to be effective, they are also obliged to display coherence if they cooperate with others: the hypothetical imperative of individual action corresponds to a categorical imperative of collective action. It should be added that, historically and genetically, these two imperatives are in the beginning one; the hypothetical imperative is distinguished later, because individualized action can only gradually be distinguished or felt to be different from joint action.

Second, the social fact is seen in the form of the exchange of values. The individual in isolation is aware of certain values, determined by interests, pleasures, pains, and affectivity in general. These values are spontaneously systematized within the individual due to systems of affective regulation, and these regulations tend toward the reversible equilibrium that characterizes the will (in parallel with its intellectual operations). The individual's own activity, moreover, is sufficient to bring about a certain quantification of values; which, as we shall see shortly, is of an economic type: the 'law of least effort' expresses the relationship between minimum work and [p. 33] maximum result; the work itself, and the energy expended by the subject therefore constitute values for the individual, which are balanced against the objects of use, and which condition these objects. The role of rarity in the mechanism of choice equally leads to an individual quantification of value. But these values, whether qualitative or partially quantified, remain variable and fluid as long as they do not lead to exchanges. Exchange value is therefore the new fact which socially consolidates values and transforms them by making them dependent, no longer only on the relationship between a subject and objects, but also on the total system of relationships between two or more subjects, on the one hand, and objects, on the other hand.

Exchange values include, by definition, everything which could give rise to an exchange, from objects used in practical action to the ideas and representations giving rise to an intellectual exchange, and inter-individual affective values. These various values remain qualitative (that is, subjected only to intensive quantification), in so far as they result not from calculated exchange, but from exchange which is simply subject to whatever affective regulations of action may be relevant – either altruistic or egoistic. In contrast, they become economic[5] when they give rise to extensive or metric quantification, the latter based on the measurement of exchanged objects or services. For example, an exchange of ideas between a physics student and a philosophy student is not an economic exchange, because it is a matter of free conversation[7] (even if the exchange is 'interested' on the part of one or other student), but the exchange of an hour of physics against an hour of philosophy becomes an economic exchange, even though the ideas exchanged may be the same as in the previous case: this is because the exchange has been intentionally 'calculated', and the duration of the conversation has been measured (regardless of the reason, or importance, of the ideas). The quantification of economic value may be simply extensive, as in bartering, where evaluation is a matter of judgment, or it may become metric (with the construction of common measures in the form of different varieties of coinage).

The relationship between rules and values is complex. Followers of Durkheim identify these two terms, while allowing that all social constraints comprise an obligation in their form (therefore a rule), and a value in their content. It is true that a 'field' of social values is never observed which does not have a framework of rules: thus economic values are regulated by a set of moral and legal rules, even though elastic, which proscribe certain forms of theft (theft nevertheless [p. 34] resulting in the maximum profit for the minimum loss, as Sageret has nicely pointed out); intellectual values are regulated by the rules of logic, and when the set of rules is completely formalized these rules become the sole source of the values of truth and falsity, etc. But it is none the less true that values can be regulated to different degrees, a fact which is sufficient to demonstrate the duality of these two kinds of social fact. In the extreme case, a value may even momentarily escape any regulation at all, such as an idea capturing the mind independently of any constraint. At the other extreme, there are values that can be called normative because they are solely a function of rules, such as moral, legal, or logical values. The essential function of a rule is to conserve values, and the only social means of conserving them is to make them obligatory. Therefore any value which is conserved over time becomes normative: a credit exchange gives rise to the idea of a security and of debt, which are legally regulated values; a scientific hypothesis gives rise to a logical conservation which is obligated by the reasoning which pertains to it, etc.

Finally, the third aspect of the social fact is the sign, or means of expression serving to transmit rules and values. The individual *qua* individual, i.e.

independently of all interaction with others, is able to create 'symbols' by means of resemblance between the signified and the signifier (e.g. mental images, ludic symbols as in imaginary games, dreams, etc). The sign, in contrast, is arbitrary and therefore presupposes a convention, either explicit and free as in the case of mathematical signs (usually called symbols, but in reality signs), or tacit and obligatory (ordinary language, etc.). Sign systems are numerous, and essential to social life: verbal signs, writing, gestures of affective expression and politeness, modes of dress (indicating social class, profession, etc.), rituals (magic, religious, political, etc.) and so on. Furthermore, many signs are accompanied by symbolism (in the sense defined above), and this tendency is greater the more 'primitive' the society, and therefore the less abstract, i.e. the less thoroughly socialized the system of collective representations. Sign systems even include some more complex, semi-conceptual collective symbols such as myths and legendary tales, which are signifiers rather than signifieds (even though they are, themselves, signifieds in relation to the words which express them): they are, in effect, the bearers of mystical and affective meanings larger than the stories themselves, and of which the story is the signifier. Religious myths develop into political myths: all social ideologies, including metaphysics, thus form part of the system of signs over and above rational collective [p. 35] representations and constitute, from this point of view, a kind of symbolic thought whose unconscious significance largely surpasses the rational concepts which are its signifieds. In effect, in any objective collective representation, value derives from the concept, whose adequate utilization is thus expressed, while in the case of ideology, the concept is only a symbol of values which have been attached to it in a contingent fashion.

All social interaction, therefore, is manifested in the form of rules, values and signs. Society itself, on the other hand, is a system of interactions beginning with relations between two individuals, extending to interactions among each of these and the set of others, and extending also to the actions of all previously existing individuals, i.e. of all interactions in history, upon existing individuals. The question arises, then, of the sense in which sociological thought uses the term 'totality'. Excluding the notion that a totality is reducible to a sum of individuals, since these are modified by interaction, and also excluding the notion of an 'emergent' totality, there are two other solutions, both acceptable either separately or jointly. The social totality can be constituted by the addition of all social interactions in play. Alternatively, it could consist in a 'mixture' (in the probabilistic meaning of the term) of interactions, with complex inter-relationships and more or less probable specific outcomes. Finally, the social totality could be partially additively composed of interactions, and partially in a state of statistical mixture.

The choice among these three solutions depends on a separate consideration of sign, value, and rule systems. Whether we are concerned with different types of state, revolution, war, class struggle, or any phenomenon which a practical sociology must study, antagonisms as well as forms of relative equilibrium are always reducible to questions of norms, values (qualitative or economic) and signs (including ideologies), because conflict due to the harmony of action and forces is necessarily polarized according to the three aspects of social reality. But the restoring of equilibrium could not take place in the same way regardless of which or other of these three aspects is important, because the obligation to be found in distinguishing between them indicates, of itself, the different ways in which they function, and [p. 36] it is important to demonstrate this in order to characterize the notion of a social totality, however idealized it may be. The problem, from this point of view, may be stated in the following way: are signs, values, and rules all reducible to logical compositions? It is when seen from this viewpoint relating to structure that the sociological problem about the totality takes on its epistemological significance.

To take the case of norms and rules, first of all, we notice that, although there are certain exceptional domains in which rules really do constitute rationally or logically composed systems, there are many other areas in which the rules have not attained such a state of coherent equilibrium, because they are a mixture of heterogeneous elements inherited from various periods of social history or prehistory. It is instructive to compare, for a given epoch, the system of intellectual norms governing scientific thought with the system of moral norms in force at the same time. Both may derive from very different historical periods, and contexts which would be currently incompatible as wholes. But the systematization of rational norms is currently both flexible and strict, i.e. it sacrifices old principles without hesitation when they are contradicted by more recent ones. In contrast, the morality of a society is like geological stratification, in which the remains of successive epochs are superposed or juxtaposed. Certain minds, or certain sections of society may reach a relative coherence, comparable to the logical systematization produced by the intellectual élite, but this moral élite will encounter greater resistance to its innovatory efforts, because of respect for established traditions. In the case of law, the situation is an intermediate one: from the formal point of view, the hierarchy of legal norms which extends from the constitution of a state to 'individualized norms' is a coherent unity; but in their content, it is possible for these laws to be partially contradictory, or at least to consist of a patchwork of elements of diverse origins and conflicting intentions. In sum, rule-systems themselves oscillate between the two possible aspects of social totalities: logical composition or mixture, a point which leads to [p. 37] the two questions of the influence of the historical development of norm systems on their present structure, and on their characteristic form of equilibrium.

In the case of values, the problem is much more complex. In so far as these are not normative values, i.e. regulated by norms which are logically composable, but relatively free in their exchange, it is quite clear that a system of spontaneous values is oriented in the direction of totalities of a statistically mixed, random character. Economic values, in a non-directed economy, as well as the qualitative values current in a political system dependent on the fortunes of parties, and in a situation of fluctuating literary and philosophical fashions, are all models of random, not additive composition. Only the subordination of values to norms can ensure their systematization in the form of logical totalities.

Signs, as is well known from the work of linguists, form systems which result from the interaction of historical factors and the equilibrium of linguistic systems. In particular, the regularities of intellectual language are always liable to be overturned by the values of affective language. A language can therefore never result in the constitution of logical coherence unless two conditions are met: that the signifiers correspond completely to the signifieds, and that values are completely subordinated to norms. In fact this never happens, except in the case of exclusively conventional languages expressing the relations among concepts which are themselves completely rigorous, i.e. logical and mathematical symbolism. Apart from such strictly limited fields, all sign systems oscillate between a totality which is logically composed, and one which is a 'mixture' totality. This is true also of the symbolism of myths and ideologies, even though they may only have the appearance of rationality.

To conclude, social totalities oscillate between two types. At one extreme, the interactions are relatively regular, polarized by norms or permanent obligations, and constituting composable systems which may be compared with operatory groupings in the cases where the latter would apply to exchanges and inter-individual interactions set in hierarchies, as well as intra-individual operations. At the other extreme, the social totality is a mixed conglomerate of reciprocally [p. 38] influencing interactions, whose modes of composition are similar to the regulations or rhythms of individual action. In this case, the social whole is no longer the algebraic sum of these interactions, but an over-arching structure analogous to psychological or physical 'Gestalts', i.e. systems in which new forces are added to the elements, because of the probabilistic character of the system's composition. 'Society', in the current meaning of this term, is a compromise between these two sorts of totalities. In explaining the social facts relative to such totalities, sociology encounters two types of problem, whose epistemological interest consists particularly in their correspondence to the two central questions confronting psychological explanation. These are: the problem of the relationship between history and equilibrium (between the diachronic and the synchronic view-points), and the problem of the mechanisms of equilibrium itself (rhythms, regulations and groupings).

3. EXPLANATION IN SOCIOLOGY. A. THE SYNCHRONIC AND THE DIACHRONIC

The difficulties distinctive to the problem of the social totality, which we have just seen from the standpoint of rules, values, and signs, essentially reduce to those of the relations between the history of social facts and the equilibrium of a society at a particular moment in its development. Does this equilibrium depend on the historical sequence of interactions, or solely on the interdependence of contemporary relations? It is immediately obvious that this problem will be posed in different terms for rules, values and signs, since the function of rules is above all to ensure continuity over time, while non-normative values essentially express a momentary state of equilibrium of exchanges, and signs are similar to both of these.

This question of the relation between history and equilibrium certainly exists in biology and in psychology (and, in a general way, wherever there is development over time, i.e. a history); but it is a much more subtle problem in sociology than in psychology. In individual evolution, beginning with birth and ending with the adult state, or death, intellectual and affective equilibrium appear as the end-point of development itself, in such a way that this final equilibrium can be seen as ensured by mechanisms related to those which bring about the sequence of evolutionary stages. In a society, whose death is only metaphorical, and [p. 39] whose apogee could only be compared in a literary way to human adulthood, the questions of the relation between equilibrium and development are differently posed, and are associated with a set of essential problems. Should social evolution be considered as tending toward a final equilibrium, with or without preceding revolutions, or does it consist in an alternation of phases of equilibrium and disequilibrium? In either case, is it possible to apply the same modes of explanation to the social future, and to the interdependencies among simultaneous phenomena?

From the beginning of sociology, Auguste Comte contrasted static sociology, or the theory of 'order', that is to say of social equilibrium, with dynamic sociology, or the theory of 'progress', i.e. evolution, and this distinction has been preserved in many different forms. The sociology of Marx comprises both an evolutionary theory, linked with economic and political history, and an equilibrium theory, linked with the final advent of socialism – the nature of this equilibrium differing radically from that of the mechanisms in operation during the preceding evolution (subsumption of law under morality, disappearance of the state as the result of complete nationalization, etc.). Even authors like Durkheim and Pareto who tend to sacrifice one of these aspects to the other (the first emphasizing genetic or historical processes, the second the mechanism of equilibrium) are obliged to distinguish between two types of relationship. Durkheim postulates, among other rules, that the history of a social structure does not explain its present function (a rule which has not always been observed, as we shall see later); and Pareto distinguishes between the permanence of 'types' in history and the unequal distribution of the same 'types' according to social class in a society considered statically.

But it is only in linguistics, without doubt the most exact of the social sciences, that the distinction is made systematically between the two viewpoints. As de Saussure[6] has shown, it is possible to study language not only from the 'diachronic', viewpoint, i.e. its historical evolution, but also from the 'synchronic' viewpoint, i.e. as a system of interdependent elements in equilibrium at a particular moment in history. It is important to notice that these two viewpoints are not in one-to-one correspondence, because the etymology of a [p. 40] word is in no way sufficient to fix its meaning in the present language system. This meaning depends on the needs of communication and expression at a specific moment in time, and the nature of the synchronic system of needs is such that semantic values can be modified partially independently of the history of words and their previous meanings. (For example, 'without doubt' has come to mean 'with doubt'; the French 'puisque' derives from 'puis', meaning temporal succession, but expresses a non-temporal relation of logic or reason.) The general character of this problem raised by Saussurian linguistics will be seen immediately. In biology, an organ can undergo changes of function, and the same function can be carried out successively by different organs: thus in some dipnoi the swim bladder acts as a lung,[8] etc. In psychology, the development of motives (or intra-individual values) can lead to complete rearrangements: what began as a simple compensation behaviour can become an individual's dominant motive, etc. In sociology, the history of myths and rituals, in so far as these are sign systems, abounds in transformation of meaning, as when a new religion gradually absorbs the native traditions of areas in which it has been introduced.

It can be asked, then, to what extent does the dualism of the synchronic and the diachronic dominate the different aspects of social life? If we manage to encompass in a single synthetic vision the totality of social facts at a particular moment in their history, we can be sure that each state depends on the previous one, in a continuous evolutionary sequence. But we will also see the influence of interactions upon each other, this 'mixture' leading to changes in function (i.e. in values and their meaning) of certain structures, quite independently of their previous history. Since the demands of analysis initially require the separate study of each different aspect of society, and it is impossible to know in advance the importance of these reciprocal influences, we are bound to distinguish systematically between the synchronic viewpoint, associated with equilibrium, and the diachronic or developmental viewpoint. This is the reason for the existence of two different types of explanation in sociology, whose compatibility cannot be guaranteed in advance: genetic or historical explanation, [p. 41] and functional explanation relating to forms of equilibrium. Two examples will demonstrate the necessity of this distinction: one from Durkheim, who based his whole theory on the historical method at the expense of synchronic problems, and the other from Pareto, who sacrificed development to the analysis of equilibrium.

It is well known how deeply convinced Durkheim was of the spiritual continuity linking contemporary societies to their past, even as far back as the most elementary stages, which he diligently sought in the so-called 'primitive' societies ('primitive' in the ethnographic, not prehistoric, sense). This is why, in his attempts to explain our logic, our morality, our religious and legal institutions, he always resorted systematically to the analysis of primitive, or 'original' collective representations. This sociogenetic method, apart from the problems it raises concerning the exact reconstruction of elementary social phenomena, and the line of descent from them to contemporary phenomena, leads to quite different results depending on the type of relationship studied. When used to explain the structure of rational, moral, legal, etc. notions, the method is undoubtedly fruitful. In any stated proposition, it is not simply the individual words which derive from preceding languages and which therefore have affinities, eventually, with the most ancient and primitive human expressions, it is also the concepts themselves, carried in language, whose roots extend into an indefinitely remote past, or which are the result of differentiation from elementary concepts. But when we wish to change focus, from the history to the contemporary value of a notion, a general difficulty is encountered, of which Durkheim was well aware, but not always able to avoid: the sociogenesis of structures does not explain their eventual functions, because, when they are integrated into new totalities, their meaning can change. In other words, while the structure of a concept may well depend on its previous history, its value depends on its functional position within the system of which it forms a part at a given moment in time, and it is only in the case where history consists of a succession of totalities oriented toward an increasing equilibrium that their genesis determines the contemporary value of notions.[7] A good example is the prohibition of incest, which Durkheim traced back to totemic exogamy. Suppose we accept this as a hypothesis: immediately the further question occurs as to why, amongst all the innumerable totemic taboos, this one should have been conserved. Obviously, all the other taboos have lost [p. 42] functional significance, while the incest taboo has kept its value in our societies because of contemporary (or still-contemporary) factors, such as those revealed by Freudian psychology.

It is this synchronic aspect of social interactions that Pareto paid particular attention to. His theory of social equilibrium was based on the idea of interdependence of factors at any one given moment in a society, and of the constancy of laws of equilibrium, quite independently of the history of particular societies. On this view, society is comparable to a mechanical system of interacting forces, these forces constituted not by norms, collective representations, etc. but by an underlying reality (a hypothesis suggested by the Marxist infrastructure), which is the 'residue' or set of constant interests, analogous to the instincts which are responsible for all animal social organization. After splitting these 'residues' into six large 'classes', and each class into particular types, Pareto tried to show that, while these types vary according to the levels of social development, the variations are self-compensating in such a way that the 'classes' themselves remain constant (except from one level, or one class to another in the social pyramid, at each stage of history). It is obvious, however, that this law of the constancy of 'residues' over time is completely relative to the classification adopted: it would be possible to construct any classification in such a way that the 'types' vary while leaving the 'classes' invariant, so long as the elements of the latter are arbitrarily chosen to compensate for the correspondingly necessary variations. Pareto's classification thus has, precisely, an arbitrary character, because each of his 'classes' is peculiarly heterogeneous, as if it contained just those elements necessary to maintain the constancy of the whole, in spite of variations in detail. The only way of avoiding this fault would be to look for (as Pareto did not) the real genetic ancestry of affective or intellectual drives, and categorize them accordingly. This would require historical research using Durkheim's method for norms and collective representations, or the Marxist method, for basic needs and technologies.

Clearly then, the essential difficulty for all sociological theories is to reconcile the diachronic explanation of phenomena, i.e. of their genesis and development, with synchronic explanation, i.e. that of equilibrium. Both sorts of explanation are necessary, because each is insufficient to account for the mechanisms in the other's domain, yet they are not easily compatible. [p. 43] It is this incompatibility which makes the problem interesting, independently of the particular theories we have examined. We need, then, to seek the reasons for this dualism between explanations of genesis and of equilibrium, without becoming involved in the debates within sociology itself, but remaining at the level of the structures of knowledge as such which are used by sociologists.

There are two reasons for this duality. The first has to do with the concrete content of sociological thought, i.e. the nature of the social totality, which is not completely analysable (because of the element of randomness and disorder in it). The second reason has to do with the formal structure of sociological thought: while the explanation of genesis becomes more causal as one approaches the real actions from which social facts arise, a different type of explanation is required for the relationship between history and equilibrium, because rules, values, and signs each call for a separate analysis, due to their basis in the domain of logical implication. In a state of equilibrium, the set of signs and values is unified and subordinated to normative necessity, and equilibrium thus requires a logical form of explanation. It is this transition from the causal to the logical that essentially constitutes the second reason for the inherent difficulties of sociological explanation.

If the social totality were a completely composable system, by means of the logical analysis of the interactions which constitute it, and there were no element of randomness and disorder involved, it is clear that its historical development would be sufficient to explain the set of present relations. That is, diachronic relations would completely determine synchronic relations. However, in so far as there is an element of randomness in interactions, the history of a totality does not determine the arrangement of elements in any present equilibrium: each particular state is a novel statistical totality, not deducible in its detail from the preceding statistical totalities. It is only in the case where it is possible to predict the form of the over-arching equilibrium of a system, independently of the detail of the relations among its elements, and, a further condition, where evolutionary change itself is highly probable (such as evolution in the direction of entropy in physics) that the history of a statistical system [p. 44] (mixture) determines later forms of equilibrium, and even in this case deviations are always possible. But in a system consisting neither in additive or logical composition, nor in complete randomness, but simply oscillating between the two types (like the history of language), chance excludes the one-to-one progression from the diachronic to the synchronic as far as the detail of the relationships within the system is concerned.

From this first point of view, the necessary condition for a synthesis of the diachronic and the synchronic would be the submission of the set of social facts to the laws of a directed evolution, i.e. their gradual equilibration, as in the sequential stages of individual development. This was certainly the goal of the constructors of these grand 'laws of development' which, like Spencer's or Comte's, were meant to embrace the totality of social facts. But such efforts have been somewhat inconsistent, partly because of the vagueness of the notions employed (the three stages, the transition from the homogeneous to the heterogeneous, growing integration, etc.), and partly because of their rather alarming optimism. The Marxist conception of an unfolding of social facts in the direction of a final stable state, in contrast, indicates the existence of continual struggle and opposition, and thus arrives at a conception of history as a sequence of more or less profound disequilibria, preceding subsequent equilibration. In this case, there is indeed over-arching prediction of the system, but not of the detail, because of the disorder which itself characterizes the constituent interactions – a point which confirms the incompatibility of the synchronic and the diachronic.

But the problem of the diachronic and the synchronic is mostly located in the structure of sociological explanation itself, which oscillates, like psychological explanation, between causality and implication. Rules, values and signs, in fact, all issue from action itself – joint action on nature, but all three additionally give rise to relationships which transcend causality and become implications. A relationship of causality, clearly, is diachronic, since it involves a sequence in time, while a relationship of implication is synchronic, since it consists in timeless necessity. The synthesis of the diachronic and the synchronic, therefore, will depend on the correspondence envisaged between the elements of causality and of implication [p. 45] in the explanation of the different types of rules, values and signs at the core of social life.

Obviously these three sorts of interaction will have very different significance in such a synthesis. The distinctive feature of rules is to generate conservation through time, and, where transformations occur, regulation is obligatorily invoked. A rule therefore has a causal aspect, related to the actions which precede it, and to the constraint it exercises, as well as an implicational aspect related to the conscious obligation which characterizes it. The evolution of a system of pure rules thus tends, in and of itself, toward a state of equilibrium, and, to the extent to which its transformations are themselves rule-governed, equilibrium can only increase as the system develops. In this case, diachronic and synchronic factors converge. The case of non-normative values is very different. Stemming also from action (needs, work accomplished, etc.), values, when they are not regulated, depend on the system of exchanges and its fluctuations; they therefore reflect particularly closely the process of equilibrium itself, and mark the *maximum* disjunction between the synchronic and the diachronic, as is demonstrated by the sudden devaluations and revaluations in which economic and political life abound. This is why the history of a non-normative value has no bearing on its present situation, while the history of a norm is predictive of its present obligatory status to the extent that it has been part of a regulated system. Finally, the system of signs requires both diachronic and synchronic explanations; both are necessary and each complements the other in this domain, though without any possibility of fusion, as can happen in the cases of norms and rules.

If the foregoing is correct, it becomes apparent that the diversity of sociological explanations will be even greater than that of psychological explanations. Recall that the latter oscillate between causality and implication, according to whether they approach the organicist or the logical type (operatory explanation seeking to establish the transition from action to conscious necessity). The same is true of sociological explanations, which oscillate between recourse to material factors (population, geographical environment and economic production) and recourse to 'collective consciousness' with, between these two, operatory explanation [p. 46] which links implicational interactions to the actions themselves in their causality. But in this case there is the added complication, which does not exist in psychology, that each of these varieties can be attributed to the social totality as such, conceived as the sole cause, or as the crucible of all these norms, values, and symbolic expressions, or to the individual, or yet to the interactions among individuals.

Three examples will demonstrate this necessity for sociological explanation to tie causal connections to systems of implication, in the case of the totality, the individual, or interactions. These are taken from Durkheim, Pareto, and Marx, in other words, three types of scientific thought as different as it is possible to find.

The Durkheimian model of explanation is simultaneously centred on norms and on the totality itself. On the one hand, all social causality is reduced to 'constraint', which is the pressure of the totality upon the individuals which compose it. On the other hand, all the implications inherent in the 'collective consciousness' (or set of representations engendered by social life) are reduced to relations among norms, the values themselves being only the content or the inseparable complement of these norms (such as moral goodness in relation to duty, or economic value in relation to the pressure of

institutions of exchange, etc.). Finally, the causality inherent in the social totality, and the system of implications in the collective consciousness are seen as one, since social constraint is a force or a cause, objectively conceived in its materiality, and it is at the same time obligation and attraction, i.e. norm and value, conceived subjectively in its effect on consciousness. Thus, Durkheimian explanation is both causal and implicational (having a dual character, like all sociological explanation), but its originality consists in its monolithic character: there is no gradation between lower level, where causality would lead the explanation toward implication, and higher level where this direction would be reversed. Furthermore, this explanation *en bloc* is attributed to the social totality itself, without any analysis of particular, concrete, interactions. If we look at the detail of Durkheim's explanation, one example, though chosen from many similar ones, is particularly striking from these various viewpoints: the account he gives of the division of labour by the increase in volume and density of segmented societies, whose divisions are thus broken down to form larger units; individual differentiation and competition then bring about the division of economic work, and 'organic' solidarity. Notice first of all that, [p. 47] although this explanation appears to be exclusively causal, since it refers to a demographic factor, in reality it involves as many implicational as causal relationships. If the breakdown of divisions among class, and social concentration, lead to the emancipation of individuals, etc., this means, in effect, that certain forms of obligation and certain values (respect for elders, traditions, etc.) are modified under the influence of the volume of new intrapsychic exchanges, i.e. are changed into different values and obligations. On the other hand, the role of these norms and values, i.e. implicational relationships themselves, is essential from the beginning, according to Durkheim's hypothesis, since they all emanate ultimately (whether differentiated or not) from the sentiment of the sacred linked with the exaltation of the collective consciousness. It is in fact this exaggerated role assigned to the collective consciousness, at the expense of economic production factors, which is the weak point of Durkheimian explanation. Although the effects of social density on the emancipation of individuals are obvious in some situations (e.g. in large towns compared to small towns or villages in the same country) this is not sufficient by itself to account for mental and economic differentiation, as is demonstrated by the large oriental empires which had great density, yet little differentiation of population. The role of economic causation, therefore, cannot be ignored. In general, the weakness of Durkheimian explanations lies precisely in first situating norms, values, and material causes all at the same level, basing them on a single undifferentiated totality of a statistical nature, instead of analysing the various types of interaction, which could be heterogeneous and have variable relations between their causal and implicational elements.

A second example of sociological explanation comes from Pareto's analysis. He did, in fact, appeal to interactions, but he also had a tendency to consider innate in the individual what could be conceived rather as the very result of these interactions: logic, on the one hand, and affective constants or 'residues' on the other (whose constancy was moreover to be established). At first sight, Pareto's explanation appears essentially causal: social equilibrium is assimilated to mechanical equilibrium, i.e. an arrangement of forces. But these forces are, themselves, reduced to a sort of instinctive tendency, manifest in the consciousness of individuals in the form of feelings and even ideas ('derivations'), in other words, implications of all kinds. It is true that the higher forms of implications, such as moral and legal norms, and collective representations of all kinds, play no role, according to Pareto, in social equilibrium, unless as the vehicles of elementary feelings which are thereby reinforced. By analogy with the Marxist distinction between infrastructure and [p. 48] superstructure, Pareto in fact considered that ideologies (for him the domain of everything normative) are a simple reflection of real interests, including within their system the 'derivations', in contrast to the 'residues' which make up the infrastructure. However, even if we accept Pareto's hypotheses, these residues act only in so far as they are affective drives or permanent interests, that is, they represent not only causes, but also, and essentially, values – which leads us back to a system of implications. Apart from this, the weakness of Pareto's analysis results from his treating these residues as constants, instinctive drives of individuals. Thus, logic (which he did not even suspect could be a social product) as well as residues are treated as given in advance; while a psychological analysis, or even a more extended sociological analysis, would have convinced him that norms and values are the result of interaction, not merely factors within it. In both Durkheim and Pareto, then, though they are poles apart, the difficulties of their systems stem from the fact that causes and implications are given from the outset in a constant proportion; for Durkheim in the social totality (constraint), and for Pareto in individuals. This distorts the analysis of interactions, in both cases, by failing to attribute a constructive reality to them.

With the explanatory model of Karl Marx, we find in contrast an example of analysis focused on interactions as such, and striking a better balance between causal and implicational elements. The point of departure of Marxist explanation is causal: these are the factors of production, conceived as a close interaction between human work and nature. These factors determine the earliest forms of the social group. But even at this first stage, an implicational element appears, because elementary values are attached to work, and a system of values is an implicational system; and because work is action, and the efficacy of actions carried out collectively determines a normative element. In principle, therefore, the Marxist model places itself on a ground of operatory explanation, in that human behaviour in society determines representations, and not the reverse, and implication detaches itself gradually from a pre-existing causal system which it partially overlaps with, but does not replace. With the differentiation of society into classes, and with the various relationships of cooperation (within a class) or struggle and constraint, norms, values and signs (including ideologies) give rise to various superstructures. One might be tempted to interpret the Marxist model as a devaluation of all these elements of implication, in contrast to the causality which characterizes the infrastructure. But it is sufficient to consider the way in which Marx interprets social equilibrium, which, according to him, is attained with socialism, [p. 49] to see the role he assigns to moral norms (which will absorb legal rules and the State itself) and rational norms (science for its part absorbing metaphysical ideologies) as well as to cultural values in general and the increasing role he assigns to conscious implications in interactions. Norms and values are made possible by a causal and economic mechanism subordinated to such ends and will constitute, in a state of equilibrium, a system of implications liberated from economic causality, and no longer distorted by it.

Three explanatory models as different as those of Durkheim, Pareto and Marx, then, can be seen to involve both causality and implication in sociological explanation. The epistemological problem raised by this fact is a fundamental one, linked with what was observed above about the diachronic and the synchronic. If diachronic explanation is largely causal, and synchronic explanation largely implicational, it is not surprising that Durkheim and Pareto, whose doctrines absorb the synchronic within the diachronic, or the reverse, fuse together causality and normative or axiological values. Marxist explanation, in contrast, separates the diachronic and the synchronic much more, and also differentiates between causal and implicational elements in the various types of interaction it distinguishes. The epistemological problem, therefore, is to understand how causality and implication are bound together in the characteristic structures of the levels of social interaction. This question is as important from the standpoint of the analysis of sociological explanation as it is from that of the application of sociology to genetic epistemology. In individual mental development, which is a progressive equilibration and therefore does not involve the essential duality between diachronic and synchronic factors, the transition from causality to implication involves three basic steps having distinct proportions of these two sorts of relationship: rhythms, regulations and groupings. Is it the same in sociology?

4. EXPLANATION IN SOCIOLOGY. B. RHYTHMS, REGULATIONS AND GROUPINGS

We do in fact find, in the analysis of forms of social equilibrium, these same three structures. There is, however, a difference which is that, since social evolution does not consist [p. 50] in regular equilibration, the sequence of these three structures does not appear as necessary, except in the single domain where directed evolution is possible: that of rational norms.

Just as, in psychology, rhythm marks the frontier between the mental and the physiological, so the limited ground between material facts of interest to society and social behaviours is the location and the origin of elementary social rhythms (as opposed to more or less regular alternating phenomena where periodicity characterizes certain, secondary, types of rhythm). Thus, economic activity of the simplest form (hunting and fishing, later agriculture) is tied to the natural rhythm of the seasons and the growth of animals and plants. These natural rhythms which are incorporated into the rhythm of production by virtue of the interaction of work and nature are the point of departure of many properly social rhythms: seasonal labour and seasonal migration, festivals fixed by the calendar, etc. These rhythms derive from the level of technical activity, yet have repercussions as far as the original collective representations, the level at which Mauss and Granet in particular have analysed them with such sagacity.

A particularly important sociological rhythm, which is perpetual and at the border between the biological and the social, is that constituted by the succession of generations. Each new generation in its turn goes through the same educational process, formed by the pressures of preceding generations, and also creating norms and values for the next generation. This periodic sequence is both a perpetual re-beginning and an essential instrument of transmission, linking through repetition the most developed and the most primitive societies. The importance of a rhythm of this kind derives from, among others, the following considerations: it is certain that, if such a rhythm were sufficiently modified, in the sense that the generations succeeded each other much more rapidly or much more slowly, the whole society would be profoundly transformed; thus it is enough to imagine a society in which almost all individuals were contemporaries, having experienced little of the family and school constraints which affected the preceding generation and exercising hardly any on the next generation, to see the nature of such possible transformations, especially in respect of the diminishing influence of 'sacred' traditions, etc. [p. 51] But as soon as we leave the areas of overlap between physical or biological nature and the social fact, to trace the processes of the latter domain, rhythm gives way to multiple regulations which are the outcome of the interactions among many various kinds of rhythms, and hence are the result of transformations into more complex structures. These are regulations, as opposed to groupings (which we will discuss later), which structure most interactions of exchange, in addition to most of the constraints of the past upon the present. Their intervention plays a dominant role in the statistical totalities, based on mixture, that were discussed in Section 2. In order to distinguish among the various types of regulations, we need to consider separately the mechanisms of exchange and of constraint.

Any exchange between two individuals x and x' is already, in itself, a source of readily apparent regulations (independently of whether the exchange is genetically primitive or not). In its most general form, the exchange schema can be represented in the following manner: each action of x on x' constitutes a 'service', i.e. a value $r(x)$ given away by x (time, work, objects or ideas, etc.) which leads to satisfaction (positive or negative) on the part of x', i.e. $s(x')$. Inversely x' gives away certain values $r(x')$ in acting on x, who in turn experiences satisfaction $s(x)$. But these actual values, consisting in current services or satisfactions are not the elements involved in a simple exchange, because the action $r(x)$ of x on x' can not be (or not immediately, at least) succeeded by a return action $r(x')$.[9] The result is that two sorts of potential value intervene: x', having received satisfaction $s(x')$, contracts a debt $t(x')$ toward x, while this same debt constitutes a credit $v(x)$ for x (or inversely there is a debt $t(x)$ from x to x', and a credit $v(x')$ in favour of x'). These virtual values have a significance which is completely general. The values $t(x)$ or $t(x')$ may take the form of gratitude and recognition (in all the senses of that word), which obligate the individual in different degrees (in the sense that one feels 'obligated' toward someone), as well as the form of economic debt. Furthermore, the values $v(x)$ and $v(x')$ express success, authority, moral credit, acquired through the actions (r), as well as economic credit. Even in the case of a real immediate exhange, $r(x)$ for $r(x')$ and $s(x')$ for $s(x)$, current [p. 52] services and satisfactions may be prolonged in the form of virtual values of recognition, t and v, or give place, under the same form t and v, to the anticipation of future real values, i.e. new services or satisfactions. The equilibrium of the exchange is determined by the conditions of equality: $r(x) = s(x') = t(x') = v(x) = r(x') = s(x) = t(x) = v(x')$. But it is obvious that such an equilibrium will rarely be attained; rather, all the inequalities $r(x) \gtrless s(x')$; $s(x') \gtrless t(x')$; $t(x') \gtrless v(x)$ are possible,[10] [8] according to whether one under- or over-estimates the services rendered, whether one forgets them or exaggerates their importance in memory, whether one distorts memory into a greater or lesser estimate of the partner, etc. Since there is no obligatory conservation of such exchange values (compelled by moral or legal rules) they are only subject to simple regulations, i.e. intuitive evaluations which oscillate around equilibrium but do not attain it, and recognizing only an approximate conservation. Furthermore, each new context will lead to a displacement of the equilibrium briefly achieved, by giving rise not to logical compositions of the new values with the old, but to approximate compensa- tions, once more of a simple regulatory character. If we now pass from consideration of a relationship between two individuals to that of a system of interacting relations, for example the system of innumerable evaluations which result from the success or reputation of an individual in a social group, we see immediately that the relation between an individual x and a collectivity B, or X, is not an additive composition, but rather constitutes a mixture; and that this mixture of interactions, each of which is already subject to regulations (and not to reversible operations) constitutes an over-arching system or ensemble of the type of a statistical totality, i.e. such that the whole is not the algebraic sum of the individual parts, but is a simple probabilistic composition.

These are the system regulations found in the fluctuations of economic values in a liberal regime, independently even of the objective factors of production, abundance or scarcity of raw materials, and money supply. When they are not subject to a system of norms, economic values such as prices result from a statistical equilibrium between supply and [p. 53] demand, and are no more than the symptom of the working of regulations analogous to those indicated by the spontaneous mechanism of interests, or any other non-economic exchange interaction. It is easy to demonstrate that elementary economic exchange is only a special case of the general form described above, in which only real values occur (*r* and *s* in our symbolism); but the evaluation of both services and satisfactions (the 'ophelimities' of Pareto) itself depends on pre-existing or anticipated virtual values, and this alone demonstrates the role of regulations in what could otherwise appear to be the simple reading of an immediate need or interest. The importance of potential values is particularly clear in the mechanism of crises due to overproduction. While small gaps between production and consumption give rise to small oscillations around the point of equilibrium between these two processes, large gaps bring about periodic crises which, in contrast, result in a displacement of the point of equilibrium itself. Small oscillations are due to the spontaneous corrections of the economic collectivity reacting to its own errors of prediction, which is purely and simply the mechanism of regulation (anticipation, then correction). Large oscillations, in contrast, represent the failure of these regulations in detail, hence the crisis and the displacement of equilibrium, but also the creation of a new equilibrium, momentarily, by means of compensatory reactions – i.e. once again by means of regulation (but of the whole system). We see how, then, in the case of periodic crises, the failure of regulation can take on the nature of rhythm, but a more complex and less regular rhythm than the elementary ones discussed above.[9]

The general character of regulations, occurring in interactions of exchange among two, or a growing number of individuals, up to the complete collectivity, is such as to lead to partial compensations, but without complete reversibility and therefore with either slow or sudden displacements of equilibrium. It is only in the case of values rendered normative by a system of rules, and in the case of these norms themselves, that composition goes beyond the level of simple regulations and reaches the complete reversibility and permanent equilibrium which characterize operatory groupings. But no system of norms can, by virtue of its normative character, attain this level of reversible grouping, because there are semi-normative systems of interactions which remain in the state of regulations. More specifically, the partial compensations which define [p. 54] regulation extend to the lower bound of completely reversible structures, and it is only systems of completed rules, which are logically composable, which attain the quality of operatory groupings. This fact implies the existence of a series of intermediaries between the two structures.

It is in this way that the pressure exerted by public opinion, or political constraints, lead to the creation of imperatives which go beyond simple spontaneous evaluation, and attain a normative character in varying degrees. These imperatives arise, in part, from the interests entering into exchanges, but they also impose all kinds of rules, ranging from those of simple usage to those of moral and intellectual constraint. But this is more a matter of an external and legalistic morality, and of rationality related to reasons of state, than of reason itself. Public opinion, of which Durkheim said accurately that it always lagged behind the deeper currents within society, therefore constitutes the model of a totality which is simultaneously statistical, in so far as it is the nexus of multiple and haphazard interconnections, yet partially normative, in so far as it obligates individuals in various ways. Public opinion, then, given its simple probabilistic and relatively little ordered character (in contrast to well-structured intellectual, moral, and legal systems), clearly arises from simple regulations, and not from an operatory grouping. As for political constraint, it is similar to the extent that interests and calculation interfere with norms, and that norms are imposed by various pressures, instead of conquering minds by virtue of their internal necessity alone. Hence the existence of compromise, which is the conscious or intentional form of regulation, as opposed to the logical or moral operation.

Exactly the same must be said of a whole set of forms of constraint whose historical and contemporary importance in relation to the formation of norms cannot be exaggerated, yet whose functioning in general does not go beyond the level of regulation, in spite of an appearance of rational composition. They are the constraints arising in sub-collectivities which each have their own special means of pressure: social classes, churches, families, and schools. We will return to the question of class ideology in Section 5, since it raises the whole question of the relation between infrastructure and superstructure. Family and school constraints, in contrast, illustrate in a particularly simple way the mechanism of moral or intellectual rules remaining mid-way between regulation and a completely normative composition. In fact, to the extent that ethical or rational truths, [p. 55] even when they converge in their content toward the norms of the moral and scientific elites of society at the time, are imposed by an educational constraint due to the family or schooling, instead of being re-lived or rediscovered through a process of free participation, they change their character *ipso facto* in being subordinated to a factor of obedience or authority which arises from regulation, and no longer from logical composition. Moral obedience, as is observed in a partiarchal family, or in the modern conjugal family during the first years of life of children, and the intellectual authority of tradition or of the 'master', as this is perpetuated in the discontinuity of the 'initiation' practised in 'primitive' tribes as well as in contemporary school life (at least in those schools not yet transformed by the so-called 'active' methods)[11] all in effect make use of a common factor of transmission, which is unilateral respect. Such a sentiment, by subordinating the good and the true to the obligation to follow a model, leads only to a system of regulations, not operations. The question of obedience, in fact, always reduces to this alternative: is reasoning an act of obedience, or is obedience an act of reason? In the first case, obedience drives reason and therefore constitutes only an incomplete norm, of a regulatory and not operatory nature. In the second case, reason drives obedience, to the extent of eliminating the element of spiritual submission, and this system is therefore entirely normative, the norm of unilateral subordination resulting from a delegation of the rational norm.

Such a conflict is particularly clear in the problem of legal norms. This is a very curious problem since it is clear that, formally, a system of legal rules is the very model of a set of social interactions having acquired the structure of an operatory grouping; yet it is nonetheless evident that, in its content, a system of law can justify anything, and legitimate the worst abuses by conferring a legal form on them. By virtue of its content, then, the grouping of legal norms could equally validate either a set of behaviours themselves already normative (moral, rational, etc.) or the kinds of interactions mentioned immediately above, which remain at the level of regulations. But this problem is not unique to law, and it seems to result from the distinction between form and content itself, which marks the advent of the operatory structure, as distinct from regulatory structures whose form and content are indissociable. In the domain of logical rules, also, we find systems of propositions which are formally correct but false in their content because they derive from false premises. Before situating legal norms in a table of equilibrated forms of ascending stages, rhythm, regulation and grouping, it is important to situate first the systems of logical and moral rules. [p. 56]

Intellectual interactions constitute, without doubt, the most instructive example from the point of view of the transition from regulations to operatory groupings. To the extent that elements of constraint such as tradition, opinion, power, social class, etc. enter into the construction of systems of collective representations, thought is subject to a movement of values and obligations that it has not engendered of itself, which is to say that it does not, then, consist in a system of autonomous norms. In this case, its heteronomy alone is sufficient to indicate its dependence on the regulations previously discussed. More specifically, a collective mode of thought with the function of justifying the viewpoint of a particular social group consists of a system of intellectual regulations whose laws are not those of pure operation, and which only attain the forms of unstable equilibrium, due to the workings of momentary compensations. As we shall see again in Sections 6 and 7, the condition of equilibrium of rational rules is that they express the autonomous mechanism of pure cooperation, that is, a system of operations carried out in common or by reciprocity between those of the partners. Instead of the translation of a system of obligatory traditions, the cooperation which is the source of 'groupings' of rational operations is simply the continuation of the system of actions themselves, and of techniques.

It is the same transition from authority to reciprocity, or from constraint to cooperation, which marks the transition from semi-normative morality, still dependent on the regulations inherent in unilateral respect, and the autonomous groupings of rules of behaviour founded on mutual respect. In the moral domain, as in the domain of logical norms, equilibrium is therefore linked to cooperation resulting from the direct reciprocity of actions, as opposed to constraints referred to above.[10]

Returning to the problem of the grouping of legal rules, it is now possible to understand the paradox whereby there is a dualism between their form and their content. In its form, a system of laws certainly constitutes the model of a set of social interactions grouped together by additive and logical composition. A set of rules of law constitutes, in effect, a structure such that each individual belonging to the social group concerned is linked to every other individual by means of a well-defined set of obligations and rights, with nothing else contained within this set over and above the logical sum of these interconnected relationships. This does not at all imply, as was emphasized in Section 2, that such a totality consists in the simple union of the individuals composing it, as if these individuals possessed rights in advance, or were related in advance through obligations which existed before the construction [p. 57] of the system (as theoreticians of natural rights believe). Nor does it imply that any given relationship, isolated from the system, could exist as such outside the system. But it does imply that the totality of the system of relations can be analysed into elementary relations, either coordinate or subordinate vis-à-vis each other, whose additive composition would completely re-constitute the system. In this sense, the system is an operatory grouping, the relationships conferring rights and simultaneously imposing obligations being brought about by the constructive operations of legal reality. Such operations include the decrees of a sovereign, the orders of hierarchical superiors, the votes of a chamber of representatives, the votes of a people as a whole, etc., and these operations themselves have the validity of the rules of their composition (defined by a constitution, etc.).

Only if such a system truly has the form of a grouping, do two questions arise as to its content. These questions are interdependent with each other, and their solution allows us to distinguish between the apparent coherence of some legal structures, and the real coherence of others: they are the question of legal equilibrium, and that of the relationships between the legal norm and intellectual or moral norms.

As to the question of equilibrium, it is obvious that no legal system, no matter how coherent its form, can have the power of constraint or conservation if its contradictions with other values and norms in society lead to conflicts and revolution. It would therefore seem that equilibrium in a legal system of norms is a matter of content, rather than form, i.e. what matters is the role played by legal rules as instruments of, or obstacles to, the distribution of values. There is certainly an equivalent here in what happens in the case of a system of collective representations, in which intellectual equilibrium is not assured merely by formal coherence, but also by adequate fit with reality. But this analogy between legal and logical norms shows precisely that the question is more complex from the standpoint of form alone, because the rules ensuring logical coherence imply possible fit with any content whatsoever, and they are not disturbed by the simple fact that erroneous content is replaced by something true: the proper character of a formal structure in equilibrium is therefore, in the intellectual domain, to ensure the possibility of a transformation of the principles themselves, without rupturing the continuity of the system. Now, comparing legal systems in equilibrium with those which are not, we see that if the equilibrium does depend on the fit of the formal structure with its reality content, it can be ensured by form alone, in the sense that, in the legal domain as in all operatory domains, the stability of the equilibrium is a function of mobility: a form [p. 58] in equilibrium is, in law as elsewhere, that which ensures the regulation of its own transformations (e.g. a constitution regulating changes to itself, etc.), while a static and closed form is in unstable equilibrium and thus displays, despite appearances, only an incomplete operatory grouping, because it allows no possible transformations with reference to higher norms.

This leads us to the relationship of legal rules with logical and moral rules. If the equilibrium of the former is tied to their capacity for transformation and adaptation, it is clear that they will converge toward these two other sorts of norms, as a function of their equilibration alone. Otherwise, there would be a contradiction between form and content, arising from the failure of the content of legal norms to adapt to the other aspects of social life. The convergence between legal and logical norms is clear: contradiction within the set of legal norms would in fact invalidate the whole structure, in that lower norms would be in conflict with higher ones at different levels of elaboration of the structure, and this necessary logical structure of legal construction is sufficient to demonstrate its correspondence with rational norms as displayed in a given society. The only difference between legal and moral norms is that law is not concerned with the relations between persons, but only considers individuals in their functions (position in the social group), thus establishing transpersonal rules. Morality, in contrast, is concerned only with personal relations, in such a way that different persons are never entirely substitutable for each other in cases. This is why legal rules can be codified in detail, but moral rules remain essentially general: they only attain pure forms like those of formal logic, without regulating, as do legal codes, the manner of their own application. We can understand then how, though they are relatively undifferentiated at source, law and morality come to separate from each other in step with disequilibria and social conflicts, readjusting their correspondence at each equilibration. At the limit, a legal form flexible enough to express the real interactions in play in an [p. 59] equilibrated society would converge with the system of moral norms.[11]

In summary, we have shown that the large structures open to sociological explanation, like those of psychological explanation, are those of rhythms, regulations, and groupings. Rhythm marks the frontier between the material and the spiritual; regulation characterizes statistical totalities, with interference from the factors of interaction (values and certain rules); and 'grouping' characterizes the structure of reversible operations seen in legal, moral, and rational constructions, i.e. in totalities which are additive in their composition.

This sequence is essential for the understanding of the mechanism of sociological explanation itself. It leads us to conceive of the relationship between causality and implication, discussed at the end of Section 3, as a genetic relationship calling for an operatory explanation and not as a merely statistical relation given at the outset. Only normative groupings constitute pure systems of implication such as inter-coordinated rules which are inter-nested and inter-generated by virtue of relations expressible as necessary connections. Regulations contain a variable component of implication, and foreshadow reversibility as well as retaining an effective causality (in the form of constraint, etc.). But rhythms are embedded in full material causality, encompassing within this causal context the first logical liaisons (elementary signs and values, with the very minimum normative element). Groupings are the limiting state of previous regulations, where the latter rest on the complex play of rhythms. Both sociological and psychological explanation, then, could succeed only by proceeding from material and causal action to the implicational system of the collective consciousness. It is through this exclusive condition that we will attain in the superstructure that which effectively extends the causal actions at work in the infrastructure in contrast to merely symbolic ideologies which reflect and deform. [p. 60]

5. EXPLANATION IN SOCIOLOGY. C. REAL EXPLANATION AND FORMAL (OR AXIOMATIC) RECONSTRUCTION

There are, then, three and not two systems of notions to be distinguished within sociological explanation (as within psychological explanation). These are causal actions, the operations which complete and systematize these actions, and ideological factors (comparable to introspective egocentric phenomena in psychology) which distort perspectives when properly operatory mechanisms are not dissociated from this sociocentric symbolism. In complete parallelism with what is the case in psychological explanation, operatory mechanisms in sociology can be studied using two methods, both of which lead to the detachment of these mechanisms from the ideological elements which almost always accompany them, and affect their status in consciousness. One of these methods is real explanation, which puts the operatory aspects of thought or of collective morality in relation to concrete work, the techniques and modes of collaboration occurring in causal actions; while the other aspects of the collective consciousness then appear as being tied to the symbolic interpretation which society offers of its own conflicts. The other method is the formal or even axiomatic reconstruction of the implications involved in operatory mechanisms. Although at first sight this method appears to have little relevance to sociological explanation (any more than the relations between logic and psychological explanation are imme-diately apparent), in fact it does have a useful role to play, in that it, also, leads to a rigorous dissociation between the ideological and the operatory in 'groupings' of rules. Furthermore, it is possible to show a one-to-one correspondence between the questions this method raises, and those raised by 'real' explanation, which adds substance to the latter.

There is an undeniable epistemological interest to be derived, both in sociological and in psychological explanation, from the general problem of the relationship between axiomatic systems and the corresponding concrete sciences. This is all the more instructive if we consider that, in social science, there are actually two different types of axiomatization; the one concerned with regulations which is forced to simplify, no doubt to excess, the real [p. 61] data; the other concerned with normative groupings, and therefore perfectly adequate to explain the operatory mechanisms involved.

In the domain of regulations, it is well known how the 'pure economics' of Walras and Pareto used mathematical deduction to try to explain the equilibrium and dynamics of economic exchanges in the same way as rational mechanics translates the composition of forces. To achieve this aim, these authors were naturally forced to simplify and idealize real phenomena, and thus to replace the inductive analysis of the facts themselves with hypothetico-deductive reasoning with formally defined concepts. They were, in other words, on the road toward axiomatization, though without carrying out an actual axiomatization, while nevertheless providing the elements which could have been used to construct one. Furthermore, like quantifiable economic value, this semi-axiomatic construction was mathematical from the outset, therefore transcending the logical or qualitative level which the models of law we shall be considering later could not transcend.

But what is the import of such a method, applied to economic facts? It should of course be understood that the question does not prejudge the laws expressed through it and is not dependent on the doctrines due to Pareto. The method is very useful as an analytical instrument for the analysis of reality itself, and is a fine example of precise deduction applied in a social domain. However, it has two very instructive deficiencies, due no doubt not to the inadequacy of the elaborated analysis, but to the inadequacy of axiomatic deduction applied to regulations as such, rather than to operatory or normative groupings.

The first deficiency is that the analysis of Walras and Pareto constitutes a static state, rather than a dynamic interpretation of economics. The reason for this is clear: the point at which a regulation attains a state of equilibrium is definable by means of a set of simple equalities which momentarily coincide with a system of reversible operations. The sole difference between regulations and operations consists in the fact that equilibrium is permanent in the case of groups or groupings, while it is not in the case of regulations, where 'displacements' and merely approximate compensations occur instead. But when equilibrium is attained *ex hypothesi*, the system does not differ from an operatory system. Pure economics thus teaches that an exchange attains equilibrium when a certain number of conditions are met: equality (for each party to the exchange) of the 'weighted ophelimities' of the quantity of merchandise possessed after the exchange, equality (for each party to the exchange) of receipts and expenses, [p. 62] expressed numerically, and equality (with respect to the merchandise) of the quantity existing before and after the exchange.[12] Such an equilibrated exchange is nothing more than a system of substitutions, with complete conservation of values (ophelimities) and objects. It represents, therefore a 'group': the equilibrated exchange AB is composed with the equilibrated exchange BC, equivalent to the equilibrated exchange AC; these exchanges are associative. The exchange AB has the inverse BA, and the product $AB \times BA$ is either identity or null. Hence this is a 'group', as though the exchanges thus defined were proper operations, and this is why the theory of equilibrium is easily axiomatized. What, then, is the dynamism of economics?

Here we see the second deficiency, which compounds the first: even within the static domain, and *a fortiori* in the dynamic domain, 'Pure Economics' over-simplifies even the process of regulations. The equilibrium of exchange is defined as the point at which, in fact, equilibrium terminates. But suppose that a real exchange never reaches this state through rigorous equalization of the 'ophelimities' (a concept substituted for 'value' through pure fear of words!) – the needs, desires, and evaluations, whose momentary compensations constitute this fragile equality, in fact are constantly changing in such a way that a durable equilibrium is never attained. The real problem is therefore that of the dynamic exchanges, in which the regulations should be expressed in mathematical equations. It would not be a simple logical formulation, but rather differential and integral calculus which would best express these variations. Yet the real transformations taking place in economic exchange are remote from a formal or axiomatic analysis, and this is why the latter is not a sufficiently accurate image of reality in the domain of regulations.

The situation is quite different where we have a system of rules, since the property of a norm is precisely to assure the conservation of values, and in this case axiomatization applies to states of permanent equilibrium or to transformations which will be regulated in advance. In this case, the axiomatization has a purely qualitative character, i.e. it is logical and not mathematical, but it is nonetheless interesting from our point of view. Since axiomatization conforms totally to the operatory structure of the rules considered, it leads, in fact, [p. 63] to a rigorous separation between the mechanism of the formal construction of rules, and all the ideological factors that the collective consciousness and metaphysical interpretations attach to the interpretation of these rules. It is particularly from this critical standpoint that the method of axiomatization corresponds in a fruitful way to causal sociological explanation, by bringing into relation the various moments of real operatory explanation with those of the deductive construction of the implications themselves.

The situation of 'pure' theory in law is particularly suggestive when seen from this viewpoint. There is general agreement that law is an essentially normative discipline, in which all questions are reduced to a matter of validity, and not of fact. This is why law is not a science, and as such is not the concern of sociology. But belief in and submission to law are social facts which must be explained like any others, and rules judged to be 'legally valid' by the collectivity constitute essential social interactions, that sociology must study as 'normative facts' like moral or logical interactions, i.e. by considering these norms as facts. Corresponding to this concrete study there is, in legal research, an attempt to produce an axiomatization analogous to that for which logicians have provided the logical rules, and which can, therefore, facilitate sociological explanation in exactly the same way that logical axiomatization facilitates the analysis of collective representations of a rational or scientific character. In fact, while most over-arching theories of law try to found law on metaphysical preoccupations or (what amounts to the same thing for sociology) on politico-social ideologies, a certain number of writers, following the work of Roguin on 'the rule of law', have tried to limit their analysis to the formal or normative structure of law. Thus, Kelsen[12] has posed the problem in terms of Kantian epistemology: 'how is law possible?'. Instead of proceeding historically, as in sociology, Kelsen carried out an *a priori* analysis, and even maintained (what is very interesting for us, and will facilitate the argument) the absolute irreducibility of the 'pure' theory of law to sociology. In fact, while sociology is necessarily causal, and therefore considers social phenomena, including rules of law, as simple facts, the 'pure' legal method consists in directly relating to each other the norms of law, and therefore depends on a particular type of implication called 'imputation' by Kelsen. Since a norm is essentially an 'ought', a 'sollen',[13] while a fact is an 'is', a 'sein'[14] and since neither of these can be [p. 64] derived from the other, there cannot be, according to Kelsen, any legal sociology, and the science of law can only be a science of the pure construction of norms. Here we have the whole problem of the relationship between implication and causality, which arises simultaneously with that of the relationship between an axiomatic system and the concrete science which corresponds to it.

From this point of view of axiomatization, what does the process of legal 'construction' consist in? The essential character of law, according to Kelsen, is to regulate its own generation. A legal norm, in effect, is the source of new norms: a parliament legislates, a government decrees, an administration regulates, a tribunal judges, and these laws, decrees, regulations and judgments are all norms elaborated without discontinuity within the framework of superior norms which confer their validity upon them, through the intermediary of legislative, executive, or legal organs, all acting according to superior norms. From top to bottom of the hierarchy of legal organs, new norms are continually being created, but, by virtue of the same process, but seen as proceeding in the opposite direction, there is also continual application of previous norms. More exactly, each norm is both the creation of norms at levels lower than itself, and the application of norms at higher levels. Simultaneous creation and application, then, are the two essential characteristics of legal construction. There are only two exceptions to this. These norms which validate each other form a pyramid in which every level is supported by the links of 'imputation' which assure its validity; but the two extremities of the pyramid have a different character. The base of the pyramid is made up of innumerable 'individualized norms', in Kelsen's felicitous phrase: the judgments of tribunals, administrative orders, university degrees, etc. – i.e. norms, each of which applies in the last analysis only to a single individual, and thus determined by right, or by specific obligation. The consequence of this is that these individualized norms represent pure 'application', and are no longer generative since, beyond the individual, there is no further legally imputable term. As for the peak of the pyramid, it is characterized by a unique form, which is pure generation, without application, since there is no higher level. This 'basic norm' should not be confounded with the constitution itself, which is the source of all norms of state law, since the validity of the constitution itself must also be established. The basic norm is, therefore, the source of the constitution itself, and is the necessary *a priori* condition of the validity of the whole legal order.

Law, then, is a system of nested norms, all depending on a single fundamental norm, extending in a stepwise fashion to the set of individualized norms. Law, [p. 65] according to the 'pure' theory of Kelsen, is nothing more than this system of norms envisaged in this way – that is, there exists no legal reality which does not form part, as an essential and necessary tier, of this system of pure norms. The 'subject of law' itself is nothing more than a 'centre of imputation' of norms, and, beyond this character, it is a pure fiction of an ideological, not a legal nature. 'Subjective law' is thus a matter for metaphysicians, and is excluded from pure theory. The 'State', on the other hand, is nothing other than the legal order itself, envisaged in its totality, and any attempt to confer any other than a purely normative reality on it oversteps the bounds of law and goes into the domain of political ideology.

One can see the close ancestry between such a conception and any formal theory expressing the structure of a system of operations. If the system of law is nothing more than a hierarchy of nested norms linked by a formal relation of imputation, by considering imputation as a special case of implication, we can place this system in relation to a set of real propositions formally bound to each other in a pyramid of implications. Legal propositions are imperatives, of course, while logical propositions are indicatives. But this difference has little importance with respect to the formal structure of the system; imperatives can be translated into propositions expressing the existence of an obligation or of a law. Furthermore, the relations between logical propositions are norms, and therefore include a normative element. Lalande has given expression to this by pointing out that *A* implies *B* 'for an honest man'. Law, like logic, may, then, be structured in the form of a system of 'groupings', and it would be easy to express the whole hierarchy of norms in logical formulae expressed as showing the groupings of asymmetrical relations (nested imputations), symmetrical relations (reciprocal co-imputations or contractual relations) and classes, which completely constitute it. Furthermore, legal propositions, instead of being contained fully within each other, are constructed out of each other, which would put on display the parallelism between legal construction, made up of indissociable applications and creations, and logical constructions carried out through properly constructive operations.

A system of operations may be studied in two ways: using the psycho-sociological method, which would analyse causally its concrete construction; and using the axiomatic method, which [p. 66] would only express the relations of implication among these operations, or the propositions which translate them. From this point of view, the pure theory of law obviously consists in an axiomatization, since Kelsen explicitly opposes legal 'imputa-tion' to sociological causality. It remains, then, to determine the relationship between the axiomatic structure, which is the pure science of law, and the corresponding concrete science, which is legal sociology, or that branch of sociology concerned with the causal explanation of norms as 'normative facts' (as Petrazycki would say), i.e. as imperative rules whose origin is social interactions of all kinds, and which act causally, in their turn, in the context of individual interactions.

The point of overlap is seen immediately. While a formalized theory develops in a purely deductive manner, once its axioms are laid down at the outset, with no appeal to the actual world, the initial axioms themselves always, in a more or less disguised form, translate real operations of which they are the abstract schema. This appears very clearly in Kelsen's legal formalization: the 'basic norm', which expresses formally the *a priori* condition of the validity of the whole legal order, is nothing other than the abstract expression of the concrete fact that society 'recognizes' the normative value of this order; it corresponds, therefore, to the social reality of the exercise of power, and of the 'recognition' of this power or of the system of rules which are the expression of it. If formal legal construction could be axiomatized in the purest form possible, it is doubtful whether the basic norm itself could ever be pure, because 'real' recognition is an indispensable intermediary between abstract law and society. No doubt it is the role of the axiomatizer to cut the umbilical cord which attaches formal construction to the actual world, but it is the part of the sociologist to remind us that this link has existed, and that it has a vital function in the nourishment of embryonic law.

If this is the situation with regard to the 'pure' theory of law, we can foresee another discipline which, though it does not yet exist, would be interesting to elaborate; this is the 'pure' theory of moral relations. Contrary to Kelsen's own expressed opinion, it is entirely possible that the construction of moral norms is a process analogous to that described by [p. 67] him for the legal sphere; but this would be a construction of personal, no longer transpersonal, relations, as well as a much slower elaboration, bringing in the succession of generations (each transmitted norm being the application of preceding norms and the generator of new norms), and above all a much greater differentiation of 'individualized norms' without the intervention of the state organs which create norms. Whatever may result from these differences, it would be worth the attempt at comparison, with the support of a precise and logical formalization.

Finally, it is obvious that the rules regulating rational collective representations also give rise to a precise axiomatization, which is logic itself, as the common expression of the intra- and inter-individual operatory mechanisms. We will see this in detail in Section 7, although from a different viewpoint, since logic is not only one of the axiomatized forms of sociological explanation – it is also a product of social life, and therefore constitutes one of the domains where sociological explanation extends in its explanation of human knowledge.

In summary, all systems of norms which have arrived at a state of flexible and relatively permanent equilibrium can be axiomatized in a way which both adds to and complements concrete sociological explanation, though without replacing it, since an axiomatization detaches only implicational structures, leaving social causation behind. Once this point is appreciated, as well as the usefulness of this type of formalization for the separation of properly operatory mechanisms from the ideologies which are attached to them in the common consciousness, we can proceed to the consideration of concrete sociological explanation (as opposed to formal) of socialized and collective thought. This discussion has been reserved for the end of this chapter, because it has relevance for epistemology not only from the standpoint of the structure of sociological explanation, seen as a particular type of scientific thought; but also has significance for epistemology given the subject matter itself, since here thought itself is the object of sociological analysis. In other words, sociology extends naturally to become the sociology of knowledge (just as psychology extends naturally to become the psychology of knowledge), and this sociology of knowledge in turn is part of the [p. 68] subject-matter of genetic epistemology.

There are two fundamental problems: the sociological explanation of sociocentric forms of thought (from ideologies in general to metaphysics in particular); and the sociological explanation of the operatory forms of collective thought (from technology to science and logic).

6. SOCIOCENTRIC THOUGHT

The analysis of the individual development of thought leads to the essential observation that the operations of mind derive from action and sensory-motor mechanisms, but also require for their constitution a gradual decentration of the initial forms of representation, which are egocentric. In other words, the explanation of operatory thought in the individual requires the consideration of three, and not only two, cognitive systems: first, there is the practical assimilation of the actual world to the schemes of sensory-motor activity, with the beginning of decentration in so far as these schemes are coordinated with each other, and action is coordinated with the objects on which it is carried out. Next, there is the representational assimilation of the actual world to the initial schemes of thought, which remain egocentric in so far as they do not consist of coordinated operations, but in isolated interiorized actions. Finally, there is assimilation to operations themselves, which continues the coordination of actions, but by means of a systematic decentration with regard to the self and subjective notions. The progress of individual knowledge does not, then, consist simply in a direct integration of early into later schemes, but in a fundamental reversal of direction which detaches relations which give priority to one's own point of view to bind them in systems which subordinate this point of view to the reciprocity of all possible points of view, and to the relativity inherent in operatory groupings. Practical action, egocentric thought, and operational thought are therefore the three essential moments of such a construction.

The sociological analysis of collective thought leads to exactly parallel results. In the many and varied human societies there exist techniques, tied to material work and to the actions that man carries out on nature, and these techniques constitute the first type of relation between subjects and objects – relations which are efficacious, and therefore objective, but [p. 69] whose entry into consciousness is only partial, because they are tied to the results obtained, and have no bearing on the understanding of the connections themselves. There also exists scientific or operational thought, which is partly an extension of technology (and enriches it in return), but which essentially completes it by adding to action an understanding of relationships, and above all by replacing concrete action with the interiorized actions and techniques which are the operations of calculation, deduction, and explanation. But between techniques and science there is a third term, whose role has sometimes been that of an obstacle: this is the set of collective forms of thought which are neither practical nor operatory, but proceed from simple speculation; these are ideologies of all kinds, cosmogonic or theological, political or metaphysical, which are placed between the most primitive collective representations and the most refined contemporary systems of thought. The most important result of the sociological analyses which have been carried out on this middle and neither technical nor operatory term has been to show that it is essentially sociocentric. While technology and science constitute two kinds of objective relationship between man in society and the universe, ideology in all its forms is a representation of things which centres the universe on the aspirations and conflicts of human society. Just as the advent of operational thought in the individual requires decentration with respect to egocentric thought and to the self, which is necessary for operations to continue the actions from which they derive, so scientific thought has always required social decentration from ideologies and from society itself, a decentration which is necessary to permit scientific thought to continue the work of technology, in which its roots go deep.

The significance of this necessity for fundamental decentration can be seen most clearly by comparing idealist conceptions of collective development (such as Comte's law of three stages[15] later to become Durkheim's theory of collective consciousness) with the Marxist concepts of technological infra-structure and ideological superstructure, inspired by the lively awareness of disequilibrium and social conflict. These three authors are in agreement as to the sociocentric [p. 70] character of ideologies, but while Comte and Durkheim see science as the natural extension of sociomorphic thought, an operatory sociology such as that of Marx, in contrast, attaches science to the domain of technology, and provides a remarkable critical instrument for the analysis of ideologies which discerns the sociocentric element even in the most refined products of contemporary metaphysical thought. The objectivity pursued by scientific thought is thus subordinated to a pre-existing and necessary condition, which is the decentration of concepts in relation to superstructural ideologies, and the placing of them in relation to the concrete actions on which social life depends.

The distinctive feature of a sociology of knowledge which ignores the necessity for such a decentration is that it will sooner or later attach scientific thought to primitive mystical and theological notions; in fact, if the evolution of this notion is traced back through its successive levels, one always finds, if the domain of superstructure is not abandoned, certain early forms of the notion which are religious in nature. Thus, the idea of cause was first magical and animistic, the idea of natural law was for a long time confounded with that of obedience to the will of supernatural beings, the idea of force had initially several occult aspects, and so on. The question is, then, to find out whether this type of derivation is direct, or rather whether scientific thought has gradually decentred from these sociocentric notions, and adjusted them to their practical basis. To adopt the first point of view would be to affirm the continuity of the collective consciousness, viewed as a monolithic unity. To adopt the second, in contrast, would be to separate the ideological from the concrete, and to begin the analysis of interactions with regard to the three categories of technique, ideology, and science, with the necessary decentra-tion of the third with respect to the second. Comte, and pre-eminently Durkheim, adopted the first of these viewpoints, and it is even possible to state that the central idea of Durkheimism is the derivation of all rational and scientific notions from religious thought, conceived as the symbolic or ideological expression of the constraint that the primitive social group exercised over individuals. On the other hand, no-one has insisted more than Durkheim on the 'sociomorphic' character of these primitive collective representations. If he was able to maintain two such incompatible [p. 71] positions, it is obviously because, instead of proceeding to the analysis of different types of social interaction, he constantly reverted to the global language of 'totality'. Hence, in order to demonstrate the collective nature of reason, he alternated between two sorts of argument, very different in fact, but used simultaneously under the cover of this undifferentiated notion of the social totality exercising constraint over individuals. The first type of argument is of a synchronic nature, and consists in showing that individuals could never attain the generality and the stability distinctive of concepts such as homogeneous time and space, the formal rules of logic, etc., without a constant exchange of thought regulated by the entire group. The second type of argument is diachronic, and tries to establish the continuity between contemporary collective representations and 'original' collective representations; the 'sociomorphic' character of these primitive representations is, then, one more proof, in Durkheim's eyes, of their social origin, and, since he fails to distinguish between the cooperative character of the rules of practical work, or of joint intellectual work, and the coercive character of unilateral transmissions or traditions, this primitive sociocentrism is no impediment to his interpretation of rational collective representations, and does not seem to him to require any decentration or reversal in the direction of scientific thought with relation to sociomorphic ideology.

Now the first of these two types of argument is perfectly valid, as we shall see in more detail in Section 7, but this is so only on two conditions. One is the acknowledgement that the collective work which leads to the constitution of rational notions and logical rules is action carried out in common, before it becomes thought in common. Reason is not only a matter of communication, speech, and sets of concepts; it is first a system of operations, and it is joint action with others which leads to operatory generalization. The second condition is the acknowledgement that this is a heterogeneous process, when compared to the ideological constraint of tradition. Of course, there exist 'consecrated' practices, such as the notions imposed by respect for opinion; but it is not this consecration which determines their rational value. It is impossible to assimilate the 'universal' to the collective, except through the notion of [p. 72] cooperation in material or mental work, i.e. through a factor of objectivity and reciprocity entailing the autonomy of the participants, and quite different from the intellectual constraint of sociomorphic representations imposed by the whole group or by certain social classes. When Durkheim replied to the criticism that he subordinated reason to public opinion, he asserted that public opinion was a poor reflection of social reality, and always lagged behind its deeper currents. This assertion reveals that he in fact recognized the irreducibility of cooperation to constraint, and the necessity for concrete sociology to analyse the social totality into a variety of processes (which would mean the analysis of types of activity, inter-individual relations, class constraints and oppositions, relations between generations, and so on).

The second of Durkheim's arguments was the discovery of 'sociomorphic' collective representations. It would be difficult to underestimate the interest of such a discovery, but it does not entail the conclusions which Durkheim deduced from it. Furthermore, sociocentrism is not limited to primitive societies. In fact, the 'primitive classifications' described by Hubert and Mauss, and traced to the distribution of individuals into tribes and clans; the modelling of qualitative forms of time and space on the sequence of festivals or the topography of the social territory; the emanation of the notions of cause and force from the energies of group constraint, etc., are all well-established facts of the greatest interest for sociology. But what do they prove, exactly? That the principal categories of mind are shaped by society, or that they are deformed by society? Or both simultaneously? Do they show that the sociomorphic forms of thought are the origin of reason, or only of collective ideologies?

There is a common misunderstanding which threatens to confuse a discussion such as this: because the 'original' collective representations are sociomorphic, and above all because these are transmitted complete and ready made by means of the educational constraint of one generation on the next in societies with no division of labour, social classes, or intellectual differentiation among individuals, it is supposed that they are somehow more socialized than ours (more socialized, for example than the autonomous reason of a mathematician using notions [p. 73] invented by himself) or at the very least as socialized as ours. To dispel such a fallacy, it is sufficient to observe that, if the development of rational operations presupposes cooperation among individuals, which liberates them from their initial intellectual egocentrism, then sociocentric collective representations are the social equivalent of individual egocentric representations.[16] Thus the small child, at the level of intuitive thought, believes that the stars follow him as he walks, and that they turn about with him when he retraces his steps. When the primitive believes that the course of the stars and the seasons is regulated by the sequence of social events, and that the Son of Heaven, among the ancient Chinese studied by Granet, ensured their regular course by walking round his kingdom, and then round his palace, centration on the tribe or even on the empire replaces centration on the self, in other words sociocentrism is substituted for egocentrism. But there remains an undeniable ancestry of structure between these two sorts of 'centrism', in contrast to the decentred operations of reason. There is a finality, an animism, an artificialism, a magic, a 'participation' in the egocentrism of the child, and despite all the differences between these fluid and unstable notions and the great collective crystallizations which characterize the same attitudes on the ideological plane of primitive life, there is once more a convergence between the intellectual egocentrism of the individual and the sociocentrism of 'primitive' representations.

We can now answer the questions raised earlier. It is not the sociomorphic character of primitive collective representations which demonstrates the social nature of reason, but rather the necessary role of cooperation in practical action (as we have just seen, and will see further in Section 7) and its continuation in the effective operations of thought. Sociomorphic collective representations are only an ideological reflection of the following fundamental reality: they express the way in which individuals represent to themselves, in common, their social group and the universe, and it is because this representation is only intuitive or even symbolic, and not yet operational, that it is sociocentric, in conformity with a general law of all non-operational thought, which is to remain centred on its subject (individual or [p. 74] collective). Further, since it is transmitted and consolidated by the constraints of tradition and education, it is precisely opposed to the formation of rational operations, which entail the free play of cooperative thought founded upon action. The sociocentric collective representations found in primitive societies are, then, not the origin of scientific reason, in spite of the apparent continuity revealed by Durkheim, who confined his vision to the continuous production of superstructures, without understanding that decentration of thought is essential for science to be possible, to the extent that, as Brunschvicg remarked[13] he imposes a respect for the notion of 'force' on modern physicists because it derives from the 'mana' of the Melanesians, or the magic 'orenda' of the Sioux![17] In reality, primitive sociomorphism is at the origin, not of reason, but of the sociocentric ideologies of all times, with the single difference that, with the division of labour, the sociocentrism of social class has gradually replaced global sociocentrism. To subordinate physical time to the calendar of festivals is, in effect, for the universe to be represented as centred on the social group, in the same way in which the theoretician of 'natural law' imagines an order of the world conferring on the individuals in society the innate possession of certain rights (which legitimates the law of property, etc.), or the same way in which the theologian or the metaphysician constructs a universe whose centre coincides with man himself, i.e. with the way in which society is organized, or is thought to be best organized, at a given moment in history.

Before looking at the way in which Marxism and neo-Marxism interpret contemporary ideologies, consider once more Tarde's doctrine. This sociologist was poorly served by a dangerous facility he had, which led him to ignore both historical reconstruction and precise ethnography, as well as the indispensable psychological information he should have used in his studies of inter-individual interaction (a notion he substituted for the Durkheimian 'totality'). Nevertheless, his work is replete with suggestive remarks on matters of detail. In Tarde's general analysis of interactions ('imitation', 'opposition', and 'adaptation' or 'invention'), logic has two specific functions, common to both individual activity and interactions themselves. First, there is a function of 'equilibration': logic is a coordination of beliefs, which excludes contradictions [p. 75] and ensures the synthesis of compatible tendencies. Second, there is a function of 'optimization': logic takes us toward ever greater certainty. These two functions may have only two settings: either individual consciousness, seen as a momentarily closed system, or the whole society also seen as a unique system. Hence, there is an 'individual logic', the source of coherence and reflected belief (logic in the ordinary sense of the term), and a 'social logic', the means of unification and reinforcement of beliefs in society. Tarde often glimpsed the interdependence between individual consciousness and society: thus social oppositions are transformed, in the individual, into internal conflicts; external deliberations into internal reflection; social adaptation into mental invention and so on, with a shuttle working between the external and internal poles, and each of the particular pairs of activity. Yet, curiously enough, he did not specify this question about logic itself, and did not ask whether 'individual logic' derives from 'social logic' or the reverse, or whether both are constructed simultaneously. He limited himself to noting the antagonisms between the two, though in a very suggestive manner, but never looked at the question from a genetic standpoint. In 'individual logic' as Tarde called it, equilibration and optimization proceed side by side: a belief will be supported in so far as it forms part of a more coherent system, and does not encounter any contradiction. In 'social logic', it seems at first as though the same is true: 'optimization' leads to accumulation of the 'belief capital', as Tarde called it, made up of religion, moral and legal systems, political ideologies, etc., while 'equilibration' tends to suppress conflicts by eliminating heresies or idosyncratic opinions. But, precisely because each individual is led to think and re-think the system of collective notions, these two tendencies of social optimization and equilibration are in the long run irreconcilable, and they alternate in dominance: when beliefs are too unified socially (orthodoxy due to equilibration) individuals cease to hold them and, when they seek to reinforce their personal convictions (optimization), they fall into heresy and thus threaten the unity of the system. The history of religions, etc., and even of systems of verbal signs (the conflict between correct speech and expressiveness) furnishes Tarde with numerous examples of this alternation, which leads him to the conclusion that societies always either subordinate 'individual logic' to 'social logic' (as in the so-called primitive societies, oriental theocracies, etc.) or the reverse (western democracies). These two logics are, then, incompatible, and in fact they are based on opposed 'categories': spatio-temporal notions and material object, in individual logic, and legal-moral notions and the idea of God as the [p. 76] origin of values in social logic.

It is interesting to note that Tarde, with some reluctance and almost in opposition with the whole of the rest of his doctrine, was forced, as soon as he approached the sociology of knowledge, to recognize the existence of a fundamental dualism between the sociocentric ideologies resulting from the constraint of the social group and rational logic. It is obvious, in fact, that Tarde's 'social logic' is nothing other than the ideological superstructure expressing the sociocentrism of all collective spiritual constraint. The equilibration and optimization which are its laws are nothing other than a barely veiled translation of Durkheim's 'social constraint', the source of both obligatory transmissions and 'sacred' values. As for Tarde's 'individual logic', his great mistake was not to have understood that this is much more social than sociocentric thought itself, and that, far from being innate in the individual, it presupposes a continuing cooperation: in individual thought in the process of socialization (childhood egocentrism) there is neither equilibration nor systematic optimization of beliefs, due to the absence of operations which are coordinated both individually and socially (see Section 7). On the other hand, the impossibility of reconciling socially optimization and equilibration is only true of ideologies, and then only of societies sufficiently differentiated beyond a certain point. On the level of social cooperation, the equilibrium of beliefs and their optimization is not contradictory, as is demonstrated by the collective relations which characterize technological and scientific cooperation. In short, the 'individual logic' of Tarde is social logic itself, and his 'social logic' is sociocentric ideology.

In contrast to the idealist realism of Durkheim and the individualism of Tarde, Marx's essentially concrete conception of the problem of ideologies and logic (leaving aside the political passions attached to a name which has become symbolic, and taken in turn as that of a prophet and of a sophist) fits exceptionally well with the actual facts of both psychology and sociology. Marx's merit, in fact, is to have distinguished within social phenomena an infrastructure and a superstructure which oscillates between symbolism and full conscious realization, in the same way in which (as Marx himself explicitly said) psychology is obliged to distinguish between actual behaviour and consciousness. The substructure is formed of practical actions or operations, i.e. work and activity which bind men in society to nature: or 'material' relations, as Marx [p. 77] called them. But it must be clearly understood that even in the most material behaviours of production, there is exchange between people and things, i.e. inseparable interaction between active subjects and objects. It is this activity of the subject in interdependence with the reactions of the object which essentially characterize the 'dialectical', as opposed to classic materialism (Marx made this clear by criticizing Feuerbach for his receptive or passive conception of sensation).[18] The social superstructure is, then, to the infrastructure what individual consciousness is to behaviour. Just as consciousness can be a form of self-justification, a symbolic translation or an inadequate reflection of behaviour, or a continuation of behaviour in the form of interiorized actions and operations arising out of real action; so the social superstructure oscillates between ideology and science. While science pursues and reflects on material action at the level of collective thought, ideology essentially consists, in contrast, of a sociocentric symbolism, centred not on the society as a whole, which is divided and prey to oppositions and struggle, but on the sub-collectivities of social classes with their special interests.

Once one has managed to attain a certain objectivity in sociology, it is striking to realize that this distinction between the infrastructure and the superstructure has also been made by one of the greatest opponents of Marxist theory, which in itself is sufficient to demonstrate the necessity of such a notion in the sociological analysis of ideologies and metaphysics. In his great *Treatise of general sociology*, Pareto in effect insists, over more than a thousand pages, on the essential need, if social mechanisms are to be understood, to study 'discourses', pseudoscientific theories, ideologies in general, so as to distil from the apparent rationality of this gigantic production of metaphysical concepts the hidden intentions and real interests which are at stake. The Marxist concepts of superstructure and infrastructure, then, are found in Pareto in the following form: on the one hand, a variable element, depending on the philosophical ideas or spiritual fashions of the time, and consisting in the conceptual and verbal 'derivations'; on the other hand the real interests, the unconscious source of collective ideation which is manifested in the form of constant 'residues'.[19] But the weakness of Pareto's attempt, however interesting his use of 'residues' as the components of a mechanical equilibrium, and the objective analysis of the oscillations [p. 78] and displacements of equilibrium, lies in two fundamental errors. First, he conceived of the 'residues' as a sort of innate instinct in the individual, categorizable once and for all and therefore unchanging in the course of history, without understanding that they were, themselves, the result of interactions which accompany the multiple activities of people in society. Second, his analysis of ideological 'derivations' was extremely brief, due to the lack of an adequate philosophical background and he was not able to distil the symbolism contained within the conceptualizations of changing super-structures.

The contemporary disciples of Marx in sociology are dedicated to precisely the systematic analysis of this ideological symbolism, and the value of Marxist hypotheses will be judged by the results of these new methods. But the work of Lukács and of Goldmann already gives an idea of what may be expected from the sociology of literature, and above all, from the point of view of epistemology, from the sociological critique of metaphysical thought.

In his several essays, Lukács has shown the role of 'class consciousness' in all philosophical and literary production, and the process of 'reification' which he attributes to bourgeois thought. In particular he has shown, in the mechanism of literary production, the idealized projection of the social conflicts experienced by authors. His most remarkable analyses concern the repercussions of the French Thermidor on German culture, especially on Hölderlin, Goethe and Hegel.

In the area of criticism of metaphysics, the work of Goldmann continues that of Lukács by showing, using examples as significant as Kant and Pascal, that the creation of large speculative systems is essentially the satisfaction, through thought, of certain dominant needs within the development of a social class in a particular period of the history of national societies. Thus, the struggle of the European bourgeoisie against feudalism, then its enfranchise-ment, entailed the establishment of a certain number of ideas which dominate the whole of western metaphysics. These are, first of all, the fundamental concepts of liberty [p. 79] and individualism, entailing legal equality, and leading to rationalism, which is essentially the philosophy of autonomy and individual rights. But ultimately, and to the extent that this enfranchisement of the individual succeeded, it is the tragic sentiment of rupture between the individual and the human community, and the consequent search for an ideal of totality, conceived simultaneously as both necessary yet unattainable. To this is added the diversity of different national viewpoints: the broad outlines point to a clarity in French thought, while English empiricism reflects the spirit of social compromise: 'a compromise is a limitation, accepted under the pressure of external reality, of desires and hopes held at the outset. Where the economic and social structure of a country is the outcome of a compromise between two opposed classes, the world-view of the philosophers and poets will be much more realist and less radical than in countries where a long struggle has existed in opposition to the dominant class. This seems to us to be one of the main reasons why the philosophical thought of the English bourgeoisie has become empiricist and sensationalist, and not rationalist, as in France.'[14] In the case of Germany, the considerable delay in the advent of liberalism places the writer and the humanist philosopher in quite a different position, characterized by solitude and the feeling of the impossibility of a rapid realization of the rational ideal. Hence the following explanation of Kantian philosophy: 'the importance of Kant lies above all in the fact that, on the one hand, his thought expresses in the clearest possible way the conceptions of the individualistic and atomistic world inherited from his predecessors, and pushed to their limits, and these limits become for Kant the limits of human existence as such, of the thought and the action of human beings in general; and that, on the other hand, his thought does not stop (like most neo-Kantians) with the statement of these limits, but having already made the first hesitant but nonetheless decisive steps toward the integration into philosophy of the second category, the *whole*, the *universe* . . . .'[15]

The importance, both sociological and epistemological, of such an analysis, will not fail to be seen. From the sociological point of view, it allows us to give an [p. 80] adequate interpretation of ideologies and their real extent, while avoiding the twin errors of either placing them on the same level as scientific thought itself, or of depreciating them and denying them any functional significance (by treating them as simple reflections or 'derivations' etc.). In fact, an ideology is the conceptualized expression of the values that a group of individuals believe in, and as such it has a positive function distinct from that of science: ideology represents a particular stance, defends and justifies it, while the function of science is to observe and explain. The psychology of the novelist is thus quite different from that of the psychologist, even though the former can advance an analysis to an equal, if not greater degree of subtlety; even a novelist who is a realist always expresses a particular point of view on the world and on society, while science seeks to know only the viewpoint of the object. A metaphysics is an apology or an evaluation, whether it is a theodicy or a glorification of nothingness. As such, an ideology conforms to laws of special conceptualization, which are those of symbolic thought in general, but of collective, rather than individual symbolism. Through thought, it satisfies common needs, and leads to a realization of values in the form of an ideal world-system, which corrects the real universe. Its symbolism is therefore necessarily sociocentric, since its function is to translate into ideas the aspirations born of social and moral conflicts, i.e. to centre the universe on values elaborated by the group or by the sub-collectivities which oppose each other within the social group.

From the epistemological point of view, this sociological explanation of metaphysical thought furnishes an essential instrument for the criticism of knowledge. Far from dividing human knowledge into two distinct categories, that of sociocentric thought and that of objective thought, this instrument allows us to see the ideological element wherever it is applied, even in the metaphysical halo which surrounds all positive science and which science only gradually differentiates itself from. On the one hand, it demonstrates the duality between a type of thought whose function is to justify values, and another whose function is to reveal the relations between human beings and nature. But, on the other hand, since these values [p. 81] constitute the aims of the actions of human beings in society, and since the objective relations between people and nature are known only through the intermediary of such actions, all possible transitions between these two opposed poles exist. Hence the difficulty, even for science, to dissociate itself from ideology, and the absolute necessity for science to be decentred with regard to sociocentric thought, as well as to egocentric thought.

Overall, sociological analysis of collective thought leads to the discernment of three, not two, interdependent systems: real actions, which constitute the infrastructure of society; ideology, which is the symbolic conceptualization of the conflicts and aspirations arising out of these actions; and science, which continues actions as intellectual operations, permitting the explanation of nature and of human beings, and decentring human beings from themselves in order to re-integrate them into the objective relations that they create by means of their activity. Thus, by an extremely revealing paradox, the process of objective knowledge requires a similar decentration in both society and in the individual; just as individuals become liberated from intellectual egocentrism by becoming conscious of their own point of view and situating it among others, so collective thought becomes liberated from sociocentrism in discovering the ties which bind it to society, and situating itself in the set of relations which link it with nature itself. The problem which remains is to find out whether this decentred structure of thought which constitutes logic is also social, or whether it is only individual, and the way in which it may appear as collective in a different sense than sociocentric symbolism.

7. LOGIC AND SOCIETY: FORMAL OPERATIONS AND COOPERATION

Just because we found reason neither on a Platonic conception of universals, nor on an *a priori* structure of transcendent subjectivity, there remains only the possibility of identifying the 'universal' with the collective. Whether reason takes its forms from experience, or constructs them in the course of interactions between the subject and objects, there is only one criterion of truth (either experimental or formal) and that is the agreement among minds, as long as any reference to an external or internal absolute is excluded. It is true that this assimilation of [p. 82] truth to collective acknowledgement is at first repugnant to reason, because the rigour of a logical proof or experimental demonstration, if carried out by a single individual, is without any common basis in relation to the value of common opinion, even if general and multisecular. But such an argument raises two questions, and the answer to them determines the meaning of any social interpretation of logic: what is the nature of the agreement of minds which guarantees logical truth (as opposed to other possible sorts of agreement) and what is the nature, collective or individual, of the instruments of thought by means of which an individual, even isolated and momentarily contradicted by all others, may demonstrate a logical truth or the existence of a fact?

The first of the two questions has given rise to the most serious misunderstandings, on the part of both the defenders and the opponents of the sociological conception of logic. From the notion that truth resides in agreement among minds, it has been concluded that any agreement among minds engenders truth, as though history (both past and contemporary) did not abound in examples of collective errors. In fact the Durkheimian conception of the unity and continuity of the 'collective consciousness' leads to such an assimilation of truth to 'universal consensus': *quod ubique, quod semper, quod ab omnibus creditur*[20] thus becomes the criterion of truth for the sociologist, as for St Vincent of Lerins. But a formula of this type rests on a confusion of ideology and rational logic (i.e. scientific logic), and it is sufficient to introduce the distinction between these two forms of thought for any equivocation to be avoided. The agreement between minds which provides the foundation for truth is not the static agreement of common opinion, it is a dynamic convergence resulting from the use of common instruments of thought; it is, in other words, agreement established through the use of similar operations in many individuals. The second question emerges directly from the discernment of the first.

The second, and sole question reduces to this: do logical operations (whether carried out by a single individual, or by several, does not matter) constitute individual actions or actions of a social nature, or both simultaneously? Once the question has been posed in these terms, the notion of operatory 'grouping' allows us to give a simple answer, using an analogy with what has [p. 83] already been said about the relations between logic and psychology. Still, in order to clarify this answer, it must be placed separately and in sequence in relation to the two points of view which are both necessary in sociology (as we saw in Section 3), namely the diachronic or genetic viewpoint, and the synchronic viewpoint, which is concerned with the equilibrium of exchanges themselves.

I. The diachronic viewpoint

The study of the development of reason shows a close correlation between the constitution of logical operations and that of certain forms of cooperation. It is the detail of this correlation which must be specified, if we wish to grasp the true relation between reason and society, rather than stopping at the global and essentially static method of description, such as the notion of 'collective consciousness' comprises. Now, this detail can be analysed in two ways, one relatively well known, the other still not sufficiently developed, which are that of the socialization of the individual, and that of the historical and ethnographic relations between the operatory structures of thought and the various forms of practical cooperation and intellectual interactions. Both of these domains should be considered with equal care, because they stand to each other in the same relationship as embryology and comparative anatomy in biology, with the difference only that the factors of transmission involved are here of an external and social nature, and not internal or hereditary.

The growth of logic in the child, first of all, shows two essential facts: that logical operations proceed from action, and that the passage from irreversible action to reversible operations is necessarily accompanied by the socialization of actions, itself proceeding from egocentrism to cooperation.

First of all, considering logic from the point of view of the individual, it appears, essentially, as a system of operations, i.e. actions which have become reversible and composable in accordance with the various 'groupings'; and these operatory groupings themselves constitute the form of final equilibrium attained by the coordination of actions, once internalized. The psychological point of departure of such operations (logical addition or subtraction, seriation through ordered differences, correspondence, implication, etc.) is therefore to be sought well before the moment when the child becomes capable of logic properly called. [p. 84] Individual thought is only capable of concrete operations (understanding that a whole is conserved independently of the disposition of its parts, etc.) between 7 years on average and 11–12 years, depending on the particular notions concerned, and does not reach formal operations (reasoning on propositions presented solely as hypotheses) until after the latter age. Logic is therefore a mobile form of equilibrium (whose reversibility attests its equilibrium character) characterizing the peak of development, and is not an innate mechanism present from the beginning. Logic asserts itself, it is true, after a certain level of development, and with the consciousness of necessity, but this is the necessity of a final equilibrium toward which practical and mental coordinations necessarily tend, and not an *a priori* necessity. Logic becomes *a priori*, as it were, but only from the time of its achievement, and without having been present at the beginning! Without doubt, the coordinations between actions and movements, from which logic proceeds, themselves rest in part on hereditary coordinations (as we have insisted elsewhere), but these do not in any way contain logic in advance: they contain certain functional relations which, once abstracted from their context, are reconstructed in new forms during later stages (without this abstraction from previous coordinations of actions, nor this reconstruction, representing any *a priori* structure). In order to understand, psychologically, the construction of logic, we must follow very closely the processes by which the final equilibration constitutes this logic; but all the stages before the final equilibrium are of a pre-logical character. This is a functional continuity of development, conceived as a progression toward equilibrium, but with heterogeneity of the successive structures marking the different levels of this equilibration; these are the two essential aspects of the individual development of logic.

With regard to the successive structures themselves, if we recall the four major ones, this will allow us to demonstrate afterwards their intimate correlation with the socialization of the individual. There are first of all, before the appearance of language, the sensory-motor structures, which have their roots in hereditary reflex organization, and which lead to the construction of practical schemes, such as that of the object, displacement in space, etc. From the time of the appearance of language and the symbolic function in general, until around 7–8 years, (second period) the effective actions of the preceding stage are accompanied by mentally executed actions, i.e. imagined actions, on the representations of objects and no longer only on material objects themselves. The higher form of this imaged representation is 'intuitive' thought, which appears between 4–5 and 7–8, in which is evoked over-arching and relatively precise configurations (seriation, correspondence, etc.,) though [p. 85] only figurally, and without operational reversibility. Now, although this imaged or intuitive thought realizes an equilibrium superior to that of sensory-motor intelligence, since it completes action through anticipation and representational re-arrangements, this equilibrium is unstable and incomplete, compared to that of the next level, because it is tied to figural evocation, and does not have complete reversibility. Toward 7–8 years, in contrast, (third period) the mental actions of intuitive judgments lead to a stable equilibrium, corresponding to the beginning of logical operations themselves, but in the form still of concrete operations. Two new aspects characterize this equilibrium, and they appear simultaneously (and often suddenly) as the final stage of representational articulations: these are reversibility and over-arching composition in operatory 'groupings'. A grouping is a system of operations such that the product of two operations of the system is still an operation of the same system; such that each operation has an inverse; such that the product of an operation and its inverse is equivalent to a null or identical operation; such that the elementary operations are associative; and, finally, such that an operation composed with itself is not modified thereby. Once constructed in the concrete domain, these operatory groupings can finally, but only toward the age of 11–12, be translated into propositions, and give rise (from this fourth level) to a logic of propositions, linking concrete operations by means of new operations of implication or exclusion of propositions, which constitutes formal logic in the current meaning of the term.

With these four structures in mind, corresponding to the four successive periods of the equilibration of actions and operations of individual thought, we can consider the problem of the sociology of knowledge which arises in relation to them, which is the following: if logic consists of an organization of operations, which are internalized actions which have become reversible, must we admit that the individual alone arrives at the organization, or is the intervention of social factors necessary to explain the sequence of four types of structure, as described? Are these social factors reducible to simple educative pressure from the adult, transmitting from outside the inter-individual notions and operations comprising various types of possible relations, and of which educational transmission (through language, teaching in the family, school, etc.) is only one type? Now it is the case that, to each of the four stages of development of operations there correspond, in a relatively simple way, stages of social development. The two preceding questions may, then, be answered through the analysis of the intellectual socialization of the child – whether this socialization is the cause of operatory development, whether it is the result, or whether a more complex relation exists between them. [p. 86]

If socialization begins at birth, this can have little effect on intelligence as such, since this is the sensory-motor period which precedes language. It is true that the infant learns to imitate before being able to speak, but only those gestures are imitated which the child can already execute spontaneously itself, or those of which a sufficient understanding has already been acquired. Sensory-motor imitation, therefore, has no influence on intelligence; rather, it is one of its manifestations. This pre-verbal intelligence is thus essentially an organization of the perceptions and movements of the individual, still centred on the self entirely. In the second period, in contrast, the intuitive and pre-operational structures mark the very important beginning of socialization, but with characteristics intermediate between the individual nature of the preceding period, and the cooperation proper to the third, just as intuitive thought remains intermediate between sensory-motor intelligence and opera-tory logic. With regard to the means of expression, necessary both for the setting up of representations and for exchange of thought, first of all, it is the case that, while language offers the child a complete system of collective 'signs', these are not all understood from the beginning, and they are for a long time complemented by a system no less rich in 'symbols' of an individual nature, which are seen in games of imagination (or symbolic play), in representational imitation (deferred imitation), and in the multiple images which are the support of thinking.[21] From the point of view of meaning, i.e. thought itself, it is also the case that the inter-individual exchanges of children between 2 and 7 are characterized by an egocentrism which remains mid-way between the individual and the social, and which may be defined as a lack of differentiation between one's own point of view and that of others (thus the child does not know how to discuss nor how to set forth its own thought in a systematic manner, the child speaks for itself as much as for others and even plays in the absence of coordination in collective games). Now there is a close relation between the egocentric character of intellectual exchanges and the intuitive or pre-operational character of thought at the same ages: all intuitive thought is, in effect, 'centred' on a privileged perceptual configuration corresponding either to the momentary point of view of the subject or to his activity, but without mobility with respect to other possible operational transformations, i.e. without sufficient 'decentration'. As for the constraints exercised by elders and adults, their content is assimilated to egocentric schemes, and only transforms these superficially (this is why schooling, properly speaking, does not begin before 7). To the third period, characterized by concrete operations (from 7–11) there corresponds, in contrast, well-marked progress in socialization: the child becomes capable of a more sustained cooperation with peers, of the exchange and coordination of points of view, of discussion, etc. The child thus becomes sensitive to contradiction, and capable [p. 87] of conserving previous data, i.e. the first stages of cooperation in action and thought are of a piece with a systematic and reversible grouping of relations and operations. From this results the possibility of understanding the teaching of adults: the latter are not, properly speaking, the source of logic, since the assimilation of externally transmitted notions is conditional upon the structuration, both intellectual and individual, which characterizes the formation of thought. The close correlation between the social and the logical is even more evident during the fourth period, in which the grouping of formal operations on simple 'propositions' corresponds to the necessities of communication and speech, when they go beyond immediate action.

In summary, each progress in logic is equivalent, in a non-dissociable way, to a progress in the socialization of thought. Should we say, then, that the child becomes capable of rational operations because social development renders cooperation possible, or should we say, instead, that it is these logical acquisitions which allow the child to understand others, and which thus lead to cooperation?

This unbreakable circle of the development of the actions or operations of intelligence and of individual interactions among the members of any collectivity is also found in the domain of the historical evolution of techniques, and the evolution of pre-scientific and scientific thought. But although we can see, in every constituted society, that the modes of exchange of thought correspond to the level of thought itself, without it being possible to tell which is cause and which is effect in this circular process, the most important period of all is lost to view: that which extends between the primal horde, comparable to troupes of anthropoid monkeys, and organized society possessing collective techniques and an articulated language. In chimpanzees, the most social of the anthropoids, there is a nascent symbolic function,[16] and a certain degree of collaborative action, but the essential act of intelligence remains sensory-motor, with neither operational nor social structuring; imitation, in particular, remains, as in the baby, subordinated to sensory-motor intelligence. It is between the Chelleen 'punch'[22] and Neolithic man's working of metals that we should [p. 88] seek the interplay of technical progress, communication by verbal signals, and the transformations of intelligence, but here we are reduced to inferences about effects due to particular tools, all that we know without being in possession of the three sorts of factors in play.

By contrast, the paradox of 'primitive mentality' is still extremely instructive, and it is the great merit of Lévy-Bruhl to have posed this problem, even if he ignored one of its essential aspects which is the relationship between techniques and 'primitive' collective representations. Confining attention first to these representations, there is certainly something essentially correct in the hypothesis of 'prelogic', in spite of the eventual retraction of this idea expressed in the posthumous *Notebooks* of Lévy-Bruhl. No doubt he went too far in not distinguishing between the functioning of thought and its operatory structure. From the point of view of functioning, the thought of the 'primitive' is comparable to our own: the needs of coherence (independently of the level actually attained), adaptation to experience, explanation, etc., are functional invariants which are independent of development. But from the point of view of operatory structure, the notion of participation seems to us to have survived criticism remarkably well. When Durkheim replied that the logic of primitives is the same as our own, since they have classification, and when Reymond and Meyerson maintained, respectively, that primitive peoples possess the principles of contradiction and of identity, but apply them differently from us, they were obviously right with regard to function: primitives classify, and consequently use certain modes of systematization and assimilation which prefigure non-contradiction and identification. But this does not resolve the problem of structure. Do the intellectual schemes of primitive people already constitute logical classifications and logical system-atizations? From the point of view of an atomistic logic,[23] the question cannot, it is true, have a very precise answer, because it is possible to find, if one looks, all the elements of our logic in any primitive form of thought, even if other elements are erroneous or illogical. From the point of view of a logic of totality, on the other hand, there are certain criteria: can primitive classifications be reduced to groupings of operations, and their rules of coherence and assimilation to operatory principles, either formal or concrete? Thus posed, the problem suggests its own solution: if it is true that primitive schemes are mid-way between objects which are not individualized in their substantial identity and non-generalized sets in the form of disjoint and nestable classes, it is not possible to speak of groupings, nor, of course, of formal operations, nor even of concrete operations. Participation would then be [p. 89] comparable to intuitive thought and pre-operational thought in the child (level II), and not to the structures of levels III and IV.

However two points remain undecided, and it is in relation to them that the work of Lévy-Bruhl is still incomplete. In the first place, it is necessary to distinguish, in primitive prelogic, between collective ideology, in the sense of ready-made representations, transmitted obligatorily from generation to generation, and the interactions among individuals reasoning concretely (about a lost object, which road to take, etc.). In the second place, and it is here that the study of the first question will eventually lead – the essential problem, if we are to place primitive thought in its true perspective, is to understand the relations between primitive thought and practical or technical intelligence. The paradox, pointed out by Lévy-Bruhl himself, of the intellectual situation of primitive peoples consists in the fact that, while they are prelogical in their representations, they are highly intelligent in action: their technical skill, their understanding of practical relations (including orientation in space) are incommensurate with their deductive or reflexive capacities. It is clear, then, that a link is missing: either their operatory intelligence has already attained the level of concrete operations, but it is held in check by a coercive ideology, or, in action itself, such intelligence remains intuitive and pre-operational, but the articulations of their practical intuitions are closer to operations than their verbal and mythical representations. It will only be when, for every society, the relations between technical action, operatory intelligence, and ideology are known that we shall be able to determine the true levels.

With regard to the question of the relations between logic and social life, from the outset the import of the paradox of primitive mentality is clear, as is the general problem, thus posed, of the relations between techniques and logic. Alongside exchanges of thought properly speaking, depending on verbal communication and the transmission of existing truths, there are exchanges of action consisting in the reciprocal adjustment of movement and work, with the transmission of procedures, though this is a transmission which, even in the case of 'consecrated' techniques, presupposes effective cooperation, rather than simple submission to authority. To each of these levels of intellectual interaction there corresponds an intuitive or operatory structure of intelligence, and it is this correspondence which constitutes the analogue of what can be observed in individual development.

The problem is, then, the following: on the one hand (both in the mental development of the individual and in the historical sequence of mentalities) there are [p. 90] successive levels of logical structuration, i.e. practical, intuitive, and operational intelligence; on the other hand, each of these levels (of which several can co-exist within any one society) is characterized by a certain mode of social cooperation or interaction, whose sequence represents the progress of technical or intellectual socialization itself. Must we conclude that it is the logical or prelogical structuration of a level which determines the corresponding mode of social collaboration, or that it is the structure of interactions which determines the nature of intellectual operations? Here, the notion of operatory groupings helps to simplify this apparently unanswerable question: it is sufficient to specify, for a given level, the exact form of the exchanges between individuals, to see that these interactions are themselves constituted by actions, and that cooperation itself consists in a system of operations in such a way that the activities of the subject acting on objects, and the activities of subjects when they interact with each other are reducible in reality to one and the same over-arching system, in which the social aspect and the logical aspect are inseparable, both in form and in content.

II. The synchronic viewpoint

If logical realities do not extend beyond the field of thought, as opposed to action, and if the defining feature of concepts, judgment and reasoning is to be reducible to isolable elements, according to an atomistic model, then it is clear that logic and social exchange have nothing in common, other than the possibility that one may affect the other. But if, rather, logic consists in operations which arise out of action, and if these actions by their very nature constitute over-arching systems of totalities, whose elements are necessarily integrated with each other, then these operatory groupings will also express equally well the reciprocal and inter-individual adjustments of operations, and the internal operations of thought of each individual.

Let us start with techniques, whose forms of equilibrium are constituted simultaneously by cooperation in actions themselves, and by groupings of concrete operations, which we have discussed earlier. Take the case of two individuals, who are proposing to construct on both sides of a river a pillar of stones in the form of a ramp, and to join these pillars with a horizontal plank, forming a [p. 91] bridge. What does their collaboration consist in? There is mutual adjustment of certain actions: some actions are similar, and correspond by virtue of their common nature (for example, making the pillars in the same shape and of the same size), other actions are reciprocal or symmetrical (e.g. orienting the pillars in relation to the stream, in such a way that the two face each other with the vertical sides facing the river and with the sloping sides behind; other actions, finally, are complementary (one of the banks of the river being higher than the other, the corresponding pillar needs to be smaller, while the other will need extra height so as to reach the same level). But how is this adjustment of actions achieved? First, through a series of qualitative operations; the correspondence of actions with common elements, the reciprocity of symmetrical actions, the addition or subtraction of complementary actions, etc. Thus, if each of the actions of the collaborators is regulated by the laws of reversible composition, and so constitutes an operation, the adjustment of actions by one collaborator in relation to the other (i.e. their collaboration itself) equally consists of operations; these correspondences, these reciprocities or symmetries, and these complementarities are, in effect, operations like others, in just the same way as each of the actions of the collaborators. Subsequently the concrete operations of measurement will intervene: in order to obtain an equal size, the partners will measure their respective pillars, and must then adjust their measure, but this adjustment will once more consist in an operation of the same nature, since they must use a middle term, or common measure, in order to equalize their individual measures. Finally, they will have to ensure, together, the horizontality of the plank, each by adjusting one end. In order to do this, each partner can choose an idiosyncratic system of reference, but both systems must be coordinated into a single system, which once more amounts to making a correspondence, by means of an operation, properly called, between their individual operations.

In short, to cooperate in action is to operate in common, i.e. to adjust by means of new operations (qualitative or metric) of correspondence, reciprocity, or complementarity. This is true of all concrete collaborations: the choosing together of objects according to their properties; the construction of a topographic schema, etc., is to coordinate the operations of each party into a single operatory system in which the very acts of collaboration constitute integral operations. But which is the social, and which is the individual, factor here? The analysis of cooperation as such (i.e. once the ideological or sociocentric elements which could accompany or distort it have been excluded) becomes identical with that of the same [p. 92] operations seen in states of equilibrium in individual action. But these operations within the individual, once at the level of equilibrium of concrete operational groupings, are they themselves individual in nature? They are not, and for reciprocal reasons. The individual begins with irreversible, not logically composable actions, which are egocentric, i.e. centred on themselves and on their results. The transition from action to operation therefore presupposes, in the individual, a fundamental decentration as a condition of operatory grouping, which consists in adjusting actions with each other until they can be combined in general systems applicable to all transformations; it is precisely these systems which permit the linking of operations among individuals.

It is obvious, then, that there is just one and the same over-arching process intervening in all these different situations. On the one hand, cooperation constitutes the system of inter-individual operations, i.e. operatory groupings permitting the reciprocal adjustment of individuals' operations. On the other hand, individual operations constitute the system of decentred actions which are also capable of being coordinated with each other in groupings which can include the operations of others as well as one's own. Cooperation and grouped operations are, therefore, one and the same reality viewed from two different standpoints. There is thus no case for asking whether it is the constitution of groupings of concrete operations which allows cooperation, or the reverse: 'grouping' is the common form of equilibrium of individual actions and of inter-individual interactions, since there are not two ways of equilibrating actions, and action on others is inseparable from action on objects.

But, what is already transparent in the domain of concrete operations is more so in that of formal operations, i.e. of exchanges of thought which are independent of any immediate action. In fact, the groupings of formal operations constitute the logic of propositions: a 'proposition' is an act of communication, as the Vienna Circle[24] have insisted from a formal point of view, which reduces logic to a general 'syntax' and 'semantics', hence to the [p. 93] coordinations of language, and as the school of Mannoury have insisted from the psychological point of view, leading to a conception of logic as a set of concrete acts of social communication. The logic of propositions is therefore, by its very nature, a system of exchanges, and whether the exchanged propositions are those of internal dialogue[25] or of distinct persons does not matter. The problem is, then, one of determining what this exchange consists in, from the sociological and concrete point of view, and then comparing its laws to those of formal logic itself. Now, the exchange of propositions is surely more complex than that of concrete operations since the latter reduces to an alternation or synchronization of actions leading to a common goal, while the former presupposes a more abstract system of reciprocal evaluations, definitions and norms. Nevertheless, we shall see that this exchange, as well, consists in a grouping of operations, and that these are the obligatory conservations proper to such a grouping, which impose on the logic of propositions its fundamental rules of grouping.

It is clear first of all that an exchange of ideas, i.e. of propositions, must conform, in its external form, to the analysis of exchanges whose general description we have already given above (Section 5). But, in the particular case of propositions, the real values r and s, and virtual values t and v, resulting from exchanges between two individuals x and x', take on the following significance: $r(x)$ expresses the fact that x states a proposition, i.e. communicates a judgment to x'; $s(x')$ indicates agreement in return (or disagreement) on the part of x', i.e. the current validity attributed by x' to the proposition from x; $t(x')$ indicates the manner in which agreement or disagreement is conserved (or not) by x' i.e. that current validity recognized or denied by him but which he may ignore later; finally $v(x)$ is, but this time from the point of view of x, the future validity of the proposition stated in $r(x)$ and recognized (or denied) in $s(x')$. That is, we have $r(x) \rightarrow s(x') \rightarrow t(x') \rightarrow v(x)$, etc.[26] In the case where x' communicates a proposition to x, we have inversely $r(x') \rightarrow s(x) \rightarrow t(x) \rightarrow v(x')$; these two sequences give the values attributed successively to the propositions stated by the partners x and x'. In other words, an exchange of propositions is, from the outset, a system of evaluations like any other, and, without the intervention of special rules of conservation will only conform to simple regulations. Thus in any dialogue, each person may forget what the other has said even if having previously indicated agreement; or inversely may retain what was said, while the partner has since [p. 94] changed position. How, then, can any exchange of ideas be transformed into a regulated exchange, and thus become a real cooperation of thought?

First, we must specify the final state of the virtual values $v(x)$ and $t(x')$ or $v(x')$ and $t(x)$: when the validity of the proposition stated by x in $r(x)$ has been acknowledged by x', who conserves this acknowledgement in the form $t(x')$, then x can later invoke this acknowledgement value in the form $v(x)$ in order to act on the propositions of x'. Hence the sequence $v(x) \rightarrow t(x') \rightarrow r(x') \rightarrow s(x)$; or, inversely, (if x' invokes $v(x')$ in order to act on x); $v(x') \rightarrow t(x) \rightarrow r(x) \rightarrow s(x')$. In other words the virtual values of order t and v have the role of obliging the partner continuously to respect the propositions previously recognized, and to apply these to later propositions. It should be noted as well, that, in conformity with a general law of social interaction all conduct initially addressed to another is later applied by the subject to himself, in such a way that x, in stating the proposition $r(x)$, should be satisfied with it himself, hence $s(x)$, and will be obliged, himself, later to recognize its validity again, hence $t(x)$ and $v(x)$.

Such a schematization is instructive in two ways: first we can look for the conditions of equilibrium and exchange, i.e. the nature of the state in which the interlocutors are agreed or intellectually satisfied; second, we can show that these conditions for equilibrium imply precisely, a *groupement* of propositions, i.e. a set of rules constituting a formal logic. It is this second point we want to stress, since this is a matter of showing that the very exchange of propositions *qua* social conduct, embodies by its own laws of equilibrium, a logic coinciding with that used by individuals to group their formal operations.

The equilibrium of exchanges, it is easy to see, has three necessary and sufficient conditions. The first is that x and x' possess a common scale of intellectual values, expressible using common and unambiguous signs. This common scale must, then, have three complementary properties: (a) a language, comparable to the system of monetary signs in economic exchange; (b) a system of defined notions, whether the definitions of x and x' completely converge, or whether they partly diverge, but such that x and x' are in possession of the same means of translating the notions of either partner into the system of the other; (c) a certain number of fundamental [p. 95] propositions placing these notions in relation to each other, determined by convention, to which x and x' can refer in cases of discussion.

The second condition is the general equality of values occurring in the sequences $r(x) \rightarrow s(x') \rightarrow t(x') \rightarrow v(x)$ or $r(x') \rightarrow s(x) \rightarrow t(x) \rightarrow v(x')$. In other words, the second condition is (a) agreement on real values, i.e. $r = s$; and (b) the obligation to conserve previously recognized propositions (the virtual values t and v, which may be realized in the sequence of exchanges). In fact, if there is no agreement, either $r(x) = s(x')$ or $r(x') = s(x)$, there could be no equilibrium, and discussion continues. On the other hand, if agreement is constantly put in question, there could not be equilibrium either. Without the intervention of rules, i.e. an obligatory conservation, the previously acknowledged validities would disappear with every new exchange, and one would have, e.g. $s(x') > t(x')$ or $s(x) > t(x)$; or inversely, previous negations would be forgotten and we would have $s(x') < t(x')$, etc. Discussion is only possible, then, through conservations $s(x') = t(x') = v(x)$ and $s(x) = t(x) = v(x')$, which demonstrates the normative character of all regulated exchanges of thought, as opposed to exchanges of ideas based on simple fleeting interests.

The third necessary condition of equilibrium is that the virtual values such as t and v may be actualized at any time, in other words previously acknowledged validities may be invoked at any time. This reversibility takes the form: $[r(x) = s(x') = t(x') = v(x)] \rightarrow [v(x) = t(x') = r(x') = s(x)]$ and entails the reciprocity $r(x) = r(x')$ and $s(x) = s(x')$ etc.

Before showing how these equilibrium conditions bring about the constitution of logic, it should be noted that these three conditions are only realized in certain types of exchange, which we call cooperations, as opposed to exchanges which are deviant, whether through egocentrism or constraint. In fact, equilibrium could not be attained if, due to intellectual egocentrism, the partners do not succeed in coordinating their points of view: in this case the first condition is missing (common scale of values) as well as the third (reciprocity), and hence the second (conservation) cannot be attained, since obligation is not felt on either side. The words are understood in a different sense by each, and no appeal is possible to propositions previously recognized as valid, since the subject does not feel obliged to hold to what [p. 96] was said before. In the case of intellectual relations where there intervenes an element of constraint or authority, the two first conditions seem to be met. But the common scale of values is then due to a sort of 'fixed market' under the authority of tradition and usage, while, because of the absence of reciprocity, the obligation to conserve preceding propositions operates in one direction only. For example, x will oblige x', but not inversely. The result is that, however crystallized and solid in appearance may be a system of collective representations which has been imposed by constraint from generation to generation, it is not in a state of true or reversible equilibrium, due to the absence of the third condition, but in a state of 'false equilibrium' (as apparent equilibria due to viscosity etc. are termed in physics). The advent of free discussion is sufficient to disrupt it. The state of equilibrium, as defined by the three conditions described, is thus dependent on the existence of a social situation of autonomous cooperation, based on equality and reciprocity of partners, simultaneously detached from the anomy of egocentrism and the heteronomy of constraint.

However it is important to make it clear that cooperation, as we have just defined it by its laws of equilibrium, and its contrast with the double disequilibrium of egocentrism and constraint, is essentially different from simple spontaneous exchange, i.e. 'laisser-faire', as it is conceived by classic liberalism. It is only too obvious, in fact, that without a discipline ensuring the coordination of viewpoints by means of a rule of reciprocity, 'free exchange' is continually held in check, whether by egocentrism (individual, national, or due to social class polarization) or by constraint (due to struggles between classes, etc). In contrast to the passivity of free exchange, the notion of cooperation thus includes the double activity of decentration, with regard to intellectual and moral egocentrism, and liberation from the social constraints that such egocentrism causes or maintains. Like relativity on the theoretical level, cooperation at the level of concrete exchanges therefore involves a continual conquest over factors of automatization and disequilibrium. Autonomy, as opposed to anomy and heteronomy is, in fact, disciplined or self-disciplined activity, at an equal distance from inertia or forced activity. It is because of this character that cooperation implies a system of norms, unlike so-called free exchange, whose liberty is shown to be illusory by the absence of such norms. This is why true cooperation is so fragile and so rare in a social condition fragmented by special interests and domination, just as reason is so fragile and [p. 97] rare, in contrast to subjective illusions and the weight of tradition.

The equilibrium of exchanges thus described is essentially, then, a system of norms rather than simple regulations. But it is clear that these norms constitute groupings which coincide with those of propositional logic itself, even though they do not presuppose this logic in their own creation.

In the first place, independently of the initial conditions determining the propositions x; either $r(x)$, and the agreement of x', or $s(x')$, or the inverse, the obligation to conserve recognized values, i.e. the obligatory conservation of the virtual values $t(x')$ and $v(x)$, or the reverse, entail *ipso facto* the constitution of two rules, which thus appear as rules of communication or exchanges, leaving aside the internal equilibrium of individual operations: the principle of identity, holding a proposition invariant during later exchanges, and the principle of contradiction, conserving its truth if the proposition is recognized as true, or falsity if it is false, without the possibility of simultaneous assertion and denial.

In the second place, the ever-possible actualization of the virtual values v and t obliges both partners to refer constantly to the past in order to bring present and previous propositions into agreement. The obligatory conservation just discussed does not, then, remain static, but entails the development of the fundamental property which opposes logical to spontaneous thought: operatory reversibility, the source of the coherence of all formal constructions.

Finally, regulated by reversibility and obligatory conservation, later productions of propositions $r(x)$ or $r(x')$, and the possible agreements between partners, $s(x')$ or $s(x)$ necessarily take one of the three following forms: (a) the propositions of one may simply correspond to those of the other, hence forming a grouping of the form of one-to-one correspondence between two isomorphic series of propositions; (b) those of one partner may be symmetrical with those of the other, which presupposes agreement about a common truth (of type a) which justifies the different points of view (for example, in the case of two spatial positions reversing left–right relations, or two kinship relations such that the brothers of one [p. 98] partner are the cousins of the other, and vice versa; (c) the propositions of one partner may simply complete those of the other, by addition between complementary sets.

Thus, even the exchange of propositions constitutes a logic, since it entails the grouping of the propositions exchanged: a grouping relative to each partner, as a function of exchanges with the other, and a general grouping due to correspondences, reciprocities or complementarities in their joint groupings. Exchange as such therefore constitutes a logic, which converges with the logic of individual propositions.

Once more the question arises: does this logic of exchange result from pre-existing individual groupings, or is the inverse true? But the answer this time is much simpler than in the case of concrete operations, since a 'proposition' is by definition an act of communication at the same time as its communicative content contains an operation carried out by an individual: the grouping resulting from the equilibrium of individual operations and the grouping expressing exchange itself are constituted together, and are only two aspects of a single reality. The isolated individual would never be capable of complete conservation or reversibility, and it is the exigencies of reciprocity which allow this double conquest, through the intermediary of a common language and a common scale of definitions. But at the same time, reciprocity is only possible between subjects capable of equilibrated thought, i.e. of the conservation and reversibility imposed by exchange. In short, however the question is approached, individual functions and collective functions require each other in the explanation of the conditions necessary for logical equilibrium. As for logic itself, it transcends both, since it is part of the ideal equilibrium toward which both are directed. This is not to say that there exists a logic in itself, which could legislate simultaneously individual and social actions, since logic is only the form of equilibrium immanent in a process of development of these actions themselves. But actions, in the course of becoming composable and reversible, and raising themselves to the level of operations, acquire the power of being inter-substitutable. [p. 99] The 'grouping' then, is only a system of possible substitutions, whether within the thought of an individual (operations of intelligence), or between one individual and another (social cooperation, understood as a system of cooperations). These two types of substitution constitute a general logic, both collective and individual, which characterizes the form of equilibrium common to both social and individual actions. It is this common equilibrium that is axiomatized in formal logic.

AUTHOR'S NOTES

[1] E. Durkheim, 'Représentations individuelles et représentations collectives', *Revue de métaphysique et de morale*, (1898).
[2] J. Piaget, *Introduction à l'épistémologie génétique*, Vol.1 (Paris, Presses Universitaires de France), Introduction, p. 16.
[3] A. Koyré, *A l'aube de la science classique* (Paris, Herman, 1898, p. 15).
[4] K. Marx, *Le Capital*, ed. Kautsky, p. 133. Cited by L. Goldmann, 'Marxisme et psychologie', *Critique*, June–July 1947, p. 119.
[5] This volume, Chapter 2.
[6] F. de Saussure, *Cours de linguistique générale* (Paris, Payot, 1916).
[7] This is the case in individual psychogenesis.
[8] See the article cited above on the 'Theory of qualitative values in static sociology'.
[9] For economic regulations, see the works of E. and G. Guillaume on 'rational economics'.
[10] See J. Piaget, *The moral judgment of the child* (London, Routledge & Kegan Paul, 1932).

[11] It is no doubt in this sense that Karl Marx conceived the absorption of law into morality in an economically regulated society.

[12] See V. Pareto, *Cours d'économie politique*, Vol. 1 (1896) p. 22; and Boninsegni, *Manuel élémentaire d'économie politique* (1930) pp. 27–29.

[13] L. Brunschvicg, *L'Expérience humaine et la causalité physique* (Paris, Alcan, 1922, pp. 106–107).

[14] L. Goldmann, *La Communauté humaine et l'univers chez Kant* (Paris, P.U.F., 1948, p. 10).

[15] Ibid. p. 8.

[16] See P. Guillaume, 'La psychologie des singes' in Dumas, *Nouveau traité de psychologie*.

TRANSLATION NOTES

1 Piaget uses *psychogenèse* (psycho-genesis), *sociogenèse* (sociogenesis) and *psychologie génétique* (genetic psychology) both in *Sociological studies* and in other texts (for example, a literal translation of the title of *The child's conception of number* (London: Routledge & Kegan Paul, 1952) is *The genesis of number*). In the anglophone world, the three French expressions are more familiarly known as mental development, social development and developmental psychology. Note, however, that these English terms mask substantive disputes as to what counts as *developmental*. The diversity is evident in R. Campbell and M. Bickhard, *Knowing levels and developmental stages* (Basel: Karger, 1986); J. Flavell *et al.*, *Cognitive development*, 3rd edition (Prentice Hall, 1993); B. Inhelder and G. Cellèrier, *Les Cheminements des découvertes de l'enfant* (Lausanne: Delachaux et Niestlé, 1992); A. Karmiloff-Smith, *The modularity of mind* (Cambridge, MA: MIT Press, 1992); R. Kitchener, *Piaget's theory of knowledge* (New Haven: Yale University Press, 1986); D. Leiser and C. Gillièron, *Cognitive science and genetic epistemology* (New York: Plenum, 1990).

2 Piaget here uses *stade* and, in the next sentence, *étape* which are translated as *stage* and *level* respectively. The distinction drawn in Chapter 4 between general–universal aspects of knowledge is relevant here. Piaget's account addresses the question of whether any specified developmental mechanism is such that it makes possible the acquisition of knowledge of universals, whether or not that knowledge is also generally and regularly used by the knower in all epistemic contexts. As Piaget put it in his novel *Recherche* (1918): is the universal knowable? Universal knowledge is important for reasons given by philosophers from Plato to Popper in their rejection of radical scepticism. See also M. Chapman, *Constructive evolution* (Cambridge: Cambridge University Press, 1988) and L. Smith, *Necessary knowledge* (Hove: Erlbaum, 1993) for discussion.

3 Piaget uses the Greek term ἀντιπερίστασις

4 Bossuet, not Rousseau, is the author of this text.

5 Comte uses the French *état* (English *state*) which is customarily translated as *stage*.

6 The quotation may be from Karl Marx, *German ideology*. Reprinted in *Karl Marx: Collected works* (London: Lawrence & Wishart, 1970) [original publication in 1845].

7 There is an error in the French text, where 'conservation' appears instead of 'conversation'.

8 Thanks to Trevor Piearce for clarification of this point.

9 $r(x)$ erroneously appears in the French text.

10 The French text omits the first term of the second inequality, viz. $s(x') \geqslant t(x')$.

11   See Piaget's discussion of 'active methods' in his 1935 paper reprinted in *Science of education and the psychology of the child* (London: Longman, 1970).

12   Hans Kelsen published his *Pure theory of law* in 1934 and gained a chair at the University of Geneva in 1936.

13   'Sollen' is the German verb equivalent to English 'should'.

14   'Sein' is the German verb 'to be'.

15   Although Comte uses the word 'état', it is customary to translate this phrase as 'the law of three stages'.

16   Compare here the early claim: 'children think and act more egocentrically than adults' (Piaget, 1923/1959, p. 38). If adult thinking is less egocentric than children's thinking, then Piaget is making a comparative claim which has the implication that that egocentric thinking is a persistent feature of adult thought. In the present passage, Piaget is making a comparable claim about sociocentric thought in human societies. See also Translation Note 2 in Chapter 8.

17   This may be a reference to the work of E. Durkheim, *The elementary forms of religious life* (London: Allen & Unwin, 1915, p. 193).

18   The reference is probably to Karl Marx, *Theses on Feuerbach*. Reprinted in *Karl Marx: collected works*, Volume 5 (London: Lawrence & Wishart) [original publication in 1845].

19   The reference is probably to the work of Vilfredo Pareto, *A treatise on general sociology* (or *The mind in society*, New York: Dover, 1963, Section 868ff). Note in this regard Pareto's claim about the residue which is the hunger for logical development: 'this residue explains the need people feel for covering their non-logical conduct with a varnish of logic' (Section 975). It is precisely Piaget's claim in *Sociological studies* that intellectual development occurs as the differentiation of logical from non-logical elements due to mind and society.

20   'That which is believed everywhere, always and by everyone.' St Vincent of Lerins, *Commonitorium*, ii.

21   See J. Piaget, *Play, dreams and imitation in children* (London: Routledge & Kegan Paul, 1951).

22   For commentary on neolithic man, see P. Bowker, *Theories of human evolution* (Oxford: Blackwell, 1986).

23   The reference is probably to the work of B. Russell, *Introduction to mathematical philosophy* (London: Allen & Unwin, 1919). Piaget elaborates his criticism of atomistic logic in *Traité de logique opératoire* (Paris: Colin, 1949).

24   The reference is probably to the work of Rudolf Carnap, *The logical syntax of language* (London: Routledge & Kegan Paul, 1937).

25   In *The Sophist*, Plato defined thinking as the mind's dialogue with itself.

26   An extra bracket appears erroneously in the French text: $t((x')$.

2   Essay on the theory of qualitative values in static ('synchronic') sociology

[p. 100] It seems that one can reduce all 'social facts' to interactions between individuals, and more precisely to interactions which modify the individual in a lasting fashion. Sociology would thus appear as clearly distinct from psychology, although complementary to it: whilst the latter envisages individuals in so far as they are fashioned by hereditary influences (biological and internal) and by adaptation to the physical milieu, sociology only considers them in so far as they are structured by external influences (generations acting on each other) and by their reciprocal adaptations.

From this point of view the three fundamental social realities are rules, values and signs. Every society is a system of obligations (rules), exchanges (values) and conventional symbols serving to express these rules and values (signs). Now although the study of social rules (constraints, norms, etc.) and that of signs (linguistic sociology, symbolic usages, rites, etc.) have been fairly extensively developed, it seems to us that that of social values has not been developed in the same degree, and this for two reasons which basically reduce to one.

The first is that the independence of values in relation to norms (to rules) has not been adequately grasped. Thus the Durkheimians consider all values as imposed by a single system of constraints and so reduce them to the rules themselves. Now, if this is true of certain values, which for this reason we will call 'normative values' (moral values, legal values, etc.) this is no longer true of simple exchange values: economic values, for example, can show regularities, but they are [p. 101] not felt as 'obligatory' (they are only 'determined') and therefore cannot be thought of as largely imposed by norms or rules.

Second, despite the important distinction which Auguste Comte foresaw between static sociology and social dynamics, sociologists have not been sufficiently inspired by linguists of F. de Saussure's school, to be able to distinguish with him between 'diachronic' questions or evolution in time, and 'synchronic' questions, the equilibrium between simultaneous phenomena. Now, and this is precisely the point, if the validity of norms depends on their history, exchange values are only meaningful from the synchronic point of view, and it is the relative confusion between problems of equilibrium and problems of development which has thus resulted in values being linked to rules in an exaggerated manner.

In the short note which follows we propose at first to show the existence of social exchange values as distinct from economic ones, the former being conceived as qualitative, whilst the latter result from quantification, and thus constitute a particular class of social values in general. It is thus that the success of a politician, or a scientist or an apostle of such or such a cause, the reputation which his fellow citizens create for him or the gratitude they acknowledge; his works or writings, the debts of gratitude which he has himself contracted with respect to other individuals, in short, all the 'services' which he has rendered or profited from – they all constitute exchange values or result from it. Some of these values can be quantified, that is to say, that certain of the services which occur can be given a monetary value; but however important economic values may be, they only form a fraction of this vast circulation of values of all kinds which form social life considered from the synchronic point of view, that is to say, from the perspective of its equilibrium at a given moment of history.

Now, we would like to sketch the preliminary outlines of a theory of these values, and in the following way. Faced with the immense domain which we need to take into account, and above all by the impossibility of proceeding statistically (by evaluations of the volume of exchanges, production and consumption, of budgets, crises, etc.) as do economists, since we are concerned here precisely with qualitative values, and not with ones that have been quantified due to material exchanges, we [p. 102] therefore ask whether it would not be useful to proceed at first axiomatically in the way in which Walras[1] and Pareto[2] have tried to formulate mathematically the laws of equilibrium of exchanges in 'pure economics'.[3] It goes without saying that in economics or sociology an axiomatic schema or an 'abstract model' cannot replace observation or experiment, no more than it can in chemistry (crystallography, etc.) or in physics. But equally it has no such pretension. Its sole function is to fashion new tools of analysis and comparison, and from this point of view all consistent axiomatic systems have proved useful. We have recently observed this in a completely different field, when using the schemas of the algebra of logic for studying the psychology of thinking. Similarly in the case of the qualitative values which characterize social exchanges other than economic ones, it could not be a question of mathematical schemas. We will therefore employ a logical axiomatic system, that is to say, one dealing with 'classes' and 'relations', and not with 'numbers', in order to express precisely the mechanism of the exchange of qualitative values.

1. SCALES OF VALUES

Let us start from the elementary fact that in every society there exists a more or less great number of *scales of values*. These values can have different origins (individual interests and tastes, collective values imposed, for example, by fashion, prestige, the many constraints of social life or again by moral, legal rules, etc.), it matters little for the moment. The scales can be variable or more or less permanent, heterogeneous with each other or able to lead to a kind of average price, as is the case, for example, for the values which correspond to elementary needs of activity, security, individual freedom, mutual confidence, etc., without which no society is viable. Even if these scales are multiple and unstable, it is nevertheless possible to analyse them in so far as they possess value at a determinate moment, just as we can in economics reason about average prices or about the variability of prices recorded during a day and at determinate intervals.

Without wishing to study here the fundamental operations which give rise to values, we can verify that for each individual, according to the ends which he wishes to attain and [p. 103] the means he employs or reckons to employ in pursuing these ends, all the objects and persons which interest him (including his own), as well as all actions, tasks and in a general fashion all the 'services' actually or virtually rendered by them, can be evaluated and compared according to certain value relations, relations which form such a scale.

From the formal point of view we can represent a scale of values by a system of *asymmetrical relations*. Let $A, B, C, \ldots$ etc. be a series of terms of increasing value. We then have the relations $O \uparrow aA = $ 'A is greater in value than O'; $A \uparrow a'B = $ 'B is greater in value than A', etc., and the following two operations (see Figure 1):

I   Addition of values $\uparrow a + \uparrow a' = \uparrow b$ (or $a + a' = b$); $b + b' = c$; etc.
II   Subtraction of values $b - a' = a$; $c - b' = b$; etc.

But a scale of values does not necessarily appear in this simple form. Thus it is possible that the value B_1, represents an end which can be arrived at by several different means A_1; A_2 or A_3; B_1 may itself be a means in relation to

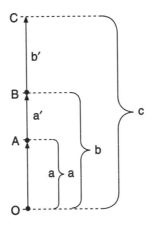

Figure 1

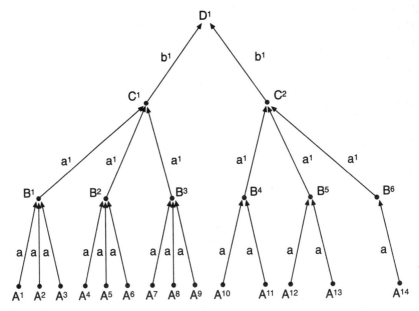

Figure 2

the value C_1, and other means B_2 and B_3 may equally lead to it. Whence Figure 2. In such a case if the means leading to the same end are substitutable, they are of equivalent value. Thus in economics two interchangeable commodities (for example, two kinds of luxury article) tend to the same price. Similarly, if an ambitious man only regards two careers, between which he is unable to make up his mind, as [p. 104] two means merely of arriving at the same end, these two careers will have the same value for him.

Let us finally note that the same individual can know at the same time several different scales, according to his different levels of activity, although he may establish a more or less stable hierarchy among the ultimate ends of each of them. In order to represent these hierarchical scales, it will be convenient to represent them three-dimensionally and no longer on a plane; for example, on the different faces of a pyramid.[1] But in what follows, in order not to complicate matters, we will restrict ourselves to the schema of Figure 1.

2. INTER-INDIVIDUAL EXCHANGE OF VALUES

Generally every action or reaction of an individual, evaluated according to his personal scale, necessarily has repercussions on other individuals: it is useful, harmful or indifferent to them, that is to say, that it marks an increase (+) of their values (= *satisfaction*), a decrease of their values (= *loss*) or a null difference.[4] Each action will therefore produce on the part of other individuals a return action. Now these can consist in a material action ('actual value'), such as a transfer of objects in exchange for a service rendered, or a virtual action such as approval or blame, an encouragement to persevere or a request to stop, a promise, etc.: we then speak of 'virtual values'. [p. 105] The existence of scales of values is thus translated by a constant reciprocal *valorization*[5] of actions or 'services' (positive or negative).

Let us assume, for example, that individual α renders a service to α' (that is to say, that the result of the action of α is a value for α'). There are then three possibilities:

1 α' has rendered in return a service to α. For example, α has given α' information about his scientific techniques, and α' has done the same.
2 α' has as yet not given anything in return, but merely valorizes α. For example, α has lent a work to α': who is grateful to him, and α knows that he will be able to count on him in analogous circumstances. Or suppose α is a politician who acts zealously on behalf of a group of constituents α': he asks for no actual payment but he knows he can count on their votes, that his 'stock rises', etc. Or again α has made a scientific discovery or published a new novel: his 'success', his 'reputation', etc. then beomes as such an 'investment', a 'value' he can draw upon in certain circumstances, however disinterested he be.
3 α' neither returns anything to α nor valorizes him. In this case it is α' who is himself devalorized by α: he will be considered as ungrateful or unjust, or unstable, or insecure, etc.

In each of these three cases there has therefore been an exchange of values. What is the nature of this exchange? Before we try to answer this question we must make the following points.

In the first place, the service rendered by α to α' is for α a sacrifice or an *actual renouncement* and for α' an *actual satisfaction* (or gain). By lending a work to α' the individual α renounces it temporarily whilst α' enjoys it. The politician α runs risks in acting on behalf of the α', whilst the latter benefit from it. The scientist or the novelist α, sacrifice their time and leisure for the work from which the α' derive an intellectual or aesthetic satisfaction.

On the other hand, the valorization of α by α' constitutes a *virtual satisfaction* for α. For example, if α' is grateful to α for having lent him a work, then α knows that he can when the time comes ask α' for a service in return. The politician α acquires a prestige and a moral position through the gratitude of the α' towards him. [p. 106] The scientist α acquires an authority and reputation to the extent in which the α' appreciate his work, etc. and this reputation will be of use to him sooner or later.

Conversely, the valorization of α by α' constitutes for α' a promise, an obligation, etc., in short a *virtual renouncement*. It is thus that after having returned the borrowed work to α, α' remains 'obligated' to him. Similarly, the political followers α' of the leader α cannot 'cut loose' from him without justification. The colleagues of α, the author of a scientific discovery, or even the readers of α, who has written a worthwhile novel, are 'forced to recognize' his success, to listen to him, etc.

In short, the service rendered by α to α' is a loss for α and a gain for α', whilst the valorization which results from it of α by α', is a credit for α and a debt for α' (which, moreover, common language meaningfully expresses by speaking of an individual's moral 'credit', of an 'indebtedness', etc.). On the other hand, it follows that each of these values can exhibit itself in a negative form.

In order to express these values in the form of a logical schema, (it would be useless to use mathematical schemas, since such values are 'qualitative' and would not be 'measurable' without a set of disputable statistical conventions), it will be enough to apply to the exchanged values correspond-ence rules,[2] in basing ourselves on the hypothesis that individuals α and α' share the same scale of values.

> Let r_α = action (or reaction) of α on α'
> $s_{\alpha'}$ = satisfaction of α' engendered by action r_α
> $t_{\alpha'}$ = debt of α' resulting from the satisfaction $s_{\alpha'}$
> v_α = valorization of α by α'

and let us use the symbol '=' to designate the relation of qualitative equivalence.

We then have in the case of simple equivalences, the following logical equation.

> Eq. I $(r_\alpha = s_{\alpha'}) + (s_{\alpha'} = t_{\alpha'}) + (t_{\alpha'} = v_\alpha) = (v_\alpha = r_\alpha)$

[p. 107] whence by hypothesis, the individual α is valued by α' proportionally to the service he has rendered to him.

In what follows we will make do with this crude notation, which deletes the signs. Taking account of the signs we would have the following notation:

> $(\downarrow r_\alpha) + (\uparrow s_{\alpha'}) + (\downarrow t_{\alpha'}) + (\uparrow v_\alpha) = 0$

This is symbolized more clearly in Figure 3, which is therefore an illustration of Equation I.

From this it follows that the only thing which constrains the individuals α and α' to respect the equivalences $r_\alpha = s_{\alpha'} = t_{\alpha'} = v_\alpha$, is precisely the moral and legal norms we will refer to in Sections 6 and 7. So long as only the dynamic of spontaneous feelings and inter-individual interests enters into play, we can have in addition to the general equivalence, a series of other combinations, of which it is interesting to consider the following:

> 1 If $r_\alpha > s_{\alpha'}$ (the other terms being equivalent to $s_{\alpha'}$), we have $(r_\alpha > s_{\alpha'})$
> $+ (s_{\alpha'} = t_{\alpha'}) + (t_{\alpha'} = v_\alpha) = (r_\alpha > v_\alpha)$

That is to say, α works at a loss and his social action is unsuccessful or frustrated. In this case there are two possibilities. Either the individual accepts the valuations of which he is the object and ceases to act, or changes his activity, rectifies his scale of values, etc. Or, on the other hand, he continues,

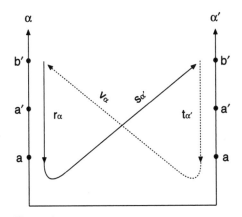

Figure 3

but devalues his judges in the hope of turning and convincing public opinion. [p. 108]

2 If $r_\alpha < s_{\alpha'}$ (the other terms being equivalent to $s_{\alpha'}$), we have $(r_\alpha < s_{\alpha'}) + (s_{\alpha'} = t_{\alpha'}) = (t_{\alpha'} = v_\alpha) + (v_\alpha > r_\alpha)$

There is in this case a gain for α, whose easily completed work is crowned by a success greater than his effort. In this case α, of course, continues, and his action is thus canalized or rather polarized by this social approval encouraging him to continue in his chosen path.

3 If $s_{\alpha'} > t_{\alpha'}$ whilst $r_\alpha = s_{\alpha'}$ and $t_{\alpha'} = v_{\alpha'}$, we have $(r_\alpha = s_{\alpha'}) + (s_{\alpha'} > t_{\alpha'}) + (t_{\alpha'} = v_\alpha) = (r_\alpha > v_\alpha)$

Individual α again works at a loss, as in (1), but this time because α' does not wish to admit or else forgets his satisfaction $s_{\alpha'}$. A case in point would be the politician who has been unable to exploit his success in time, whose credit has therefore become exhausted before he has used it, and who can then only record the 'ingratitude of the masses'.

4 If $s_\alpha < t_{\alpha'}$ whilst $r_\alpha = s_{\alpha'}$ and $t_{\alpha'} = v_\alpha$ we have $(r_\alpha = s_{\alpha'}) + (s_{\alpha'} < t_{\alpha'}) + (t_{\alpha'} = v_\alpha) = (r_\alpha < v_\alpha)$

In this case there is an over-evaluation of α by α'. As an example we may cite those political friendships by means of which an incompetent individual has been made a success, and about whom nobody has any illusions as to the real services rendered. There is thus overestimation of his worth, with consequent temporary inflation of value, with the risks of a sharp deflation which all inflation involves.

It will be asked what justification do we have for deriving these equalities and inequalities. We repeat they are not measurements, otherwise the exchange would no longer be qualitative but quantifiable, and we would enter into the field of economics: it is a question simply of qualitative relationships perceived directly by each individual consciousness. We can each take account of whether our acts are valued higher or lower than they have cost us, or whether the result and the effort expended are equivalent. It may be that these subjective evaluations are without an objective foundation (psycho-physiological), but this does not concern our problem: however subjective they be, they constitute insofar as they are the driving power in social interaction, essential social facts, and it is as such that we ought to analyse them, exactly as the economist studies the laws of exchange without asking, for example, if the price of a precious stone corresponds to a real psycho-physiological 'utility' for the buyer who attributes to this merchandise a subjective utility. [p. 109]

Use of virtual values

Up to now we have examined how the action of α (r_α) on α' ends in a valorization of α by α' (v_α); in other words, how a real value r_α is exchanged against a virtual value v_α. It remains to show how α is able 'to realize' these values v_α.

Let us therefore assume that α has been successful in his enterprises, that is to say, that he achieves $v_\alpha = r_\alpha$ or even $v_\alpha > r_\alpha$. He is thus in possession of values of approval, of gratitude, of reputation, of authority, etc. From his point of view we will call these virtual values 'credits', independently of whether they will be recognized or not, whilst they will constitute 'rights' as soon as they are recognized by α' (Section 7). Conversely, for α' they correspond in α to the evaluations $t_{\alpha'}$ made by α', which we will call 'debts', from the point of view of α, and which will become 'obligations' if they are recognized by α'. At a given moment α can therefore realize his credits, that is to say, ask of α' services in return for those he has rendered or 'use his authority' in order to compel α' to perform an action $r_{\alpha'}$. In the case of equivalence we then have the logical equation:

$$\text{Eq. II. } (v_\alpha = t_{\alpha'}) + (t_{\alpha'} = r_{\alpha'}) + (r_{\alpha'} = s_\alpha) = (s_\alpha = v_\alpha)$$

This means that (1) if α' acknowledges a debt equivalent to the credit of α, i.e. $v_\alpha = t_{\alpha'}$; and (2) if he pays his debt under the form of an equivalent service, i.e. $t_{\alpha'} = r_{\alpha'}$; and (3) if this service satisfies α in an equivalent fashion, i.e. $r_{\alpha'} = s_\alpha$; then (4) the satisfaction of α equals his credit, i.e. $s_\alpha = v_\alpha$.

We are concerned here with the inverse transformation of Equation I, whence the reversal of signs:

$$(\downarrow v_\alpha) + (\uparrow t_{\alpha'}) + (\downarrow r_{\alpha'}) + (\uparrow s_\alpha) = 0$$

This is symbolized by Figure 4. To pay a debt is a positive operation, whence $\uparrow t_{\alpha'}$; and to use a credit is to decrease capital, whence $\downarrow v_\alpha$, since α thus loses by his actual satisfaction s_α, a right v_α which he possessed up to then.

It follows from this, on the other hand, that we can discover here all the inequalities just distinguished appropriate to Equation I, according to [p. 110]

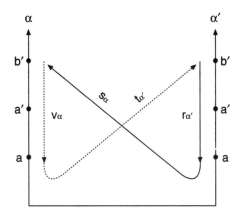

Figure 4

which α' does not acknowledge his debt, or acknowledges it without satisfying α, etc. etc. In reality all combinations occur and play a clear role in the social equilibrium (see below Section 5). But from now onwards, what we need to note is that except in the case of low volumes of economic exchange (of small tradespeople), and of certain very particular cases of qualitative exchange (in the usages of the strict forms of politeness; in a ceremonial protocol where questions of etiquette and of prestige are tied to a symbolism covering important interests) we never claim all our due (v_α) and never pay all our debts ($t_{\alpha'}$). The circulation of social values rests, on the contrary, on a vast credit, continually maintained, or rather constantly disintegrating through attrition and forgetting but constantly reconstituted, and which only disappears at a time of revolution or grave social crisis, that is to say, when there is complete devaluation of all the values up to then known.

3. THE LAWS OF EQUILIBRIUM OF ECONOMIC EXCHANGE AND OF THE EXCHANGE OF QUALITATIVE VALUES

Before continuing it can be interesting to show very briefly how the laws of equilibrium of economic exchange can be deduced as a particular case of the preceding forms of exchange, as soon as one quantifies the 'actual' qualitative values, and one defines the 'virtual' values solely as a function of that quantification.

Let us imagine an exchange that is immediately duplicated, and therefore obeys simultaneously Equations I and II. It is clear that this dual operation if carried out as one, cancels out the virtual values v and t. We thus have have:
[p. 111]

Eq. I $\downarrow r_\alpha + \uparrow s_{\alpha'} + \downarrow t_{\alpha'} + \uparrow v_\alpha = 0$
Eq. II $\downarrow v_\alpha + \uparrow t_{\alpha'} + \downarrow r_{\alpha'} + \uparrow s_\alpha = 0$

Whence $\downarrow r_\alpha + \uparrow s_{\alpha'} + \downarrow r_{\alpha'} + \uparrow s_\alpha = 0$, cancelling out $\uparrow v_\alpha$ by $\downarrow v_\alpha$ and $\downarrow t_{\alpha'}$ by $\uparrow t_{\alpha'}$.
There remains therefore $(r_\alpha = s_{\alpha'}) = (r_{\alpha'} = s_\alpha)$.

In other words, in exchange for a service by α (r_α) which satisfies α' $(s_{\alpha'})$, α' immediately renders a service to α $(r_{\alpha'})$ which satisfies him in return (s_α). For example, let r_α and $r_{\alpha'}$ mean that α gives wine to α' whilst α' gives wheat to α until they are both satisfied. If $s_\alpha = r_\alpha$ and $s_{\alpha'} = r_{\alpha'}$ (equality of satisfactions and of sacrificed values), we then have what economists call 'equality of final utilities', or in Pareto's terms equality of 'elementary ophelimities', that is to say, the satisfaction connected with the last lot of wine (or wheat) received tends to equal the satisfaction connected with the last lot of wine (or wheat) given. One can then quantify s_α and $s_{\alpha'}$ or r_α and $r_{\alpha'}$ by measuring the objects exchanged: for example, three hundred kilo of wheat against two hectolitres of wine. From this fact the relationship between the values is translated in terms of price, and will thus express the quantity of a commodity that has to be given in order to obtain a unit of another. So we can see how the quantification of exchange with the cancellation of virtual values suffices to transform the operation into an economic one.[3] If, on the other hand, the exchange is made over time and credit replaces immediate payment, the virtual values will reappear under the form of credits and debts, but equally quantified since they preserve in this case the actual quantitative values (plus the payment of interest equivalent to the time difference). Only, as we will see (Sections 6 and 7) such a 'conservation' of values presupposes the operation of legal norms.

The 'pure economics' of the Lausanne school[4] has determined the laws of equilibrium of such elementary exchanges, that is to say, the point at which such exchange comes to an end; and it has reduced these laws [p. 112] to six conditions of equality: (1 and 2), equality for each exchanger of elementary ophelimities balanced by the commodities possessed after the exchange (condition of maximum satisfaction); (3 and 4) equality for each exchanger of receipts and expenditure evaluated numerically (balance of exchangers); (5 and 6) equality for each commodity of the quantities existing before and after the exchange (balance of commodities). Now it is striking that these conditions of equilibrium are precisely those which govern the exchange of purely qualitative values, such as that for which our Equation I gives the formula. To begin with, the equality of the elementary ophelimities is to be found in the equality of the values s_α $(= r_\alpha) = v_\alpha$.[5] So long as one has $v_\alpha > r_\alpha$, the individual α will have the tendency to continue his action r_α, whilst if $v_\alpha < r_\alpha$ he will have gone beyond the point of *optimum* satisfaction; conversely, for α' the maximum satisfaction is $s_{\alpha'} = t_{\alpha'}$. For example, when a lecturer α speaks to an audience α' he will tend to continue as long as his success v_α exceeds his effort r_α, and his audience will listen to him as long as its pleasure $s_{\alpha'}$ is greater than its obligations $t_{\alpha'}$, equilibrium being achieved for $r_\alpha = v_\alpha$ and $s_{\alpha'} = t_{\alpha'}$, a limit, alas, often exceeded! And secondly the balance between the exchangers is, of course, determined by the equalities $\downarrow r_\alpha + \uparrow v_\alpha = 0$ and $\uparrow s_{\alpha'} = \downarrow t_{\alpha'} = 0$, that is to say, there is equilibrium when efforts and gains counterbalance one another. Finally, the balance of commodities corresponds in the qualitative exchanges to this essential condition of equilibrium, which we will find in Sections 6 and 7 and which is the 'conservation of values', i.e. $r_\alpha = s_{\alpha'}$ and $t_{\alpha'} = v_\alpha$: if the values exchanged are not conserved during their transformations, there occur the different disequilibria referred to in Section 2, to which we will return in Section 5.

As for the way in which the price or the qualitative values are established, we will find another parallel between these two fields in the famous law of supply and demand. We know that in a market, if the supply is greater than the demand, the competition which occurs between the sellers has the effect of lowering the price offered; and that if the demand is greater than the supply the competition between the buyers has the reverse effect of increasing the initial price. Now it is clear that this phenomenon is not peculiar to the economy: for example, the same [p. 113] literary gifted individual will be overvalued in a social milieu lacking such individuals and rich in literary appreciation as, for example, in a small provincial town, whilst he risks being undervalued in a large town where there are many such individuals. In a general manner from the axiomatic point of view, one can reduce such an empirical law to a very simple principle resulting from the very structure of the scales of value described under Section 1. Let us assume a scale based on the many–one correspondence between means and ends (Figure 2): many means A will correspond to each end B, several means B to each end C, several means C to each end D; ... etc. giving the hierarchy $A \rightarrow B \rightarrow C$; etc. ($A \uparrow B \uparrow C$ ... etc.). It follows that the greater the means, the less their value, since the use of one devalorizes the others. Value would therefore seem to be like 'scarcity' in the qualitative field, as Walras has already noted in economics. This inverse relationship between value and quantity, which is the basis of the law of supply and demand, can even be considered as corresponding on the plane of values, to that which is general in qualitative logic, the inverse relation between the extension (cf. quantity) and intension (cf. value) of concepts.

We could amuse ourselves by constructing a series of other analogies between the mechanism of economic exchange and that of qualitative values. Every group for the production of values (scientific society, etc.) could, for example, be compared to an 'enterprise' and would give rise to a study of internal exchanges (among the collaborators themselves) and external ones (between the group and the public). Loans and interest also find their equivalent in the way in which men in public life hire out their authority (act as a figurehead, etc.) and calculate the advantages and risks of these operations. The capitalization of values thus gives rise to a technique of loans and interest largely going beyond the political sphere. Finally, between the free exchange of values, the monopoly of some of them, and the 'fixed market'[6] due to state control and the corresponding economic phenomena, many 'common mechanisms' may be found.

4. INTER-INDIVIDUAL AND COLLECTIVE VALUES

Let us now proceed from the exchange between two or several individuals to exchanges of values between whole societies. [p. 114]

Let us assume a dual qualitative exchange between two individuals, but such that there may be *reciprocal gain*, i.e. $v_\alpha > r_\alpha$ and $v_{\alpha'} > r_{\alpha'}$

$$(1)\ (r_\alpha < s_{\alpha'}) + (s_{\alpha'} = t_{\alpha'}) + (t_{\alpha'} = v_\alpha) = (r_\alpha < v_\alpha)$$
$$\text{and (2)}\ (r_{\alpha'} < s_\alpha) + (s_\alpha = t_\alpha) + (t_\alpha = v_{\alpha'}) = (r_{\alpha'} < v_{\alpha'})$$

(see Figure 5)

Such a dual valorization relation empirically constitutes what can be termed 'sympathy'[6] between α and α': everything that one does satisfies the other more than it has cost him in the first place, and reciprocally. (Inversely 'antipathy' is a reciprocal devaluation.) Now the prerequisite condition for the existence of such collectives of reciprocal valorization, even only of two individuals, is that they possess a *common scale* of values, without which the exchange is made at random and cannot take place. We assert this when we

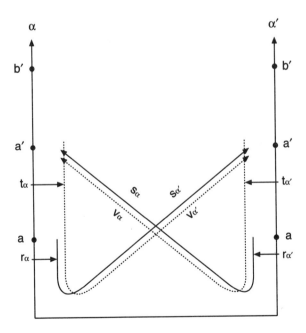

Figure 5

say that two individuals 'understand each other', or 'agree', 'that they have the same tastes', etc.

Now this prerequisite condition is not peculiar to inter-individual exchange, but constitutes a condition of existence for every collective, including nations, even international communities. Conversely, we can say that every scale of values corresponds to a collective of [p. 115] *co-valorization* constituted by the set of individuals, co-exchangers according to that scale. But in fact there exist a relatively large number of scales in contemporary societies, which leads to difficulties of coherence between them. There are, for example, political scales, and every 'ideology' can be considered in this respect as a conceptual system, whose real function is to serve to express values, which it presumes to justify rationally, but for which it simply provides a scale in a symbolic form. Thus a democratic regime will recognize as essential values, the dignity of the human person, freedom of thought, respect for popular opinion, etc. If the valuation and everyday exchanges do not conform to such a scale, the finest constitutions will remain a dead letter and the regime will not be able 'to become part of the people's way of life'. There are also religious scales whose symbolic expression is provided by systems of dogmas, but which go beyond this ideological framework: thus societies where the Church has long dominated can effectively preserve the character of 'Christian civilizations', to the extent where actions are generally judged there according to a common evaluation inspired by the morality[7] of Christianity. There is moreover a host of aesthetic, literary, etc. scales which follow rapidly or interfere with each other in different ways.

We will therefore call the 'class of co-valorizants' every set of individuals exchanging their values according to a common scale. Let the class A be a class formed of the individuals α, α', α'' who accept the same scale of values. We can then conceive the following different possibilities, in considering exchanges no longer solely between two individuals α and α', but between all individuals belonging to the class A (the algebraic sum of exchanges according to the principle of the algebra of relations, such that $v_A = v_\alpha + v_{\alpha'} + v_{\alpha''} \ldots$ etc):

1 If there is a *reciprocal gain* $v_A > r_A$, i.e.
$$(r_A < s_A) + (s_A = t_A) + (t_A = v_A) = (v_A > r_A),$$

then the collective is naturally stable, since it is a condition of mutual enrichment of individuals. Thus in Switzerland, despite considerable differences in languages, cultures, and interests, the federal bond represents for everyone a moral and intellectual enrichment. In this case the collective A becomes itself a positive value for the individuals who make it up. [p. 116]

2 If there is a *reciprocal devaluation* $v_A < r_A$, i.e.
$$(r_A > s_A) + (s_A = t_A) + (t_A = v_A) = (v_A < r_A),$$

then the collective is not viable and only represents an artificial bond surviving its stage of real existence. Naturally the exchange of values is not the only factor to be considered, and legal and ethical norms can forcibly conserve the collective bond without any positive values corresponding to it. (Thus a marriage, a political alliance, etc., can survive through obligation whilst involving no more than exchanges exhibiting a deficit.)

3 If there is an *exact equilibrium*, $v_A = r_A$, i.e.
$$(r_A = s_A) + (s_A = t_A) + (t_A = v_A) = (r_A = v_A)$$

The collective can continue to exist as long as competing values do not prevail over them in disequilibrating it.

Many other combinations could be considered, but it is preferable, in order to analyse them, to distinguish within a whole collective B, two partial collectives, the class A and the class A' conditioning B's equilibrium. This is what we intend to do in the following section.

5. THE CIRCULATION OF VALUES AND SOCIAL EQUILIBRIUM

It is well known that Pareto has tried to represent the equilibrium of a society as a mechanical composition of co-occurring forces, these forces being themselves constituted by the feelings or instincts of individuals and which reveal themselves under the form of constant 'residues' and variable 'derivations'. The equilibrium of values formulated in our equations I and II coincide in principle with Pareto's social equilibrium, since according to him the resultants X, Y, etc. of the residues A, B, C, etc. represent the maximum utility for 'society' when one chooses as a reference system the 'ends', that is to say, the scale of values of any individual α whatsoever. But Pareto's system appears to us to raise some difficulties, which perhaps a schema based on the exchange of values escapes. In the first place, in order to define the forces in equilibrium, Pareto is obliged to distinguish real ends of actions (needs and feelings exhibited by the 'residues') from fictitious ends (the 'residues' themselves and the derivations). Now the distinction is always arbitrary and depends on the subjective interpretations of the sociologist. Second, [p. 117] it has never been very clear if the 'residues' result from individual instincts or from the interactions themselves. And, third, the Paretian equilibrium is always relative to a total 'utility' ('of' or 'from' society), but this utility is necessarily arbitrary, as Pareto himself admits, since it is relative to the very *content* of this value (to such an 'end', arbitrarily chosen, as the author puts it). On the other hand, for us, there is no need to distinguish objective and subjective ends, since we only study *exchanges* and not the content of values. For example, a pharmaceutical product having an illusory effect can have a real exchange value independently of its medical value: similarly, the mutual valorizations of a small African tribe believing in magic can obey the same laws as our own without our having to ask what the attributed values objectively mean. The social equilibrium which we study is therefore solely based on the dynamic of exchanges and not on the nature of the co-occurring 'forces' (feelings), which only constitute the content or the subjective driving force of the exchange. We also do not have to determine whether a feeling widespread in a society is 'logical' or 'non-logical': it is only translated socially by values, and it is these values and not the feelings or the 'residues', which are the real constituents of the social equilibrium. These values actually depend on the exchange, that is to say, on an essentially collective mechanism and not on illusory 'instincts' or individual 'residues'. To the extent in which we maintain the notion of 'residues', we shall have to conceive them as the resultant of exchanges and not as explaining the latter, since their active value depends on these exchanges.

The conclusion of Section 4 is that at least two conditions are necessary in order that a collective be conserved: (1) the collective exhibits, *at least*, a common scale of values and, (2) that the exchanges lead to reciprocal gains or to a state of equilibrium. Now it is clear that the basic fact is that of reciprocal valorization: a scale of values is nothing but the comparison or seriation of satisfactions already obtained or yet to be obtained. We might therefore believe that the devalorization $r_A > s_A$ constitutes the same phenomenon as the rupture of the common scale, but if the first of these processes sooner or later entails the second, there can be [p. 118] a shift or *décalage* between the two and a revalorization without a rupture. We shall therefore distinguish different forms of disequilibrium in the exchange of values, and show that they correspond to the principal kinds of social *crises* that observation allows us to analyse:

1   Crises of type $r_A > s_A$, manifest themselves when in a collective B, a class A renders fewer services to the rest A' of society than was previously the case: either the class A' has no longer the same needs, or the class A has become too large in relation to its needs (too many intellectuals, etc). In this case the common scale of values is not necessarily altered, but the satisfactions $s_{A'}$ diminish whereas the work carried out and supplied r_A remains constant or increases. Such crises normally end by a simple readjustment of the equilibrium of supply and demand. This is a contemporary economic phenomenon (cf. overproductions, etc.) but which also governs qualitative values, as can be observed in the crises of literary and cultural movements, etc.
2   Crises of type $v_A < r_{A'}$. The reader will recall (Section 2) that the simple exchange of values (Equation I) leads to a kind of capitalization of values (when $v_\alpha > r_\alpha$) or of qualitative credit, which credit can be then used to obtain return services (Equation II). Now when the shuttling between the credit and the new work is interrupted for too long, that is to say, when an individual or a group relies too much on its credit without using and reconstituting it, *the capital becomes eroded*. Thus a literary man or a scientist who lives too many years on his reputation devalues himself. This periodic devaluing of dead capital can affect a whole class A within a collective B. The most contemporary example is the erosion of political

parties in power: party A, very active in opposition, renders service to the rest A' of the collective B by defending it and acting as a check, whence $(r_A < s_{A'}) + (s_{A'} = t_{A'}) + (t_{A'} = v_A) = (v_A > r_A)$. On coming to power it at first enjoys its credit v_A whilst inevitably creating discontent. If it does not then increase its credit by new activities, this credit becomes exhausted, and falls to $v_A < r_A$. Here again the phenomenon does not necessarily entail the rupture of the common scale, since the A are devalorized in the name of the same values which have produced their earlier success. [p. 119] But if the parties very quickly exhaust their credit without reconstituting it, then inevitably the regime itself is threatened. We then have the following situation.

3   Crises of type $r_B < s_B$ and $v_B < r_B$. It can happen finally that the services rendered by the A to the A' and conversely, no longer satisfy either, whether because they follow from negative intentions, or what was appreciated earlier ceases to be appreciated (as between two individuals who no longer love each other and for whom even the memory of the past satisfactions ceases to be a value). It is then that the exchange becomes impossible on the old scale of values, or in other words, this scale is broken. Such a crisis, of course, covers the two preceding forms; but precisely because it combines the actual dissatisfaction (type I) with the loss of the capitalized values (type II), it leads to a more severe disruption.

The rupture of the common scale appears characteristic of political or social *revolutions*, and it would be possible to conduct an instructive study of their mechanism from this point of view of valorizations. It is thus that the most important aspect of the revolution is the construction often very speedily of a new scale of values, which replaces that whose survival no longer corresponds with the actual exchanges. This is why, if we cannot stop a revolution at its start by force, nothing will then prevent it except another revolution. Contrary to mild crises which constitute simple oscillations between two co-occurring forces (alternate rise and fall of values), revolution always intensifies more by the elimination of the moderates and their outbidding by the extremists. Now this is precisely explained by the presence of two scales, one of which is breaking down and no longer allows the habitual satisfactions (the payments, if one can thus put it, effected by its means no longer reach their normal rate), whilst the other in constituting itself allows all 'speculations' and all higher bids. On the other hand, sooner or later there occurs a process comparable to that which in economics is described by Gresham's famous law:[8] just as bad money drives out good because we try to pay others with the former whilst we hide the latter, so when two qualitative scales oppose each other, we [p. 120] publicly approve all the valorized actions that conform to codes still dubious or even fictitious (such as 'slogans' of 'authority', 'order', etc.) whilst conserving in private the old values, which thus lose their power of exchange. Finally one ends up with grossly inflated values ($t_B > s_B$), that is to say, with reputations and promises greater than the actual or possible services, at an 'artificial' confidence exceeding the feelings of security really experienced, etc. After this, liquidation occurs by the elimination of false values and a return to equilibrium, according to a scale generally halfway between the old and that which has been at the forefront during the crisis.

These are some current examples of social crises which it is possible to mention without entering into detail. One observes at first their analogy with mild and 'normal', or serious economic crises which result in a change of regime. It is undeniable, to quote only one type of example, that after the military defeat of a great nation, the resultant social actions exhibit all the characteristics, not only of a devaluation of certain ideals and of certain individuals, but also and above all of a sharp breakdown of the whole scale of values and of manifold efforts at reconstructing a scale of values allowing renewed internal as well as external exchanges. We would equally have to analyse closely the interference of different phenomena of this order with the different modes of the circulation of values, from free competition to monopoly and from this to complete state control. One can then conceive a sociology of values for which the laws of economics, because quantifiable, would provide a particularly interesting model. Although, of course, qualitative exchanges are not only more complex than economic exchanges because of their non-quantitative nature: they are so also in virtue of their closer dependence upon the system of norms, from which we have made abstraction thus far, and which it is now advisable to examine as a function of the general problem of values.

6. THE NORMATIVE COORDINATION OF VALUES. I. MORAL COORDINATION

One general fact overshadows the preceding considerations: it is that easy as it may be to define the equilibrium of social values in terms of conditions of qualitative identity or equivalence, nothing in fact is more unstable than such values and [p. 121] such an equilibrium. Not only do the satisfactions vary without relation to the work done, but also the acquired values are continually frittered away and remain at the mercy of unforseeable devaluations either in detail or as a whole. This is why besides the exchange mechanisms, every society exhibits a set of general operations (an apparatus, one could almost say) for the conservation of values, whose role is to ensure the equilibrium, no longer by the automatic balancing of spontaneous exchange, but by means of a series of increasingly precise obligations according to whether they are of a moral or legal order.

Now it is esential to understand from the very first that these rules of moral and legal conservation are not superadded from outside the exchange of values: it is within the very interior of the field of these exchanges that they constitute themselves and in virtue of valorizations which extend the earlier ones, but with this one difference, that in place of remaining exclusively tied to one's own point of view, they separate themselves from it in order to constitute a coordination of points of view. In order to clarify this transition, we are going to start from simple exchange in order to derive from it the laws of normative reciprocity of the moral order, then only after this will we examine heteronomous obligations or moral duties, although these are genetically earlier; and finally we turn to legal obligations, which will bring us to the whole[9] problem of social equilibrium.

A. Normative reciprocity

In order to understand how normative equilibrium differs from a simple exchange of values, one can compare the relationship which exists between them to that which unites, in the field of thought, a system of simple perceptions (= non-normative representation) to reasoning (= system of normative operations of a logical order). Let us suppose, for example, that we give a child three small rulers A, B, C, leaving all three on the table, within the subject's visual field. After having compared the relationships $A = B$ and $B = C$, the child will naturally conclude that $A = C$, but reasoning is then in no way necessary, since the subject can compare directly A and C: the perceptual or empirical observation is sufficient. Let us now assume that the subject has not seen the three small rulers together, but that after we have made him verify that $A = B$, we hide A under the table; we then make him verify that $B = C$, [p. 122] and still not showing A, we ask whether $A = C$ or if $A > C$? It is clear that in this case the intervention of reasoning becomes necessary, but what does it consist in? It simply consists in conserving the perceptual values $A = B$ and $B = C$ as given, even if the perception no longer exists, and to draw from this the conclusion $A = C$ corresponding to a new possible perception which is coherent with the earlier ones, i.e. non-contradictory (logical norm) with them. Now the situation is exactly the same in the exchange of values, where one can distinguish the *actual exchange* directly controlled by the interested parties and which thus corresponds to an immediate perception of values, and the *exchange in time* or the *enduring exchange* which goes beyond the frameworks of verification and actual perception, and thus requires the intervention of stabilizing norms, that is to say, operational reversibility.

For example, in a cash sale there is no moral merit in the exchangers not stealing from each other, if each is observing the other. Similarly, when a service rendered is paid for in the form of thanks and in the immediate expression of a felt gratitude, the actual character of this qualitative exchange does not require the intervention of moral norms, and the exchange remains a matter of mutual sympathy. On the other hand, in a credit sale, the debt becomes the object of a legal and moral obligation. (If the debtor remains for any accidental reason whatsoever safe from prosecution, or if he is ruined in the meantime, his moral worth increases if he wishes to discharge his debt.) In the same way, to acknowledge, after a lapse of time, a service received presupposes a moral attitude, particularly if, for example, the person rendering it was highly placed and has since 'fallen'.

In short, simple or spontaneous exchange only implies a lived or intuitive reciprocity, whilst if exchange is effected in time (or at a spatial distance, that is to say without direct contact between the exchangers), then all *enduring equilibrium* requires the occurrence of particular norms and there is consequently *normative* reciprocity (comparable to operational reciprocity, which makes up the logic underlying the stabilizing of irreversible perceptions). From the sociological point of view, one can therefore consider legal and moral norms as *the set of operations tending to the conservation of values in exchanges of types I and II.* [p. 123]

Consider, for example, Equation I: $(r_\alpha = s_{\alpha'}) + (s_{\alpha'} = t_{\alpha'}) + (t_{\alpha'} = v_\alpha) = (v_\alpha = r_\alpha)$. The co-occurring values can change in a multiplicity of ways, changes which will thus prevent an enduring equilibrium. For example, action r_α will not satisfy α' $(s_{\alpha'})$ or will satisfy him in an illusory manner; or α' fails to acknowledge what he owes to α $(t_{\alpha'})$, etc. In short, the values v_α and $t_{\alpha'}$ can increase unduly or be eroded by affective forgetting. Observation clearly shows that where values are destroyed, there is an inter-individual reaction tending to bring about conservation or to censure such destruction. For example, if $s_{\alpha'} > t_{\alpha'}$, that is to say, if α' does not acknowledge the satisfactions which α has given him, he wil be accused of faults ranging from ingratitude to deceit; if the action of α ends by hurting α' (negative values), one will meet all forms of censure according to the type of action. If there is immediate reciprocal gain it will not be judged blameworthy (except if it is obtained at the expense of a third person) but will remain outside the moral sphere, in so far as it is the outcome of simple sympathy: but even then, once the values are acquired, their destruction will be censured (infidelity, etc.)

How does this conservation of values then become assured? It does so through a system of operations assigning in a permanent manner certain relations and conditions of equivalence to the co-existing values. These operations of a formal order will be called *norms*, whilst we will continue to call the content of these forms values: a *normative value* will therefore be the value which results from the application of a norm. (For example, an act is invested with a moral value when it is enforced by α or 'approved' by α' by reference to the same norm.) Thus the norm is the rule or obligation itself. One can conceive two possible methods of conservation. One which forms legal norms consists in simply transforming, as a result of the operations of 'acknowledging', of 'enacting', etc., the values of virtual exchange v_α and t_α into 'rights' and 'obligations' (codified or non-codified), and this whatever be the interested or disinterested character of the norms thus stabilized. The other, which constitutes morality, ensures a more radical conservation as a result of operations coordinating means and ends, or actions and satisfactions according to a disinterested point of view, that is to say, each person evaluates himself reciprocally as a function of his partner and no longer from a personal point of view. [p. 124]

It is thus that the 'moral' conditions of conservation in the case of Equation I are found to be the following. (1) *Indefinite satisfaction of α' by α.* Whilst the simple act of exchange is effected from one's own point of view, the moral act locates itself at the other's point of view. In simple exchange, α acts (r_α) with a view to his own success (v_α); on the other hand, in the reciprocity of the moral order, α acts with a view to the satisfaction of α', which therefore constitutes an end and no longer a means. The limits of the action r_α of α are no longer determined by his own interest, by the hedonistic law of the equality of the 'ophelimities' r_α and v_α, but only by the possibilities open to α in his desire to satisfy α': α will seek therefore to satisfy α' as much as he can and not simply to the extent in which his own success compensates his effort. This is what we will call the 'indefinite satisfaction of the other' (indefinite because non-determined as a function of the relationship $r_\alpha \leftrightarrow v_\alpha$). (2) *Evaluation of r_α by α' in the light of the intention of α.* On the other hand, if α acts from the point of view of the scale of α', α' will reciprocally evaluate the action r_α of α from the point of view of the scale of α, namely, according to the intentions of the latter (and not from the result of the action valued according to scale α').

One can reduce these two conditions to a single one, which we will call *the reciprocal substitution of scales* or *the reciprocal substitution of means and ends,*[7] $s_{\alpha'}$ becoming an end for α and r_α a value in itself for α'. This suffices to demonstrate the disinterested character of moral action as against the utilitarian ends of simple exchange. From this it follows that if this dual condition is fulfilled, we will always have $r_\alpha = s_{\alpha'}$, each of these two terms being evaluated according to the partner's scale. As for the terms $t_{\alpha'}$ and v_α, they then acquire the following meaning. In v_α α is valorized by α' according to r_α, from which $v_\alpha = r_\alpha$, which no longer means, as in the case of simple exchange, that α has the right to a service in return from α', but only that it is 'approved'. And the 'moral approval' consists in the scale of normative values of α being acknowledged by α' and the very person of α being invested with a 'moral value' in the eyes of α'. [p. 125] On the other hand, the term $t_{\alpha'}$ is the obligation that α' has thus incurred to act according to the normative scale of α.

The normative equilibrium of moral reciprocity is therefore attained in an exchange of type I, when each of the partners conserves the values of the other according to the latter's scale, α tending to the indefinite satisfaction of α', and α' acknowledging the moral values of α. This normative exchange can, of course, be duplicated.

It follows therefore that in exchanges of a moral order, Equation II $(v_\alpha = t_{\alpha'}) + (t_{\alpha'} = r_{\alpha'}) + (r_{\alpha'} = s_\alpha) = (v_\alpha = s_\alpha)$ only holds in a particular sense which is that of the 'reciprocal substitution of means and ends'. One does not find among the 'moral feelings', 'rights' which the individual attributes to himself in an interested sense ('rights' that he would have, for example, to get others to value his services or even his previous credits, in his own self-interest). The term v_α which represents the moral value of α in the sight of α' (= the way in which he has been 'approved' by α') only involves therefore for α the disinterested right to make α' acknowledge α's scale of moral values, that is to say, to acknowledge his own obligation as 'having value'. And if this right v_α obligates α' in $t_{\alpha'}$, this obligation results directly from the fact that α' 'approves', esteems (and as we will soon say 'respects') α. If α' therefore acts via $r_{\alpha'}$ according to the obligation $t_{\alpha'}$, he gives in return to α, a 'moral satisfaction' s_α as a function of the intention of $r_{\alpha'}$ (this intention itself depends on the valorization of α by α'): α thus 'approves' α' in return, which closes the circle of normative reciprocity.

One then immediately sees how moral conservation, based on the substitution of points of view, differs from legal conservation which only takes account of the interested party's scale, and ignores the condition of disinterested reciprocity. It can therefore be said that in this sense morality is the obligatory conservation of values in Equation I, and law in Equation II; on the other hand, Equation II therefore appears as derived from morality, and Equation I as derived from law.

Finally, it is possible that in an exchange of type I, α' does not subject himself to the norm of reciprocity whilst α remains faithful to it. In this case there is an inequality and no longer an equivalence, but for someone who respects the norm, the obligation remains the same independently of the other's reaction. In this case it is α himself who will acknowledge the value of his own action, in the form of [p. 126] 'internal satisfaction', his 'good conscience' constituting a kind of 'self-approval'. Moral exchange therefore has this interesting character for the sociologist: it constitutes an internalized exchange in consciousness, such that the value v_α depends only on the intention of α and no longer on the reaction of α' (or the partner's valorization). How is this new character of exchange to be explained?

A first solution, often correct in part, would consist in saying that in acting morally we are not really disinterested but seek the pleasure provided by the approval of others; and that in the absence of the partner's approval one always hopes for that of public opinion. But if observation effectively shows that sometimes the most apparently altruistic acts involve this egoistical element in the search for approval, on the other hand, other observations underline the existence of conflicts of conscience between disinterested obligation and the approval of others, the honest man preferring to rely on his conscience rather than on contemporary opinion, even of that of his closest and dearest. But is it then based on the approval of non-present witnesses? No doubt, but they are not necessarily future witnesses, whose praise will satisfy, despite everything, his egoism: it can be of absent witnesses, whose examples and past benefits still ' obligate' him in the present.

For still stronger reasons, we cannot consider as an explanation of the 'internalization' of moral exchange, the crude utilitarian interpretation of common sense. For common opinion, the moral value v_α is often conceived as a value of exchange analogous to that of spontaneous exchange (v_α = possibility of future satisfactions s_α, and the right to be recompensed by others $r_{\alpha'}$), but like an indeterminate exchange value, indefinitely postponed.

It is in this way that persons professing a certain common morality reason when they speak of the future recompense that every good action merits, either in this world or the next. And they even add that the merit increases with the delay in compensation, which recalls the economic notion of 'interest' conceived as the price of the difference between the actual and future value (the actual enjoyment given by the idea of a future recompense constituting a lesser satisfaction than the immediate recompense). But such conceptions merely prove that there exist all the intermediaries [p. 127] between spontaneous (or 'interested') exchange and purely normative (or 'disinterested') exchange and therefore do not provide an explanation of the latter.

In fact, the obligatory and internalized character of normative exchange can only be understood if the disinterested action r_α results from earlier obligations t_α contracted by α with regard to α' or persons other than α', and which will bind him in the present to certain values to be respected. One therefore sees how the intervention of norms in the exchanges introduces directly the notion of the 'diachronic', not only because the norms conserve values in time, but also because the obligatory character of the norm is only explicable as a function of its history. This is what we are going to examine briefly.

B. The two forms of respect and moral obligation

The hypothesis from which we start is therefore that a *norm* results from an equilibrium in time; that it is the obligation ensuring the equilibrium between present exchanges and all the earlier exchanges.

We call *respect* the feeling tied to positive *valorizations* (and absence of respect to that joined to negative valorizations) *of persons* (individuals), as against the valorization of objects or services. To respect a man thus means to attribute to him a value, but one can attribute a value to one of his actions and to one of his services without valorizing him as an individual. To respect a person therefore amounts to recognizing his scale of values, which as yet does not mean to adopt it oneself, but to attribute a value from the point of view of this person. Let us at first note that to respect an individual does not simply mean to respect the rules which he embodies (as Kant and Durkheim thought, for whom respect is a feeling concerned with the moral or collective law and not one concerned with individuals). As P. Bovet has shown, it is respect for the person which engenders the obligations and not the opposite (a thesis which it is easy to verify in the young child). There is therefore no vicious circle in making respect the origin of normative values and obligations in general, since respect is initially nothing more than the expression of the value attributed to individuals as opposed to things or services. Further, it is easy to see that this valorization [p. 128] of individuals as such, in terms of 'respect', necessarily leads to the disinterested behaviour which characterizes moral norms, and leads to it alone: to say that α' respects α, is to say that in his behaviour relative to α the individual α' puts himself at the point of view of α and of his scale. The 'reciprocal substitution of scales' or of 'means and ends' is therefore nothing else than the expression of a mutual respect.

The first form of respect (first in the order of psychological genesis) is *unilateral respect*, or the non-reciprocal valorization of two individuals. Let us start, for example, with the continuous exchanges observed between parents and their young children. If α is a parent and α' a child, the dual exchange produced between them is in constant disequilibrium, because the actions of α are valued by α' more than those of α' are by α.

1. $(r_\alpha < s_{\alpha'}) + (s_{\alpha'} = t_{\alpha'}) + (t_{\alpha'} = v_\alpha) = (r_\alpha < v_\alpha)$
2. $(r_{\alpha'} > s_\alpha) + (s_\alpha = t_\alpha) + (t_\alpha = v_{\alpha'}) = (r_{\alpha'} > v_{\alpha'})$

In simpler terms, this means that α appears to α' as superior to him (stronger, cleverer, wiser, etc.) and inversely. To be sure the small child can give his parents satisfactions as intense, or more, than they can give in return, but in this case we are concerned with particular values which are specifically affective, whilst the valuing of the parents by the child begins by being general. Now this total value attributed by the child to his parents leads to two results. The first, of course, is (and this is bound up with the unilateral valorization of individuals) that the child will adopt the scale of values of the respected person, whilst the converse is not true (or to a lesser extent): thus the child will imitate the examples one has set him, espouse adult points of view, etc., whilst the reverse hardly ever occurs. The second is that the respect of the adult indicated by the value v_α is translated in the child into the acknowledgement $t_{\alpha'}$ of a permanent right to give commands, orders, etc. For the child therefore the term $t_{\alpha'}$ stands for the obligation of having to conform to the examples and orders of α; and this is precisely what the psychological analyses of Bovet have shown. The obligations of conscience appear in α' to the extent that α who gives α' his orders is respected by α'. And Baldwin even says that the obligation $t_{\alpha'}$ is constituted as a function of the [p. 129] examples of α' (a point of view that psychoanalysts have taken up in their theory of the 'super-ego'). Finally, the obligation $t_{\alpha'}$, at first undifferentiated, will become 'moral' as soon as the orders of α fulfil the condition of disinterested satisfaction.

The second form of respect, on the other hand, is *mutual respect* or the reciprocal valorization of two individuals, and its product is the normative reciprocity to which we are thus brought. Just as unilateral respect results from the inequality of the valorizations between two individuals, mutual respect arises from the equivalence. Let us assume that α feels that α' is superior to him in a certain field, whilst the reverse is the case in another. Or again, when collaborating with one another on an equal basis, α and α' consider themselves as being of equal value. In either case (and, of course, all variations are conceivable between unilateral and mutual respect) it follows that α and α' either accept a common scale of values, or in the case of divergence, mutually recognize the legitimacy of the other's point of view (resulting from more general common values from which the particular divergent values will appear as both derived). From then, there will no longer exist between them relations of authority (to obey commands, orders, etc.) but relations of simple mutual agreement.

The valorizations (v_α and $v_{\alpha'}$) of each by the other being equivalent, the acknowledgements ($t_{\alpha'}$ and t_α) indicate only a common obligation to put oneself at the other's point of view; but precisely because this obligation results from a reciprocal valorization of persons, the valorizations acquire the normative character which spontaneous exchange does not exhibit, and which renders values permanent. This obligation characteristic of normative reciprocity is explicable by the fact that neither α or α' would be able without contradiction to value the other, whilst acting at the same time towards him in a way which would devalue the agent himself. For example, α cannot at the same time respect α' and lie to him, because α' then will stop respecting him and there only remains in this case for α either to give up respecting α' or himself. Now even if α' overlooks α's lie and retains his respect for him, the same mechanism of normative reciprocity will operate within α's consciousness to the extent in which α valorizes α' and acknowledges his scale of values: in the case of reciprocity as in that of unilateral obedience, the obligations t_α, in becoming general, are therefore internalized, [p. 130] and as a result become applicable to all the cases assimilable to those occurring at the time at which the norm first arose.

In short, the norms due to unilateral respect constitute a *morality of duty*, and the norms due to mutual respect a *morality of reciprocity*. This difference derives uniquely from the form of the obligation or of the norm and not from its content. It is clear that the morality of duty can lay down rules whose content has been fashioned by the morality of reciprocity. For example, there are the norms of equality or of distributive justice which arise spontaneously, with each new generation, from the relations of reciprocity between peer groups such as children of 7 to 12 years of age or adolescents, but which can also be imposed in the guise of duties by elders or parents. But even then there remains this essential difference, that in the case of obligation by duty the norm is received as ready made and is thus heteronomous, whilst in the case of construction by reciprocity the individuals obligated by the norm have themselves cooperated in an autonomous fashion in its elaboration. On the other hand, it follows from this that the morality of duty can impose all kinds of prescriptions and imperatives of any content whatsoever, and without relationship with those of the norms of reciprocity. One can quote as an example the 'taboos' pertaining to the morals of social constraint and the prohibitions of the same form imposed upon children (not to speak certain words, not to touch certain furniture, papers, etc.).

Now we can ask in the case of normative exchange, whether the morality of duty constitutes a phenomenon comparable to *monopoly*, or the 'fixed market' of simple (non-normative) exchanges, so that the morality of reciprocity would correspond to free trade. It could be the case that a system of pure heteronomous obligations would lead like monopoly to a relative destruction of values. The 'indefinite' action r_α which is presupposed by the norm of reciprocity, does not by definition have limits, since to satisfy the other as one would wish to be satisfied oneself is an essentially indeterminate and 'open' programme; on the other hand, to do one's maximum duty when this duty has no content of reciprocity, but constitutes a simple prohibition, can constitute a 'closed' action having a finite limit. Conversely, whilst the sanction of the norms of reciprocity is never more than a remission in the productive state, the repressive sanction tied to the norms of heteronomy, which [p. 131] consists in redeeming an offence by a punishment, can consist in unproductive values.

On the whole, and however schematic this outline remains, one sees how the normative coordination of the moral type constitutes a system of operations ensuring the conservation of values. Both the clause regarding 'indefinite satisfaction of the other' and that concerning evaluation according to intention, result in the integration of values in a set of 'groupings'[8] of reversible substitutions, some asymmetrical (morality of duty) and the others symmetrical (reciprocity), but all formally analogous to the logical 'groupings' themselves.

7. THE NORMATIVE COORDINATION OF VALUES. II. LEGAL COORDINATION

It is well known that legal theorists disagree about the nature of the foundations or 'origins' of law. For some like Kelsen, law constitutes a unique normative system deriving its origin from the State. For others, there exists a law given independently of the State, of a metaphysical ('natural law') or of a social nature. (Petrazycki, who appears to us to be the most profound of the defenders of non-State law, even speaks of psychological origins, in other words, inter-individual ones.) We will distinguish therefore between state or codified law, whose formal and normative structure has been so well analysed by Kelsen, and that which we will call, for lack of a better description, 'non-codified' law or 'deontology', that is to say, the relations of law not fixed by written laws or the practices recognized in the precedents of the courts. To fix our ideas let us, to begin with, consider a completely verbal promise made without witnesses, by α' to α: we will say that this promise gives α a non-codified right over α'. But we must be clear as to this classification, about whose origin we do not offer any hypothesis. A large number of legal theorists would prefer to classify such a right under morality and exclude it from the 'legal' domain. This is not important for us, but it will be necessary in this case to distinguish two domains of moral order: first, that of relations termed 'disinterested' [p. 132] in the preceding section, where obligations are ordered by the condition of this reciprocal substitution of scales; second, another domain in which obligations are determined by conventions or inter-individual agreements based on personal interests, and where we have the notion of the 'right' that an individual can have over his partner, a notion absent from the first domain. For example, let us assume that α' has promised α an article for a future number of his Journal. We then consider the following cases: (1) If there has been a contractual agreement and the defaulting of α' is deterimental to α, the latter can call in his lawyer or even serve a court summons on α': this case therefore involves codified law, a situation which we will not for the moment examine. If the promise is legally informal and α', taken up with unexpected tasks, has not been able to start on the article on time, two cases are again possible. (2) α' placing himself at the point of view of α feels in spite of everything the obligation to keep his promise; whilst α placing himself at the point of view of α' wishes to release him from it. (3) α reckons to be able to make use of his right and claim the article, whilst α', surprised by the attitude of α, acknowledges his right (or, on the other hand, challenges it, claiming that the promise was tied to circumstances which have changed, etc.). We would all agree to consider case 1 as being of a legal order and case 2 as being of a moral one, but what is to be made of case 3? If it is connected with the moral order, we will nevertheless recognize that it differs from case 2 as it deals with 'rights' like case 1, and not with disinterested obligations like case 2. From the point of view of the exchange of values, it has therefore more of a relationship with 1 than with 2, and this is why we speak of 'non-codified law' or deontology, in order to designate this kind of relationship. On the other hand, we will classify professional deontologies, once they are recognized by the courts, under 'codified law'.

We will therefore first study the exchange of values characteristic of non-codified law, and we will then try to analyse the formal structure of the relationships of statute law.[9]

A. Non-codified or deontological legal relations

Just as normative coordination in the moral sphere appeared [p. 133] to us as an obligatory conservation of values in the case of Equation I, so the normative conservation of a legal order will constitute a conservation of values in the case of Equation II, but without the condition of indefinite satisfaction of the partner and with the scales of value being unified only from the point of view of the rightful claimant.

Let us assume Equation II: $(v_\alpha = t_{\alpha'}) + (t_{\alpha'} = r_{\alpha'}) + (r_{\alpha'} = s_\alpha) = (s_\alpha = v_\alpha)$.

In the case of the necessary conservation of values, the meaning of the terms are the following:

v_α = right of α acknowledged by α'.
$t_{\alpha'}$ = correlative obligation of α'.
$r_{\alpha'}$ = services of α' intended to fulfil his obligation $t_{\alpha'}$.
s_α = satisfaction of α resulting from the services of α'.

For example, α' having promised a journal article to α, the term v_α will refer to the right which results from this for α; the term $t_{\alpha'}$ the obligation α' has to write his article; the term $r_{\alpha'}$ the action of writing the article; and s_α the satisfaction of α.

We can immediately see that each of these equivalences postulated by the legal relation can be vulnerable to disturbance: (1) We can have the cases $v_\alpha > t_{\alpha'}$ or $v_\alpha < t_{\alpha'}$, that is to say, that α and α' fail to agree as to their rights and obligations. (2) If $t_{\alpha'} \gtreqless r_{\alpha'}$ is the case, they do not see eye to eye as to the way in which α' has fulfilled his obligations. (3) $r_{\alpha'} \gtreqless s_\alpha$ means that α may not be satisfied with the services received; and (4) $s_\alpha \gtreqless v_\alpha$ expresses the non-equivalence between the satisfaction obtained and the right possessed by α. In fact in legal actions relating to contracts of private law, the court proceedings will be concerned precisely with these different points.

Now, the legal relation (both codified and non-codified) in the case of Equation II consists precisely in ensuring the conservation of values. This can be expressed by saying that two conditions have to be fulfilled for equilibrium to be achieved.

Condition 1: $v_\alpha = s_\alpha$, whence the equation of the rightful claimant: $(v_\alpha = t_{\alpha'}) + (t_{\alpha'} = s_\alpha) = (s_\alpha = v_\alpha)$
Condition 2: $t_{\alpha'} = r_{\alpha'}$, whence the equation of the liable party: $(r' = r_\alpha) + (s_\alpha = t_{\alpha'}) = (r_{\alpha'} = t_{\alpha'})$.

As for the origins of this right v_α, one recalls that in spontaneous exchanges, the origin of the value v_α is the satisfaction [p. 134] $s_{\alpha'}$ that α's action r_α has given to α'; but a value which is non-normative and consequently subject to variations and erosion could not as such constitute a right. On the other hand, in normative exchanges of a moral order, the origin of the obligation $t_{\alpha'}$ is always a value attributed by α' to a person α, a value such that the orders of α become obligatory for α' (heteronomous duty), or such that the reciprocal valorizations of α by α' and of α' by α, obliges α' to act towards α in accordance with this mutual respect (autonomous reciprocity); but, in these two cases the value v_α only constitutes a right for α in a particular sense, that of the 'disinterested' right to make α' acknowledge his scale of moral values and to make α' act in accordance with this, and not in the sense of a right to obtain for himself services (personal or 'interested' satisfactions). In order that there be a right v_α and an obligation $t_{\alpha'}$ in the (non-codified) legal order, there must therefore have been a prior acknowledgement of v_α and $t_{\alpha'}$: either α has given α' an order which has been accepted by him; or α' has made a promise to α or entered into an engagement with respect to him; or both have come to a mutual arrangement; or finally α' in giving himself a right which obligates α has tacitly conferred on α the same right over himself. The part played by acknowledgement is therefore the same in the normative coordination of a legal or deontological order, as that of respect in the moral coordination; and explicit or tacit convention corresponds to a command or a mutual agreement in the case of moral behaviour.

As we shall see, this non-codified normative law is none other than that which the eminent philosopher of law L. Petrazycki has analysed. According to him four conditions are necessary and sufficient in order that there may be 'normative fact' of a legal order.[10] (1) the person who has the right to demand or receive the service (therefore person α) (2) the person subject to the obligation (i.e. person α'); (3) the idea of what ought to be done by the owner of this right (v_α); (4) the idea of what ought to be done by the subject of this obligation (i.e. $t_{\alpha'}$). Petrazycki concludes from this that the legal relation is a *bilateral imperative–attributive relation*, which corresponds well with the equivalence $v_\alpha = t_{\alpha'}$ on which our Equation II is based. However, Petrazyski claims in this way to be able to [p. 135] differentiate law from morality, as the latter only implies a 'unilateral imperative relation'. Thus in the example quoted by Sorokin, the moral precept which an individual α sets himself of 'giving away his fortune to the poor' in no way gives the poor the right to claim the wealth of others! Now on this interpretation of the moral norm we must part company with Petrazycki: we believe that the moral relation like the legal relation is necessarily bilateral. In the case of duty it is the value v_α attributed by α' to α (unilateral respect) which is the origin of the obligation $t_{\alpha'}$, and in the case of moral reciprocity this bilateral relation is even duplicated. It is true that if α ordered α' to behave well towards α'', the relation between α' and α'' does not constitute a right for α'', but to the obligation $t_{\alpha'}$ there nevertheless corresponds a right, that of α to give his commands, or more generally, to see that his own scale of moral values is respected. However, as the characteristic of moral obligations is to become internalized and to exist independently of the partner's reactions, it is possible, on the other hand, that they remain unilateral in a unique sense. For example, if α' has accepted the orders of α because of his respect for him, then later on loses it, he may still heed[10] these orders. Or again, α can act on a basis of reciprocity towards α' even if α' does not do likewise and does not deserve this treatment. The relation then remains bilateral 'in principle' even if no longer in fact, just as in a legal relation the right of α exists even if α' refuses to provide the services to which he is obligated. What distinguishes the moral relation from the legal one is therefore not its unilateral character: it is its 'disinterested' character, that is to say, the dual proviso of indefinite satisfaction and of valuation according to intention (reciprocal substitution of scales).

Finally, we need to note that we can conceive, on the model of the preceding schemas, a non-codified legal relation between the individual and the collective of which he forms part, providing, of course, that each recognizes the other's right either by agreement or by means of a tacit or explicit convention. For example, it can happen that an individual α acknowledges that a collective A has the right v_A to impose on him the obligation t_α to accept a public office which he does not desire: or after meritorious service, the collective A gives α the right v_α to hold a privileged position, etc. [p. 136] It is undoubtedly on facts of this kind that Duguit has tried to base his notions of 'objective law' or of 'joint responsibility'. Now although these facts appear to us inadequate to explain the 'origins' of codified law, they nevertheless unquestionably provide a content for certain relations of non-codified law.

B. The relations of codified law

Codified or statute law, in spite of the considerable development that it has had compared to the informal and elementary character of non-codified relations, obeys, in reality, the same formal mechanisms as the latter. The essential difference between them is therefore that the scale of values of codified law or of the hierarchy of rights and correlative obligations, is determined by *statute* or *common law*, and is therefore ultimately based on the system of legal norms which is the *State*.

In the domain of codified law we possess a contemporary study which has axiomatized law as far as this is possible: H. Kelsen's 'pure theory of law'. It is therefore interesting to ask whether his formal system can be expressed axiomatically in terms of the preceding equations.

Let us first remember that H. Kelsen (who, of course, reserves the term 'Law' for codified law and who, it goes without saying, does not accept natural law, nor even any spontaneous and extra-statute law) conceives the pure theory of law as a study of the simple validity of norms (as against their causal explanation). In this respect he defines a relation different from a causal relation but comparable to logical implication, and which he calls 'imputation': 'peripheral' imputation when an act is imputed to the norm, in the case of a misdemeanour, for example, or 'central' imputation when a state of affairs is attributed to a norm: in this sense, the physical and *a fortiori* moral 'person', is to be conceived as a centre of imputations. On the other hand, the State is merged with the legal order itself, and there can be no dualism between State and law, every norm entailing in a unique system those which are of a lower order to it and itself being grounded in those of a higher order, up to the constitution itself.

Now, in this complete system, of which the obligation to acknowledge the validity constitutes the basic norm, the application of norms is merged with the ediction of new norms, since the law [p. 137] regulates its own creation. It is thus that a Parliament applies the norms of the Constitution in making laws: 'to make a rule is thus at the same time to enforce another'. The only exceptions are the two extremes, the final act of individual enforcement (no creation) and the basic norm (no enforcement). This process is absolutely continuous: there is therefore no difference in nature between the enactment of laws, administrative decisions and court judgments, all of which are at the same time the enforcement of higher norms and the creation of new ones to enforce. As for private law, it differs from public law in that the latter imposes on individuals ready-made norms, whilst in a contract the contracting parties are associated with the creation of the norm which obligates them; but contractual norms are, on the other hand, sanctioned by the State. Finally, this participation of those subject to the law in the creation of norms, differentiates the constitutional regimes, from the minimum of participation (autocracy) up to the maximum (direct democracy).

We see that to the extent in which the pure theory of Law reduces the latter to a simple system of norms, it is easy to express the legal relations which will exist between any group of individuals (or centres of imputations) A possessing the right to enact v_A and any group A' bound by the obligation to fulfil $t_{A'}$, where the A' can be separate from the A, or include them or indeed merge with the A themselves (depending on whether we are concerned with a norm of the A which only obligates the A', which also obligates the A or which obligates only the A).

We then have the general condition of equilibrium:

Eq. II $(v_A = t_{A'}) + (t_{A'} + r_{A'}) + (r_{A'} = s_A) = (s_A = v_A)$

where v_A = the right of the A to 'enact' norms (laws, regulations, orders, judgments, etc.)

$t_{A'}$ = obligation of the A' to 'comply with' these norms.
$r_{A'}$ = the act of the A' complying with the norm of the A.
s_A = satisfaction of the A resulting from compliance with the norm.

If there is the inequality $r_{A'} < s_A$, then $s_A - r_{A'} = (s_A - d)$, where the difference d constitutes a *misdemeanour* for which amends are made by a *penalty* equally determined by the norm. This penalty always consists [p. 138] in depriving A' of an asset, a value which we will call $r'_{A'}$. From this follows the re-establishment of the equilibrium.

If $r_{A'} < s_A$, then $r_{A'} + r'_{A'} = s_A$.

Thus put, it is easy to apply these equilibrium conditions to all the possible legal relations of a codified order. For example, in a purely hierarchical system, such as the regime of an absolute monarchy, the sovereign S will possess every right over the whole of his subjects S' without any obligation with respect to them, whence $(S \downarrow v_s S')$. His direct representatives R_1 will have only obligations towards him (whence $R_1 \uparrow t_{R1} S)^{11}$ but a body of rights over their inferiors, etc., and all the relations will be thus of the asymmetric type $\downarrow v$ or $\uparrow t$, $\downarrow s$ or $\uparrow r$. On the other hand, where the constitutional norms are voted by a party A (adult males or both sexes) of the collective B, this enactment of norms constitutes a right for the A over the B (whence $A \downarrow v_A B$), and there result for the whole of the B (the A and the A') the obligations $B \uparrow t_B$, etc. etc. One can thus conceive at the limit a collective B which possesses at each moment the right to obligate itself or to modify its earlier obligations by new norms: $B \downarrow v \uparrow t_B$. Finally every contractual relation between individuals constitutes a dual symmetrical relation $(a \overset{v}{\leftrightarrow} a')$ resulting from $(a \overset{v}{\rightarrow} a') + (a \overset{v}{\leftarrow} a')$ and $(a \overset{t}{\rightarrow} a') + (a \overset{t}{\leftarrow} a')$. It is therefore easy, but this is not our aim in this article, to constitute a complete logic of legal values, the 'groupings' thus constructed fluctuating between the purely asymmetric type (hierarchical) and the purely symmetrical type (contractual and egalitarian).[11]

What interests us here is simply the similarities and differences of functioning between these codified legal relations and the relations of a non-codified or moral order. Clearly, there is a great difference (of degree, but not in kind) between the non-codified and the codified ones: in the former, inter-individual relations are of the essence (promises, agreements, etc.) and the relations between the individual and the collective as such are much more diffuse, whilst in the latter, the relations between the individual and the State [p. 139] are what matters and the inter-individual ones are less important. The matter is self-explanatory: since the function of legal coordination is to conserve values, where non-codified relations adequately ensure this conservation, codification remains unnecessary, whilst it is effected everywhere where the equilibrium is not spontaneously established.

Second, it is very interesting to note how the formal structure of the legal relations of a hierarchical order ($\downarrow$ and $\uparrow$) corresponds to that of the moral relations of heteronomy and pure 'duty' whilst the legal relations of a contractual order formally correspond to the moral relations of reciprocity (setting aside the differences that we have emphasized as far as the mode of valorization is concerned: reciprocal substitution of scales). We therefore believe that on these questions of the relations between law and morality, both H. Kelsen and L. Petrazycki have exaggerated the opposition between them. According to the former moral norms evaluate by their 'content' and proceed only by a deduction from the general to the particular, whilst legal deduction is constructive, the new norms being valid to the extent in which they are enacted according to a method fixed by higher norms. We believe that moral obligations are equally only valid because of their form, whether they have been imposed as duties by respected persons on those who respect them, or result from a reciprocity of valorization. On the other hand, they equally give rise to a progressive construction, but obviously rather during the course of an individual's lifetime than during that of societies viewed as wholes. But even from this latter point of view, the hierarchy of respects, in terms of which we explain the fact that in the succession of generations each constructs the morality of its successor, constituting the same flow of simultaneous 'enactments' and 'enforcements' of interlocking norms as in a comprehensive legal system; and as no received norm is sufficiently precise to be applicable to each particular action, individual applications in the long run always involve in the moral as well as the legal domain, what H. Kelsen has so aptly called an 'individualization of the norm', the last term of the creation of norms before the final enforcement.

Now, not only does there thus exist a formal parallelism of a general order between legal construction and moral construction, [p. 140] there are also the following two important convergences. In the two domains, the symmetric inter-individual normative relations are formed only within the framework of hierarchical (asymmetrical) relations. Thus in law the contractual relation comes to be inserted in the set of obligations linking the individual with the State, and in morality reciprocity only develops within a complex system of duties (which have moulded the individual as the result of the action of unilateral respect). But, conversely, in the two domains the symmetrical relations once constituted tend to supplant the asymmetrical relations by either replacing them or determining the content of their norms (whose form alone then remains asymmetrical). Thus in morality at a given moment in the history of each society reciprocity tends to prevail over heteronomous duty or to provide a content for it, and in law the bilateral relation tends with democracy to dominate unilateral respect or to inspire its norms. But the equilibrium thus attained remains in the two domains subject to perturbations and reversals. This leads to the last point which remains to be examined.

8. NORMATIVE EQUILIBRIUM AND SOCIAL EQUILIBRIUM

The preceding attempts at formal or axiomatic analysis should do two things: they should bring out the similarities and differences of structure between the diverse domains of social exchange, and they should also determine the respective functions of legal, moral, economic or simply qualitative exchange in the social equilibrium.

In this respect, legal coordinations raise a particularly interesting problem. Formally it is obvious, that for any legal organization whatsoever, equilibrium is attained when between any two individuals α and α', selected at random in the society, when we have $r_\alpha = t_\alpha$ (fulfilment of the obligations of α with respect to α') and $s_\alpha = v_\alpha$ (satisfaction by α' of the rights of α) thus $r_{\alpha'} = t_{\alpha'}$ and $s_{\alpha'} = v_{\alpha'}$. This simply means that the laws, administrative decisions, judgments, etc. are applied. But this in no way implies that $v_\alpha = t_\alpha$, namely that the rights of α over α' are equivalent to his obligations towards him, or in general that the set of obligations of α is equivalent to the totality of his rights. In other words, the (codified) legal equilibrium necessarily coincides neither with the equilibrium of non-codified [p. 141] law nor with the moral equilibrium, or with that of (economic and simply qualitative) spontaneous exchanges. This is why, as a result of these interdependent diverse coordinations, codified law may appear just or unjust from the point of view of deontology or ethics. Besides the problem of intrinsic legal equilibrium (= application or enforcement of the laws, etc. in a given society) there is, therefore, a problem of extrinsic legal equilibrium, or equilibrium between the codified values (rights and obligations), non-codified normative values and spontaneous values.

We need to put ourselves at this extrinsic point of view if we ask whether a constitution or a legislation is stable or whether it is at the mercy of political disruption. From this second point of view, there can be legal equilibrium in a given society, even if for the great majority of individuals obligations prevail over rights, when the feeble value of these codified rights is compensated by the existence of non-codified rights, by moral reciprocity or by beneficial economic and qualitative exchanges.

As for moral equilibrium, which thus necessarily enters in, we need to distinguish heteronomous norms and reciprocity. In a general fashion moral equilibrium is never reached since it is linked to the condition of the indefinite satisfaction of the other, which continuously raises the ideal pursued. But in the case where heteronomous duty prevails increasingly over reciprocity, morality is little differentiated from legal obligations and satisfaction is possible (equilibrium). On the other hand, in the case of reciprocity, morality by its disinterested character acts as a factor of social equilibrium, even if the specifically moral equilibrium is unobtainable.

On the whole, the problem of legal equilibrium in its relations with social equilibrium in general appears therefore to manifest itself as follows. The rights and obligations of which any individual whatsoever is the 'centre of imputations' only constitute one class of all the values, positive or negative, which he holds. It is, therefore, through relations to other values, with respect to which legal values play the role of means (or of obstacles), that these rights or obligations are translated in terms of satisfactions or dissatisfactions. Extrinsic legal equilibrium will thus be [p. 142] determined by the balance of all its values. Two extreme cases are particularly interesting.

The first (autocratic, theocratic regimes, etc.) is that in which the subjects A' are submitted to the *maximum* of obligations and possess only a minimum of rights $(t_{A'} > v_{A'})$. Here the legal structure allows no free exchange of values. But it will nevertheless conserve its equilibrium if those who have the rights and impose the obligations are, at the same time, the origin of moral values (if there is respect for superiors), or if the social hierarchy gives rise to the constant valorization of inferiors (Stendhal in *Le Rouge et le noir*[12] speaks, for example, of the manner in which the hirelings of the restored monarchy, after 1815, 'distributed considerations'); and finally if the distribution of wealth remains proportionate to the hierarchical order, and allows the great 'to keep their station' without the masses knowing destitution.

On the other hand, when rights tend to equal obligations $(t_B = v_B)$, and norms are therefore elaborated with the participation of those they obligate, these then tend to become simple instruments for the regulation of exchanges, regulations which are modified as necessary adaptations. But in this case disequilibrium is liable to arise anew in the form of a progressive excess of rights or more precisely of satisfactions over obligations. Only the norms of a moral order are able then to redress the balance of the opposing forces, and to do so by ensuring through their own distinctive mode of operation, the general function of every normative system: the conservation of values.

AUTHOR'S NOTES

[1] Each face of the pyramid would thus be constituted by a scale of the type shown in Figure 2.

[2] Serial correspondence or 'qualitative similarity' based on the multiplication of asymmetrical relations.

[3] Other examples: 'to buy a politician' α is again to quantify a qualitative exchange by eliminating the virtual values t and v, where a certain quantity either of money, or of some other service corresponds to the service r_α. Diplomatic 'deals' similarly illustrate all the stages between qualitative and quantitative exchange.

[4] See Pareto, *Cours d'économie politique*, vol. I (1896), p. 22 (para. 52) and Boninsegni, *Manuel élémentaire d'économie politique*, (1930), pp. 27–29.

[5] r_α is the sacrifice by α of a value s_α of which, if $r_\alpha = v_\alpha$, the *ophelimity* equals that of v_α.

[6] See Pierre Janet, 'Les fatigues sociales et l'antipathie' in the *Revue philosophique* of 1931.

[7] It is this condition which therefore defines 'normative reciprocity' of a moral order.

[8] We have elsewhere called a 'logical grouping' any system of operations having the properties of composition, associativity, reversibility and identity, as is the case with 'mathematical groups', but different from them in that each operation plays the role of 'identity' in relation to itself and to those of an order either lower or higher than itself. See *Compte rendu des séances de la Société de Physique et d'Histoire naturelle de Genève*, séance du 20 Mars 1941 (Vol. 58, no. 1).

[9] On the relationships between law and values, see the interesting pamphlet of de Maday, *Essai d'une explication sociologique de la origine de droit* (Paris: Giard et Brière, 1911). The author, however, takes up the genetic point of view, which we will not do, the present essay being solely of a synchronic order.

[10] See P. Sorokin, *Les Théories sociologiques contemporaines*, (trans. Verrier, Paris: Payot, 1938, p. 518).

[11] *Droit et état*, p. 32 (*Annales de l'Institut de Droit comparé de l'Université de Paris*, 1936). [There is no reference in the text to this note which occurs at the foot of p. 138 in the French text – trans.]

TRANSLATION NOTES

1   Marie-Esprit Louis Walras (1834–1910), of French origin, was professor of political economy at the University of Lausanne. He started life as as an engineer, is best known for his mathematical theory of economic equilibrium, and was one of the founders of of marginal utility theory. Walras based his theory of economic value on scarcity (*rareté*). As he put it: 'An individual who owns some scarce thing can obtain something else in exchange for it; if he does not own something he can obtain it only by exchanging something else for it, and if he has nothing to exchange he must go without. This is the concept of value in exchange.' He regards value in exchange to be a natural concept: 'If wheat and silver have some given value relative to each other it is because they are relatively more or less scarce, that is more or less useful' (cf. Michael Allingham: *Value*, Macmillan, 1983, p. 100). For Walras the value of commodities is then determined by the market conditions prevailing at any one time, and can be quantified in terms of the exchange process. Thus we may be willing to exchange, to quote Piaget's example, three hundred kilos of wheat against two hectolitres of wine.

   Piaget's theory of social exchange, in which economic exchange is included as a subset, also includes qualitative values, which, as he puts it, can have different origins; individual interests and tastes, group values imposed by fashion, prestige, social constraints and legal and moral rules. One can exchange compliments, gifts, ideas, etc., just as one can exchange commodities in economic exchange. Social values of a non-normative kind seem to have an affective origin, whilst legal and moral values or norms contain an intellectual element and are conserved through time. In both cases they are manifested through our actions directed to others. Piaget's picture of society as a vast circulation of values arises from his view that social behaviour is built up from the interactions of individuals, which are basically of an exchange nature – and not necessarily imposed from outside as Durkheim thought. For further discussion, see W. Mays, 'Piaget's sociological theory', in S. Modgil and C. Modgil (eds) *Jean Piaget: consensus and controversy* (London: Holt, Rinehart & Winston, 1982).

2   Vilfredo Pareto (1848–1923), Italian economist and sociologist, succeeded Walras as professor of political economy at the University of Lausanne. Like Walras he started life as an engineer and developed the latter's general economic equilibrium theory. In utility theory he replaced Walras' notion of scarcity by that of ophelimity (*ophelimité*). Ophelimity defines a more restrictive meaning of utility in that it refers to satisfactions from economic causes only. Further, for Pareto ophelimity is primarily concerned with the attributes of things which may be desired by an individual even though they might have harmful effects (e.g. drug-taking), as opposed to the attributes of things beneficial to society. Ophelimities as personal satisfactions are heterogeneous in nature and thus exclude interpersonal comparisons. In other words, one's likes and dislikes will not necessarily be shared by others.

3   Walras and Pareto in their respective accounts limit themselves to equilibrium in economic exchange. In this chapter Piaget widens his investigation to include equilibrium in social exchange, which is what 'qualitative values in static sociology (synchronic)' refers to in the chapter title: namely, that social or qualitative values, which include moral and legal norms, are the resultant of a diachronic exchange process. But this does not mean that they do not also have an experiential basis for Piaget. In the case of the morality of duty he locates it in the feeling of respect the child may have for his parents.

From his earliest writings Piaget has used the notion of equilibrium to explain how our behavioural activities, as a result of our interactions with the environment, take on an invariant structural form (by analogy with the static balance of forces reached in a physical system). But there is this basic difference, behavioural activities on the biological and psychological level undergo a reconstruction as a result of such interactions. In other words, to use Piaget's terminology, the organism assimilates certain characteristics of its environment in order to accommodate itself to it. The notion of equilibrium when applied to the biological, psychological and social fields, would seem to involve different levels of explanation, although Piaget claims that isomorphisms can be established between these levels. Piaget's approach in the biological field might be termed Bergsonian, since he starts with a flux of biological activities from which are constructed the basic structures of behaviour and experience, which he regards as equilibrium states. Thus the child will start by exploring his surroundings with trial and error movements and finally construct definite schemata in terms of which he manipulates objects. On the normative level one may quote Piaget's statement, 'I have always maintained that a structure can become normative *qua* necessary, and can only become so at the end of its development once its closure has been achieved through its final equilibrium.' (cf. footnote 3 in Preface to this book). A question of interpretation arises here: is such necessity attained or is it merely attainable? Piaget does claim that necessity is attained: 'the main problem of any epistemology, but principally of any genetic epistemology, is in fact to understand *how the mind succeeds in constructing necessary relationships*, which appear to be "independent of time", if the instruments of thought are merely psychological operations that are subject to evolution and are constituted in time' (in L. Smith, *Necessary knowledge: Piagetian perspectives on constructivism* Hove: Erlbaum, 1993, p. 1). Even though attainment may be a matter of degree, the attainment of lower levels of modal understanding may still amount to a valid form of understanding. However, if necessity is achieved through final equilibrium, the latter is an ideal limit which is never reached. If the necessity Piaget is after is unachievable, at least in its ideal form, it raises questions as to the status of necessary knowledge in his system and whether, as he claims, he has freed himself from psychologism. It is difficult to see how it can be avoided if norms are taken as the resultant of a diachronic process of exchange. In his later work Piaget related his concept of equilibrium to feedback activity (regulations), which might be said to have a learning element built into it. (See e.g. Jean Piaget: *The equilibration of cognitive structures*, (Chicago University Press, 1985).

4   Piaget uses the phrase *différence nulle* which is translated as null difference. It could equally have been translated as indifference. Piaget is referring here to our preferences for certain things rather than others. In economic theory preferences are defined as follows: given any two commodities *a* and *b*, whether *a* may be preferred to *b*, *b* to *a* or *a* and *b* are considered as indifferent to each other, one of these possibilities must apply. Thus in addition to our greatest and least preferences there must be indifference, i.e. the case where *a* or *b* will equally satisfy us. An apocryphal example of the economic notion of indifference is that given by the scholastic philosopher Buridan, of the ass who could not make up his mind which to choose between two equally succulent bundles of hay and consequently died of starvation. From the point of view of economic choice the ass was indifferent to his situation, but physiologically he was not.

5   In French the term is *valorisation*, which is here given the American spelling 'valorization', since according to the *Oxford English dictionary* the term originated in the US. It is defined as 'The act of or fact of fixing the value or price of some commercial commodity.' *Chamber's English dictionary* defines valorize as 'to fix or stabilise the price of (esp.) of a policy imposed by a government or controlling body.' *Harrap's standard French and English dictionary* translates *valorisation* as 'Valorization (of product, etc.); stabilization (of price of commodity).' It appears that Piaget is using the term here in the sense of valuing in conformity with a common scale, which may be said to fix the values we use. And this comes close to its economic meaning, where the values are fixed in terms of prices. Thus Piaget talks of 'the class of co-valorizers', which he defines as 'every set of individuals exchanging their values according to a common scale'. Such commonly shared scales of value may be of an aesthetic, ethical, religious or political kind.

6   The French phrase is *cours forcé* which could be translated as *controlled market*. This refers to the way in which a monopoly controls and fixes prices of a product in the market. In the moral sphere Piaget compares this with the morality of duty, where the parents impose their commands on the young child.

7   French, *morale*. Note that *morality* is ambiguous since it can mean either an ethical system or actual moral conduct depending on the context. Thus an alternative translation would be *ethics of Christianity*.

8   Sir Thomas Gresham (1519–1579), English financier and philanthropist, made the observation known as Gresham's law 'that of two coins of equal exchange value, that of the lower intrinsic value would tend to drive the other out of use', or more colloquially 'bad money drives out good money'. For example, when paper money was introduced, gold coin was hoarded since it had a greater intrinsic value.

9   French, *d'ensemble*. An alternative translation used in other chapters in this volume is *over-arching* by analogy with *structure d'ensemble* (*over-arching*

structure). Note that although *structure d'ensemble* is sometimes interpreted to mean *general structure*, Piaget has in mind the logical universalizability of any such structure and not its inductive generalizability (cf. the distinction drawn by Piaget between universal/general on p. 178 together with his discussion of moral universals on pp. 166–7).

10   Piaget's use of *conserver* here is linked to his technical notion of 'conservation'. He is concerned here with the way our concepts and norms obtain their invariance or constancy. Insofar as Piaget refuses to regard them as Platonic objects, arbitrary conventions or mere names, he has to explain how the norms of logic, mathematics and morals, etc., obtain their universality and intersubjectivity over and above the flux of our feelings and perceptions. He does this by positing that during intellectual development such norms are constructed from more primitive experiential structures.

In this way he tries to explain how on the moral level the child ceases to follow his immediate impulses based on feeling, and comes to act according to moral precepts, either according to the morality of duty or that of reciprocity. As an example of conservation in morals, one may quote the case of an individual who may still continue to heed the requests of his parents, though he may have lost his respect for them.

On the cognitive level Piaget shows how the child develops an understanding of conceptual criteria such as classes, relations, etc., in terms of which he orders objects. Piaget claims that in the absence of such criteria a child's judgments will depend on his immediate perceptions which can lead him into error. When he develops such criteria or conceptual frameworks he comes e.g. to understand that a quantity of liquid remains the same even when it is poured into differently shaped glass containers. He is thus able to correct the illusions of perception. Critics of Piaget who maintain that children can make conservation judgments at an earlier age than Piaget says they can, often try to prove their case by constructing experiments where the experimental set-up provides the required invariance through perceptual cues. In this way the child does not need to have developed the necessary conceptual structures to give the correct response.

11   Where $(S \downarrow v_s S')$ refers to the sovereign's (S) rights (v_s) over his subjects (S'), and where $(R_I \uparrow t_{R_I} S)$ refers to the direct representative's (R_I) obligations (t_{R_I}) to the sovereign (S).

12   In his novel *Le Rouge et le noir* (The Red and the Black) Stendhal (psuedonym of Henri Marie Beyle, a French novelist (1783–1842)) gives a sharply focused picture of the political ferment in France in the post-Napoleonic era when the monarchy was restored. It deals with the life and times of Julien Sorel, a brilliant young opportunist, who finally came to a tragic end on the scaffold. The title appears to refer to two forces which struggled within him: the desire to be a fighter for liberty and republicanism (symbolized by the soldier's red uniform) and the desire to conform to the forces of conservatism and the monarchy (symbolized by the priest's black dress).

3 Logical operations and social life

[p. 143] The aim of this brief article is to re-examine the question, so often discussed, of the social or individual nature of logic. We propose, however, to do so while at the same time placing a new fact in the folder. Specifically, we refer to the existence of the operatory '*groupements*'[1] whose role in the formation of reason genetic psychology permits us to discern.

We must excuse ourselves all the more for coming back to the problem of logic and society because we have already dedicated numerous pages to it in two special works[1] as well as in our studies of the development of intelligence in children. However, after more than twenty years of research in the latter domain, we have begun to glimpse in what the logical fact consists when it is conceived as an experimental result rather than an axiomatic rule. We cannot, therefore, resist returning to this question from which we started long ago. And this is even more the case because the operatory interpretation of that fact, far from complicating the relationships between reason, individual intelligence, and social life, appears to simplify the terms of the debate in an important way.

I. THE SOCIOLOGICAL PROBLEM

There is no need to recall in detail by what arguments Durkheim, following numerous predecessors (Espinas, Izoulet, de Roberty, etc.), defended the thesis of the social nature of logic. Individual thought is shaped by the group, he said, since, thanks to language and to the pressures each generation exerts on following generations, the individual is always dependent [p. 144] on the whole of prior acquisitions transmitted via the 'external' path of education. Left to his own devices, the individual would only develop practical intelligence and images. By contrast, the interplay of concepts, mental categories, and the rules of thought consist in 'collective representations'. These are produced by social life that has continued from the beginnings of humanity up to the hotbeds of spiritual creation constituted by the great contemporary civilizations.

To support this thesis, Durkheim invoked two sorts of proof. One simply amounted to showing how the principal notions of thought and logical rules go beyond the limits of individual activity and presuppose a collaboration of minds. Thus, space and time infinitely exceed the spatial or temporal experience of individual perception and constitute environments common to all such perceptions. Logical rules, on the other hand, consist in normative laws necessary for exchanges of thought. Consequently, they are imposed by social necessity and work against the anarchy of an individual's spontaneous representations. Durkheim, who had been instructed in Kant's philosophy, opposed the *a priori* of reason to individual experience, but he interpreted the 'universal' inherent in the Kantian *a priori* in terms of 'collective consciousness' superior and prior to individual consciousness.[2]

Durkheim's second sort of proof was historical or ethnographic in nature. In effect, 'primitive', as opposed to 'derived', collective representations are completely 'sociomorphic'. In other words, they are copies traced from the structure of the social group. Thus, primitive classifications do not divide up objects according to their natural similarities and differences, but rather according to arbitrary classes drawn from social classifications, e.g. clans, sub-tribes, and tribes. (This is a little in the manner in which we verbally lend gender to things, for example *'le'* (masculine definite article) sun and *'la'* (feminine definite article) moon. [p. 145] We, however, do this without attributing logical value to this linguistic classifying, while the 'primitive' believes that minerals, plants, and animals truly belong to social units.) Likewise, time is conceived as interdependent with the collective calendar which ensures the rhythm of things through seasonal celebrations, and space is organized as a function of tribal territory, etc.

From all of this, Durkheim concluded that reason has a social origin. Far from deducing a possible plurality of collective 'mentalities' from this, however, he believed the sociomorphism seen initially simply presages common thought. Logic is singular, permanent, and universal, because 'beneath civilizations there is Civilization'. Thus, truth[2] reduces to what everyone agrees to, and the celebrated formula, *Quod ubique, quod semper, quod ab omnibus creditur*[3] could serve as the definition of truth according to Durkheim.

Considerations of this sort led Durkheim to a problem of the greatest importance. Auguste Comte believed that in sociology the whole cannot be explained by but must, instead, explain the parts. Applying this principle with the greatest rigour, Durkheim brought clearly into view the fact that individual thoughts are shaped by the entire social body, both in its current and in its past aspects. However, a collective whole is not identical with the sum of the individuals of which it is composed for the simple reason that this whole exercises modifying constraints on individual consciousness. One, therefore, may conclude nothing about the unanalysable nature of the whole as such. In fact, three rather than just two types of interpretation are possible. First, there is atomistic individualism where the whole results from individual activities that would be present even if society did not exist. Since Durkheim has done justice to this point of view, we shall not discuss it. Second, there is totalitarian realism where the whole is a 'being' that exercises its constraints, modifies individuals (e.g. imposes logic on them, etc.) and therefore remains heterogeneous to individual consciousness as it would be independent of its socialization. Third, the whole may be conceived as the sum of relationships among individuals, which is not the same thing as the sum of individuals. According to this relativism or to this 'interactive' point of view, every relationship constitutes, on its own scale, a 'whole' in Durkheim's sense. Even in the case of two individuals, [p. 146] an interaction that brings about lasting changes may be considered a social fact. Society would, therefore, be the expression of the set of interactions among *n* individuals, *n* starting from 2 and being indefinitely extendable such that, at the limit, it includes the unidirectional actions of the most distant ancestors on their social heirs. But it is essential to understand that this in no way comes back to individualism. The primary fact, from this point of view, is neither the individual nor the set of individuals but the relationships among individuals, a relationship constantly modifying individual consciousnesses themselves, as Durkheim desires.

Now, if one agrees to this third formulation – which can express everything contained in the second while making analysis possible instead of speaking in a totally global fashion – one will no longer be content to say that 'society' is the basis of logic but will ask exactly what social relationships are involved. In effect, it is clear that not just any action of 'society' on the individual is the source of reason. If that were so, reason would be confused with the 'reason of the State'. Contemporary events have demonstrated in the clearest manner how generations stemming from a great people can be shaped by collectivity up to the point of adopting, without discussion, entrenched ways of thinking and, no doubt, can do so for the entire lifetime of an individual. Assuredly, in contrast to the simplistic idea of 'race' – which is in good part a social myth! – such a fact confirms the Durkheimian thesis of the action of the group on individual consciousness. But even more, it proves that 'social constraint', far from including all social relationships in a single heap, only constitutes one relationship among others and ends in very special intellectual and moral effects that are quite distinct from other possible interactions.

In effect, there exist two extreme types of interpersonal relationships. On the one hand, there is constraint, which implies authority and submission and leads to heteronomy; on the other, there is cooperation, which implies equality under law or autonomy as well as reciprocity among differentiated personalities. It is a matter of course that between these two extremes an entire series of relationships can be seen and that in mass action, like that of the 'whole' of a society on the individuals who compose it, mixing is possible with simple [p. 147] statistical predominance of one or the other extreme type. It nevertheless remains that when Durkheim assimilates things to the collective 'universal' of constituting reason, he refers implicitly to cooperation. In other words, he refers to a factor of objectivity and reciprocity, eliminating the subjective by relating things to one another. By contrast, when he invokes the sociomorphism of primitive collective representations, he makes a certain type of intellectual constraint come into play. It is interesting, then, to remark that the tribal mentality formed in this way hardly differs in its logical structure from the 'egocentric' mentality of children's logic. In other words, it hardly differs from the logic of individuals whose socialization is incomplete, except that egocentrism is then extended to a small social group and thus becomes sociocentrism. Constraint, then, transforms the individual much less than cooperation does and is limited to covering him with a thin layer of shared common notions whose structure differs little from egocentric notions.

Lévy-Bruhl's critical work provides decisive arguments in favour of this interpretation. From the social nature of the higher forms of thought, Lévy-Bruhl draws the hypothesis of a possible plurality of mentalities. To the logical mind of the elite belonging to civilized societies, he opposes the 'prelogic' of primitive mentality which he characterizes by a different intellectual structure. If one re-establishes, no doubt more than Lévy-Bruhl wished to, the functional continuity linking so-called primitive thought to our own, it seems incontestable that the logical structure belonging to the small gerontocratic societies that ethnography has made familiar testifies to original characteristics that are irreducible to rational operations. Thus, one cannot translate 'participations' into systems of logical classes or relations capable of being 'grouped' by means of additive or multiplicative operations like the classes or relations that a normal individual, in our society, uses from 7 or 8 years for concrete operations or from 11 or 12 for formal operations. On the other hand, one can compare these 'participations', so fully described by Lévy-Bruhl, to the 'preconcepts' that, in our societies, children employ from 2 to 4 or 5 years of age and that manifest both a systematic difficulty in understanding the substantial identity of individual objects and an incapacity in constructing the hierarchical inclusions of logic.[4] Here again, then, one must wonder whether the [p. 148] prelogic due to primitive social constraints does not consist in a collective crystallization of infantile mentality manifest at a given stage before achieving the operatory mechanisms defining reason.

Let us once again recall the doctrine of G. Tarde who attempted to analyse the social whole in terms of interactions. Tarde was poorly served by a dangerous facility that turned him away from both the systematic effort of historical and ethnographic reconstruction – of which the Durkheimian school has made a specialty – and the psychological information indispensable for the study of such interactions. His general schema of social actions is quite familiar: 'imitation' propagates examples in the manner of physical waves running through the population in every direction; 'social opposition' arises, then, from the shock of opposing imitative currents; and 'social adaptation' or 'invention' overcomes oppositions by reconciling different or opposed impulses. As for logic, it fulfils, in its over-arching mechanism, two special functions common to individual activity and to collective interactions. To begin with, it serves the function of equilibration. From that perspective, logic is a coordination of beliefs that sets aside contradictions and ensures the synthesis of reconcilable impulses. Second, logic serves the function of 'optimization',[5] from which perspective it always tends toward greater certainty and thus seeks to replace fragile with more stable beliefs. Equilibration and optimization of beliefs can, however, be seated either within the individual consciousness envisioned as a momentarily closed system or within the whole collectivity considered as a system of higher order. From this fact stems an 'individual logic', source of coherence and reflected belief at the heart of each personal consciousness (simply logic in the classical sense of the term)[6] and a 'social logic', source of the unification and reinforcement of beliefs at the heart of a given society. The curious thing is that Tarde, who so often glimpsed the interdependence of the individual consciousness and society in so many areas in which he worked, did not see it clearly as far as logic was concerned. He did not wonder whether individual logic derives from social logic or vice versa or whether both are correlatively constructed. He limited himself to pointing out the antagonisms and that, moreover, in a very detailed way without ever entering genetic terrain. In individual logic, equilibration [p. 149] and optimization go hand in hand. A belief is all the better ensured to the degree that it is part of a coherent system and does not encounter contradictory beliefs. In social logic, it at first seems that the same is true. Optimization leads to accumulation of the varieties of 'belief capital'[7] constituted by religions, moral and legal systems, political ideologies, etc., and equilibration tends to suppress conflicts by eliminating singular opinions or heresies. In the end, however, precisely because each individual is called upon to think and rethink the system of collective notions on his own account and by means of his own logic, these impulses toward social equilibration and social optimization become irreconcilable and alternately hold sway. When beliefs are too unified socially (orthodoxies due to equilibration), people no longer believe in them. When they seek to strengthen their convictions (optimization), they fall into heresy and thus threaten the unity of the system. The history of religions, of language, etc., furnish Tarde with numerous examples, from which he draws the conclusion that societies always end either in subordinating individual to social logic ('primitive' societies, oriental theocracies, etc.), or the inverse (western democracies). These two logics are, therefore, incompatible and, in fact, rest on opposing 'categories'. For example, theological notions, etc., are based on social logic; and objective spatio-temporal ideas, etc., are based on individual logic.

However different it may be from preceding systems, Tarde's system is interesting for our proposal since, against his will and almost in opposition with his starting principles, Tarde himself ends in a dualism reducing to the opposition between constraint and cooperation. In effect, it is clear that Tarde's 'social logic' is the expression of the group's constraint, even though he never wished to grant importance to that fundamental idea. Inversely, one can wonder whether his 'individual logic' does not necessarily presuppose social life for its development and whether, therefore, it is not a product of cooperation. On the one hand, child psychology shows that logic is not innate in the human being but that it is constructed as a function of reciprocal relationships. On the other hand, the impossibility of socially reconciling the optimization and [p. 150] equilibration of beliefs is only true of societies of the constraint type and then only when they are sufficiently dense and voluminous. On the plane of social cooperation, the equilibrium of beliefs and their optimization are in no way contradictory as is shown, for example, by the collective beliefs involved in scientific collaboration or even in a normally functioning democracy. In short, during children's egocentrism when individual thought is being socialized, there is neither systematic equilibration nor optimization. These functions lead to a real transformation of the mind only at the level of personalities that are at once autonomous and reciprocally obligated to other people through cooperative relationships. This leads us, then, to examine the genetic psychological data.

II. THE PSYCHOLOGICAL FACTS

Let us, then, wonder how logic is constructed within individual activities, that piece of information being necessary to develop Section III where we link the operations of the individual mind to cooperation.

A. Individual factors

Artificially and for the sake of exposition only, let us begin by envisioning the individual as a closed system, open only to exchanges with the physical environment without bringing interpersonal relationships into play. From this first point of view, logic appears as nothing more than the final equilibrial form of actions – it would almost be necessary to speak of movements or sensory-motor processes – that have come to be completely coordinated with one another and that constitute, therefore, a system of reversible compositions. More briefly, one might say that *logic is a system of operations in the sense of actions that have become both composable and reversible*. In effect, to reason is to unite or dissociate according to simple (addition or subtraction) or multiple (multiplication or division) inclusions. And this is so whether it is a matter of classes (union of objects according to their similarities), of asymmetrical relations (seriation of objects according to their ordered differences), or of numbers (generalized similarities and differences). To reason, therefore, is to effect on objects, materially or mentally, the most general actions possible [p. 151] while 'grouping' those actions according to a principle of reversible composition.

The psychological starting point for such operations is to be sought on the sensory-motor side of the moment when the child becomes capable of logic properly so-called. On average, the child is only capable of concrete operations (understanding that a whole is conserved independently of the disposition of its parts, seriating objects, etc.) between 7 and 11 or 12 years of age, depending on the ideas at issue, and he only arrives at formal operations (reasoning by syllogisms, by transitive relations given as hypotheses, etc.) after the latter age. Logic is, therefore, essentially a form of 'mobile' and reversible equilibrium characteristic of the end of development and not an innate mechanism provided at the start. To be sure, logic imposes itself with necessity, but by way of a final equilibrium toward which practical and mental coordinations necessarily tend and not by way of necessity at the start. In order to understand the construction of logic psychologically, then, it is necessary to track the processes whose final equilibrium constitutes logic from their source, even though all of the phases prior to the final equilibrium are of a 'prelogical' order. Moreover, in order to explain the construction of logic psychologically, two essential notions must be grasped. These are the functional continuity of development, conceived as a progressive march toward equilibrium, and the heterogeneity of the successive structures that mark the steps in that equilibration.

It is, therefore, from the initial sensory-motor functions that one must try to tease out the processes whose later equilibrium will lead to logic. Starting from primitive perceptual and motoric structures and before any language, the infant succeeds in constituting a 'sensory-motor intelligence' sufficient for discovering the schemes of the permanent practical object, of the organization of spatial displacements in his immediate vicinity (with detours and returns to the starting point), of causality, and of elementary time. Without, naturally, being structurally comparable to concepts belonging to later thought, the organization of sensory-motor 'schemes' presages such thought from the functional point of view. It thus constitutes a sort of logic of movements and perceptions.[3]

[p. 152] Subsequently, from 2 to 7 years, the effective actions of the preceding period are matched by actions executed mentally or, in other words, by imagined operations bearing on representations of things and no longer only on material objects themselves. In effect, representation consists in the capacity to evoke 'signified' realities by means of symbols serving as 'signifiers'. In the elementary forms of representative thought, these realities are not yet objective relationships among things themselves but, rather, the actions that the subject can carry out on things. Thought, therefore, is at first only a 'mental experiment' or translation into symbols or images of possible actions prolonging actions that were or are still being really effected on the sensory-motor plane.[8] The higher form of imaged thought we call 'intuitive'. Between 4 to 5 and 7 to 8 years, this sort of thought makes it possible to evoke some relatively precise over-arching configurations (seriations, correspondences, etc.) but only figuratively and without operatory reversibility.[4]

There is no doubt that imaged or intuitive thought achieves higher equilibrium than sensory-motor intelligence. Instead of being limited to what is, in actual fact, given by perception and movement, it goes beyond the actual by means of representative anticipations and reconstructions. However, compared to the thought of the following stage, the equilibrium reached by intuitive thought remains unstable and incomplete, since it is linked to figural evocations without reversibility properly so-called. Thus from 5 to 6, the child will be able to make six red counters correspond to six blue ones and to consider these collections equal when he can see them, but he will no longer believe in their equivalence when the elements in one row are spread out. There is, therefore, no conservation of the whole because the elementary reversibility is lacking that would make the subject understand how to return to the initial configuration by means of an operation inverse to spreading the counters.[5]

By contrast, toward 7 or 8 years of age, 'intuitive' judgments in the form of actions effected mentally end in a stable equilibrium defined by reversibility and thus constitute the beginning of logical operations themselves. To unite or dissociate, to seriate in [p. 153] one direction or the other, to make correspond, etc., acquire, therefore, the rank of composable and reversible actions permitting anticipation and reconstitution, no longer only in terms of images or intuitions but in terms of necessary deductions. Whence the great discovery that marks, in the child, the beginning of operatory thought, that is, the conservation of a whole (of a set of elements or of a quantity of liquid, of modelling clay, etc.) whatever may be the internal transformations effected on its parts.[6]

How, therefore, can this transition from irreversible sensory-motor or intuitive action to reversible operations be explained? The fundamental fact is that an operation is never present in an isolated state. It is not a particular action that at a given moment is conceived as reversible. The growth of operations is linked to a sort of over-arching reworking that occurs at the end of the progressive equilibration of intuitive anticipations and reconstitutions and that is comparable to a total structuration of the system. It must be understood, however, that it is a matter of a mobile structure dissolving, so to speak, rigid imaged configurations by subordinating them to every transformation possible. Thus, it is only after having slowly constructed the first numerical sets 1, 2, 3, 4, and sometimes 5, in intuitive terms that the child suddenly understands the indefinite sequence of whole numbers $n + 1$. Thus again, it is only after having understood certain relationships $A < B$ or $B < C$, but without linking them to one another, that the subject discovers the seriation $A < B < C < D \ldots$, etc.

Over-arching systems of this sort, which engender operations by basing them on one another,[9] always either take the form of what mathematicians call 'groups' (when it is a matter of mathematical entitites such as number, etc.), or of what we have called *groupements* (when it is a matter of qualitative or simply logical relationships).[7] The conditions for such systems are four in number for groups plus a fifth for *groupements*:

1   Two operations of the set, composed with one another, give yet another operation of the set. For example, the addition of two classes $A + A'$ gives a new class B [p. 154] $(A + A' = B)$. Psychologically, this composition is

only the expression of the possibility of coordinating two actions of uniting or seriating, etc.

2   To the direct operation $+ A$ there corresponds an inverse operation $- A$. This indicates psychological reversibility, the progress of which can be followed from the sensory-motor level up to the end-point of articulated intuitions.

3   The operations are associative in so far as it is a matter of different elements: $+ A + (A' + B') = (A + A') + B'$. This indicates the fundamental characteristic of intelligence of being able to take 'detours' and to arrive at the same result by several different paths.

4   The product of the direct operation and its inverse engenders a general 'identity' operation: $+ A - A = 0$, which assures the identity of the objects of thought.

5   In addition, logical *groupements* (in opposition to mathematical groups) presuppose that an operation composed with itself remains identical ('special identity' or 'tautology'):[8] $A + A = A$.

When the child deductively discovers the conservation of a whole, it is easy to show that he really carries out these operations. They do not, therefore, simply constitute mathematical or logistical possibilities. Rather, they express psychologically the effective end-point of thought where different imaged intuitions of the prelogical period come to be 'grouped' so as to constitute systems of logical operations, properly so-called.

But between 7 and 11 years of age, logical operations are only understood in the concrete domain where deduction is accompanied by effective or imagined manipulations. As is quite apparent, operations during this period constitute the final equilibrated form of intuitive thought, since they still rest on real or possible movements. By contrast, toward 11 to 12 years, the symbolization of operations is completed in the sense that the subject can carry them out on simple verbal hypotheses. [p. 155] In other words, the logic of propositions finally takes over from the logic of concrete actions. Even in this form, however, it is a matter of course that logic, in its psychological essence, remains a system of virtual actions. Either language is only pure parrotry or it expresses a possible transformation of reality, and it is this system of composable, reversible, and associative transformations that all logic and all elementary mathematics reflect.

In conclusion, if one envisions the individual and his relationships with the physical environment as a closed system, it is necessary to conceive the development of logic as a progressive transition from irreversible effective actions to the reversible virtual actions that are operations. One can, therefore, interpret logic as the final equilibrated form of actions toward which all sensory-motor and mental evolution tends. This is because there is equilibrium only in reversibility. The *groupement* appears to be the structure manifesting that equilibrium, and that is why it was necessary to formulate it in order to understand what follows.

B. Interpersonal factors

Let us now give up the artifice by which we considered the individual and his relationships with the physical environment to be a closed system and ask ourselves what intellectual relationships he enjoys with other individuals. The problem then becomes the following: if logic consists in an organization of operations which, in the final analysis, are internalized and reversible actions, does the individual arrive at this organization by himself, or is the intervention of interpersonal factors necessary to explain the development we have just described?

In order to answer this question, we must first analyse the steps in the individual's intellectual socialization in the same way that we just reviewed the steps in his logical development. Only after that is accomplished will we be able to ask whether socialization causes logical development, whether it results from it, or whether the two are related in more complex ways.

Now, the principal steps in the development of logical operations correspond in relatively simple fashion to correlative stages of social development. Both start at a level where the individual is still committed to himself. In effect, during the sensory-motor period preceding language, one cannot yet speak of the socialization of intelligence. In fact, it is [p. 156] only during this period that one may speak of anything like a purely individual intelligence. True, the child learns to imitate before knowing how to speak. But he only imitates gestures that he already knows how to execute by himself or of which he has acquired, by himself, sufficient understanding. Sensory-motor imitation does not, therefore, influence intelligence but is, rather, one manifestation of it. With regard to the baby's affective contacts with his surroundings (smiles, etc.), these are not exchanges of interest to the intellect as such.

We have characterized the period extending from the appearance of language to 7 or 8 years as pre-operatory (imaged and intuitive thought). This period presents a very significant beginning of socialization, but with characteristics intermediate between the purely individual character of the sensory-motor period and the cooperative character of the operatory period to follow. This is parallel to intuitive thought which remains intermediary between sensory-motor intelligence and operatory logic. From the point of view of the means of expression necessary both for the constitution of representations and for exchanges of thought, we first establish that if language, learned from the surroundings, gives the child a complete system of collective 'signs', these signs are not all understood immediately. In fact, they are rounded out with a no less rich system of individual 'symbols' which proliferates in imaginative or symbolic play, in representative imitation, and in the multiple images that the child expresses as best he can. On the other hand, from the point of view of meanings, which is to say of thought itself, we establish that interpersonal exchanges in children from 2 to 7 are characterized by an 'egocentrism' which remains halfway between the individual and the social and which can be defined by a relative non-differentiation of the individual's and the other's points of view. Thus, the child speaks as much for himself as for other people, does not know how to discuss things, cannot exposit his thoughts in systematic order, etc. In children's collective play, one likewise sees everyone playing partly for himself without over-arching coordination.[9]

Interestingly, there exists a close relationship between the egocentric character of interpersonal exchanges during this period and the imaged and intuitive, and therefore pre-operatory, character of thought [p. 157] of the same ages. On the one hand, all intuitive thought is 'centred' on a privileged static configuration, e.g. optical correspondence between two rows of superimposed objects, and knows nothing of the mobility of the operatory transformations that are possible. In other words, it never arrives at an adequate 'decentration'. One sees, therefore, how intuitive 'centration' implies egocentrism in the sense of a primacy of the immediate subjective (perceptual) point of view over decentred relationships. On the other hand, all egocentric thought consists in centring on objects as a function of one's own immediate action, which specifically implies thinking in terms of images or intuition in opposition to objective relationships of an operatory order.

As for the intellectual constraints practised during this same period by adults or older children (imposed knowledge, examples, etc.), they are assimilated to this same egocentric mentality and, therefore, transform it only superficially.

By contrast, the period of operations properly so-called (from 7 to 11 or 12 years) is accompanied by clear progress in socialization. The child becomes capable of cooperation, which is to say he no longer thinks only in terms of himself but also in terms of real or possible coordination of different points of view. Thus, he becomes capable of discussion (and of the sort of internalized discussion with himself that is reflection), of collaboration, and of ordered expositions that a listener can understand. His collective games give evidence of common rules. And finally, his understanding of reciprocal relationships (e.g. the inversion of right and left in an individual facing him, the coordination of spatial perspectives, etc.) shows the generality of these new attitudes and their connection with thought itself.

Just as there exists a close connection between the egocentrism of thought and its intuitive character, there also exists an intimate correlation between cooperation and the development of logical operations. An operatory *groupement* is a system of operations with compositions exempt from contradiction, reversible, and leading to the conservation of the totalities envisioned. Now it is clear that thinking jointly with others facilitates non-contradiction. It is much easier to contradict oneself when one thinks only for himself (egocentrism) than when partners are present to recall what one has said previously and what one has agreed upon. Reversibility and conservation [p. 158] are, on the other hand, contrary to how things appear and only become rigorous on the condition of replacing objects by signs, which is to say by a system of collective expressions. In a still more general way, a *groupement* is a system of concepts (classes or relations) implying a coordination of points of view and a pooling of thought. This is even clearer on the formal plane which begins after 11 or 12 years, since hypothetico-deductive thought is, more than anything else, thought based on a language (common or mathematical) and, therefore, on a collective form of thought.

In this way, but in more precise terms, the problem anticipated at the beginning of this section above again appears. If logical progress goes hand in hand with progress in socialization, is it because the child becomes capable of rational operations due to the fact that social development makes him capable of cooperation; or, on the contrary, is it because his individual logical acquisitions permit him to understand other people and thus lead to cooperation? Since the two sorts of progress go completely hand in hand, the question seems to have no solution except to say that they constitute two indissociable aspects of a single reality that is at once social and individual. It is in exactly this way that one must respond, but with some provisions making it possible to completely apply the means of analysis offered by the concept of *groupements*.

III. LOGICAL *GROUPEMENTS*, THE INDIVIDUAL, AND SOCIETY

Considered from the point of view of their psychological development, logical operations constitute the final equilibrial form of actions reached when they are 'grouped' into mobile systems that are both indefinitely composable and rigorously reversible. Now, social cooperation is also a system of actions, interpersonal rather than simply individual, but actions all the same and consequently subject to the laws of action. One can say, therefore, that social actions that end in cooperation are themselves ruled by laws of equilibrium and that they will, like individual actions, only attain equilibrium on condition of becoming organized into composable and reversible systems. Will, then, the laws of the *groupement* be simultaneously the laws of [p. 159] cooperation and of individual actions on the physical world? And is cooperation not, therefore, to be conceived in the final analysis according to the very etymological meaning of the term that designates it, that is, as a set of co-operations?

The individualist thesis consists in saying that logic is constructed at the heart of individual activities and, once achieved, permits the establishment of cooperation. The problem with this is that it is only by cooperating with others and not beforehand that the individual elaborates his logic. The current sociological thesis opposes a global interpretation to the individualist thesis, that is, social relationships constrain the individual to recognize a logic. While we agree with this, it is on the condition that these relationships themselves present such a logic. The decrees of a dictator do not engender it necessarily, whereas free cooperation leads to that reciprocity of perceptual judgments and representations which, alone, make the objective operation possible. It is, then, a matter of understanding how social relationships end in logic. The solution at which we arrive is the same one we found on the psychological plane. Individuals' actions on one another, which lie at the basis of every society, only create a logic on the express condition that they themselves acquire a form of equilibrium analogous to the structure whose laws may be defined at the end-point of the development of individual actions. And even that is a matter of course, since individual actions are more and more socialized and since cooperation is a system of actions like any other. In sum, the social relationships equilibrated into cooperation constitute *groupements* of operations exactly like the logical actions exercised on the external world by the individual, and the laws of *groupements* define the form of ideal equilibrium common to both social and individual actions.

A. The mechanism of intellectual exchange

First of all, it is necessary to show briefly that an exchange of thought constitutes an exchange comparable to all other exchanges and that, in consequence, such exchanges belong to the schema[10] of qualitative exchanges in general. In other words, they belong to the schema of exchanges that do not necessarily bear on material objects.[10] [p. 160] In any exchange between two individuals α and α', it is necessary to distinguish four different moments which can be expressed in the language of qualitative values. (1) Individual α exerts an action on α' that we shall call r_α (or α' exerts action $r_{\alpha'}$ on α); (2) This gives α' (or α) a positive, negative, or neutral feeling of satisfaction that we will call $s_{\alpha'}$; (3) This feeling obligates α' to α (or the inverse), or, in other words, constitutes a debt $t_{\alpha'}$; (4) This debt or obligation constitutes a virtual value for α, say v_α (or $v_{\alpha'}$ for α').

The conditions of equilibrium (still for an arbitrary qualitative exchange) are therefore the following:

1   It is first of all necessary that there exist between α and α' a common scale of values, making the evaluations of r_α and v_α by α comparable to the evaluations of $s_{\alpha'}$ and $t_{\alpha'}$ by α'.
2   Equilibrium is then attained if one has the equivalences:

$$\text{Eq. I: } (r_\alpha = s_{\alpha'}) + (s_{\alpha'} = t_{\alpha'}) + (t_{\alpha'} = v_\alpha) = (r_\alpha = v_\alpha)$$

and, reciprocally, if the virtual values $t_{\alpha'}$ and v_α[11] sooner or later lead to the real values $r_{\alpha'}$ and s_α:

$$\text{Eq. II: } (v_\alpha = t_{\alpha'}) + (t_{\alpha'} = r_{\alpha'}) + (r_{\alpha'} = s_\alpha) = (v_\alpha = s_\alpha)$$

3   Finally, equilibrium presupposes that one may reverse the order of the two series:

$$\text{Eq. I': } (r_{\alpha'} = s_\alpha = t_\alpha = v_{\alpha'})^{12}$$

$$\text{Eq. II': } (v_{\alpha'} = t_\alpha = r_\alpha = s_{\alpha'})$$

Where exchanges of thought, our only interest here, are concerned, these different terms and relationships take on the following meanings: (1) Individual α states a proposition r_α (true or false in varying degrees); (2) Partner α' finds himself in agreement (or not, in varying degrees), his agreement being designated by $s_{\alpha'}$; (3) The agreement (or disagreement) of α' is binding for the series of exchanges between α' and α, whence $t_{\alpha'}$; (4) This engagement of α' confers value or validity v_α (positive or negative) on the proposition r_α or, in other words, renders it valid or not insofar as future exchanges between the same individuals are concerned.

One, then, again finds the same three conditions of equilibrium, but transposed onto the plane of intellectual exchange:

1   To begin with, it is important that α and α' possess a common scale of intellectual values or, in other words, that they understand one another on [p. 161] the meaning of the words they employ and on the definition of the ideas that constitute those meanings. The common scale will, therefore, have to include two complementary aspects:

  (a) A language, comparable to the system of monetary (fiduciary) signs used for economic exchanges and also comparable to the system of signs and symbols used to express qualitative values in non-economic exchanges that are not intellectual, e.g. political, social, and affective exchanges, etc.
  (b) A system of well-defined ideas such that the definitions of α and α' completely converge or that they diverge in part but in such a way that α and α' possess some key allowing the ideas of one partner to be translated into the other's system.

2   This first (or double) condition fulfilled, the second condition of equilibrium is assigned by Equation I but with the following meaning:

  (a) The equality $(r_\alpha = s_{\alpha'})$ means either that α and α' can agree on the same proposition or that they agree on a common truth justifying the difference of their points of view (e.g. a law of perspective making legitimate the fact that one sees to his left what the other sees to his right and vice versa).
  (b) The equality $(s_{\alpha'} = t_{\alpha'})$ implies that α' feels himself to be thereafter obligated by the proposition that he has recognized as valid or, in other words, that he does not contradict himself.
  (c) The equivalence $(t_{\alpha'} = v_\alpha)$ attributes to the proposition r_α a validity capable of being conserved, which is to say that α will be able to keep proposition r_α self-identical as a permanent value.

But Equation I invested with these meanings only leads to the equilibrium of intellectual exchange if, in return, it makes possible the series of equivalences expressed by Equation II:

  (d) $(v_\alpha = t_{\alpha'})$ means, then, that the conserved value of proposition r_α is still recognized by α'.

(e) $(t_{\alpha'} = r_{\alpha'})$ means that the obligation conserved by α' is applied by him to a proposition $r_{\alpha'}$ that he in turn formulates and which is by virtue of this application equal in validity to r_α[13] and, therefore, to $t_{\alpha'}$. [p. 162]

(f) $(r_{\alpha'} = s_\alpha)$ implies that α agrees to the equality of $r_{\alpha'}$ with r_α and, therefore, with $t_{\alpha'}$, whence the equilibrium $v_\alpha = s_\alpha$.[14]

3   Finally, there is equilibrium only in the case of reciprocity or, in other words, when the preceding relationships are applied to the propositions of α' in relation to α. In effect, it is a matter of course that Equations I and II must be capable of being written by permuting all of the indices of α and α' or, in other words, the initiative can start from α' with a proposition $r_{\alpha'}$ (Equations I' and II').

In sum, equilibrium of thought exchanges presupposes: (1) A common system of signs and definitions; (2) Conservation of valid propositions obligating whoever recognizes them as such; and (3) Reciprocity of thought among partners.

The problem now is to determine whether these conditions of equilibrium can be fulfilled in no matter what type of interpersonal exchange or whether they presuppose a particular type of relationship. We are going to try to show that, in fact, the common scale, the conservations or obligations, and the reciprocities in play differ from one type of exchange to another. Only in the case of equilibrated exchanges does the structure of the processes of exchange consist of a system of reversible operations. In consequence, only the equilibrated exchange will lead to the formation of operatory thought, and that because it already itself conforms to the laws of *groupements*. In the final analysis, there is a fundamental identity between individual operations and cooperation from the point of view of the equilibrial laws that rule both.

B. Disequilibrium due to egocentrism

A first reason for disequilibrium may simply be that partners do not succeed in coordinating their points of view. This happens systematically with young children who conceive things and other individuals in terms of their own activity. Naturally, this occurs at all ages when interests or acquired inertia oppose objectivity. The three conditions necessary for equilibrium in intellectual exchanges cannot then be fulfilled for the following reasons: [p. 163]

1   There is not yet or there is no longer a common scale of reference because partners employ words in different senses or implicitly refer to individual images or symbols or to private meanings. Without common or sufficiently homogeneous concepts, lasting exchange is impossible.

2   There is insufficient conservation of previous propositions because partners lack feelings of obligation. Nothing better demonstrates the roles

intellectual obligation and conservation play in the equilibrium of exchanges than discussing something with a subject too young or with a mentally handicapped person when they have to some degree implicitly systematized the issue using images or uncommunicable symbols. As such discussions proceed, subjects forget what they momentarily recognized as valid, and, consequently, they endlessly contradict themselves without knowing that they do so. Everything goes along as if they lacked some regulation essential to reasoning, a regulation that obliges them to take account of what they have agreed to or said and to conserve that value in later constructions.

3   There is, therefore, no ruled reciprocity. Each partner, starting from the tacit postulate that his point of view is the only one possible, refers to it in his discussion with others instead of ending up either with propositions shared in common or with distinct but reciprocal propositions that can be coordinated with one another.

C. **Disequilibrium due to constraint**

Completely different from this are systems of exchanges based on unified collective thought imposed from the outside through constraints of traditional opinion or of elders or ancestors. In current life, this is seen wherever autonomous search for the truth does not come into play. It is also seen in so-called 'primitive' societies as well as in young children at the age where they oscillate between egocentric thought and imitation of the adult entourage. (In the latter case, the two phenomena are, moreover, complementary and due to the same lack of differentiation of the self and others.)

At first glance, thought crystallized by social constraints appears to present *maximum* equilibrium, since it is capable of lasting and even of taking on multisecular forms. Beside this, the agreement of minds on the shaky terrain of autonomous research appears quite fragile. During scientific collaboration, for example, [p. 164] accepted principles and truths seem to be constantly called into question. But it is the same for collective thought as for social equilibrium altogether. The most rigid totalitarian edifices are not always the most solid; free cooperation leads to a mobility whose suppleness is often a gauge of the greatest resistance. It is necessary, therefore, to distinguish between true or stable equilibria, recognizable in terms of their mobility and reversibility, and 'false equilibria', as one says in physics, where viscosity, multiple adherences, and frictions ensure what might be called external permanence for a system without internal stability.

1   From this point of view, it is undeniable that collective thought crystallized by the constraint of previous generations on those that follow ends in a common scale of intellectual values, in the form of a uniform language and a system of general concepts with fixed definitions. But there also occurs a phenomenon analogous to what, in political economy,

is called a 'fixed market'.[15] Here, instead of resulting from spontaneous exchanges ending in free determination of prices and markets, the scale of values becomes stabilized by measures of constraint. Under such conditions, the system of notions with which one starts and which one uses as a scale for exchanges has not been constructed in the course of previous exchanges under free and mutual control. Rather, it is a system simply imposed by the authority of usage and tradition.

2   Regarding the various conditions of equilibrium expressed by Equation II, if one agrees to call α the partner who exercises authority over another α' (as, for example, when an older individual transmits received truths to a younger individual), the following questions arise:

(a) In what way will the proposition r_α stated by α meet with α''s agreement? Only three possibilities exist. On the one hand, α and α' may both think in their own ways, in which case agreement is neither necessary nor even probable. (This is exemplified by the egocentrism examined in Section B above). On the other hand, α' may be brought around by α's proofs. For example, he may establish the same facts or effect the same operations independently of α's authority. In this case, it becomes a matter of cooperation and no longer constraint. And finally, α' may adopt α's [p. 165] point of view because of the latter's authority or prestige. In that case, intellectual constraint occurs, and two circumstances limit equilibrium. In the first place, the relationship is not reciprocal or, in other words, α will not agree with α''s propositions (Equations I' and II') for the same reasons that α' agrees with α's propositions. In the second place, α and α''s agreement lasts in so far as the second is submissive to the first and ends the moment that α' begins to think for himself, that is, it ends with social differentiation.

(b) The obligation ($s_{\alpha'} = t_{\alpha'}$) only endures as a function of α's constraint on α' and does not constitute a mutual obligation, lacking Equations I' and II' (where one has $r_{\alpha'} = s_\alpha = t_\alpha$).

(c) The conservation of values or of the validity of the propositions admitted ($t_{\alpha'} = v_\alpha$) is, therefore, determined only by the external factor of constraint. Because of this, it is a 'false equilibrium'. Although social structure can ensure its indefinite duration (in (d), (e), and (f) above), it does not constitute a stable internal equilibrium.

3   Because reciprocity is lacking, the conditions of equilibrium implied in the possibility of Equations I' and II' cannot be fulfilled. Since α is never obligated by α''s propositions, obligations function in one direction only and not in the reciprocal sense provided by Equations I' and II'.

In sum, then, there is an absence of internal equilibrium in the case of constraint not because condition (1) above is not met (the fixed market replacing the scale established spontaneously by previous exchanges), but because the system of obligations is not reciprocal. Lacking that reciprocity, the process of constraints is irreversible and for that reason cannot lead to truths of an operatory order. In effect, the conservation of propositions in a system of constraint does not consist in invariants resulting from a series of mobile and reversible transformations. Rather, it consists in a body of ready-made truths, the solidity of which is due only to their rigidity (as is seen in intuitive as opposed to operatory structures) and the transmission of which is in one direction only, e.g. action of older on younger children. [p. 166]

D. Cooperative equilibrium

It remains to be demonstrated not that equilibrium is ensured only in the case of cooperation (which is in part obvious from the preceding remarks) but that this equilibrium attained through cooperative exchanges of thought necessarily takes the form of a system of reciprocal operations and consequently of *groupements*.

1   To begin with, it is clear that a common scale of well-defined concepts – if it is truly common (in opposition to the non-coordinations due to egocentrism) and if it does not result from a fixed market imposing notions ready-made in advance – can only consist in a system of conventions or 'hypotheses' that do not prejudice possible constructions.

2   As for exchange itself, one must ask what real conditions correspond to the ideal conditions of equilibrium anticipated by Equations I and II:

(a) In the first place, how will a proposition r_α expressed by α meet with α''s agreement if that agreement is not due to external factors of authority? The only way this could occur is through a convergence between α and α' concerning the facts invoked by α and recognized by α'. But how can such a convergence be established? Two subjects α and α' necessarily have different, non-interchangeable perceptions. One can exchange ideas or, in other words, verbal judgments bearing on perceptions, but one can never exchange the perceptions themselves! It is the same with the movements that α and α' are able to execute in relation to the object, with their mental images, with their memories, and in short with the whole of their private symbolism in so far as it is not translated into conceptualized ideas. However, once the conventions determining the meaning of words and the nominal definition of concepts (see point 1 above) are agreed to, conceptualized notions can only give rise to communications in the form of judgments or reasoning. In so far as such judgments cannot be given operatory form and remain at the level of intuitive propositions, agreement between partners cannot be certain, since all perceptual or imaged intuition contains an egocentric residue. Certain agreement will, therefore, take on the form of a double operation. While the operation effected by α in his proposition r_α is obvious, it must be understood that, lacking external authority, α' can only certify his agreement with or even grasp the thought of α on the [p. 167] sole condition of being able to effect the same operation on his own account.

On the one hand, the initial equality ($r_\alpha = s_\alpha$) presupposes two individual operations (those of α and α'); on the other hand, it also and necessarily presupposes correspondence between those operations. This correspondence can take two forms. Either it will be a matter of the same operations on the part of α and α' and nothing more, and there will be simple correspondence with direct equivalence. Or it will be a matter of reciprocal operations (as in the example already cited of the individual who sees on the right what another individual sees on the left and vice versa), and there will still be correspondence but with reversed equivalence. In both cases, therefore, the correspondence is itself an operation which makes the cooperative process an operation from the start. In brief, the proposition r_α[16] is an operation of α, the agreement of s_α is due to a second individual operation, and the equivalence $r_\alpha = s_\alpha$ is due to a third operation which is nothing other than the correspondence making exchange possible and constituted by it from the start.

(b) In the second place, α' is obligated to continue to recognize the validity of r_α,[17] say ($s_\alpha = t_\alpha$). In what does this obligation consist if it is not due to the authority of α? It is now due to the 'principle of contradiction'. But as we sought to show a long time ago, one does not apply a logical principle in the manner of a legal law as if there were, on the one hand, the principle and, on the other, its subsequent application.[18] Non-contradiction is a direct effect of the reversibility of thought, because to think without contradictions is simply to think using reversible operations. Therefore, if α' remains obligated by r_α,[19] that means not only that he himself thinks in terms of reversible operations but that the correspondence between his operations and those of α constitute, as a system of correspondences assured by the exchange, a sequence of reversible operations.

Moreover, it is precisely because the operatory and reversible character of correspondence is involved in the exchange itself that non-contradiction becomes in this case a 'rule' or, in other words, a social norm of exchange and no longer only a form of equilibrium internal to the individual. That is why it is accompanied by a feeling of obligation and no longer only by a feeling of internal harmony. But this obligation is one that results [p. 168] from reciprocity and not from the authority of one partner over another, whence its difference from obligation of the coercive type. Again, this amounts to saying that exchange in its cooperative form acquires a normative character of operatory and no longer simply intuitive order.

(c) Third, conservation of the validity of the proposition r_α is ensured in the subsequent correspondences between α's and α''s operations and, therefore, throughout the exchange ($t_{\alpha'} = v_\alpha$). This 'identity' gives rise to the same reflections as do non-contradictions. The 'principle of identity' only constitutes a rule by virtue of exchanges. In individual thought, identity is the product of direct operations composed with inverse ones. If there is subsequent identity of the valid propositions exchanged, it is because the operatory mechanism is in this case constituted by the exchange itself and not just by individual thoughts.

(d) The proposition r_α is subsequently applied by α' to his own propositions ($v_\alpha = t_{\alpha'} = r_{\alpha'}$). If there is in this more than simple repetition by constraint, it is because, again, a new operatory construction comes into play.

(e) This new proposition $r_{\alpha'}{}^{20}$ meets with α's agreement ($r_{\alpha'} = s_\alpha$), which presupposes a new correspondence analogous to (a) above.

3   As for the reciprocity implied by Equations I' and II', it simply leads to reversing the correspondences and reciprocities just examined or, in other words, it generalizes them in the case where the initial propositions start with the subject α'. Thus the *groupement* is ensured in both directions.

Thus, one sees that the exchange of thought, when it reaches equilibrium, is led by that very fact to constitute an operatory structure. In other words, the form of equilibrium attained by exchange is nothing other than a system of simple correspondences or reciprocities; it is nothing other than a *groupement* including the *groupements* elaborated by the partners themselves. [p. 169]

CONCLUSION

Individuals' actions on the external world, as we have seen, obey a law of development such that the equilibrium toward which they tend takes on the mobile and reversible form of the *groupement*. Social relations consist in the actions of one individual on another. In exchanges of thought, such relations also tend toward a form of reciprocity, which implies the reversible mobility belonging to the *groupement*. In other words, cooperation is only a system of operations carried out in common; it is only a matter of co-operation.

Must we say, then, that operations 'grouped' by the individual are what make cooperation possible or that operatory *groupements* implied in cooperation as a social fact determine individual *groupements*? Posed in this way, the question loses all meaning because the *groupement* as a logical structure is a form of equilibrium and that form of equilibrium applies necessarily to the process as a whole.

Therefore, the problem simply becomes: does the individual reach equilibrium in the form of the *groupement* by himself, or is cooperation with others necessary for this to be achieved? Or conversely, does society reach intellectual equilibrium without an internal structuration unique to individual actions?

As far as the individual is concerned, the question presents itself in two forms. Can individuals construct for themselves a system of stable definitions constituting what one might call a set of self-conventions? And once in possession of this system, will they come to use it by means of grouped operations implying reversibility and consequently rigorous conservation of the totalities in play? That would mean, therefore, that one accords the individual the power to make conventions with himself or, in other words, to link his present thought with his thought to come, as if it were a matter of different people. Now if one sees the extent to which individuals, in the process of being socialized, constantly change the meaning of the notions they employ, there is no way to avoid supposing that agreement with oneself is an internalized social conduct. On the other hand, how will the individual come to conserve the [p. 170] totalities on which his operations bear? How will he attain complete reversibility? In effect, sensory-motor processes cannot suffice to explain reversibility, since they are essentially irreversible and only succeed in reversing themselves in part and doubtless under the action of factors of higher order. Complete reversibility presupposes symbolism, because it is only by reference to the possible evocation of absent objects that the assimilation of things to action schemes and the accommodation of action schemes to things reach permanent equilibrium and thus constitute a reversible mechanism. The symbolism of individual images fluctuates far too much to lead to this result. Language is therefore necessary, and thus we come back to social factors. What is more, the objectivity and coherence necessary for an operatory system presuppose cooperation. In short, then, in order to make the individual capable of constructing *groupements*, it is first necessary to attribute to him all of the qualities of the socialized person.

Inversely, it is clear that cooperation can lead to the formation of *groupements* not only by means of language, since the logic of operations is not a verbal logic, but also by means of individual psychomotricity in the exact measure where operations are a system of actions.

In short, in whatever manner one turns the question, individual and collective functions make appeal to one another in explaining the conditions necessary for logical equilibrium. As for logic itself, it goes beyond both of these functions since it arises from the necessarily ideal equilibrium toward which they both tend. This is not to say that there exists a logic in itself that simultaneously rules individual and social actions, since logic is only the form of equilibrium immanent in the processes of development of these actions themselves. But actions, becoming composable among themselves and reversibile, acquire, by being elevated to the rank of operations, the power of being substituted for one another. Thus, the *groupement* is only a system of possible substitutions either within a single individual's thought (operations of intelligence) or within thought exchanges from one individual to another (cooperation). These two sorts of substitutions constitute, therefore, a general logic, at once collective and individual, that characterizes the form of equilibrium common to cooperative as well as to individualized actions. [p. 171]

If the logician can axiomatize his science without worrying about sociology or even psychology, it is because he operates in the 'ideal'. As a logician, he has a right to stay in the ideal realm dealing with a form of equilibrium never wholly realized in fact. By contrast, when sociologists and psychologists seek to understand how this realization is effected, they can only appeal to one another. One might say the same for those other axiomatics, morality and law, to whose values the notion of *groupement* is equally applicable. Let it suffice for us to have sought to show here how the notion of operation, taken in its fullest sense, allows us to analyse certain forms of equilibrium that are common to the respective fields of psychology and sociology while at the same time safeguarding the rights of logic on a plane at once parallel and superior to both. The plane in question is that onto which this very equilibrium is 'projected' (in the geometric sense of the term), as if it were realized in fact.

AUTHOR'S NOTES

[1] (1928) 'Logique génétique et sociologie', *Rev. Phil.* (Paris), pp. 167–205 (this volume, Chapter 5), and 'L'Individualité et le développement de la raison', in M. Caullery, C. Bouglé, P. Janet, J. Piaget, and L. Febvre, *L'Individualité* this volume, (Paris: Alcan, 1933) Chapter 6.

[2] In a remarkable thesis (*Théorie de la société internationale*, Geneva, 1941), M. Papaligouras, a talented young jurist, has recently sought to oppose to Durkheim's society an 'existential' society of a priorist inspiration without doubting that Durkheim had followed an analogous path. It is all the more interesting to establish that he rediscovers, as essential postulates of sociology, the Durkheimian hypotheses of a 'social time', of a 'social space', of a system of collective logical norms, etc.

[3] See Piaget (1936) *La Naissance de l'intelligence chez l'enfant* and Piaget *La Construction du réel chez l'enfant* (Neuchâtel: Delachaux et Niestlé, 1937). In English, Piaget, *The origins of intelligence in the child*, trans. M. Cook (London: Routledge & Kegan Paul, 1953); and Piaget, *The construction of reality in the child*, trans. M. Cook (London: Routledge & Kegan Paul, 1954).

[4] See our work *La Formation du symbole chez l'enfant* (Neuchâtel: Delachaux et Niestlé, 1945). In English, *Play, dreams, and imitation in childhood*, trans. C. Gattegno and F. M. Hodgson (London: Routledge & Kegan Paul, 1951).

[5] See Piaget and Szeminska, *La Genèse du nombre chez l'enfant* (Neuchâtel: Delachaux et Niestlé, 1941). In English, *The child's conception of number* (London: Routledge & Kegan Paul, 1952).

[6] Piaget and Inhelder (1941) *Le Développement des quantités chez l'enfant* (Neuchâtel: Delachaux et Niestlé, 1941). In English, *The child's construction of quantities* (London: Routledge & Kegan Paul, 1974).

[7] See our work, *Classes, relations, et nombres: Essai sur les 'groupements' de la logistique* (Paris: Vrin, 1942).

[8] Whence the special rules of calculation regarding associativity. Again see, *Essai sur les 'groupements' de la logistique* (Paris: Vrin, 1942).

[9] See *Le Langage et la pensée de l'enfant* 2nd edition, (Neuchâtel: Delachaux et Niestlé, 1930) and *Le Jugement moral chez l'enfant* (Paris: Alcan, 1932). In English, *The language and thought of the child*, trans. M. Gabain, 3rd edition, (London:

Routledge & Kegan Paul, 1959); and *The moral judgment of the child*, trans. M. Gabain, (London: Routledge & Kegan Paul, 1932).
[10] See our *'Essai sur la théorie des valeurs qualitatives en sociologie statique'*, reprinted as Chapter 2 of this volume.

TRANSLATION NOTES

1 A *groupement* (grouping) is a logical structure one of whose defining properties is reversibility, where the latter 'constitutes the principal feature of logical thought . . . . Through the notion of reversibility, I have effectively defined logical intelligence.' (J. Piaget (1939) 'Les groupes de la logistique et la réversibilité de la pensée', *Revue de théologie et philosophie*, 27, 291–295) Piaget's continued commitment to this structure is qualified, but evident, in his recent studies (J. Piaget and R. Garcia, *Towards a logic of meanings* (Hillsdale, NJ: Erlbaum, 1991, pp. 3, 121 respectively) on the grounds that it is a necessary, though not sufficient, element in an intensional model. For discussions of Piaget's logic, see L. Apostel, 'The future of Piagetian logic', reprinted in L. Smith (ed.), *Jean Piaget: critical assessments*, vol. 4 (London: Routledge, 1992); W. Mays (1992) 'Piaget's logic', *Archives de psychologie*, 60, 45–70; and S. Papert (1963) 'Sur la logique Piagetienne', in L. Apostel *et al.* (eds), *La Filiation des structures* (Paris: Presses Universitaires de France).
2 *Le vrai* presents many problems of translation as well as the substantive problem stated in the first paragraph of Chapter 5.
3 'That which is believed everywhere, always, and by everyone.' St Vincent of Lerins, *Commonitorium*, ii.
4 See Chapter 7 for an empirical study of hierarchical classification in the social domain.
5 The word in French is *majoration*. Clearly, this is related to Piaget's theory of *équilibration majorante*, that Brown has elsewhere translated as 'optimizing equilibration'. His reasons for doing so appear in the footnote on page xvii of Piaget, *The equilibration of cognitive structures* (Chicago: University of Chicago Press, 1985).
6 'Logic in the classical sense' here refers to common language usage, not to the syllogistic meaning of the term.
7 In the French text: *capitaux de croyances*.
8 Cf. Piaget, *La Naissance de l'intelligence chez l'enfant*, Chapter 5, Sections 1 and 2 (Neuchâtel: Delachaux et Niestlé, 1936). In English, Piaget, *The origins of intelligence in children*, trans. M. Cook, (London: Routledge & Kegan Paul, 1953).
9 In the French text: *engendre les opérations en les appuyant les unes sur les autres*.
10 *Schéma* is used in the text although it does not adhere to the distinction that Piaget makes between *schéma* and *schème* in the 'Author's Preface' to G. Seagrim's translation of *Les Mécanismes perceptifs*. In English, Piaget, *The mechanisms of perception* (New York: Basic Books, 1969). In the text referred to, Piaget states: 'In our usage, [*schème* and *schéma*] correspond to quite distinct realities, the one operative . . . the other figurative'.
11 There appear to be several errors in the notation given in the French text. In this case the text reads '*si les valeurs virtuelles t_α et $v_{\alpha'}$ entraînent tôt ou tard en retour les valeurs réelles $r_{\alpha'}$ et s_α*'. In order to be consistent with the equation that follows, we have reversed the subscripts on t and v.
12 In the French text from which this article was translated, this equation reads '(r_α = s_α = t_α = $v_{\alpha'}$'. (The final parenthesis is missing.) Since the general idea is to

reverse the partner indicated by the subscripts, we have made r the action of α'.

13 The French text reads 'r_α'. The statement would then be completely tautological: α would formulate $r_{\alpha'}$ equal in validity to $r_{\alpha'}$. It seems clear that the validity of $r_{\alpha'}$ needs to be equivalent to the validity of r_α, for $t_{\alpha'}$ to equal v_α. We have, therefore, changed $r_{\alpha'}$ to r_α.

14 The French text reads '$(r_\alpha = s_\alpha)$ *implique que α soit d'accord avec $r_{\alpha'}$ de r_α donc de $t_{\alpha'}$ d'où l'équilibre $v_\alpha = s_{\alpha'}$)*'. The sentence is ungrammatical and unintelligible. We have, therefore, introduced changes to make the translation coherent.

15 The French text uses the term *cours forcé*.

16 The French text reads 'r'_α'. This has never been referred to in the previous formalism and makes no sense. In consequence, it has been changed to 'r_α'.

17 Again, for reasons of coherence, the notation has been changed: '$r_{\alpha'}$' has been made 'r_α'.

18 See Chapter 5 this volume for a discussion of the psycho-logic of the principle of contradiction.

19 Again, for reasons of coherence, the notation has been changed: '$r_{\alpha'}$' has been made 'r_α'.

20 The French text reads 'r'_α'. For reasons stated in Note 16 above, this has been changed to 'r_α'.

4 The relationship between morality and law

[p. 172] In this article we propose to extract certain mechanisms common to moral facts and legal facts, as well as certain differences or contrasts between them. The problem of the relationship between law and morality gets taken up over and over again, either from the point of view of practical delimitations (in particular among jurists, for whom the question of boundaries arises daily) or from the point of view of the philosophy of law or moral philosophy. But it is undoubtedly also interesting to pure sociology. It is to this sociological terrain that we will restrict ourselves, but the special and well delimited formulation of the questions perhaps calls for some preliminary explication for the reader for whom the jurisconsult's or the moralist's or the philosopher's habits of thought would draw him far away from that specific to a sociologist. The sociologist must explain sociological facts as facts, while constraining himself constantly not to evaluate them, even from the standpoint of his own metaphysical system.

I

The sociology of law is a discipline very different from the science of law or the philosophy of law. The science and philosophy of law necessarily take a normative approach: they reduce the knowledge of rules of law to the analysis of their validity, without seeking to explain them in terms of psychological or historical facts external to the law. The sociology of law, by contrast, considers rules as facts among facts and sets out to interpret them as a function of the set of the other social facts taken together. Instead of studying what is legally valid, as pure jurists do, the sociology of law simply asks how mankind in society has come to elaborate rights or obligations and consider them to be [p. 173] valid. Instead of asking these questions in the context of an over-arching speculative system, as the philosophy of law does, it stays within the territory of observation and experiment. By the same token, moral sociology does not ask, with the moralist, what is good and what is evil. It limits its curiosity to studying, not in the name of what principles, but by what causal process, mankind in society has considered certain thoughts and actions to be good or bad (without itself evaluating those thoughts and actions) and by what mechanism mankind has come to place sanctions on such thoughts and actions. In brief, just as sociology and psychology of thinking study how reason develops, while logic studies what is true or false, so moral and legal sociology analyse the progressive construction of rules pertaining to social conduct,[1] while ethics and law determine the validity of those rules. More briefly still, sociology explains without seeking foundations, whereas law, morality, and logic aim to establish foundations without pursuing causal explanations.[2]

This difference between those sciences that deal with empirical facts and 'real' causality, like sociology or psychology, and those normative disciplines that deal with relations of 'ideal' implication (and, in the legal field, relations of 'imputation' as Kelsen calls them), like law, morality, and logic, might be better understood as follows. Let us draw an example from a domain where the conflicts between the normative and the causal scarcely exist at all – the study of reasoning, which is shared between logic and the psychology of thinking. Consider a proposition like $A = B$; $B = C$; therefore $A = C$. The logician confines himself to studying why this proposition is true or logically valid, whereas the proposition $A = B$; $B = C$; therefore $A < C$ is false and logically invalid, but he will not ask how these propositions are constituted in real live concrete thought. He will search for principles that may give grounds for the first proposition and at the same time render the second one invalid, but he will tend to abstract these principles or foundations from factors of experience and axiomatize them as purely ideal, *a priori* connections in order to make them more certain. The psychologist, on the contrary, will ask how these propositions appeared in the mind and how they are constructed. He will note that the ability to handle the first proposition arrives later in development[1][3] [p. 174] rather than being innate. He will note especially that it is tied to certain mental conditions that make it possible and explain it (which does not necessarily mean that they provide foundations for it): for instance, the conservation of number and quantity and reversibility in thought. In brief, there cannot be any conflict between two very distinct sciences like logic and the psychology of thinking. On the contrary, one illuminates the other because one is the axiomatic enterprise for which the other is the corresponding empirical science. The relationship between law and sociology of law works in the same way. The 'science of law', which seeks to provide foundations for legal norms, has recourse to principles which in reality are axioms; this gradual axiomatization can be seen all the way from Roguin to Kelsen. But the science that provides foundations cannot at the same time be the science that provides causal explanations. The problem remains of understanding how human societies have come to constitute and recognize law, that is, to construct rules that the social group considers valid and obligatory.

It is true that a doctrine (one of many produced by the philosophy of law as opposed to the pure science of law) has been offered that claims to attain simultaneously the goal of giving foundations for law and the goal of explaining it in terms of human nature. This is the theory of 'natural law', under the many forms it has assumed over time. But the principles of natural law, which seem tautological to 'pure' jurists,[2] cannot now be satisfactory to the sociology of law. Interestingly enough, the problem is the reverse. The principles of natural law assert too much, making claims that are beyond the reach of scientific verification. Doubtless, all sociologists will agree that in every human society there is a belief in justice that stands higher than positive law, and that this aspiration can play an important causal role in transforming the law. Even Pareto, who pokes fun at Justinian for granting a 'natural right' of marriage to earthworms and fleas, is obliged to classify among the essential 'residuals' the sentiments of justice and injustice and thus to recognize their causal action on society. But once this fact has been acknowledged, it needs to be explained. Our discussion begins at this point, without necessarily giving preference to natural law interpretations. [p. 175] One possible solution: this constant aspiration toward justice results from human nature as willed and created by God. It is thus that neo-Thomists, and in our times F. Guisan, conceive of Law as an over-arching metaphysical system. It is clear that sociologists can neither approve nor criticize this point of view because it is outside their domain. All the same, they will remark that natural law has curiously metamorphosed into supernatural law, and that such a position can be of no help in giving particular explanations of sociological facts. Explaining law by reference to divine will is a little like seeking to characterize physical laws by stating that causality is a product of God's will – we still have to understand the details of the phenomena in question. Sociology concerns itself with secondary causes, not with the First Cause.

A second solution: natural law is innate and is the hereditary expression of a human nature that is being thought of on its own, independently of any metaphysical hypotheses. Here we are definitely in the realm of facts and empirical verification, but the entire demonstration still needs to be supplied. Indeed, moral realities, like logical realities, do not seem to be subject to hereditary transmission; they are constructed as a function of interactions or contacts between individuals. And there is no reason to suppose that legal realities are a breed apart from other human norms and possess an innate basis unknown elsewhere. Besides, the claim that the principles of law are innate is supported only by those authors who hope to draw from it an argument in favour of the theological hypothesis that we mentioned above. But why should we want the divine will to manifest itself through hereditary transmission instead of through social laws external to the individual? Hereditary transmission may seem more certain than sociological laws, but perhaps only if we have not looked very closely at either. In the truly 'naturalistic' approach adopted by sociologists in their rivalry with philosophers of law, a group of human beings is capable of being governed by laws (in the scientific sense) that are just as stable as the laws applicable to a group of genes. The study of law[4] gains nothing by preferring one set of laws to the other. [p. 176]

A third solution: the aspiration toward justice characteristic of all human societies is the expression, not of factors prior to social evolution (a 'human nature' innate in the individual) but of laws of equilibrium immanent in society. In effect, whatever rules of positive law might be in force in a particular society, they never succeed in bringing into equilibrium all of the current interests or values. We might always suppose that beyond the received rules, and consequently at the source of certain new rules, lies a permanent tendency toward more equality, more reciprocity, more justice, because all of these are forms of a more complete or advanced[5] state of equilibrium. In this case the so-called principles of natural law would result from a *terminus ad quem* and not a *terminus a quo*,[6] from a necessary state of equilibrium toward which social relations tend, and not from a structure prior to every society. The practical value of believing in natural law is thus safeguarded and the theoretical difficulties of the doctrine are eliminated. But we must realize that at this point we exit the domain of classical 'natural law' hypotheses. By a semantic paradox which we leave to the curiosity of linguists, we abruptly part company with the jurists who are called 'naturalists' today as soon as we consider society to be a 'natural' phenomenon. In the days of Pufendorf and Grotius, only human nature was 'natural' – society was artificial. Today's sociologists would be tempted to turn these two affirmations around, except to maintain that true 'human nature' is that of the socialized person as opposed to the pre-social individual (the infant).

To put it briefly, this third, equilibration-based solution[7] amounts to saying that two or three individuals who have lived their entire lives on a desert island would necessarily come up with the idea of justice, without implying that they had it in them to start with. As a necessary result of social interactions, law – 'natural' as well as positive – thus unavoidably requires sociological explanation. But, we repeat, the field of sociological explanations is more modest and restrained than the field of the philosophy of law. The sociology of law is restricted to the facts obtained by observation and experiment, without aiming to provide foundations for law on the basis of any *a priori* principle. It thus calls for the constitution of a complementary axiomatic system like the 'pure' science of law, and is limited to complementing it. Maybe [p. 177] one day the axiomatic theory of law will be considered to complement the sociology of law. But the relation of complementarity is reciprocal or symmetric, not unilateral or asymmetric, so no disputes are to be expected in that direction. Before the sociology of law has enough adepts to challenge the 'pure' jurists, a great deal of useful work will have to be done to move beyond the level of preliminary investigations.

II

Among these introductory questions, one preliminary problem is particularly delicate, but its solution is indispensable if we are to continue this work. To be precise, it is the problem of the boundaries between law and morality. For the rules that govern modern Western societies,[8] it is easy to make this delimitation in practice. Law can be identified with specific laws codified by the State[3][9] whereas non-codified obligations can be inferred to belong to the sphere of morality. Only jurisprudence will raise questions of frontiers when it becomes a matter of being sensitive, for instance, to subtle differences in equity, in extenuating circumstances or in immorality in the strict sense of the term. By contrast, if one tries to partition into moral and legal categories the characteristic usages of so-called primitive societies, which possess no (or virtually no) written laws, the problem becomes most difficult to get control of. Take for example customs concerning the potlatch[10] (an exchange made for reasons of prestige rather than material interests) or gifts and presents regulated by nearly ritualized customs. Are these moral or legal? And the various types of vengeance and reprisals? And the rules relative to the sexual act, etc. etc.? All of the intermediate cases tie together the extreme poles, which alone are well defined. An essential theoretical problem is thus immediately posed for the sociology of law, namely, how to distinguish law and morality. Even in the matters that concern contemporary Western societies, the ease of making this distinction in practice in no way does away with the very great difficulty of formulating it in theory.

This difficulty is attested by the multiplicity and diversity of conceptions that have been proposed by the best [p. 178] authors. We will now expound some of these conceptions, because this discussion, even in a summary form, will permit us to bring to light several of the essential aspects of this formidable question.

A first group of doctrines can be characterized by the conception of a commonality of nature between law and morality: they differ only in their greater or lesser degree of collective or public coordination. This is in summary form the opinion of Duguit as well as the view of Durkheim and his school. According to Durkheim, law, like morality, is characterized by the existence of obligatory rules, sanctioned by the collective. But legal sanctions are organized into rule systems[11] whereas the sanctions that define morality are 'diffuse' – that is, not codified. Besides the prohibitory sanctions common to morality and law, it should be added that law also knows 'restitutive' sanctions unknown to morality. (There is no blame attached to restitutive sanctions; they simply compensate for damages of a material order, as in a civil case.) But since the degree of codification concerns only the external form of rules, moral and legal realities are fundamentally identical. Both proceed from the same constraint that the group exercises on individuals. From a totally different point of view, one that emphasizes individual 'human nature' more than the social group, the neo-Thomists defend an analogous conception. Law is entirely contained within morality because it is sanctioned by morality. But morality extends beyond law. Law is limited by the administration of rules of evidence, but there are moral actions that pertain only to the individual conscience, unknown to other individuals. Thus the difference between law and morality is merely a difference of degree, not an opposition of internal natures.

But this hypothesis of a common nature looks difficult to sustain, as far as societies like our own are concerned. There are at least two arguments against it. The first is that there are frequent conflicts between law and morality. For example, a conscientious objector to military service appeals to motives that must be regarded as moral, yet he does this in order to disobey what he well knows to be the positive law. Exercising a public function can also occasion conflicts between obeying certain orders, whose legal validity is incontestable, and following one's own conscience, [p. 179] etc. Second, there are reciprocal influences between the legal life of a society and its moral life. It is thus that Ripert was able to write an interesting book about 'moral rules in civil obligations', in which he points out how the collective moral conscience[12] has transformed French law. However, a reciprocal influence, due to periodic changes in public opinion as well as the conflicts themselves, most surely attests to a duality in content and not just in form between the two sorts of social realities whose relationships we are investigating.

Conversely, certain partisans of natural law see moral and legal rules as two kinds that are distinct from the outset in both content and form, as though at every level of development there is a difference in nature between law and morality. But we must reject this other extreme position, because it seems incontestable that the two social realities have grown more differentiated in the course of the evolution of social groups, and that the difference between them is much less pronounced in 'primitive' societies than it is in modern ones.

Our point of departure, then, is neither identity in nature nor radical opposition. What we need to find is a conception that takes adequate note of both the differences and the resemblances between law and morality, without excluding either common mechanisms, or a process of progressive differentiation from an ultimate common origin. Let us examine, in this regard, a certain number of well-known points of view, such as those of Roguin, Petrazycki, and Kelsen, or the more recent ideas of Gurvitch and Timacheff. With striking regularity, these different authors, who have tried to underline the differences between law and morality, will end up showing us just the opposite. In discussing their particular hypotheses, we will see how the common ancestry of moral and legal functioning is greater than anyone could imagine without carrying out a psycho-sociological analysis of the origins of social behaviour.

Roguin[4] rightly asserts that the distinction between law and morality is as important for a sociologist as the distinction between vertebrates and invertebrates is for a zoologist. We might wish for a criterion for classifying [p. 180] law and morality that is as clear as the presence or absence of a spinal column. But the indications furnished by the great jurist from Vaud are still far removed from this desirable level of clarity. For Roguin, legal and moral realities are comparable to two overlapping surfaces – they have a common intersection but each also extends beyond the other. On the one hand, there are quite a few legal rule systems without moral interest. On the other hand, morality, to which no individual action is immune, legislates about certain actions that do not concern the law – more precisely, these are 'authorized by the law, which does not occupy itself further with them'.[5] In what does this opposition between the legal and the ethical then consist? It depends essentially, according to Roguin, on the character of the sanctions. In the domain of law, sanctions are external and coercive, because they stem from collective authority. In the domain of morality, sanctions reduce to 'internal punishments' (remorse, torments, and fear of the hereafter). No matter how clear this distinction may look, however, it does not survive empirical examination, especially from the standpoint of developmental psychology.[13] To begin with, adult morality would doubtless be more fragile than it already is, if it were sanctioned only by 'internal punishments' and blame and pressure from other people did not strengthen the internal voice of some people's consciences. Even more to the point, the sociological question is whether this interior voice and the 'internal punishments' that it brings with it are truly internal from the cradle or, on the contrary, they are products of the progressive interiorization of external influences, and thus effects of socialization by the family and through education. Now everything we know today about the origin of obligations of conscience[6] seems to indicate that the commands[14] received by the young child, as well as his or her respect for those who give them, are the determining factors in this training. It follows that, at the beginning of moral life, the sanctions are external (blame and punishment coming from parents) and coercive, just as they are in the domain of law. In particular, moral obligations, like legal obligations, have as their first source a superior authority [p. 181]: in this case that of the father and mother. In an effort to preserve the basic meaning of Roguin's proposed solution, one might reply that this authority is merely familial, whereas legal authority concerns society as a whole and is crystallized in the conception of the State. No doubt this is true in well-differentiated modern societies. But if one applies this criterion to the tribal societies of Polynesia, in which family and clan are largely the same, must we then say that the rules of the clan are moral and the rules of the tribe are legal? That would be rather simple-minded. In short, there is moral authority just as there is legal authority; there are 'external' sanctions in morality just as there are in law; and for that matter legal obligations are doubtless interiorized just as ethical obligations are. So?

Petrazycki, the great philosopher of law, seeks to make things precise, but on the point that interests us his approach is basically similar to Roguin's. For Petrazycki, the legal relationship (and such relationships exist on a scale infinitely broader than that of codified law) is 'bilateral' and 'imperative-attributive'. That is, it always presupposes at least two partners, one of whom is under obligation while the other, by virtue of this same obligation, has a right attributed to him. Every legal relationship between *A* and *B* is thus imperative for *A*, because it puts *A* under obligation, and attributive for *B*, because *A*'s obligation is equivalent to *B*'s right. Moral facts, on the contrary, are 'unilateral' and 'imperative' only, because A's moral obligation remains internal to A and confers no right on B. For example, if A is a follower of Tolstoy and feels that it his moral duty to give his fortune away to the poor, B, who is poor, nonetheless cannot claim any right to A's fortune. But this solution, despite its considerable elegance, cannot satisfy us any more than Roguin's does. The objections are the same. As we have already pointed out elsewhere,[7] once it is acknowledged that moral obligation springs not from an innate or hereditary process but from commands or examples that emanate from respected persons, moral facts themselves also constitute bilateral relationships – even double relationships when the respect becomes mutual. Petrazycki's amusing example is particularly clear in this regard. Why indeed does A, the follower of Tolstoy, [p. 182] consider it his duty to give his fortune away to the poor? This is the question that the sociologist necessarily asks, whereas the philosopher of law only asks[8] whether A's obligation constitutes a right for B (the very claim we have set out to contest). The reply is in any case easy to give. It is because A had respect for Tolstoy that he came to adopt his commandments and interiorize them as duties. (Tolstoy, in turn, would have adopted and interiorized Christ's commandments.) In consequence, the moral relationship is not so much between A and B as between A and T: the relationship then becomes bilateral because it is T's commandments that put A under obligation. This moral relationship may even become imperative-attributive because to A's respect for T and A's obedience to T's commandments there corresponds a (moral) right on T's part to formulate the commandments and to make others respect the values that he is transmitting. In the case of father and son, the point is obvious, yet we do not consider the father's right to exercise moral authority over the son to be a strictly legal one. As for the relationship between A and B (as we continue to pursue the Tolstoian example), if A gives his fortune to B, B now becomes obligated to A. Even if we consider only mutual respect, B thus assumes an obligation to give thanks and esteem, etc., to A, to which corresponds at the very least A's (moral) right to respect for the values in whose name he acted. In short, Petrazycki's criterion for distinguishing the moral from the legal, no matter how transparent it appears to be, is not adequate to bring to light the basic difference between law and morality. Under analysis, it reveals, on the contrary, a common mechanism.

The same goes for the distinction adopted by Kelsen in his celebrated system of pure legal theory. According to this profound author, legal rules draw their validity from their 'form', which is characterized by a continual creative construction, whereas moral rules draw their validity from their 'content', which is static and non-constructive. It is easy enough to understand what Kelsen means by formal legal construction, because the essential postulate in his axiomatic theory is that law regulates its own creation. Law, from Kelsen's standpoint, is a hierarchy of norms, in which each simultaneously applies norms higher in the hierarchy and creates norms lower in the hierarchy. [p. 183] Only 'individualized norms', which constitute the base of the pyramid (administrative orders, court judgments, etc.) are pure applications and create nothing further; only the 'basic norm' at the top of the pyramid is purely creative and is not derived from something else. This basic norm is the one that assures the validity of the constitution in every system of government, and thus the validity of the whole set of hierarchically nested norms that run from the constitution on down to individualized norms. One readily understands how Kelsen came to formulate this indispensable axiom because it asserts the validity of the entire legal order. From a sociological standpoint (this is our own interpretation; despite his first-rate contributions to the sociology of primitive peoples, Kelsen has always refused to draw any connections between law and sociology), it is the point at which any axiomatic system whatever must ultimately be tied to the actual world. The basic norm is the way that the society whose system of positive law is being studied normatively asserts the validity of the law and experiences the special sense of obligation[15] that assures its normative character. As for morality, Kelsen readily distinguishes it from law in that continuous formal construction is not involved and its validity is based solely on the content of its rules. Morality proceeds by deduction from general to particular, but without creating new norms in the way that legal deduction does.

Kelsen and Petrazycki have profoundly analysed the origin and even the dynamic character of the law – Kelsen strictly in the domain of governmental rules, Petrazycki in the socio-psychological territory of 'legal convictions' distributed throughout the social group.[16] But they have been content in the area of morality to describe the products of development instead of comparably reconstituting its constructive process. This disparity is easily accounted for. Law is essentially a matter of the adult consciences in a given society and the jurist can describe its contours without having to get up from his work table or leave the library. Morality, on the other hand, goes back to the cradle; to investigate its origin and dynamic character we must have recourse to methods used by child psychologists. We cannot simply look at 'primitive' people, who were also children once; ethnography cannot tell us what we need to know in moral sociology [p. 184] without help from developmental psychology.

Once we bring to bear on moral realities the same care in unearthing their constructive mechanisms that Kelsen has applied to the law, we see that, far from resulting in a fundamental opposition between the two systems of norms, Kelsen's schema applies in a highly suggestive manner to moral rules themselves. We have already made this point elsewhere,[9] so we will limit ourselves here to a few remarks. The first is that, even among adults, moral life is far from being a process of applying ready-made general rules, despite the illusions encouraged, in part unintentionally, by certain philosophers and by Kant in particular. Moral life is a continual process of construction: it is often easier to do one's duty than to discern what one's duty is, and this discernment sometimes results from interior debates in which it is impossible not to recognize the signs of constructive elaboration. Frédéric Rauh has written an entire book – and how admirable it is – on 'moral experience'. His goal is to show precisely that ethical norms have nothing 'universal' in them, in the sense of propositions so general that they apply to every individual and every situation. Rather, moral norms result from a special kind[17] of 'experience' which presupposes an inductive or deductive construction, like a scientific experiment, and an empirical test.[18] Rauh's position takes us far away from the ready-made rules that Kelsen considers characteristic of morality as opposed to law.

But above all, if this is already the case for normative construction when considering adults individually, how much stronger the case must be for taking it into account when examining the psychological development of the child or the evolution of customs in an entire society. The first duties that a child knows are the commands transmitted by his parents. Yet from these heteronomous norms the child will draw new norms, by generalization and application to other individuals, by differentiation, reinterpretation, and so on. The end result of these processes will be an autonomous and spiritualized interiorization of this set of rules that the child will have unceasingly reworked. Now let us situate these processes within society as a whole, viewed as an unbounded nesting structure of generations each of which educates and trains the next by means of this same mechanism. And let us think of the immense [p. 185] collective endeavour that extends from the 'morality of the Hottentots' (or purely heteronomous and external submission to established usages) to Christian morality, and again from current Christian morality to the morality of saints and of the most highly evolved consciences in their interior autonomy. We cannot avoid observing that each generation applies the norms that have been handed down to it while promulgating new norms in their name. From primitive obedience to the 'individualization of the norm' that each adult decision presupposes, we keep finding the same constructive process as in the elaboration of laws – in different forms, it must be understood, but with the same common mechanism. What is more, depending on whether norms are elaborated under the influence of submission and unilateral respect, or reciprocity and mutual respect, we find the two normative forms (hierarchical and contractual) that Kelsen has so skilfully distinguished and analysed in the domain of law. In the hierarchical case, the person who is subject to the law is under obligation from an already established norm; in the contractual case that person participates in the elaboration of the very norm that places him under obligation.

These remarks concerning the distinction that Kelsen has established between law and morality will permit us to be brief in dealing with another author. He is in any case quite different in his method, which is inspired by German phenomenology. Georges Gurvitch, who champions intuition and legal pluralism against Kelsen's formalism, teaches that the moral relation is 'purely spiritual', whereas the legal relation is both 'perceivable'[19] (when it takes the form of constraint, etc.) and 'spiritual'. In addition, codified law is formalized in a logical manner whereas morality is not. But Gurvitch's second criterion has nothing absolute about it; even in spontaneous 'moral experience', the rational element plays an indisputable role. As for the first criterion, that the morality of a phenomenological, intuitionist philosopher is purely spiritual we will not doubt. But we fear that Gurvitch has never looked at a child nor thought about so-called primitive tribes. Unless the educative constraint that weighs on children, and the constraints from taboos that are the essential part of morality for primitive tribes are both to be considered to be of an exclusively legal order ...

Finally, let us raise the interesting viewpoint of Timacheff, author of an *Introduction to the sociology of law*. Of the works we currently possess in this young discipline, his relies least on words and most on empirical evidence.[20] [p. 186] For Timacheff, there are different forms of power in society. Some of these forms of power can be recognized by the conscience of the community, whereas others (like pure despotism) have no validity[21] in themselves. On the other hand there are 'ethical convictions' which emanate from individual consciences and imply duty as an irreducible reality. Law in Timacheff's conception is constituted as the intersection of these two kinds of reality. It is the system of powers that are morally recognized, that is, sanctioned by the ethical convictions of the group. The essential difference between law and morality would then be that law is morality accompanied by power. No matter how solid his detailed analyses often are (and his work abounds with them), Timacheff's central thesis seems to us to be difficult to support. We will not dwell on the arbitrariness of his distinction between powers that are not recognized morally and powers that have legal validity because they conform to the ethical convictions of the group – this distinction requires Timacheff to disqualify Oriental despotisms and certain contemporary revolutions from having any legal standing. Let us limit ourselves to pointing out the erroneous claim – one that we keep finding, with a slightly disconcerting regularity, from Roguin to Timacheff – that moral obligation is independent of all external authority or 'power'. And let us reiterate that the autonomous adult conscience is a recent, exceptional social product. The authority of a father over young children in the modern family based on marriage, the authority of a *pater familias*[22] over his sons of all ages under the patriarchal system, the authority of the elders over the members of the clan, etc. etc., cannot be considered to be of a purely legal nature. They certainly involve law in part but by the same token they are sources of authentically moral obligations. The whole problem thus remains: how to distinguish moral authority from legal power during the phases of heteronomy in which the same people may well exercise both, instead of their being clearly differentiated as has been progressively the case with the constitution of the State.

In conclusion, we observe that so many subtle distinctions, elaborated by authors whose theoretical systems are sometimes of considerable value, in reality mask a fundamental common ancestry between morality and law with regard to mechanism. Far from having given us a refined criterion for differentiating the two, this discussion of various doctrines ends up doing quite the contrary. It brings to light an astonishing [p. 187] parallelism in the details of moral and legal facts. Morality, like law, presupposes an initial power or authority, along with a possible transition from this heteronomy to an autonomy which in any case is always relative. Both morality and law rest on a creative construction consisting of the continued application and promulgation of norms. Both imply bilateral imperative-attributive relationships. Both oscillate between asymmetrical relationships (or hierarchy) and symmetrical relationships (or reciprocity). Could developmental[23] analysis bring some clarity to this debate?

III

From a developmental standpoint, a suitable place to start is with the elementary affective relationships that intervene in morality and law. When Petrazycki, who is followed in this by Gurvitch, speaks of 'legal emotions', 'legal convictions', or 'normative facts', these are feelings or sentiments shared among individuals. We must analyse these affective relationships at first in their own right; later we will move beyond this limited area to situate the problem of morality and law within the problem of social relationships in general.

To begin with, as far as moral facts are concerned, authors of the most diverse inspirations find themselves in agreement on one point – and proper heed should be taken of their unanimity. They agree that the inter-individual sentiment most characteristic of moral life is the feeling of 'respect'. Their disagreements come to light when we ask how respect and the moral law[24] are related. For Kant, respect is not the cause but the effect of the moral law. When we respect a person, we do so insofar as that person embodies this moral law. The sentiment that we feel in regard to that person is not addressed to his individuality as such, but to his quality of being subject to the moral law. But because for Kant the categorical imperative has no relationship whatsoever with anything that can be perceived, the fact that it can nonetheless trigger a unique sentiment of respect, one that is unlike any other feeling, thus remains 'inexplicable', as the great philosopher himself avowed. From a psycho-sociological point of view, the inexplicability of respect prevents us from retaining the Kantian interpretation. Emile Durkheim, as is well known, drew his initial inspirations from Kantianism but went on to translate the *a priori* into the terms of a collective conscience that transcends the individual. [p. 188] Durkheim accepts the idea that respect comes from the moral law. But since the moral law is, from his standpoint, the expression of the action of the group over individual consciences, it follows that respect for Durkheim is the characteristic sentiment that the individual feels in regard to those who embody discipline and collective values. Except that if we just instantiate those abstractions, 'the individual' and 'the group', in concrete terms, we will still find ourselves at the common point of departure for feelings of respect and effective moral obligations – a well-defined relationship between an adult who is educating a child and the child being educated. It is only in this arena that we can hope to isolate the initial relationships between respect and the moral law.

It is here that Pierre Bovet's discovery shows its worth (see Author's Note [6]). Contrary to Kant, Bovet argues that from a developmental standpoint respect precedes the moral law. Respect is the complex sentiment, a combination of fear and affection, experienced in regard to a superior individual by an individual who feels inferior. It is precisely because small children experience respect for adults that they accept their orders, commands and examples, and these become obligatory – moral norms, or the moral law, have their origin in respect and do not explain it. For our part, we have tried to show that later, in the framework prepared by this unilateral respect, mutual respect becomes possible. Mutual respect explains autonomous norms of reciprocity just as unilateral respect causally accounts for heteronomous norms of obedience and duty.[25]

Let us now pose the problem in the same terms in the field of the sociology of law. Here we are concerned with the origin of a legal right or obligation, as opposed to a moral one. Is respect to be found here as well? What kind of respect? If not, what other sort of elementary sentiment?

We say 'respect a law' or 'respect the rights of others' or even 'have respect for one's obligations' but everyone immediately feels that this sort of respect is entirely different from moral respect for a person or an act. To begin with, if one respects the law, one does not respect the legislator in the same sense. One respects his decisions, which is something different. Similarly, if one respects a magistrate, one does so by virtue of collective symbolism that has nothing specifically legal about it, whereas respect for the magistrate's rulings is mixed up with the feeling of being legally obliged by them. [p. 189] In short, talk of respect in the legal domain involves an extension of the meaning of this concept. It has to do with another sentiment, though one undoubtedly related to moral respect. The important task is to analyse exactly how 'legal respect' resembles moral respect and how it differs from it.

Now two different groups of authors agree in speaking of the 'recognition' of rights, as though the fact of 'recognizing' its validity constituted the essence of respect for the law. This is true whether they seek to describe the sources of law in psychological or sociological terms or offer a purely normative account, whether they proceed from subjective data (individual or collective) or reject the whole notion of 'subjective law'. In an exact parallel with what we have seen in the moral arena, the divergence between these two groups shows up only on questions of origins. For those who adopt a psychological or sociological approach, it is recognition that entails the validity of a norm and in consequence its normative or obligatory character. For the normativists, it is the norm, itself regarded as a given, that inspires in people's consciences the sentiment of its recognition. (In this regard the members of the first camp, like Petrazycki and Gurvitch, play the same role in this debate as Pierre Bovet; Kelsen plays Kant's role!)

Let us start with the relation that Petrazycki defines in his psychological interpretation of legal facts: *A* recognizes that he has an obligation towards *B*, which translates on *B*'s part to a right that he has over *A*. It follows directly that if the legal relationship is a real-life relationship, as the great Polish philosopher wants it to be – or a legal 'emotion', as his translators even say, the source of 'normative facts' prior to all codification – then it will be necessary to interpret the obligation that *A* experiences toward *B* as a consequence of the fact that *A* recognizes *B*'s right. Without this prior recognition, the obligation would be incomprehensible; to speak concretely, obligation is confounded with recognition of the other's right, and only becomes differentiated from it as a secondary projection.[26] Indeed, it is this elementary sentiment of recognizing the right of another person that Gurvitch keeps finding when, following Petrazycki, he tries to get at the 'specific legal experience', i.e. the immediate lived experience, as opposed to any construction. The only point on which Gurvitch disagrees with his teacher is that he interprets immediate legal experience, not in individualistic language, but in terms of communal relationships.[27] [p. 190] But in his chosen arena, Gurvitch still finds that legal experience reduces to the 'the set of all acts of recognition taken together'.[10] Before any codification or intellectual coordination has taken place, it is still the case that no one can live with others without 'recognizing' their rights. It is thus that independently of any rendition into formal rules, each member of society 'intuitively recognizes' a new association to which that person adheres and thereby undertakes the obligation not to destroy or abandon.[11] Recognition is thus an elementary legal sentiment; it is an 'intuitive act', not a 'reflective' one, something given instead of constructed.

Those doctrines that explain law by reference to social constraint make no less of an appeal to 'recognition', which is the only thing that allows them to distinguish law from force. As Thurnwald has stated so profoundly in his celebrated studies of legal organization in primitive societies, 'constraint when recognized transforms custom into law'. In other words, brute constraint or pure force has no legal value *per se*. It is thus that the will of the conqueror cannot be considered valid by the vanquished as long as the vanquished has not recognized defeat. But constraint, once 'recognized', transforms a *de facto* obligation into a *de jure* (legal) obligation.

We must still deal with the normativists, for whom the recognition of a right derives from the existence of a norm and does not explain it. Kelsen has defended this point of view with considerable elegance. He shows that in international law one can consider a State to be under obligation by common norms only if it recognizes them. And it goes without saying that in the field of codified law, laid down by the State, subjective recognition carries no weight in determining validity. But though this normativist position is perfectly coherent with the status that we have already attributed to it *qua* axiomatic system of law, one might wonder whether the same claim could be maintained about the 'basic norm', the one that at some point or other must connect the axiomatic system with the actual world. What indeed is a basic norm that first assures the validity of the supreme norms of the State (constitutions) if not precisely the abstract expression of the fact that society 'recognizes' the established legal order as [p. 191] valid? We thus follow Kelsen without difficulty when he radically dissociates pure legal theory from sociology, axiomatic system from the actual world, once the basic norm has been laid down. And we will acknowledge that for all other norms, the pure legal construction of 'applications' and 'promulgations' rests on a system of implications (or 'imputations') in which recognition has no function. But we doubt that the basic norm can itself remain 'pure'. We appeal here to recognition as the only possible intermediary between society and Law in the abstract. No doubt the formulators of axiomatic systems have a duty to cut this umbilical cord in order to free their rational constructions from any empirical attachments. But it is the sociologist's job to remember that there was such a cord and that it played a highly significant role in nourishing the law in its embryonic stage!

Developmentally, we can thus conclude that law depends on recognition, just as in morality respect precedes obligation. From the standpoint of individual development, a child recognizes the validity of adult authority before having a notion of rules, just as he respects his parents before being obliged by precise duties. Sociologically, societies had to recognize the power of the elders and the authority of older generations over younger ones before they could constitute well-defined systems of law and morality. Recognition thus figures as a primary fact in the sociology of law, paralleling respect in the sociology of ethics. Would it not be possible to simplify the problem of the relationships between morality and law by analysing the relationships between respect and recognition? That is the issue to which we now turn.

First of all, it is clear that the recognition of a power that is felt to be valid cannot precede respect in the course of development, because it is a more intellectualized and abstract sentiment than respect is. Rather, recognition must follow respect or develop contemporaneously with it; recognition would then differentiate out of respect, or both would arise from a common source. But respect is a sentiment of one individual toward another. It expresses the value attributed by a person who feels inferior to a person that he judges superior (unilateral respect) or the value attributed reciprocally by one person to another (mutual respect). Respect is thus an essentially personal sentiment; that is, [p. 192] it evaluates a person as such, well differentiated from other individuals and considered as a unique whole. By contrast the recognition of an authority, a right, or a law, etc., is an impersonal sentiment, involving no evaluation of a person as an individual distinct from other individuals, but rather a 'function' or a 'service', that is, a particular abstract aspect of the person. This is why the recognition of a right cannot be thought of except by way of differentiation from respect for a person, whether it derives directly from respect or whether it is less differentiated from it in the initial phases than it will be later.

For instance, one can obey a man because of his personal authority; in this case there will be respect and obligation of a moral order. But if one complies with his orders because he is the leader, one is simply recognizing a function and the obligation points in a direction that differentiates itself from submission to a moral authority; whether a moral obligation also accompanies this recognition does not matter here. One can be grateful for a service that has been rendered and return the service in order to convey one's gratitude. One can also, by virtue of an agreement, recognize the partner's rights independently of what one might feel in this regard. In the first case, the relationship is personal and springs from mutual respect; in the second, it presupposes no more than the recognition of a debt (as opposed to gratitude which is recognition in a personal sense). One can avoid harming one's neighbour because he is one's neighbour, because the sentiments one feels in this regard are person-to-person. One can also act in the same manner while limiting oneself to recognizing rights analogous to one's own *qua* member of the same community; in this case the recognition of a right is relative to a function of the person and is quite different from respect for the person as such.

In short, in each of these cases and in every analogous example, it is easy to distinguish two poles from the standpoint of inter-individual values. Either the person is valued as such and the sentiment at issue is one of respect (unilateral or mutual) or a function or service is evaluated and the sentiment is one of recognition of a right (based on authority or reciprocity). The words 'function' and 'service' here must be understood in the broadest sense, and naturally the negative cases (like damages or infractions of the law) have to be kept in mind as well as the positive ones. We understand 'function' or 'service' to mean [p. 193] any activity on the part of the individual that is characterized either by that individual's position in the group (function) or in an inter-individual exchange (service) and that thus engages only one side of his personality,[28] not its value as a whole. From this standpoint, moral facts are to be characterized by person-to-person relationships and legal facts, even prior to any codification, by relationships of function and service. Moral respect is a sentiment of a personal order; the recognition of a right is a sentiment that tends to move beyond the boundary of the personal sphere toward the impersonal.

But there is no way that we can be satisfied with a psychological criterion, let alone an affective one, when we want to be able to distinguish the elements involved with the precision of a formal definition suitable for an axiomatic system. The analysis of sentiments can only serve as a preliminary. Now it is a matter of discovering how to develop further this distinction between moral 'personality' and legal 'functions' and 'services'. It is thus useful to distinguish what moralists consider to be personal and what those jurists who believe in subjective law – contrary to the undoubtedly definitive analyses of normativism – call legal personality. It would be a notably poor response to say that moral personality encompasses the totality of the individual self, whereas the functions or services that seemingly express legal personality cover only an aspect of the entire individual. Criteria for wholes and parts would still have to be furnished in this domain where material comparisons are mere metaphors.

Yet in the presence of seemingly insurmountable difficulties, perhaps close attention to these very obstacles would enable us to come out with a positive argument. It is an interesting fact – and one that may not have been sufficiently stressed – that the law has been capable of being codified to the point that legal positivists confine themselves to the part that has been rendered into formal rules. Morality, on the other hand, has not given rise to any codification that is even distantly comparable to a system of laws. This is not because morality is less complex; as Roguin says, nothing is indifferent to it. Nor is it because no one has tried to codify morality – moral codes are legion. The trouble with all of these moral codes is that either they remain at a level of generality which contrasts starkly with legal precision, or they sink into casuistry. The true formulation of Christian morality[29] is what [p. 194] in its impressive clarity and simplicity Christ laid down as a synthesis of all possible particular duties: to love your neighbour as yourself and to love God as a Father. 'Such are the Law and the Prophets'. So what is the source of this contrast between the relatively non-formulable character of moral rules and the limitless codification of legal rules, if it does not lie precisely in the opposition between the simple unity of the person and the multiplicity of functions and services? To tackle this question from a formal standpoint, focusing on how morality lacks fertility with regard to codification whereas the possibilities of codification in law are unbounded, we must dissociate the personal character of morality from the impersonal, or – as we shall soon see more exactly – the transpersonal character of the law.

Let us work from a concrete example. A specific child *A* respects his father *B*. The particular nuances of each one's individuality and their parent–child relationship entail habitual consequences – *A* will respect *B*'s commands and obey them – while bringing it about that neither the respect nor the commands nor the obedience will be exactly identical to those that obtain between other parents and children. Even at this elementary level of moral life, the same child will set quite different duties, in relation to his father's values, for himself to perform the same actions. He will reproach himself for the same failings in very different ways depending on the context shaped by his education. One and the same lie, told to an authoritarian father or a weak one, to an insincere father or an honest one who trusts the child, is not morally the same lie. Conversely, for the same father, the same acts coming from children of different temperaments would not be morally identical. In short, there are as many distinct moral relationships as there are situations[12] and to know them objectively we must be able to 'test the heart and the mind', to use a Biblical expression.[30] Let us suppose now that the same son *A* and father *B*, some time later, have changed their moral relationship and now find themselves in the following situation: *A*, for some reason or other, having to do with himself, his father, or both, now has a changed opinion of *B* and no longer feels the moral respect that used to make his father's commands obligatory for him. [p. 195] Notwithstanding this change of mind, he continues to obey, but simply because he recognizes that his father has the right to issue commands. On the inside, he judges his father from a detached perspective and no longer is morally obliged by a respect he no longer feels. Nonetheless he believes (not out of fear, but from a somewhat depersonalized judgment) that because he is the son and *B* is his father, his father has the right to decide and he has the obligation (no longer moral but well on the way to being purely legal) to obey. In normal cases, of course, it goes without saying that recognizing a father's rights does not necessarily entail a diminution of moral respect; we have chosen this example in which respect and recognition are dissociated to enable us to give a better formulation of the difference between them.

How, then, do we define the difference between the moral, 'personal' relationship between a son *A* and his father *B* and the simple recognition by the son *A* of the right that *B* possesses insofar as he fulfils the 'function' of being a father? Well, to put it simply, in the moral relationship the terms *A* and *B* cannot be substituted for each other. That is, there are always an individualized *A* and an individualized *B*, each endowed with unique qualities and a unique value. Whereas in the legal relationship *A* and *B* are substitutable for any other terms defined by the same functions, and are thus replaceable by any son whatsoever or any father whatsoever. Let us note right away that this opposition does not in any way mean that there are no general duties in practice (for instance, a child will always obey his parent). All we are saying is that moral relationships in which the same norm intervenes are never identical to one another because this very norm is in reality differently constituted, depending on the individuals who participate in the relationship. What the norm really amounts to is a class of analogous norms, which are unboundedly differentiated.[31] By contrast, the legal obligation incumbent on a child to obey a parent is definable in such a manner that the norm can remain identical over an indefinite number of situations. In consequence, we say that moral value is not substitutable from one relationship to another, even when the circumstances are equivalent from an external perspective. To one and the same act there can correspond merits and demerits that are infinitely varied and unanalysable from outside, as well as from the standpoint of the interested parties themselves, because of lack of introspection. Finally, moral obligations appear never to be completely fulfilled; the more [p. 196] delicate the conscience the greater the gap between real actions and ideal duties, precisely because these duties are multifarious and their internal construction is never completed. By contrast, a legal norm can be fulfilled completely, and even if infractions give rise to appraisals whose variety is somewhat like that of moral judgments, the absence of an action that violates the norm is equivalent to its complete fulfilment. Thus, fulfilment of a legal norm takes on a constant positive value that can be appraised objectively and substituted for equivalent values.

In short, the boundary between the moral domain and the legal domain, and therefore between persons and functions or services, is to be sought in the substitutability or non-substitutability of individuals taken as terms of the relationship. This amounts to saying that a legal personality always designates an x that could be replaced by a y whereas morally persons x and y remain irreducible. It becomes understandable straightaway why law is codifiable to an indefinite degree whereas a moral principle like loving one's neighbour cannot specify the multiplicity of its applications in advance. But though such a criterion might work empirically, its meaning[32] still needs to be extracted, that is, situated in an over-arching interpretation.

For this purpose let us borrow from a Russian sociologist (S. Franck, cited by Timacheff) the essential notion of *transpersonal* relationships. Let there be, for instance, a group of three individuals A, B, and C. There could be a personal relationship between A and B, and similarly between B and C or between A and C, because A's will and B's will are directly involved in the relationship $A–B$, B's will and C's will are involved in $B–C$, and A's will and C's will are involved in $A–C$. But from A's point of view, the $B–C$ relationship will be referred to as 'transpersonal' because it is independent of A's own will; the same holds for $A–B$ from C's point of view, and for $A–C$ from B's point of view. For three individuals it will thus be necessary to distinguish three possible personal relationships and three transpersonal relationships. In general, transpersonal relationships will be generated for each individual according to the formula $N(N-1)-(N-1)$; in a group of 100 individuals there will already be 4,851 transpersonal relationships.[33]

It follows that in the mechanism of evaluation and the construction of norms, transpersonal relationships play just as important a role as personal relationships. To the extent [p. 197] that A is bound to B and to C by personal relationships, A must take heed of the transpersonal relationship $B–C$ just as he takes heed of a value in which he participates. That is why, as Timacheff clearly shows, in a given social group, even if some individual does not personally submit to the ascendancy of a leader, he is still obliged to bow before the set of relationships – transpersonal from his standpoint – which bind the other individuals in the group to that leader. Hence the preponderant weight, in the formation of public opinion, of transpersonal relationships as opposed to personal ones (of which there are only $N-1$ for each individual).

Our hypothesis consists then in simply acknowledging that whereas moral evaluations are tied to personal relationships, legal evaluations are fixed by the mechanism of transpersonal relationships. The 'recognition of a right' is nothing but respect that has become generalized into something transpersonal, and it is from that generalization that the 'substitutability' of persons in legal relationships is derived. In what follows we define 'transpersonal' relationships without further ado by the substitutability of their terms and 'personal' relationships by their non-substitutability.

Let us again examine from this standpoint a moral relationship between two individuals, A and B, in the same group and a legal relationship of analogous form, like a contract between *C* and *D*. It follows directly that, beyond the direct acquaintance that *A* and *B* or *C* and *D* might have with the relationships in which they are interested, these relationships can give rise to an unbounded series of transpersonal judgments. On what criterion will we then define the relationship between *A* and *B* as simply moral and the contract between *C* and *D* as simply legal – when both could have the same object and could even be stated using the same clauses? It is that in a contract, even if the contracting parties remain unknown to the other members of the social group, their obligations remain identical regardless of whose point of view they might be judged from. 'If there has been an undertaking written in good and due form .... If there has been no fraud .... If the undertaking is not contradictory with any of the established laws .... If all of the conditions of a valid contract are fulfilled', then *C* and *D* are subject to obligations whose validity will be recognized by each party [p. 198] or sanctioned by government agencies that each 'recognizes'. The contract thus belongs to the transpersonal order, even if it constitutes an 'individualized norm', established by the two contracting parties themselves. What makes it an individualized norm is its place in a series of other norms that interest each of the parties in the same way (such as the code of civil obligations). It can be seen just how its transpersonal character is precisely equivalent to the substitutability of the terms of the relationship: if *C* and *D*'s reciprocal obligation is recognized by everyone, it is because it would be the same for *X* and *Y*. Let us examine by contrast the promise between *A* and *B* – is it the same thing? Undoubtedly, if *A* seems not to keep his word and *B* becomes indignant about it, the entire group or part of it may intervene in this case as well, with blame, criticism, and other 'diffuse sanctions'. But will truth be on their side? Will *A* and *B*, who know the situation from the inside, see things as everyone else does, without ever having the occasion to deceive others' opinions or fall victim to them? Yes, there is a general moral norm, 'You ought to keep your word', but are we certain that *A* did not keep his? And what is the relationship between the particular case of *A* and *B* and this general norm? The true moral obligation felt by *A* and *B* remains known only to themselves. Or in any case they judge it differently from its transpersonal reverberations. What is involved is a 'personal' relationship, which is the same as saying, 'a relationship whose terms cannot be substituted for others'. Finally, *A* and *B*'s moral norms doubtless come to be situated, just as legal norms are, in an indefinite series of higher norms. These higher norms are all of those that *A* and *B* have received during their education. But these higher norms are still of a personal order, even if they end up depending, more and more closely, on ethical norms that originally belonged to the common ancestors of the group. For each present member of the group has borrowed part of the substance of these ancestral norms and reworked it in his own way.

In short, the criterion of substitutability of terms for a legal relationship and non-substitutability for a moral relationship must be interpreted so as to direct us to the explanation or the reason for this essential difference. Law is constituted as the entire set of transpersonal normative relationships in a society; morality is the entire set of [p. 199] personal normative relationships.[13] This conception has the additional value of allowing us to make contact with the well-known distinction between law as laid down by the State ('positive law'), which will be defined as the 'total transpersonal', and the systems of duties or codified rules which are of interest only to smaller collectivities within a society, which could be called the 'partial transpersonal'. In the field of morality, however, we run up against the Kantian problem of 'universality', which we have already encountered. It is best to confront this problem now.

In distinguishing morality from law by drawing a contrast between personal relationships with non-substitutable terms and transpersonal relationships with substitutable terms, are we not sacrificing morality to law? And are we not rendering incomprehensible the 'universality' by which one of the greatest of all moral philosophers defined the categorical imperative? We should note first of all that not all of his successors agreed with Kant on this issue. Significantly, he was often accused of 'legalism' on this very point, as if he had been led to conflate the legal with the moral. That is the gist of Rauh's critique, which pits the particularization of 'moral experiences' against general rules. But there is still an essential truth in the Kantian thesis. It is that a moral norm adopted by one individual with regard to another cannot contradict those that the first individual applies in his dealings with a third person, etc. Nor can this norm contradict those that he wants others to apply to him. This is the essential meaning of moral universality – it is not necessarily a 'general' rule (besides, it is well known that in logic "universal" and "general" do not mean the same thing) but the internal coherence of actions or their reciprocity. Now in this regard it is sufficient for us that moral judgments are capable of being grouped, for as we have endeavoured to show elsewhere,[14] the *groupement* of moral values assures both their non-contradiction and at the same time the indefinite extension of their reciprocity, always provided this is understood in the positive sense, to mean that the grouping of moral values has conservation properties. It does not mean the negative reciprocity of the Law of Talion.[34]

This point leads us to note in addition that the criterion that we have proposed here for differentiating between law and morality converges with the one [p. 200] we were satisfied with in the paper already cited (see Chapter 2, this volume). There we maintained that moral relationships consist of an exchange of disinterested values because each of the partners takes the other's point of view in adopting his scale of values. We stated that legal relationships are based on a simple conservation of acquired values, from the standpoint of a common or general scale of value (i.e. common law or the legal code). It can be seen immediately that these are the same propositions, just stated in another language. The reciprocity of points of view that makes the moral relationship disinterested is implied by relationships of personal respect, whereas transpersonal recognition is sufficient for the conservation of values from the standpoint of a general scale. There is thus a *groupement* of values in both cases, but not of the same values.

Now that we have our criterion of the non-substitutable personal and the substitutable transpersonal, we can retain and complete what is essential in the distinctions defined by the authors that we examined in Part II (we were obliged to reject their distinctions as inadequate on their own). When Roguin opposes the 'internal punishments' of morality to the external authority of the law, all that is needed is to recast his conception of interiority; we can then recognize that remorse and repentance are personal sentiments, inherent in the moral domain, and are to be distinguished from transpersonal constraints. When Kelsen distinguishes content from form, it is perhaps the unlimited fecundity of codification by substitution that he is thinking of. Thus he opposes transpersonal rule systems to the lived character of personal relationships (which does not prevent personal relationships from having a normative form). Similarly we would agree with Petrazycki if instead of speaking of the 'attributive' character of the legal relationship and the non-attributive character of the moral relationship, he put the emphasis on the pure recognition inherent in the legal relationship, as opposed to respect. And we agree with Gurvitch that the logical formalization of law as a system of rules is opposed to the logic of morality, as long as he understands the logic of law to be a process of generalization by substitutions that unceasingly transcend the personal sphere. Finally, we would be quite close to Timacheff if he limited legal authority to the transpersonal relationships that he describes so well, and recognized the existence of distinctively moral authority. In short, the criterion at which we have arrived allows us to reunite all of the scattered elements of the solution that have been offered so many times, instead of discarding or overlooking them. [p. 201]

But one essential point still deserves notice. Though the opposition between the unsubstitutable personal and the substitutable transpersonal may constitute a well-defined criterion, it does not exclude in the slightest the possible mutual influence of law on morality or of morality on law. Instances of the influence of law on morality are quite clear: they are manifest in the tendency toward 'legalism' that has been noted in Kant and that shows up again in every moralist once he tries to extend his experience of the universal (understood in the sense of necessary internal coherence) into too broad a framework. As for the effects of moral life on the law, they are especially noticeable in the domain of punishment, principally in the systematic tendencies (albeit quite recently in the history of social sanctions) to individualize punishments and to acknowledge extenuating circumstances. However, as we must point out once again with care, no matter how similar penal and moral considerations might sometimes look, there is always the essential difference that moral values do not allow substitution. In judging a parricide, the jurist starts with the essential fact that there is *a* father and *a* son and only later looks into what circumstances could have extenuated this monstrous crime. Whereas the moralist, before judging, asks first of all *which* father and *which* son, and, perhaps out of inability to penetrate incomprehensible mentalities that lie on the borderline between the normal and the pathological, may not feel able to judge the case in depth.

Finally it goes without saying that while law and morality are distinguished from each other in civilized societies according to the criterion we have been led to select, in so-called 'primitive' societies, these two systems of norms are much closer to each other than is the case among us. That is because personal and transpersonal relationships are much less differentiated in societies that have a low population density and are segmented into many subgroups than is the case in voluminous, dense societies like our own. Indeed, 'primitive' moralities are much more legalistic than ours, and, conversely, primitive law remains impregnated with many more elements of mysticism and moral respect than is the case when the law splits off with its own independent techniques. What are the reasons for this difference?

First it must be remarked that because the elementary moral relationships are relationships between the elders and young people, [p. 202] and because the social organization of the clan or the primitive family is based entirely on a hierarchy of age groups, the 'personal relationships' distinctive to morality are much less diversified and much more homogeneous in such societies than in modern ones. Mutual respect and autonomy for individuals are subordinated or even partly thwarted by unilateral respect and heteronomy. In consequence, primitive morality presents a much higher degree of unity and generality than would be found in modern societies, which moves it closer to legalism and to the law. Moreover, for lack of psychological differentiation between individuals (economic division of labour, etc.) and of personal freedom of action, moral responsibility retains, as Fauconnet has shown, a collective and external or 'objective' character, which gives taboos a status somewhere between moral rules and legal rules.

Conversely, in a society that is much less dense, and in which the members of the clan form a big family, all of whose members know each other individually, transpersonal relationships are far less dissociated psychologically from personal relationships than is the case in societies that are both voluminous and differentiated. It follows that legal rules are much less distinct from moral rules and that 'recognition' of the legal order does not get completely dissociated from personal 'respect' for the ancestors, elders, and chiefs who are its agents. That is why, in the beginning, morality, law, and religion are part of a complex totality and differ only in nuances.[15]

By contrast, as societies grow in volume and density, and the economic division of labour and psychological differentiation between individuals follow as necessary consequences, the contrast between personal and transpersonal relationships grows ever stronger. It is to this precise extent that legal recognition, or respect turned transpersonal, is dissociated from moral respect. Thus law is dissociated from morality and both are dissociated from their common trunk, religion, which is the generalization on the supernatural plane of the most basic personal relationships.

AUTHOR'S NOTES

[1] Starting at age 6 or 7 in normal children.
[2] For example, 'Pacta sunt servanda [agreements must be kept]'. And what would the *pacta* be that were not *servanda*?

[3] Or by custom, as in Great Britain, but a custom recognized in the jurisprudence of government courts.

[4] E. Roguin, *La Science juridique pure* (Paris–Lausanne, 1923, p. 134).

[5] Roguin (1923), p. 138.

[6] See notably Pierre Bovet, 'La genèse de l'obligation de conscience', *L'Année psychologique* (1912), and Jean Piaget, *Le Jugement moral chez l'enfant* (Paris: Alcan, 1932). In English, *The moral judgment of the child*, (London: Routledge & Kegan Paul, 1932).

[7] See the 'Essay on the theory of qualitative values in static sociology', Chapter 2, this volume.

[8] In truth we read neither Russian nor Polish and cite this example only on the authority of Pitirim A. Sorokin, *Les Théories sociologiques contemporaines*, trans. Verrier, (Paris: Payot, 1938).

[9] See 'Essay on the theory of qualitative values in static sociology', Chapter 2, this volume.

[10] *Expérience juridique*, p. 72.

[11] Ibid., p. 68.

[12] Psychoanalysts who, with indefatigable patience, find in each new individual case the same parental complexes and the same problems with family relationships, know well enough that no two situations are ever identical.

[13] We speak advisedly of personal 'relationships', because this does not take us out of the inter-individual realm and does not in any case get us into the purely internal 'human nature' of classical systems of psychology.

[14] 'Essay on the theory of qualitative values in static sociology', Chapter 2, this volume.

[15] It has even been claimed that the only 'law' in force in some archaic societies consisted of the Ten Commandments and other sacred codes, which were both legal and moral.

TRANSLATION NOTES

1 French, *mœurs*.

2 Some philosophers would use the phrase 'strictly causal' here, but whether efficient-causal relationships between logically independent states of affairs constitute a stricter sort of causal relationship is itself subject to dispute.

3 Piaget is referring to the transitivity of equality, which according to his theory of cognitive development is not understood until the concrete operational period. Piaget does not, of course, deny the practical mastery (*réussir* or *success*) of the transitivity of equality during the early years of childhood. But practical mastery is not understanding (*comprendre*) – see Piaget's *Success and understanding* (London: Routledge & Kegan Paul, 1978). For Piaget's operational account, see *The psychology of intelligence* (London: Routledge & Kegan Paul, 1950, Chapter 5) and Translation Note 1 to Chapter 3, this volume.

4 French, *droit*. In this translation, *loi* and *droit* are translated as *law*.

5 Literally, *meilleur* (*better*).

6 'Limit toward which versus limit from which'.

7 That is, a solution in terms of development toward more complete or advanced levels of equilibrium in society. Equilibration was central to Piaget's epistemology and his developmental psychology as well as his sociology.

8 Piaget habitually writes *nos sociétés* or 'our societies'.

9 Piaget's references to *l'État* are translated as 'the State' or 'government' depending on the context.

10 In American Indian tribes of the Northwest, the potlatch was a ceremony in which

a person gave away furs, copper slabs, and other conspicuous signs of wealth (and sometimes destroyed items that could not be given away) in order to increase his status in the community.

11   Piaget frequently uses the term *réglements (réglementé, réglementation)* which can be translated as 'regulations' in the legal sense. But because *régulation* is a technical term in Piaget's theory of cognitive development and is always translated 'regulation', 'rule systems' is used instead, in the interest of avoiding confusion. Piaget also uses *codifié* on occasion; this is translated as 'codified'.

12   Reading *les effets de la conscience morale collective* (literally, *the effects of the collective moral conscience*) instead of *les effets et la conscience morale collective*.

13   Literally, *psychogénétique (psychogenetic)*. See Translation Note 1 to Chapter 1. Piaget also uses *psychogénétique (psychogenetic)* and *psychologie génétique (genetic psychology)* on numerous occasions. 'Development' and 'developmental psychology' have comparable meanings.

14   The term that Piaget uses is *consignes*, which is used in French for military orders and the like. This is normally translated as 'commands'. However, in the case of moral authority figures more distant in time and place than parents and teachers, 'commandments' is used instead.

15   The text reads *ce sollen sui generis* (literally, *that ought of its own kind*). This trilingual phrase puts the finishing touches on a convoluted sentence.

16   Though Piaget treats the analyses of Kelsen and Petrazycki as compatible, Kelsen would have rejected Petrazycki's enterprise. Thanks to Daniel Wueste for this point.

17   Literally, *sui generis* or *of its own kind*.

18   Literally, *a verification as a function of results*. Piaget generally characterized empirical testing as verification.

19   Literally, *sensible*, if this term is read in the old-fashioned philosophical sense as 'knowable through sense perception'.

20   Literally, *is the least verbal and and the most positive*. Piaget is using 'positive' to mean empirical and non-metaphysical.

21   *Validité*, in the context of Kelsen's philosophy of law, is properly translated as 'validity'. It is not to be confused with validity as a logical property of forms of inference; in fact, in the legal positivist tradition it is possible for laws that contradict one another to be valid, so long as they have the proper pedigree. Though 'legitimacy' would avoid the confusion with deductive logic, it would not be satisfactory because it has moral overtones that Kelsen and his followers wish to avoid. It is also to be noted that 'individualized norms' in Kelsen's scheme are not deduced from more basic norms; they are derived via the practical syllogism, which for Kelsen does not constitute deduction in the strict sense because it involves norms and not factual propositions. Thanks to Daniel Wueste for advice on these points.

22   (Male) head of family.

23   French, *génétique (genetic)* is translated as *developmental*. The French term is an adjective, corresponding to the noun *genèse (genesis)*. Piaget makes frequent use of these cognate terms: see Translation Note 1 to Chapter 1.

24   In this passage, Piaget falls into a Kantian way of speaking about 'the moral law' (sometimes *la loi normative* or the normative law, other times *la loi morale*) which is not to be confused with the law as such. 'Moral rules' might be a more perspicuous translation of what Piaget has in mind but it would dispel the Kantian ambiance.

25   See Piaget's book *The moral judgment of the child* (London: Routledge & Kegan Paul, 1932) and the other chapters in the present volume, especially Chapters 5 and 6.

26 See Piaget's model of recognition and obligation in Chapter 2 of this volume.

27 The term in French is *rapports communautaires*. Piaget adds that these are to be understood in terms of inter-individual 'communion' rather than community in the usual sense.

28 See Chapter 6, Section V, this volume.

29 See Piaget's early works, including *Recherche* (Lausanne: La Concorde, 1918) and 'La Psychologie et les valeurs religieuses', in Association Chrétienne d'Etudiants de la Suisse Romande (ed.) *Sainte-Croix 1922*, pp. 38–82, 1923.

30 Literally, *sonder les reins et les cœurs*, or 'test the kidneys and the hearts', but idiomatically translated as 'test the hearts and minds'. To complicate matters, Piaget gives *souder* (unite) for *sonder* (examine) here – obviously a misprint. The reference is to Jeremiah 11:20, 'O Lord of Hosts who art a righteous judge, testing the heart and the mind, I have committed my cause to thee'.

31 An alternative translation of this passage is *because this very norm is in reality differently understood by the individuals who participate in the relationship and so constitutes a class of analogous norms which are unboundedly differentiated.*

32 French, *signification*.

33 This is an error. According to Piaget's formula, there should be 100 (99) – 99 = 9,801 transpersonal relationships. However, the formula also yields 4 trans-personal relationships for 3 people (see Piaget's previous example), which suggests that the formula itself may be incorrect.

34 *Lex talionis* or 'An eye for an eye, a tooth for a tooth'. In this passage, Piaget is referring to his structural theory of concrete operations. The mutual adaptation of actions – such as an eye for an eye – does not require the common and shared acceptance of norms which are instantiated in those actions and for whose sake the actions are performed.

5   Genetic logic and sociology [1], [2]

[p. 203] The problem we propose to examine here can be put in the following way: do the operations by means of which we attain what rational consciousness calls truth depend on society and, if so, in what sense?

This is a perennial problem which Thales raised when he contrasted philosophical reflection with religious conformity and of which Parmenides of Elea was aware when he distinguished human opinion from true knowledge. The question is more current now than it ever was. The impetus given to the sociological study of knowledge by Durkheim[1] and Lévy-Bruhl[2] has been passed on to a group of eminent researchers. Even a sociology rather different in spirit from that of Durkheimism – that of V. Pareto – has not been able to avoid the problem, and the theory of 'residues' and 'derivations', which the author of *Traité de sociologie générale*[3] advances, attempts to provide such a solution (whether he was aware of it or not). German sociology, for example that of Max Scheler,[4] quite naturally has broached the same subject. In the second place, logicians and epistemologists have responded to these same sociologists. In 1899, Lalande[5] (in a work often cited),[6] contributed a rather detailed study of the relations between logic and sociology. Goblot[7] has taken a similar position. Brunschvicg[8] has devoted several insightful chapters of his later work to the diversity of sociological approaches.[9] In the third place, psychologists have focused their discussion on the level of individual development. Baldwin[10] (and especially Janet)[11] have [p. 204] returned our perspective to the socialization of thought; Charles Blondel[12] has provided a psychological translation of Durkheimism, and Delacroix,[13] on the other hand, has forcefully maintained the position of classical rationalism.

It may, therefore, appear somewhat unreasonable to try to add anything to what these great thinkers (from their divergent points of view) have already said. But nothing can be done today in psychology or sociology without encountering this same problem in a different guise. As limited as the realm of experience is, one always comes upon an unexpected point of view which is worth the trouble of situating in relation to other perspectives; this is valuable in completing our intellectual exploration of the social world, which no one can encompass in one over-arching view; indeed, as Durkheim has said, society extends far beyond all its aspects . . . .

I would like to approach these issues from the point of view of the socialization of the child. The development of the infant is an adaptation of its mind to its social and physical surroundings. Hence, one cannot speak of the child without asking if logic is something social and, if so, in what sense. I have been plagued by this question; I have attempted to discard it, but it has always returned. Without pretending to be original, therefore, I would like to indicate where these reflections, made during an extended study of the thought of the child, have led me. One will find few facts in these pages, but instead a theoretical orientation. I want it to be understood from the beginning that this stance is not the result of any *a priori* reflection but has been gradually imposed upon me after considerable groping and wrestling with experience. It is only because these facts are so easily forgotten that one may find some interest in this present essay.

I

Let us begin by clearing up an equivocation. When one asks if true reasoning depends on social life, one may adopt either a practical point of view – a valuational perspective – or a theoretical point of view concerning the genesis and mechanism of reasoning. It is this second point of view we adopt. However, one should also say something about the first [p. 205] in order to refute an objection which repeatedly arises, one which claims that any appeal to society in the explanation of true rationality is devastating for rationalism.

From the point of view of praxis, we develop the true because of an internal and irreducible experience, one which depends on the totality of value judgments which consciousness feels it is *obliged* to recognize, given certain conditions of information and reflection. There is, therefore, a *logical experience* strictly comparable to that of a 'moral experience', whose autonomous and constructive character has been admirably shown by Frédéric Rauh.[14]

None of this is altered by the sociological point of view. If one shows that the formation and elaboration of this internal experience is due to one's social life, then from the practical point of view, i.e. from the point of view of evaluating the true, it would still remain the ultimate criterion. Even if it were connected to belief or to collective norms, one is still referring to the same experience. It is by virtue of this experience that one always opposes his beliefs to that of another person or to general opinion, and consciousness always contrasts the universal to the collective, i.e. 'truth' to 'opinion'.

However, although one recognizes the normative autonomy of this logical experience, one ought to analyse its mechanism. The important thing to remember is that, in such an analysis, one cannot extract any new value from it. All the decisive conclusions that Rauh has made in order to extricate moral experience from 'moral theory' are also applicable here and allow one to distinguish the descriptive or analytic point of view from the normative or practical point of view. Psychological or sociological analysis prescribes nothing; it asks how logical consciousness comes to select its norms. But it is necessary to keep silent about the future course of this process. From the fact that one has always chosen in a certain way, it does not follow that one *ought* to continue to do this if circumstances happen to change. For it is always logical consciousness and not sociology that decides if this matters. From the practical point of view, therefore, nothing is altered by a sociological analysis.

It is, of course, difficult to move from facts to norms; hence 'psychologism' and 'sociologism' or, on the other hand, 'logicism',[15] all of which legislate under the guise of description (the first two under the guise of a description of the empirical mechanisms of logical experience, the third under the guise of the formal considered as creative and not merely as regulative). Against psychologism [p. 206] and sociologism, one should always affirm that the true is an ideal and hence one cannot reduce it to empirical laws. Against logicism, it is necessary to add that this ideal is not given once and for all, but is always in a state of development. One can thus ask how this development occurs. As a result, we must limit ourselves to the study of the mechanism of this development; it is this to which we must now turn.

II

The questions raised by the sociology of knowledge of Durkheim and Lévy-Bruhl are particularly difficult. One cannot approach a discussion of their views without bringing in their new kind of ethnographical data collection. Hence, we propose not to examine any of these well-known positions unless they are directly but inversely related to the question – impossible to avoid when dealing with the relations between logic and social life – of the invariance or variability of reason. In effect, even when we focus on the socialization of the child, we encounter this problem. Does the thought of the child differ in degree or in kind from that of the adult? If one discovers *sui generis* types of intellectual connections in the child, are these due to the absence of socialization or to the existence of a socially analogous relation belonging to less developed and conformist societies? Hence, the problem of the transformation of reason also arises for the thought of the child and is related, on this level as well as that of ethnographic sociology, to the question of the fundamental types of social relations.

One is well acquainted with the position Durkheim has taken on this question: reason is a social product, with truth constituting a collective norm just as the good or the just do; however, reason is uniform and invariant.

That reason is collective is attested to by a number of facts, some contemporary, others genetic. It is necessary to note, first of all, that language is more than a system of customs; it imposes on the individual a system of classification, a system of relations, in short, a logic. Naturally, language presupposes society. Second, concepts are a general and fixed means of exchange [p. 207] different from particular and changing mental images just as a social rule is contrary to an arbitrary individual one. In the third place, logical principles are moral principles which constrain consciousness without determining it, hence they attest to their character of being collective imperatives. From the genetic point of view, Durkheim has shown us how scientific reason proceeds from the collective mystique of less developed societies. The notions of cause, force, time and space, genus and species derive from religious notions whose structure is modelled on that of the group both under its material and spiritual aspects.

Moreover, and it is always a pleasure to recognize this, Durkheim has never inferred a rigid and intentionalistic rationalism from these premises. In spite of surface variations, which reflect a diversity of conscious realizations rather than a real evolution, reason is unitary. As opposed to Lévy-Bruhl, Durkheim has maintained that primitive mystical speculations are rational; in agreement with August Comte,[16] he has maintained that logic is the same in all societies.

However, if reason is one (although social), it is unitary because it is social. The constancy of our intelligence is assured by the fact that, under all the diverse types of social organization, there is a central nucleus common to all societies. As Fauconnet has said, with respect to the underlying unity of legal facts whose evolution he has so nicely described in detail, 'as diverse as civilizations may be, there is something which is civilization'.[3] It is civilization, in contrast to civilizations, that is the underlying basis of the invariance of human reason.

But here there are two interpretations, and as an examination of the texts seems to us to show, Durkheim has not been able to decide between them. At the risk of being overly schematic, we may formulate the difficulty in terms of a dilemma; it is the existence of this dilemma that seems to us to be the principal obstacle in the path of adopting an orthodox Durkheimism. Either reason is unitary because it is based upon the unity of social fact and thus the only guarantee of truth would be universal consent; or truth depends upon its own intrinsic guarantees, and thus one could not explain sociologically how consciousness successfully arrives at the truth since [p. 208] there is such a multitude of social processes, and this would amount to giving up the unity of social fact.

Durkheim is unclear on this point. He speaks both the language of universal consent and of the rational ideal. And even if the spirit of Durkheimism is more inclined toward the second of these interpretations, one would be able to retain this spirit only if, out of respect for him, one abandoned those formulas that incline one towards the former.

Consider universal consent. Durkheim often speaks as if reason contains no intrinsic criterion of truth. In any case, this is how Brunschvicg has interpreted his position, justifiably emphasizing the direct link which exists between certain pages in *Formes élémentaires de la vie religeuse* and the sociology of Bonald[17] and Joseph de Maistre.[18] The universal becomes the collective. The example usually cited here is the one mentioned by Brunschvicg: the notion of force.[4] In order to show that our rational ideals proceed from primitive mystical notions, Durkheim appeals, quite appropriately, to the idea of the dynamic causality of 'mana'.[19] But this argument can be turned back on itself, for ever since Descartes, the efficacy of the notion of force has been the scandal of physics and the effort of mechanics – which awaited the arrival of Einstein – has always been toward providing an explanation of gravitation that avoided the irrationality of action at a distance. However, Durkheim anticipated this objection by giving the rather astonishing reason that, since the notion of force has been recognized and accepted by all extant societies, it exists.[5] Consequently, this agreement trumps the opinion of physicists.

But this is not always the language of Durkheim and just because this penetrating, subtle and vigorous thinker made the remark that science does not depend on universal consent, one cannot take this as a refutation of his sociology of knowledge. In fact, most of the time Durkheim conceives of the true as an ideal in relation to collective consciousness. One can thus say of logic what is said of morality: '... the society which prescribes morality for us to will is not society [p. 209] as it appears in itself to be but society as it really is or inclines to be'.[6][20] In other words, truth is not a *de facto* law of society but a law of equilibrium that society attempts to attain without ever completely succeeding. Put somewhat differently, truth has nothing in common with opinion, for 'the awareness society has of itself in and through its opinion may be inadequate to the underlying reality'.[7] By contrast, here is an example opposed to that of force and 'mana': Socrates had good reason to be opposed to his judges who were the representatives of current opinion, for Socrates was clearly aware of this ideal equilibrium toward which society in his time was inclining.[8]

From this second aspect of Durkheimism, the argument from sociology often leads to the notion that we make the ideal intervene, an ideal conceivable only by autonomous reason, opposed to that of society. This is often claimed, since it is difficult to see how an awareness of this ideal can be conditioned by society. But here it is necessary to maintain (and this is the second horn of our dilemma) that any distinction between opinion and the ideal also presupposes a distinction between heterogeneous social processes. One can no longer speak of 'Society' when one is speaking carefully. It is always necessary to make clear what kind of society is at issue and the problem is to replace the mysterious 'whole' to which Durkheim repeatedly appeals (the 'whole' is not reducible to its 'parts') by basic and clearly defined social relations. Of course, this does not mean that social life does not transform the nature of the individual, nor that in this sense it is creative; it means only that the substantialist language of whole and part ought to be replaced by a language based on relations between individuals or individuals in groups.

From the point of view of the relations between logic and sociology, we are thus led to consider certain social processes as formative of the ideal, whereas others produce mandatory conformity to traditional opinion.

This leads us to the well-known perspective of Lévy-Bruhl[21] who, even if he has not tried to analyse these basic social processes, has studied their respective outcomes. To each type [p. 210] of social organization there corresponds a 'mentality', the mentality called primitive for conformist or segmented societies and rational mentality for our differentiated society. The unity of society, conceived as civilization underlying all civilizations, is thus severed. But, at the same time, rationalism, defined as the doctrine of the permanence of reason, is rejected. Reason is plastic, and diverse types of logical systematization are conceivable. Furthermore, these types are irreducible to each other and as a result, the evolution of reason is to be conceived as contingent. There is no necessary law of development, no 'orthogenesis': our logic comes after the prelogic of the primitive but if civilized societies had been oriented differently than they were, a third type of logic would have been born.

If we limit our reflections to what is suggested by the facts of genetic psychology, it is necessary to distinguish two questions – that of the diversity of mentality and the direction of intellectual evolution.

With regard to the first, we can only adopt the idea, so fruitful from a heuristic and theoretical point of view, of a qualitative difference between the various types of logical systematization. Reason is not given to individual consciousness once and for all; it gradually constructs itself. There are stages to mental life and when one overcomes the 'sophism of the implicit' (against which Baldwin warns), one may no longer be hindered from recognizing that the existence of our logical principles presupposes a prior work of elaboration, infinitely complex in which collective life has its own role to play.

Unfortunately here as elsewhere, language is unable to capture these psychological nuances and one may thus interpret the thesis of Lévy-Bruhl in different ways. The controversy opened up here – the question of whether all thought applies logical principles or not – runs the risk of perpetuating a misunderstanding if one does not carefully examine the meaning of the metaphors employed. It is necessary, therefore, to pause a moment to consider this point, so important for our purposes, for the question that always arises concerns the mental evolution of the child.

Logicians are accustomed to speak of the principle of contradiction as if it were a legal law, which by itself could foresee its own meaning and the extent of its application. But it is clear that the principle of contradiction does not apply itself in this way, for [p. 211] in and of itself, it does not indicate whether something is contradictory or not. We know in advance that, if A and B are contradictories, we must choose between them, but we do not know at the outset if they are. The principle of contradiction says nothing about this; in fact it is possible for us to have incorporated the two terms under the same concept without ever suspecting that this concept involved a contradiction. Thus, to repeat once again, not only does formal logic uniquely regulate the course of thought without creating knowledge, this regulation already presupposes two terms and a prior organization of these notions, and only then a formal application of the principles. In short, from the very beginning, this process inclines us to think in terms of an immanent equilibrium, one which realizes itself little by little as its jurisdiction is gradually determined externally.

If we attempt to describe these matters in psychological or biological terms which is perhaps more adequate to the life of thought than legal metaphors, we can distinguish two elements in the principle of contradiction – its *function* and its *structure* or organ.[9] This distinction has numerous advantages, since a function may be common to all the members of an evolutionary series, whereas the structure or organ may vary. For example, all living beings assimilate. Here is an immutable function essential for life. But some animals have a stomach, some do not, and the organs (structure) of assimilation vary indefinitely. Analogously, it may be that the function of the principle of contradiction is invariant in the course of mental evolution, whereas the organs of logical coherence vary. At least things seem to happen this way.

The function of the principle of contradiction is what can be called the search for coherence or the unity of thought. This function appears to us to be constant. Whenever there is thought, there is organization, and the function of this organization is to introduce unity. But in order to show how this function remains independent of what logicians call the principle of contradiction, we can go to the extreme and say that [p. 212] even in dreams and delusions this function remains the same as in logical thought. A dream, in effect, is an attempt to systematize all the diverse impressions which assail one's consciousness: kinesthetic or external sensations, feelings, etc. Suppose there is a dream: 'I am dead and yet not dead. There stands before me my friend X, who is himself and yet someone else. It is he who had killed me but I am not dead . . .', etc. In spite of the contradictory nature of these words and concepts, there is an attempt at systematization. The dual friend effectively condenses the characteristics of two persons that can be brought together. The notion of death without death is an attempt to systematize a duality of impressions which consciousness attempts to justify, to unite them into a whole. However chaotic the result, the function is there. It is the same in a delusion. Charles Blondel, who has attempted to show an irreducible and *sui generis* entity in abnormal consciousness, represents it as an attempt at a systematization of kinesthetic sensation poorly 'decanted'.[22] In short, wherever there is thought, there is the search for coherence.

This coherence, however, is purely functional, and from the invariance of this function one cannot analytically infer an inherent invariance in the structure of thought. The coherence sought for may be limited to the motor level: a coherence between organic processes or actions. It may extend to one's feelings without touching judgments as acts of thought. Thus the child may continually contradict himself in his speech so as to bring his feelings into some agreement. Similarly, coherence may be sought on the plane of beliefs, a belief being a 'promise to act' in the sense of P. Janet, and others. In short, even though the function is constant, there are diverse types of organization; and even if these types obey a unique law of evolution – even if one appeals to their logical organization to set them off necessarily from prelogical organizations – it is necessary to distinguish qualitative differences between the structures corresponding to the successive stages.

From this point of view, the primitive seeks coherence just as we do; furthermore, once certain obstacles are removed, this attempt must lead necessarily to our logic. However, from the point of view of structure, Lévy-Bruhl is perfectly justified in speaking of a prelogic in the sense that what appears coherent to the primitive appears to us to be incoherent, and vice versa. [p. 213]

What then are the conditions for what in logic is called the application of the principle of contradiction? The condition *sine qua non* of this application is a fixed and non-equivocal definition of concepts. The employment of formal logic thus presupposes an axiomatization of knowledge. But as soon as one leaves the domain of concepts as nominally defined, the principle of contradiction no longer plays a role and it is then a coherence based upon internal feeling or actions on which we are reliant. Everyday conversations testify to this. Thus two sociologists, one patriotic and the other not, may discuss their respective positions. One reproaches the other for his incoherence: 'It is not possible to be patriotic and a socialist at the same time. You have to choose between them, etc.' Now, with regard to these two things, one is either discussing concepts or attitudes. If one is discussing concepts, it is necessary to show that while one particular definition of socialism entails the negation of patriotism, some other one does not, to define the terms 'socialism' and 'patriotism' and hence formally to apply the principle of contradiction. Thus, in this case, the principle of contradiction has only a regulative role, limiting itself to excluding definitions resulting in a formal contradiction. Thus, where there is no formal incoherence, there is no property by means of which to judge coherence, nor to prescribe one particular definition rather than another. On the other hand, if one is discussing attitudes (and all definitions involve attitudes), it is not possible to see operating here the principle of contradiction as a structure related to the formal organization of thought: one party will have the 'moral experience' in which his socialistic action and a patriotic action are in harmony, while the other one will have the opposite experience. And if one of these experiences winds up prevailing over the other, this is not due to the application of the principle of contradiction but to the progressive organization of action. As Flournoy[23] colloquially put it: when you walk, you don't apply the 'concept of walking', you just put one foot in front of the other.

Traditional language, which does not distinguish function and structure, encloses us in a circle: in order to apply the principle of contradiction, it is necessary to possess well-defined and axiomatized concepts; but in order to define the concepts correctly, it is necessary to apply the principle of contradiction. This difficulty arises as soon as one admits that thought and action everywhere and always strive for coherence (of course with different degrees of success and at different rates of speed) [p. 214] but that there are different, successive types of systematization.

With regard to the primitive or the child the question, therefore, is the following. Everyone admits that, for them as for us, there is the coherent and the incoherent and that the function of their thought and ours is to seek coherence. But do they attain an adequate definition of their concepts, so that the principle of contradiction can be applied formally; or does the structure of their thought have a different type of coherence from ours?

If one formulates the question this way, Lévy-Bruhl has, in our opinion, made substantial progress in showing that the systematization of primitive thought operates on a plane different from our logic. The coherence which primitive thought seeks is much more of an affective or behavioural type than an intellectual one. If one takes the principle of contradiction to be a structure and not merely a function – the structure of concepts sufficiently defined in order to permit the elaboration of non-contradictory reasoning – one may be justified in doubting that the primitive or the very young infant possesses this principle. In an insightful discussion of the ideas of Lévy-Bruhl, A. Reymond has maintained that if the primitive contradicts himself on the physical plane, it is because he simply lacks an interest in an objective order. However, on the mystical plane, the sharp division of objects into sacred and non-sacred does allow the application of the principle of contradiction: for the primitive, an object could not in fact at the same time be both sacred and non-sacred.[10] But is the notion of the sacred a well-defined concept? Does it not involve a contradiction? The sacred is that which attracts and that which repels, the source of everything good and evil; the sacred is sometimes localized, sometimes diffuse, etc. Durkheim, who attributes such a great importance to this notion, has even defined it in opposition to the profane without being able to apprehend its intrinsic properties. From the point of view of function, it is clear that this classification leads to an organization of things and feelings, but from the point of view of structure, the conditions necessary for the application of logical principles are missing. As Lévy-Bruhl says, the primitive has, strictly speaking, no notions; [p. 215] there are just pre-notions, that is to say, judgments are related to each other not in terms of the intellectual content of what they affirm, but by the collective basis of the motor and the affective substrata, a basis from which they are not able to free themselves. But it would be a mistake to conclude that participation does not exist on the plane of thought but that it is only an affective phenomenon, for, otherwise, where would thought begin? The thought of the scientist is even laden with value judgments of a different type, it is true, but this makes illusory an absolute division of the mind into pure intelligence and affectivity, even in us.

In short, it would be false to conclude that the difference between so-called primitive consciousness and ours is a matter only of degree. Here it is useful to distinguish two questions and, assuming we are not violating biological usage, we may call them the question of epigenesis and orthogenesis.

Embryology began by studying the ensemble of organs and morphological characteristics of the adult in the egg. Ovists and spermatists agreed on this preformism and believed that, with an adequate means of investigation, one[24] would be able to find the adult in miniature in the germinal substance. But embryology made progress only by renouncing this view and admitting an epigenesis – a progressive and real formation of organs. However, preformationism is certainly not dead and Weismann's conception of 'representative particles', which persists under the guise of 'genes' among certain contemporary biologists, results only in a refinement of preformationism instead of abandoning it. It is very probable that in genetics as in embryology progress will result only if one substitutes the notion of construction for that of identity. Whatever the case, the working hypothesis of Lévy-Bruhl has replaced the preformism of classical logicism by an epigenesis. If one maintains the functional continuity of mental development, the idea of a progressive construction of structures appears singularly satisfactory.

On the other hand, we could not consider the evolution of mentality from the primitive to the scientist as contingent. We are afraid of attributing to Lévy-Bruhl more than he has actually said, but we propose to discuss an implicit aspect of his doctrine, a proposition which appears to arise out of his views, and one which he might possibly repudiate. In reading Lévy-Bruhl, it seems that our logic is related to our social condition just as primitive mentality is related to the conformist and [p. 216] theological organization of segmented societies. If this is true, a different social organization would have given birth to a different, third kind of logic, and so on. Hence, the passage from primitive mentality to ours, although necessary *de facto*[11], would not be necessary *de jure*.[25]

Even if one were to agree to the facts as described by Lévy-Bruhl, two reasons prevent us from agreeing with his thesis. The first, as we will attempt to show, is that the mentality imposed on individuals by obligatory conformism is merely *de facto*: the group dictates certain beliefs, which are either accepted or rejected, but they contain nothing more than that which they explicitly claim. On the other hand, what we can call the intellectual cooperation unique to our societies is not imposed on beliefs or opinions; instead, it is, first and foremost, a *method* given to all individuals and by its very content contains the germ of a distinction between the ideal and the factual. Similarly, the connection between mentality and one's social condition is different in differentiated societies and conformist societies.

What then is the notion of a contingent evolution of reason? Certainly, the passage from primitive mentality to ours is contingent in the sense that the development of civilization is related to a relatively fragile system of institutions just as individual reason is related to the proper functioning of the brain. Civilization might not have arisen and may have disappeared as soon as it arose; indeed, it could disappear from one moment to the next if our societies were to return to a new Middle Ages, which no one desires. But when it comes to the evolution of rational norms themselves, can one really speak of reason if the norms are indefinitely flexible in every sense? Is it not possible, even from a purely experimental point of view, that there are functional laws of equilibrium such that an individual or collective consciousness can only evolve in a certain direction if it is not to disintegrate? Of course, one cannot determine this equilibrium *a priori* since it is functional. But it is important to distinguish the existence of this ideal equilibrium from that of the successive [p. 217] structures by means of which we seek to realize it, just as it is necessary, from the biological point of view, to distinguish an assimilation, which is never completely attained and the organs of this assimilation. The sociology of knowledge provides an analysis of the formation of these organs. With respect to the functional equilibrium of reason, one can admit that everything in the universe evolves without direction, but an evolution of reason without orthogenesis is impossible to show since it is always by virtue of a purer ideal of rationality that one passes from one stage to the next.

III

Must we therefore return to the classical view and admit the hypothesis of an immutable psychological structure internal to the individual, as and regulated by the law of logic? In other words, is the functional equilibrium to which we have alluded more individual than social?

We believe that psychology itself prevents us from going backwards and that if, in certain respects, the equilibrium of thought has its roots in the biological reality of a compromise between accommodation to the milieu and assimilation of the external world, it is only in a socialized awareness that this compromise becomes an equilibrium and results in the constitution of valid norms.

What is, after all, purely individualistic thought? According to spiritualistic psychology, personality is the spontaneous extension of individuality. Ribot,[26] translating this view into physiological terms, would consider the self as the awareness of the organism. Nowadays we know the person also contains social elements, and pure individuality is to be sought at a lower level. What then would individual thought be if society did not exist? Such a question is not absurd from a genetic point of view, for although it is pointless to try to split an adult into individual and social elements, it is at the same time necessary when one asks at what point the infant becomes socialized. On this point there is a wealth of work, both psychological and logical, that has enriched our knowledge of intelligence. [p. 218]

First of all, the research of Flournoy and psychoanalysis (even if Freudianism were to be completely rejected in psychology of emotion, it would still be interesting on this point), have shown the existence of a kind of thought different from conceptual or verbal thought. This is called symbolic thought because it is composed not only of intellectual signs but also of pictorial images forming symbols. This kind of thought, manifested in play, dreams, imagination, certain kinds of delirium, etc., presents an ensemble of characteristics quite different from reason and this difference is of considerable importance with regard to the socialization of thought. In the first place, the mere fact that intelligence employs only verbal signs, i.e. a sign with a fixed and common meaning, whereas symbolic thought proceeds in terms of private images, indefinitely plastic due to the activity of condensations and displacements, shows the interesting contrast between these two types of thought with respect to the connections between society and the individual. Furthermore, symbolic thought has, as its sole function, the realization of the desires of the individual through dreams. It is thus ruled by the anarchistic pleasure of each individual, whereas reason must adapt itself to reality and to others. Finally, symbolic thought presents an ensemble of structural processes whose opposition to that of intelligence raises once again the issue of the individual and society. In short, we can state that without socialization, individual thought can hardly do those things analogous to symbolic thought. Of course, there is action and factual verification. But, as everyone knows, this verification is trivial when something like desire obscures thought, and symbolic thought really does appear to be thought dictated only by individual desire.

One may proceed to deny all power of systematization to individual consciousness in order to re-establish with Charles Blondel the primacy of pure and simple kinesthesis. But the examination of the child's first year of life and in particular the emergence of play shows an experience of spontaneous symbolism which obeys the laws to which we have just referred. If one focuses on the pathological level, the distinction between the individual and the social should, it seems to us, be marked by the heuristic distinction Bleuler[27] draws between *autism* and what he calls realistic thought. Mild cases of schizophrenia show in an illuminating way that, to the extent that a sickness turns in on itself and is cut off from everything external, [p. 219] what once appeared as rational thought gradually approaches a state we would call symbolic. If we admit that each of us is autistic and that autism is pathological only to the extent that it becomes exclusive, we can say that individual thought as such is autistic.

If the work to which we have just made reference tends to determine what is pure individuality, that of others shows the effect of socialization. It is useful here to cite the important theoretical synthesis which P. Janet[28] has sketched in his later work and which shows social behaviour to be at the root of higher 'behaviour'. Everyone knows his theses on the connection between thought and speech, on narrative memory, on promissory belief, etc. Especially important in this regard is Janet's analysis of reflection. Reflection is an interior discussion. But before the stage of reflection, the individual proceeds through a stage of intellectual impulsivity, so to speak, a phase during which he immediately believes everything that appears to him without verification or concern for coherence. This is what Janet calls the stage of belief – the pithiatic stage – whose traits resemble those of autism. Due to social shock, discussion is born; first a simple dispute and later a discussion results in a conclusion.[29] It is this latter behaviour that, once it is interiorized and applied to itself, becomes reflection.

Logicians and psychologists have also insisted on the fact that objectivity presupposes society, for objectivity is not a criterion different from that of an agreement of minds. From the genetic point of view, on the other hand, it is easy to see that the need for proof is a social need: a need initially to find agreement and then later confirmation.[30]

Furthermore, it is useful to recall here those accurate remarks of Durkheim on the analogy between logical principles and moral principles. This analogy has been recognized by everyone and in particular by Baldwin in his interesting remarks on the distinction between the syndoxic and the synnomic.

In short, there are social elements in logical knowledge. What then is the connection between these elements and the very structure of thought? Two views present themselves here, views so well known we must limit ourselves to just a few remarks on this subject before proceeding to a discussion of the relevant data concerning the psychology of the child. [p. 220]

In his *Traité de logique*[31] Goblot asks how the critical mind arises, how individual judgment becomes impartial. His answer is: 'the idea of truth is conceived and explained only by social life'.[12] One has to choose here between sociology and Platonism. The universal is what is communicable. But how can one distinguish mere agreement, the syndoxical, from rational agreement? History shows that less developed societies produce only common beliefs in which feeling predominates, whereas discussion emerges from the clash of other beliefs: thus dialectic emerges from dialogue. 'Logic properly called is thus an *indefinite* extension of social relations since the dialectical is reducible to that of the interlocutors alone'.[13] Hence, in order to distinguish correct assent from plain common belief, it is sufficient to distinguish the assertion from the feeling of communality belonging to those who are united by these various assertions. That which is unique to discussion is just the operation of this distinction. One can thus believe that it is the individual who holds onto truth against society, even though individual independence is a social fact, a result of civilization.

It is unfortunate that Goblot does not discuss these clear statements of his views any further in his *Traité*. Goblot claims (reasonably) that it is necessary to choose between Platonism and sociology. One is thus led to expect that the structure of thought will be explained by that of society, not only in general terms but in detail. But Goblot seems to limit the role of society to providing us in some way with a morality of thought – an ideal of objectivity and discussion. But when he advances his interesting thesis that deduction is construction, it is no longer a question of social life. For, can one not push the analysis back still further and ask the following question? Supposing that one puts the logic of relations on the primary level in the structure of deduction so that, as compared to Goblot, one ascribes a secondary role to the syllogism, is not this logic of relations closely related to the practice of reciprocity, which results from discussion? We will return to the question shortly. [p. 221]

The criticism can also be made that Lalande, whose grand theory is presented as one of the most powerful syntheses attempted in logic or sociology, does not invoke social life in explaining the details of the operation of thought.

Lalande's sociology is well known. As opposed to the drive toward differentiation and social organization – an evolutionary drive – it is necessary to distinguish a drive toward the suppression of differences, toward equality, hence a dissolutive drive. There are thus two kinds of societies: a society whose organization prolongs vital processes in general, and the community or assimilation of minds, which is exactly the opposite. Hence we have rather well-defined social processes and the question left unanswered by Durkheim may perhaps be resolved, for if truth is something social, how can one distinguish legitimate common representations from collective beliefs not based on reason?

The solution proposed by Lalande leaves nothing to be desired in terms of its clarity. Social organization *per se* is not a factor in intelligence. It limits the individual by requiring specialization. It is the source of strife by virtue of the pre-eminence it gives to the differentiated self and by virtue of the conflicts between groups which it occasions. It is the source of constraint but not of reason. The assimilation of minds, on the contrary, produces objectivity and is the basis of logic. Knowledge proceeds the same way that social assimilation does. It counteracts experiential differences for the benefit of an intelligible, homogeneous universe. It overrides the external world just as morality overrides biological society. The logical expression of community is thus identity.[14]

Furthermore, by the very fact of this distinction between heterogeneous social processes, the way is opened up for the hypothesis of a transformation of reason. Here one finds the subtle and profound distinction between *constituting reason* and *constituted reason*. Reason evolves; that which is generally admitted in a given period of history is rejected or overturned in the following one. There is thus an ensemble of fluctuating principles, dependent upon social evolution and the progress of knowledge, dependent also upon the varying degrees of pre-eminence, in particular eras, of social assimilation for [p. 222] its organization and constraint.[32] This changing component of reason is constituted reason. But this evolution also obeys a law and is not due to chance. Observation shows, and this is supported by reflection, that the evolution of thought consists in a progressive identification. There is thus a constituting reason at the basis of constituted reason, a constituting reason which one can explain only by a set of fixed principles, but which is only manifested in a vection. This identification is thus the supreme law of the logical as well as the moral world.[15]

Out of charity and respect for such a view, one should, we believe, distinguish the spirit of this idea from its letter. If the letter appears to contain paradoxical points, its spirit remains and ought to vivify all reflection on these significant issues. This spirit has two aspects: direction in the evolution of reason, and necessary distinctions at the heart of the social processes generative of thought.

Having said this, we must confess some difficulty with respect to the details of the views of an individual to whom we owe so much, difficulties that result all the more if the views of Lalande are trenchantly formulated, thereby losing the flexible and subtle application which is constantly made of them. Our difficulty is the following: constituting reason seems to us to extend beyond identification, and the social processes generative of rationality seem to extend beyond mere assimilation. If we insist upon this point, let us repeat, it is to show how the spirit of the doctrine may be conserved, even if the particular interpretation adopted by Lalande is rejected.

That reason extends beyond identification amounts, in our view, to a distinction between the function and the structure of reason, which we attempted to sketch above. Consider the case of mathematics. Lalande knows better than anyone that mathematical deduction involves creation, and the account, subtle and full of ideas, which he has given of *Traité de logique* shows that he agrees with Goblot that deduction is construction. How then can one call identification an ensemble of operations by which, from certain axioms, few in number, impoverished of content, one may proceed to a world of realities? Along with placing in correspondence,[33] which wholly constitutes identification, mathematical thought contains [p. 223] an ensemble of operations that diversify entirely and create intelligible entities; unless one is a Platonist, it is preferable to view these entities as produced by reason. Can one say that number carries with it an intuition irreducible to logical formula, and that identification remains the sole rational process at work, making contact with the data of this intuition? In that case, logic is not essential to rationality. Now, if one attempts to solve the problem of the relations between formal logic and numbers, one finds oneself in those difficulties which we mentioned above in relation to the principle of contradiction. Recent discussions of the scope of the principle of excluded middle[16] show that the principles of logic apply only to an axiomatized reality. But in axiomatics there is always an effective construction of thought extending far beyond a mere logical formalism. Can one determine the laws of this construction? For our part, we believe it is illusory to approach this from a structural point of view, even with respect to identification. The laws are functional, that is to say, to turn around an image borrowed from *The dissolution*,[34] the unity of acts of thought is more like a picture or an organism than a coin minted in n copies.

Now, is the elaboration of truth due sociologically to the convergence of minds, conceived as a gradual suppression of individual differences? That this fusion plays an essential role is not at issue. But is it the only thing at work? A preliminary remark must be made here, for outside of all relations between social life and thought, it is only egalitarian tendencies, which Lalande invokes as an indication of the levelling of individuals, that always go hand in hand with social differentiation, in particular with the division of labour. As Durkheim and Bouglé[35] have shown, these tendencies are not antagonistic to differentiation, but complementary to it: what egalitarianism seeks to attain is not absolute levelling but simply mobility, the power of an individual to rise above his condition if his talents call him elsewhere. It is the same with regard to those social relations which condition thought: the convergence of minds is nothing but a particular aspect of an over-arching process [p. 224] equally presupposing differentiation. Thus, in particular, where judgments of value are involved (and they intervene beginning with mathematical reasoning and increase in importance with the progressive complexity of science; they are always involved in metaphysics), reason demands not convergence in the sense of a suppression of differences, but simply reciprocity: each ought to furnish the other with the laws of perspective of his own vision of things so as to allow mutual comprehension. One can call this convergence, but one must give it a different sense. Furthermore, outside of all logic of value, the logic of relations appears to us to be a result to be rendered possible from a sociological point of view by the reciprocity of minds, and not by assimilation pure and simple. It is important to note that it is precisely the logic of relations via an indefinite fecundity of its operations (the multiplication of relations permits the creation of new relations and mathematical operations, etc.) which extends far beyond identification.

As long as the discussion remains on the level of this 'epistemological paradox', on the gap between logical identity and real diversity which both Lalande and Meyerson have emphasized with 'philosophical courage' and which we have not investigated here, the suggestions we make will concern the meaning of words more than it will involve irreducible oppositions. Let us reiterate, therefore, that reason does not evolve in a radically contingent way and that its progress is due to social mechanisms, each of which essentially presupposes the mutual comprehension of individuals.

IV

The time has come for us to take a stand by comparing these different views to the data of social development from infancy to adulthood.

The first conclusion to be drawn is that the formulation of the problem remains vague as long as one proposes to compare the individual and society. Nothing is more equivocal than these two very terms. In fact, there is no society: there are social processes, some generative of rationality, others sources of error (for 'society' may be as mistaken as the individual ...). Likewise, there are no individuals: there are individual mechanisms of thought, some generating logic, [p. 225] others producing anarchy. But there is nothing substantially in common[36] between the autism of Bleuler and the socialized person, whose functioning Delacroix has studied.

If one attempts to group the different senses of these terms from the point of view of the relations between logic and social life, one finds not two but three groups of data: autism, social constraint, and cooperation.

Let us call *autism* pure individualism, anarchistic thought governed by feeling, found, for example, in reverie, in dreams, in some states of thought of the child, and in the internalized part of the thought of the schizophrenic. Let us recall, furthermore, that we have attempted to interpret the thought of the infant as a state intermediate between that of autistic thought and the logical thought of the adult; we call this intermediate state 'egocentric'.

We call *social constraint*, in a sense a little more restricted than that of Durkheim, all relations between two or more individuals in which an element of authority or prestige is involved. Thus the respect the child has for an adult opinion or command is an educative constraint, one kind of social constraint. The hold a tradition or a common obligatory belief has on an individual consciousness constitutes another species of this genus. The difference between our definition and that of Durkheim is twofold. In the first place, we admit that constraint always results in conformism (but all conformism is not due to constraint; for example, by virtue of reasoning, the entire world may agree that the earth moves without this being due to authority). We believe this restriction in the meaning of the term is legitimate, since we admit that, in spite of Durkheim, society is not a single thing. It is necessary, therefore, to remove the equivocation due to the meaning of the word 'constraint', which sometimes applies to obligatory conformity, sometimes to the pressure resulting from cooperation and free discussion, etc. This is a purely linguistic matter and if one prefers to use another term, it is at bottom inconsequential, provided that one takes this distinction into account. In the second place, our concept employs a purely psychological criterion, since constraint may begin between two individuals but end up being an over-arching pressure of tradition on all the individuals in the group. That is not, [p. 226] however, a major point, for one may write a sociology in the language of consciousness or in the language of things. Although Durkheim favours the second method, as Lacombe[37] has recently pointed out, he often employs the first; thus, in order to make us understand the effects of the division of labour on feeling, Durkheim deals with friendship or love. In taking the sentiment of respect or prestige as the criterion of constraint, we are quite legitimately employing one of two parallel notations.

Let us call *cooperation* all relations between two or more equal, or believed to be equal, individuals, that is to say, all social relations in which no element of authority or prestige is involved. It is, of course, difficult to standardize the behaviour involved in coercion or cooperation other than in degrees; for example, the result of cooperation may also be imposed by constraint. But the distinction is, in principle, intelligible and, in practice, one can determine a very satisfactory estimate for the sake of discussion.

Having said this, we maintain that only cooperation constitutes a process that can produce reason, with autism and social constraint resulting only in prelogic in all of its forms.

In order to comprehend this proposition and to see something other than a truism or an unverifiable hypothesis, it is necessary to begin with an essential remark often forgotten: instead of being antagonistic, autism and social constraint can easily be combined. In many cases, constraint by itself 'consolidates' those mental habits due to autism. In other cases, constraint functions specifically to suppress[38] less than it seems the perspective of the autistic mind does, because of compromises and harmonies established between the two extremes as so often happens when three terms are present. It is the failure to appreciate this fact that creates the difficulty manifest in sharp affirmations concerning the relations between the individual and the society. Hence, Durkheim often reasons as if group conformism suffices by itself to elicit in the individual habits of mind, whether spontaneous, practical, or intellectual. We claim, on the contrary, that social constraint (in the restricted sense indicated) is not sufficient for the true suppression of intellectual egocentrism, although it does ally itself intimately, but also paradoxically, with this autistic element. [p. 227] One may justify these remarks by direct arguments, that is to say, by appealing to the psychology of the child. But, before proceeding to do this, let us make two remarks about a question that invariably occurs however one may try to avoid it, namely, what is the connection between the primitive and the child?

Primitive mentality is surely the most important result of social constraint. The mentality of the child, however, is closely related to the egocentrism of the thought of the child, if not entirely explainable by this lack of socialization. Now, these two mentalities are similar in certain ways and if these resemblances are correct, they would be very instructive regarding the relations between social constraint and autism. This is why it is necessary to mention the problem here.

The analogy between the primitive and the child has often been exaggerated. In its pre-sociological phase, psychology did not hesitate to make the primitive over into a simple child, even a child with no parents. Furthermore, thanks to the fascination of transformist ideas, one is tempted to see in this rapprochement a confirmation of the law of recapitulation. For example, Stanley Hall[39] has attempted to find in childhood activities the ancestor (via biological heritage) of primitive behaviour. Although all of this today seems to be weak, it is clear that to the extent that one maintains a direct relation between the child and the primitive, it is necessary, with Baldwin, to explain the primitive by means of the child and not the contemporary child by the primitive.

But if one does go this far, it is not to avoid making all such comparisons. Naturally, this comparison should not dictate the practice of research, for it is easy to find whatever one is looking for. But once certain results have been obtained, reflection may not abstain from drawing these comparisons. It is thus that P. Janet has approached the problem in his last work;[17] and, with the synthetic spirit for which he is known, has produced a global comparison between the sick, the primitive and childhood.

Now, the principal obstacle to drawing a parallel between the primitive and the child derives precisely from the element of social tradition which constitutes the basis of primitive mentality and which is absent in the case of the child. Let us examine, therefore, this obstacle and attempt to make the relations between social constraint and egocentrism more precise. [p. 228]

It is clear, first of all, that no primitive collective representation could be a simple generalization due to imitation, or to some other factor not influencing the content of that which is propagated, of an individual representation analogous to that of the child's. The participation between the Araras and the Bororos has been invented by no one, any more than a word or linguistic phrase is; if the successive transformations of an element of a collective representation or of language had their origin in the heads of individuals, it is only by analogy with the formations already in use, and under the control of this usage. All tradition, in the most general sense of that word, all the content of collective constraint, thus obeys the laws unique to *consensus*.

But is it not necessary to distinguish – and for us this is the most important distinction in sociology – between *signs* in the most general sense of that term: language, magical or religious ritual, usage, narrative, beliefs or representations serving only to support collective sentiments, myths such as interpreted by Lévy-Bruhl[18] and others – and *norms*, logical, moral, legal principles, etc., independent of signs in the sense that all signs are 'arbitrary' and all norms 'motivated'? Hence, sociology would divide itself into general semiology (the science dreamed of by F. de Saussure)[40] and theory of value. What we have just said of the characteristics belonging to all tradition, with its stylization, syntax, semantics, etc., also applies to its semiotic aspect. But it is completely different when we come to norms.

In effect, if no primitive collective representation can be considered as a generalized individual representation and if there is no one–one correspondence between primitive beliefs and the ideas of children, there are, however, astonishing functional resemblances between logical norms and the moral norms adopted by both sides. These resemblances point to a union of social or educative constraint and egocentrism, a union to which we will return later.

As examples of the tendency to affirm without proof, one can cite the affective character of thought, its global non-analytic (syncretism) character, the absence of logical coherence [p. 229] (of principles of contradiction and of identity considered as formal structures), the difficulty in reasoning deductively and the frequency of reasoning by immediate identification (participation), mystical causality, lack of differentiation between the psychological and the physical, the confusion of sign and cause, of sign and the thing signified, etc. It goes without saying that in stressing the functional aspect of thought, and to avoid brute identification, we do not pretend that each of these traits is clearly present in the same way both in the infant and the child. It would indeed require an entire book to mark out their nuances. However, we do think that, in rough outline, there are such analogies.

If these analogies are justified, how do they arise? To repeat: such common mechanisms seem to be due to social constraint in the primitive and to egocentrism in the child. Now, as paradoxical as it may seem, these two explanations are not in themselves contradictory, and the union of constraint and egocentrism appears with maximum clarity in the fundamental fact that conditions both primitive mentality and childhood mentality: the fact of educative constraint, the relation between a mind not yet socialized and a mind exercising its influence by virtue only of age or power, and not by virtue of the intrinsic truth of its affirmations.

What then are the results of this educative constraint on the mind of the child? (What we say here may be generalized to the results of social constraint on the mind of individuals.) They are twofold. First, educative constraint reinforces the mental habits of egocentricity in the child (and in a sense constraint is a factor of 'consolidation' in the sense of W. Jerusalem and not of creation). In the second place, constraint, refracted by egocentric mentality, gives rise to moral phenomena which are novel in the sense that they do not come from the individual as such but rather from the relation between individuals, and which harmonize rather well with egocentric mentality without which they would not exist (and so this second element does not change the intellectual habits of egocentrism).

Consider the first case in which educative constraint is only the consolidation of egocentric habits of thought without producing anything new. Consider a child who believes in the apparent motion of the sun and the moon. The stars seem to him to be living beings which accompany us, moving not around the earth but above us, at the level of the clouds. The child is taught [p. 230] that the sun appears to be immobile in relation to us, the earth turning around it. The child, who is much too obedient and respectful, whatever educators may think, freely repeats the latter's thoughts. But has its mentality changed? Can one say that a correct[41] idea has taken the place of a false one? I have often found in children that one could not usefully question them because their mind was full of so-called 'correct'[42] knowledge. When one asked how the clouds move, they responded: 'The clouds don't move, it is the earth that turns.' Clearly, since the sun is on the same level as the clouds, this obviously follows. But we should not emphasize such an example, which is too simple; we should try to bring out the lessons to be learned from these facts, which are numerous.

Intellectual egocentrism forces the child to affirm continuously without verification, to believe whatever comes to mind without feeling the need for verification, which is born of discussion. But this egocentrism is unaware of itself, in the sense that the child spontaneously considers his point of view as absolute and general. The child always believes the entire world thinks as he does, failing to take into consideration individual differences. What does such an assertion, even a correct one coming from an adult, produce in his mind? What does a lesson, even a well-reasoned one, given not by an equal, but a master result in? The child quickly abandons his ideas in favour of those presented to him, such that his ideas, not having been explicitly formulated and existing only by virtue of mental direction, cannot enter into competition with those of the adult. Surely, what is produced here, as in the psychology of feeling, are 'failures' in repression,[43] that is to say, drives in the child, thwarted at one point, are reasserted at another point. Yet overall the adult opinion is victorious. But what has changed? The child continues to make assertions without proof; he just substitutes adult authority as the ultimate criterion of truth for his own decision and does not see the need to verify it. Has the logical structure of his thought changed? Does the accumulation of knowledge suffice to form reason? Is it not rather that it is only when the adolescent learns to discuss on equal terms with his peers and teachers, when his internal freedom is checked, that the vague remnants of knowledge mechanically stored emerge and become something quite different? [p. 231] Contemporary pedagogy, the 'active school',[44] and innumerable experiences in this subject teach us that if something is not acquired by experience and personal reflection it is acquired only superficially, with no change in our thought. It is in spite of adult authority, and not because of it, that the infant learns. Hence it is to the extent that the intelligent teacher knows when to step down as a superior and to become an equal, when to engage in discussion and to require proof rather than merely to make assertions and to compel morally, that the traditional school has rendered its services.

A typical example of this disastrous pre-established harmony between inclinations unique to childhood egocentrism and the results of adult authority is that of verbalism. One of the principal traits of egocentric morality is syncretism, the tendency to perceive and conceive everything globally and hence to relate everything to everything else, all at the whim of subjective parallels. In the verbal domain, this tendency leads to understanding words, not by analytical reflection, but as a function of the global schema of the phrase, this schema itself being due to an immediate and completely personal perspective. Thus in the phrase 'men of small stature may be of great merit', such a child understands the word 'merit' in the following way: 'That means that they become larger later.' Again, verbal instruction or simply the ensemble of adult orders and commands does not contain anything, in itself, that would lead the child to rid himself of this syncretic verbalism. On the contrary, as soon as one attempts to understand even a little what the child has understood about adult discourse, one is dismayed at the resulting state of chaos and confusion as to what has thus been accumulated and distorted.

In short, even in our society in which what the adult imposes on the child is logical reasoning itself and an ensemble of positive knowledge, adult authority changes nothing of the egocentric mentality of the child. One can even say that it consolidates this kind of thought process. In effect, what the child can repeat in such a way to fool his peers and examiners is of little importance. What we are concerned about here is knowing how the child attains logical reasoning and takes account of the objectivity of experience. On these two points, constraint is unable to correct egocentrism: it only reinforces syncretic logic and affirmation without proof. If the child attains the intellectual autonomy of the adult [p. 232] (too few adults are really autonomous; so if one takes real life as one's criterion and not merely scholastic sanctions, our pedagogy is defective), it is to the extent that he was able to become a personality in discussion with his peers and to the extent that adults will have learned to cooperate without constraining.

Furthermore, constraint is not limited to the consolidation of autism. It also creates certain moral mechanisms, which through practice have an influence on intelligence. But as long as cooperation does not supplant constraint, these results are counteracted by egocentric mentality and the resulting combination is not always productive of rationality.

Let us consider the genesis of the feeling of obligation. Durkheim conceives moral obligation as being due to the constraint of the social whole upon the individual. Bovet, in a rarely cited study[19], discovered the psychological source of this obligation of conscience in the respect the individual has for another individual superior to him, and in particular the respect the child has for the adult. It is difficult not to consider the differences between these two theses as being due merely to terminological differences, the language of the first being objective, whereas that of the second being a description of one's internal life. Whatever the case, let us return to the fact of constraint, such as we have defined it, as the source of obligation.

Now what kind of obligation is at issue? As Durkheim himself recognized, and with some skill he has weakened his dualism, there are two moralities, that of pure obligation (duty) and that of goodness. This has been clearly seen by Bovet. In our societies and in those philosophies expressing our collective conscience (as in the moral philosophy of Kant), this opposition is diminished, for duty prescribes no more than goodness does. However, in primitive societies, the antithesis is almost complete: an ensemble of obligations and absurd prohibitions imposed by tradition and of certain principles of justice and goodness that are the conditions for all cooperation.

We see quite spontaneously in the life of the child certain aspects of this conflict. We maintain that the authority of the adult, (i.e. overlooking their possible brutality, the simple [p. 233] moral prestige of the parents), is certainly the source of obligation and this is independent of the content prescribed. The consequent obedience results in a strict morality, a morality of pure obligation (duty) and of taboo. But only mutual affection, i.e. the affective aspect of cooperation in which complete obedience is lacking, leads the mind to goodness.

For example, consider lying.[20] The command due to adult authority is that you must not lie. This command is imposed on an egocentric mind for which, as all our work has shown, lying is a natural form of thought, an aspect of fantasy governed by feeling. On the other hand, however, egocentric mentality is realistic: it does not separate the spiritual and the material, for these appear to be both intentional and physical. These two aspects of egocentrism result in the command being deformed in the following way: all lies appear as 'naughty' independently of the intentions of the liar, with the criterion of evaluation remaining completely physical. Often, as children report to us, it is much more blameworthy to assert that you have seen a dog as big as a cow than to pretend you have a pain in your foot in order to avoid a chore. There actually are no dogs as big as cows, whereas it is quite possible to have a pain in your foot! Intention thus plays no role; it is the degree of falsity of the assertion that is the only measure of culpability.

Hence, in morality as in logic, constraint is bound up with egocentric mentality. The rule of taboo goes hand in hand with that of making assertions. 'Objective responsibility' as Fauconnet calls it, is a close relative of the realism of intelligence.

To return to the structure of thought: the consequences of this morality of obedience (or pure duty) are nothing other than mystical causality and artificialism: two characteristics of the child's representation of the world that spring from a belief in adult wisdom. These facts show once again the intimate and natural union of egocentric habits of thought with the effects of constraint. Thus constraint consolidates the processes of egocentric logic or unites them in a narrow synthesis. [p. 234]

A study of ours currently under way,[45] clearly shows the complexity of egocentrism and respect for the adult, and the salutary results of cooperation. We are currently studying the development of the practice of social rules and the internal awareness of them. To show this, we play a game of marbles with the children and then, after having determined how much they know about the rules and how to apply them, we ask them if it would be possible to change the rules and why or why not. The result is paradoxical. To schematize things (and here we are speaking of children from 6 to 12 years of age), we can say that these younger children (6–8 years) have a mystical respect for rules to such an extent that their practice remains egocentric, whereas for the older ones (10–12 years) rules become rational to the extent that the cooperation of the players is stricter.

Smaller children play almost as they understand things: they have become fixated on certain notions shaped by custom concerning the manner of play. But each has retained something more than imitation of the older children. When they play together, they do not corroborate[46] each other. Each one plays for himself, as he understands things. No one seeks to win at the expense of others. 'To win' means to succeed in what one undertakes. In other words, everyone wins. This is equivalent to what we have called the 'collective monologue' of conversations between children.[47] The older children, on the other hand, obey extremely complicated and detailed rules, presupposing a code and legal precedent. When there is disagreement, they understand each other and they begin to recognize such-and-such a usage and not something else. Play is thus social. To win means to gain something over the others.

The curious thing, however, is that only the older children admit that one can change the rules. For them, a rule is something adopted along with its logical consequences. If everyone agrees to it, one can modify this one or that one. The smaller children, on the other hand, believe that everything is eternal and unchangeable. As different as their respective experiences may be, they all affirm that each one plays like the other and that they have always played like the other: 'My father played this way. My grandfather played the same way.' The children of William Tell, Noah, Adam and Eve conform to the same custom. Moreover, the older children admit that the rules have been invented by children. The younger ones believe they have come from adults. When it is a question regarding [p. 235] the origins of things, one child invokes his father, another one appeals to the first humans, a third brings in God, a fourth the 'sages of the community' as creators and legislators of the game of marbles.

Of course, this is only one piece of evidence, but it is important. It shows that childhood egocentrism is not asocial behaviour. It is rather behaviour intermediate between autism and socialization. This shows clearly that autistic mentality may remain alive under the guise of sociality. This is what makes it so easy to combine adult constraint and childhood egocentrism. For the child, each personal arbitrary whim is considered to be of universal value and each external order is interpreted in terms of the self. But cooperation frees oneself from egocentrism and the mystique of parental or social constraint.

If one thus comes to recognize some analogy between primitive mentality and the thought of the child, it would hardly be intelligible. The most important social fact perhaps of these lower civilizations is their respect for the aged, or gerontocracy. Lévy-Bruhl has again insisted on this point in his recent work where he repeats in such a fruitful way his description of the data concerning primitive mentality.[21][48] Whether this respect is innate or socially transmitted, whether there are degrees of it or not is hardly important. Whether the education of the child is by its parents or by educators (the old ones charged with initiation) is also unimportant. In a society where generations place all of their influence on each other, conditions necessary for the elimination of childhood mentality cannot appear. There is no discussion, no exchange of points of view. There is just an ensemble of individuals whose autistic views will remain forever incommunicable and whose commonality is assured by a completely external link of tradition. There are thus only personalities who do not know themselves and a group which is everything. In such a situation nothing is created by individuals, and nothing extends beyond the level of childhood thought. In letting oneself be influenced by collective representations, the individual does not substitute a different kind of logic for his own; he changes his beliefs (or rather he introduces a solid and firm belief) where there was only an inconsistent dream or play. But this belief preserves[49] the characteristics of childhood logic. From the point of view [p. 236] of reason, therefore, the intensity and permanence of belief do not add anything to its logical structure. Of course, one can say that this permanence, which originates in the collective, represents a kind of objectivity for the individual. But this is to reason only in the sense in which the child believes something subjectively. For the small child, there is nothing any more objective here than just its individual opinion. The distinction between the subjective and the objective is a product of cooperation. Before cooperation appears, the most powerful social constraint could not introduce the smallest element of reason into an autistic mind.

Let us turn, therefore, to cooperation. Everyone admits that you can find the germs of cooperation, hence the germs of rationality, in the primitive as well as in the child, and hence that a difference in nature between social processes does not exclude a factual continuity between them. Having said this, we want to claim that cooperation is opposed both to autism and constraint. It progressively eliminates the processes of autistic or egocentric thought thanks to those processes we have just mentioned. Discussion produces internal reflection; mutual verification produces the need for proof and objectivity. The exchange of thought presupposes the principles of contradiction and identity conceived as regulative of discourse, etc. As for constraint, cooperation destroys it to the extent that there is a differentiation of individuals and free discussion.

Hence only cooperation provides for the mind the psychological conditions necessary for the attainment of truth. But the question that arises is whether the objections to the theories based on constraint just mentioned do not also apply to the case of cooperation. Does not cooperation, just as constraint, lead to the primacy of belief? Do not conventions, those tacit agreements between equals, lead to results which are as devastating to reason as to authority itself? Does not Durkheim have reason to speak of constraint in both cases, even with respect to societies that are differentiated and individualistic?

We do not believe so, since whenever these conventions or received truths arise between equals, one can see there is constraint from a psychological point of view. The prestige of such an individual or the authority of such an opinion do play a role. But what seems to distinguish cooperation and constraint, and what ensures at the same time the logical value of cooperation as compared to [p. 237] constraint, is that the first furnishes a *method* whereas the second just imposes *beliefs*. In effect, constraint presents to the individual a system of rules and beliefs completely established: one either accepts them or not. All correction is contrary to constraint and when constraint purports to suggest rules of method as in classical pedagogy, it again only imposes other beliefs. On the other hand, cooperation is exclusively a method. When I discuss and sincerely attempt to understand someone else, I not only pledge not to contradict myself, not to play with words, etc., but rather to be open to an indefinite number of points of view different from mine. Thus, cooperation is not a system in static equilibrium as one finds in constraint; it is a mobile equilibrium. The commitments which I make in relation to constraint may be laborious but I know what they involve; but that which I undertake by virtue of cooperation leads me I know not where. These commitments are thus formal and not material.

Consequently, cooperation provides the distinction so necessary for reason between *fact* and *ideal*. Constraint is only a factual state of affairs; it is static, imposed by others and given once and for all. Cooperation, on the other hand, since it constitutes simply a method, forces us continually to consider along with *de facto* states, truths recognized and classified, *de jure* states, consisting in a greater agreement of opinions and perspectives.[50] The equilibrium characterizing cooperation is thus not only mobile, it is also ideal.

Certainly cooperation presupposes a pressure which alone can make the individual leave his autistic state and attain rationality. But if one considers this pressure as being like constraint in the limited sense just defined, one will perpetuate a serious misunderstanding. Certainly, one is always free to combine these two kinds of pressure into a more general concept one could call 'social constraint' (in Durkheim's sense). But unless one is to relapse into the dilemma we have previously discussed one cannot assert without further qualification that constraint in a large sense is the source of reason. It is thus always necessary to distinguish the element of method unique to cooperation from the element of obligatory belief unique to the other aspect of social relations. [p. 238]

Of course, one can ask if this methodological component is not external to the very structure of reason and hence explains only the secondary aspects of logical development. We believe, however, that in a certain sense method is everything, and that the method at issue here lies at the very heart of the functioning of reason. If one enlarges the profound view of Lalande on the parallelism between the assimilation of minds and logical identification somewhat, one can say that the method of cooperation can be translated in logic by the notion of *reciprocity*.

Now, as we have attempted to show by our particular investigation into the development of reasoning in the child, it is only by putting the points of view of other individuals into a relationship of reciprocity that intelligence can construct this logical tool, which commands all the others and which is the logic of relations. Certainly, the logic of relations has biological foundations more important than social life. The construction of those elementary notions accomplished during the first two years of infancy presupposes behavioural patterns, if not thinking in terms of these relations. Animal psychology (in particular, Gestalt psychology) has shown that perception is often a perception of relations and not a perception of absolute qualities. A chicken raised to peck grains on a light grey background, and not on a white one, will peck on a darker grey if it is given a choice between a darker grey and a lighter grey. The research of Eliasberg has shown analogous phenomena with young children. However, when one comes to action and to the dawning of consciousness[51] of action, things change: the dawning of consciousness, as we have insisted, presupposes a shift[52] of operations on the verbal plane, in effect, a complete reconstruction. It is here that the self intervenes. Experiment shows that the notions young children use, such as heavy and light, light and dark, left and right, are always taken in an absolute, egocentric sense. The child does not conceive what heaviness is in itself, nor what heaviness is for others, nor does the term 'heavy' have any meaning in terms of a relation to a system of reference. A young boy certainly knows he has a brother, but he does not understand that his brother also has a brother.[53] Someone else believes that the moon accompanies him but he never wonders whether it accompanies his friends. On the other hand, one notices that at the precise age when the social life of the child begins to develop, the possibility of entering into the point of view of others [p. 239] is opened up; hence he practises reciprocity and discovers the use of a logic of relations. Must we ask if it is the logic of relations that gives rise to reciprocity or the other way around? It is the problem of the bank and the river: they are two aspects of one and the same process – cooperation is the empirical fact of which reciprocity is the logical ideal.

That the history of thought provides us with facts from which one may extract a sociology of cooperation and hence move beyond the psychological point of view to which we have limited ourselves, has been shown with certainty in the superb work of Brunschvicg. Everyone knows the important role he attributes to the concept of reciprocity in *Le Progrès de la conscience dans la philosophie occidentale*.[54]

In conclusion, we believe that social life is a necessary condition for the development of logic. Thus, we believe that social life transforms the very nature of the individual, making him pass from an autistic state to one involving personality. In speaking of cooperation, therefore, we understand a process that creates new realities and not a mere exchange between fully developed individuals. In the domain of norms, the psychological terminology of social facts, which we prefer to an objective and external terminology, seems to be a return to Tarde.[55] Despite a stock of singularly rich insights, Tarde has made the great mistake of considering as the fundamental social process a mechanism that is not creative but one that simply prolongs what has already been elaborated. As a result, he has been led to explain society by the individual just as Durkheim has done the inverse. This dispute, which has been disastrous for sociology, is consequently based on a pseudo-problem: there are neither individuals as such nor society as such. There are just inter-individual relations. Some of these do not change the mental structure of individuals, whereas others transform both the individual mind and the group. Among the latter, some lead to rationality, some do not. It is on this point that the language of Durkheim seems to us to be problematic. With Lévy-Bruhl, we prefer to distinguish a prelogic from a logic according to the social processes which predominate in a particular collective setting. But as paradoxical as this may seem, primitive mentality seems to us to be less socialized than ours. Social constraint is only a step towards socialization. Only cooperation assures mental equilibrium, which allows one to distinguish the *de facto* state of psychological operations from the *de jure* state of the rational ideal.

AUTHOR'S NOTES

[1] [Originally published in] *Revue philosophique de la France et de l'étranger*, **53**, 1928, numbers 3 and 4, pp. 161–205.

[2] The following pages constitute approximately the text of a lecture given to the annual general meeting of the Franco-Swiss Society of Philosophy, in Rolle, June, 1927. This explains the schematic and summary character of an exposition intended merely to open up discussion and not to be a detailed argument concerning all the details. I had not anticipated publishing it. However, I have not been able to resist the pressure of kind friends, who have suggested the usefulness of compromise when attempting to produce a synthesis. This essay does not pretend to be precise in advancing our knowledge, but to constitute a general attitude and may, therefore, have some heuristic value. Besides, there is always the pleasure of sticking your neck out . . . .

[3] P. Fauconnet, *La Responsabilité* (Paris: Alcan, 1920, p. 20).

[4] *Formes élémentaires de la vie religieuse*, p. 515.[19]

[5] In this passage, Durkheim claimed that he did not look to the notion of force for its logical value but for its explanatory value. But when one attempts to demonstrate the unity of reason, it is precisely this logical value that is in question; other contexts show that Durkheim believes in the notion of force precisely because it is social.

[6] *Sociologie et philosophie*, p. 54.[20]

[7] Ibid., p. 54.

[8] Ibid., p. 93.

[9] Lévy-Bruhl has clearly pointed to this distinction concerning organ and function (along with its importance for the study of mental life) (see *Fonct. ment. soc. infér.*, 3rd ed., pp. 19–20).[21] But I do not know if it has been applied to the special problem concerning the formal principles of thought. In any case, Lévy-Bruhl, it seems to us, has considered these principles more as structures than as functions.

[10] A. Reymond, 'La Philosophie française contemporaine et le problème de verité', in *Revue de théol. et de phil.*, Lausanne, 1923, p. 250–251.

[11] It should be noted here that Lévy-Bruhl has never granted a fundamental heterogeneity to mentality since he affirms the existence of a *functional* continuity between diverse societies (op. cit., p. 175, note 1). Thus along with certain anti-rationalists, he could not admit a radically contingent evolution of reason, a pure conventionalism. The question now, however, is not merely whether there is a functional continuity between so-called primitive mentality and ours, it is whether the structure of our rationality is more adapted to the unchanging functions of reason than is the structure of so-called primitive rationality, in other words, whether there is an orthogenesis in this very structure.

[12] *Traité*, p. 31.

[13] Ibid., p. 38.

[14] See in particular A. Lalande, 'Qu'est-ce que la vérité?', *Rev. de théol. et de phil. de Lausanne*, 1927, pp. 1–27.

[15] See A. Lalande, 'Raison constituante et raison constituée', in *Revue des cours et conférences*, 1925, numbers 9 and 10.

[16] See R. Wavre, 'Logique formelle et logique empiriste', in *Rev. de Mét. et de Mor.*, vol. XXXIII (1926), p. 65. And F. Gonseth, *Les Fondements des mathématiques* (Paris: Blanchard, 1926).

[17] P. Janet, *De l'Angoisse à l'extase* (Paris, Alcan, 1927).

[18] *Fonctions mentales*, p. 434.

[19] P. Bovet, 'Les conditions de l'obligation de conscience', in *Année psychologique*, vol. XVIII, p. 55.

[20] We propose to return to these facts later and to report on them.[45]

[21] *L'Âme primitive*, p. 268ff.[48]

TRANSLATION NOTES

Information has been added about authors mentioned by Piaget through reference to works which may have been read by him before 1928.

1   Emile Durkheim (1858–1917), the most famous French sociologist, author of *Les Formes élémentaires de la vie religieuse* (1912) [in English, *Elementary forms of the religious life* (1915)], *Sociologie et philosophie* (1924) [in English, *Sociology and philosophy* (1953)], *Les Règles de la méthode sociologique* (1894) [in English, *The rules of sociological method* (1938)].

2   Lucien Lévy-Bruhl (1857–1939), philosopher and anthropologist, author of *Les Fonctions mentales dans les sociétés inférieures* (1910) [in English, *How natives think* (1926)], *La Mentalité primitive* (1922) [in English, *Primitive mentality* (1923)], *L'Âme primitive* (1927) [in English, *The soul of the primitive* (1929)].

3   V. Pareto, *Traité de sociologie générale*, 2 vols, trans. P. Boven (Paris: Payot, 1917, 1919). This is the French translation of *Trattato di sociologia generale*, 2 vols. (Florence: G. Barabera, 1916). The English translation of this is: *A treatise of general sociology: The mind and society*, trans. A. Bongiorno and A. Livingston, 4 vols. (New York: Dover, 1935).

4   Max Scheler (1874–1928), phenomenological philosopher, author of *Versuche zu einer Sociologie des Wissens* (1924), *Die Wissensformen und die Gesellschaft* (1926).

5   André Lalande (1867–1964), French philosopher of science, author of numerous works including *L'Idée directrice de la dissolution opposée à celle d l'évolution* (1899), *Les Théories de l'induction et de l'expérimentation* (1929).

6   *L'Idée directrice de la dissolution opposée à celle de l'évolution* (Paris, Payot, 1898).

7   Edmond Goblot (1858–1925), French philosopher and logician, author of *Essai sur la classification des sciences* (1898), and *Traité de logique* (1918).

8   León Brunschvicg (1869–1944), French idealist philosopher and philosopher of science, author of numerous works including *La Modalité du jugement* (1897), *Les Étapes de la philosophie mathématique* (1912), *L'Expérience humaine et la causalité physique* (1922).

9   L. Brunschvicg, *Le Progrès de la conscience dans la philosophie occidentale* (Paris, Alcan, 1927), pp. 489–584.

10   James Mark Baldwin (1861–1934), American philosopher and psychologist, author of *Mental development in the child and the race* (1900), *Development and evolution* (1902), *Thoughts and things*, 3 vols (1906, 1908, 1910).

11   Presumably Pierre Janet is meant here and not Paul Janet.

12   Charles Blondel (1876–1939), French physiologist, author of *La conscience morbide* (1914), *La Mentalité primitive* (1926) and *Introduction à la psychologie collective* (1928).

13   Henri Delacroix (1873–1937), author of *Psychologie et mysticisme* (1908) and *La Psychoanalyse* (1924).

14   Frédéric Rauh (1861–1907), French philosopher, author of *L'Expérience morale* (1890) and *Essai sur le fondement métaphysique de la morale* (1903).

15   *Psychologism* is the fallacy of deducing a normative conclusion from psychological facts; *sociologism* is the fallacy of deducing a normative conclusion from sociological facts; presumably *logicism* is the fallacy of deducing a psychological or sociological conclusion from logical norms. Logicism should not be confused with the Frege–Russell–Carnap programme of reducing mathematics to logic plus set theory. See also E. Beth and J. Piaget, *Mathematical epistemology and psychology* (Dordrecht: Reidel, 1966, p. 132) for discussion of logicism and psychologism.

16 August Comte (1798–1857), French positivistic sociologist, author of *Cours de philosophie positive* (1830–1842) [in English, *System of positive polity* (1875–77)].

17 Louis Gabriel Ambroise de Bonald (1754–1840), French philosopher, author of *Théorie du pouvoir politique et religieux* (1796), *Recherches philosophiques sur les premiers objets des connaissances morales* (1818), and *Démonstrations philosophique du principe constitutif de la société* (1827).

18 de Maistre, J. (1753–1821), author of *Essai sur le principe générateur des constitutions politiques* (1814).

19 E. Durkheim, *Les Formes élémentaires de la vie religieuse* (Paris, Alcan, 1912), [in English, trans. J. W. Swain, *The elementary forms of the religious life* (New York: Free Press, 1915)].

20 E. Durkheim, *Sociologie et philosophie* (Paris, Alcan, 1924), [in English, trans. D. F. Pocock, *Sociology and philosophy* (New York: Free Press, 1913)].

21 L. Lévy-Bruhl, *Les Fonctions mentales dans les sociétés inférieures* (Paris, Alcan, 1910) [in English, trans. L. A. Clare, *How natives think* (New York: Alfred A. Knopf, 1926)].

22 The sense intended here is something like 'to draw off without disturbing the underlying sediment'.

23 Théodore Flournoy (1854–1920), founder of scientific psychology in Switzerland and the *Archives de psychologie*.

24 Reading French *on* for *ou*.

25 Translating the French *en fait . . . en droit* as *de facto . . . de jure*. The contrast here is between the factual ('is') and the normative ('ought').

26 Théodule Armand Ribot (1839–1916), French psychologist and co-founder of French psychology, author of *Les Maladies de la mémoire* (1881), *Les Maladies de la volonté* (1883), *Les Maladies de la personalité* (1885), *La Psychologie des sentiments* (1896), *Logique des sentiments* (1905), *Essais sur les passions* (1907), *De la Méthode dans la sciences* (1909), *Problèmes de psychologie affective* (1910), and *La Vie inconsciente et les mouvements* (1914).

27 Paul Eugen Bleuler (1857–1939), Swiss psychiatrist, most famous for his *Dementia precox, oder Gruppe der Schizophrenien* (1911).

28 Pierre Janet (1859–1947), French psychologist, author of more than fifteen books, the most famous of which were *L'État mental des hystériques* (1892), [in English, *The mental state of hysteria* (1901)], *The major symptoms of hysteria* (1907).

29 This theme is also addressed in J. Piaget, *Le Jugement et le raisonnement chez l'enfant* (Neuchâtel/Paris: Delachaux et Niestlé, 1924), [in English, *Judgment and reasoning in the child* trans. M. Warden, (London: Routledge & Kegan Paul, 1928)].

30 French, *vérification*.

31 Edmond Goblot, *Traité de logique*. 4th Ed. (Paris: Colin, 1925).

32 The contrast assimilation-constraint in Piaget's (1924) text, *Judgment and reasoning in the child* (London: Routledge & Kegan Paul, 1928) is replaced in 1936 with the contrast assimilation-accommodation in *The origins of intelligence in the child* (London: Routledge & Kegan Paul, 1953).

33 French, *la mise en correspondance*. For a re-analysis of correspondence as a precursor of transformation, see J. Piaget, G. Henriques and E. Ascher, *Morphisms and categories* (Hillsdale, NJ: Erlbaum, 1992).

34 The reference here is to Lalande's *L'Idée directrice de la dissolution opposée à celle de l'évolution*.

35 Célestin Bouglé (1870–1940), French sociologist and friendly critic of Durkheim, author of *Les Ideés égalitaires* (1899), *Leçons de sociologie sur l'évolution des valeurs* (1892), [in English, *The evolution of values* (1926)], *Qu'est que la sociologie?* (1907).

36   French, *grand chose de commun.*
37   The reference here presumably is to Paul Lacombe (1834–1919), French historian, author of *History regarded as a science* (1894).
38   French *refoule.* For discussion of cognitive unconsciousness, see J. Piaget, *The grasp of consciousness* (London: Routledge & Kegan Paul, 1977) and *Success and understanding* (London: Routledge & Kegan Paul, 1978).
39   Presumably the reference here is to G. Stanley Hall, *Adolescence*, 2 vols. (New York: Appleton, 1904).
40   Ferdinand de Saussure (1857–1913), Swiss linguist, author of *Cours de linguistique générale* (1916) [in English, *Course in general linguistics* (1959)].
41   French, *juste.*
42   French, *exactes.*
43   French, *refoulement.*
44   The reference here presumably is to Johann Pestalozzi (1746–1827) and his followers, as well as to Piaget's account in his 1935 paper which is reprinted in *The science of education and the psychology of the child* (Longman, 1970).
45   See J. Piaget, *Le Jugement moral chez l'enfant* (Paris, Alcan, 1932), [in English, *The moral judgment of the child*, trans. M. Gabain (London: Routledge & Kegan Paul,1932)].
46   French, *ne se contrôlent pas.*
47   See J. Piaget, *Le Langage et la pensée chez l'enfant* (Neuchâtel/Paris: Delachaux et Niestlé, 1923), [in English, *The language and thought of the child*, trans. M. & R. Gabain, (London, Routledge & Kegan Paul, 1926)].
48   L. Lévy-Bruhl, *L'Âme primitive* (Paris: Alcan, 1927), [in English, *The 'soul' of the primitive*, trans. L. A. Clare, (New York, Macmillan, 1928)].
49   French, *conserve.*
50   See Note 25.
51   French, *la Prise de conscience.*
52   French, *décalage.* In Piaget's account, vertical *décalage* is an inter-stage shift and, as such, is taken to be a central process in intellectual construction. Such a process is distinct from within-stage shifts or horizontal *décalage.* See Piaget's 'Le mécanisme du développement mental et les lois du groupement des opérations: esquisse d'une théorie opératoire de l'intelligence'. *Archives de psychologie*, 28, 215–285.
53   See Note 29.
54   Paris, Alcan, 1927.
55   Gabriel Tarde (1843–1904), author of over a dozen books in sociology and social psychology, the most famous of which is *Les Lois de l'imitation* (1890), [in English, *The laws of imitation*, (1903)].

6 Individuality in history
The individual and the education of reason[1]

[p. 240] There is hardly a more complex subject or one more liable to misunderstanding than that whose discussion *la Semaine de synthèse*, 1931,[1] has entrusted to a simple child psychologist. Mastering such a problem requires combining a knowledge[2] of sociology and psychology with a detailed understanding[3] of the history of science and of epistemology. Now the author is a specialist in neither sociology nor in the philosophy of science, and, as far as individual psychology is concerned, his competence ends around the age of 12 or 13. Nevertheless, once having noted these limitations, it is perhaps not entirely meaningless to try to project the few rays of light that an analysis of children provides on to the sociological history of reason. August Comte stated correctly that the most important phenomenon of social life was the mutual pressure each generation exerts on the others. Now, one of the principal aims of child psychology is precisely the study of this phenomenon. So, the observation of children is not such a bad method when deciding the extent to which rationality is a matter of individual development and to what extent it is something social. We will limit ourselves here to fulfilling this task, leaving to others the problem of situating this particular perspective within the set of possible perspectives.

First of all, what is the meaning of the question we are going to examine? At first glance, its meaning seems very clear: is it the individual as such or is it the social group that constitutes the motor or, if you prefer, the 'context' of intellectual evolution? But, after analysing the already too voluminous file of these still on-going proceedings, one immediately realizes that a dispute of an epistemological nature has attached itself to the psycho-sociological discussion, [p. 241] and that a sound method is to begin by dissociating these two aspects of the debate. Why, indeed, have so many fine minds felt an immediate and almost unreflective distrust in the presence of sociological theses, other than that they seemed to diminish the value of reason itself? The passionate obstinacy which maintained that reason was exclusively the province of individual consciousness resulted, for many, from the rationalist belief in the radical autonomy and the superiority of intellectual values. But, it seems to us, that this is a first ambiguity to be dismissed. First, history shows that several 'individualist' psychologies have revealed themselves to be just as ruinous for rationalism as was the narrowest sociologism: this was the case with associationism, for example. But especially, we believe, there exists no direct relation between the problem 'of principle' or logic, which is to discover the internal conditions for a sound exercise of reason, and the problem 'of fact', or the psycho-sociological problem, which is to know whether this immanent development of reason presupposes, as an external condition, a certain social organization or the mere play of hereditary or acquired characteristics specific to individual consciousness as such.

In order to avoid any misunderstandings, let us immediately state that we believe in the irreducible and *sui generis*[4] value of reason, and we think that no argument drawn from experience could ever make us doubt this value which is specific to rational activity, as all experience is always relative to such activity. But precisely because truth is an ideal that proposes itself to consciousness, and not a datum that is imposed like a material fact, it is senseless to conceive of reason as an already constructed mechanism operating as does an hereditary reflex, an individual habit, or a collective custom, and it is pointless to hunt for whether the seat of this mechanism is biological, purely psychological, or social. Reason is an ideal, of which reflection becomes consciously aware during the course of its deepening, and the elaboration of rational norms in and of itself, since it is reflexive, is neither biological, individual, nor social. On the other hand, and here is where the factual problem occurs in all of its legitimacy, one is entitled to ask what the external conditions for this reflection are. Granted, the criterion of truth still remains to be found [p. 242] not in the constraints of heredity, habit, or custom, but in the autonomous reflection of a personal consciousness, one can and must wonder how the new-born infant that we all began as becomes capable of such reflection. Is his hereditary equipment, together with his purely individual acquisitions, sufficient for this task, or is a social interaction among individuals necessary to shape his intellectual instruments? This is the only problem that we will attempt to discuss here.

But this very question, thus brought down to its proper proportions, unfortunately remains equivocal and in part trifling. Indeed, obviously, everything in the individual is always at once biological, psychological, and social. If we consider the meanings of the term 'social', that is, as encompassing the hereditary drives that push us toward communal life and toward imitation, as well as the 'external' relationships of individuals among themselves (the word 'external' being understood in the manner of Durkheim), one cannot deny that intellectual development, from birth, is simultaneously the work of society and of the individual. Nevertheless, two now famous theses have confronted each other: for some, reason is a product of the individual superior to any collective tradition or opinion, whilst for others reason is a collective product superior to individual feeling and caprice.

If child psychology can be of some help to us here, it certainly will not be by reviving this sterile and verbal debate into which Tarde and Durkheim have already overly lapsed. Nor will it suffice to place the opponents back to back by repeating that everything is always both individual and social. These terms must themselves be analysed, and they must be analysed genetically. Indeed, the common man is not social in the same way at 6 months and at age 20, and consequently his 'individuality' cannot possibly be of the same quality at these two different levels. The internal relations that constitute individuality and the correlative relations that constitute social life are constructed gradually and one must cut into this construction in order to grasp its mechanism and direction. This is what we are going to deal with first, in order then to be able to apply the distinctions established to the problem of the relations between individuality and reason. [p. 243]

I. DISTINCTIONS AND DEFINITIONS

The terms 'individual' and 'society' are not only vague: they cover almost contradictory notions. As to their relations with reason, there is not, in fact, one single type of individuality nor one single type of social relation: there are at least two. The individual can be the *self*, when centred on himself, or *personality*, when he voluntarily submits himself to forms of reciprocity and of universality. And society can be *constraint*, to the extent that the authority of the group and of its traditions are exercised as such, or *cooperation*, to the extent that autonomous personalities elaborate a system of relations based on reciprocity.

To understand these distinctions, let us start from this observation, whose fundamental importance it remains Durkheim's great merit to have realized, that human society presupposes an increasing number of relations 'external' to the individual. Animals are social, but especially 'internally'; that is, their collective life is regulated, for a very large part, by means of hereditary biological drives. Granted, in higher animals, certain behaviour patterns are learned through educating the young, and certainly, in the anthropoid apes, imitation and even mutual understanding between individuals play an essential role in their behaviour. But what is exchanged thus by means of 'external transmission' is hardly anything compared to the social interaction permitted in man by language, family and school education, and the set of the other 'institutions' that exert pressure on the individual during his entire life. So then, if in his first year the child begins by being social only in the biological and 'internal' sense of the word, he becomes increasingly more socialized throughout the following years, in the sense of a society 'external' to individuals. No doubt affective exchanges, imitation, rules of hygiene, etc. imposed by his family circle from the cradle on, already constitute 'external' relations. But one would have to be blinded by a preconceived system of thought[5] not to admit that the number of these interactions increases with age and increases in importance relative to purely hereditary social drives. It is in this sense that the child becomes progressively socialized. [p. 244] This does not mean that the infant is not social from birth, but simply that he submits to an increasing number of external ties, that is, ties whose content is not predetermined by his biological heritage. So he becomes socialized in the same way that he adapts to his external physical environment: he adds an increasing number of acquired mechanisms to his hereditary equipment, the only difference being that in the social domain these acquisitions are made due to the pressure of other individuals instead of only being due to the sole constraint of things.

This being the case, individuality can be understood in two very distinct ways. The first is the *self*, that is, the individual as centred on himself. In fact, it goes without saying that, to the extent that society penetrates into the individual from the outside, he was not prepared to accept this without further ado: there is no pre-established harmony between each one's psycho-biological constitution and the set of intellectual and moral values proposed by communal life, and, if there naturally exists an affinity between the first and the second, this affinity nevertheless presupposes a laborious adjustment (all of 'education') to transcend the virtual and become actual. Just as a child of 2 or 3 is not able to conceive of the laws of the solar system simply by looking at the stars and his immediate horizon, so this same child cannot discover the various aspects of intellectual and moral reciprocity all at once simply by being in contact with his family circle. In both cases, a mental transformation is required that consists not just in a passive recording of external facts, but in a structural elaboration of new relations. Consequently, a set of active, intellectual, but non-socialized drives will obviously exist in the individual, either because they have not yet been socialized, or because they resist this socialization. This is the first sense of the word 'individual': it is the 'self' as opposed to other 'selves', that is, as prior or resistant to socialization.

This egocentrism, specific to each of our individualities, is all too well known in adults with whom it is largely lucid and tolerated by the social consciousness.[6] But, at the beginnings of mental evolution, it presents quite another character. Childhood individuality is not only partially resistant to socialization, as is our own: it is above all prior to it, [p. 245] to the exact extent to which society only conquers the individual progressively and from the outside in. Consequently, childhood egocentrism is unconscious of itself: it is a sort of 'innocence' not only 'of the eye' but of the whole mind, such that the immediate sight of people and things seems to be the only one possible and is not yet situated in relation to other points of view. This being the case, the young child is largely centred upon himself, but unknowingly, and so projects his subjectivity into things and into other people: he only perceives people and objects other than himself, but he sees them only through himself. Of course, this unconscious intellectual egocentrism con-stitutes only a fraction of the mind since socialization begins with growth, but the younger the child, the more important is this fraction in relation to the zone that is truly socialized.

In certain respects, the second sense of the word 'individuality' is exactly the opposite: indeed, *personality* is not the 'self' as different from other 'selves' and resistant to socialization, but is rather the individual as one who voluntarily submits to the norms of reciprocity and universality. As such, far from being on the fringe of society, personality constitutes the most refined product of socialization. In fact, the individual becomes a personality to the extent that the 'self' voluntarily renounces itself in order to insert its own point of view among those of others, and bends to the rules of reciprocity. No doubt the personality does not abolish the self, but it requires its conversion and thus condemns its egocentrism. The personality is thus a *sui generis* synthesis of what is original in each of us and of cooperative norms. In opposition to an initial egocentrism that involves taking one's own point of view to be absolute, failing to notice its specific character, personality involves consciously realizing the relativity of one's individual perspective and then relating it to the set of all other possible perspectives: so personality implies a coordination of the individual with the universal.

Now, on the other hand, to this double aspect of individuality corresponds an obvious dualism in what we globally call the social: society can be either constraint or cooperation, and a strict relation unites each of these two terms to each of the two poles of the individual.

Society is *constraint* to the extent that it is a source of heteronomy for individual consciousness. [p. 246] In fact, being 'external' to individuals, social realities can impose themselves by their very authority and without the individual who is subject to them participating in their elaboration. Such is the case when a child accepts preformed opinions and rules from an adult as given, or when there is a constraint on even adult individuals to respect the traditions of their social group simply because they are imposed. In this way, educational and social constraint implies an inequality among individuals: whereas some are cloaked in authority or prestige, because they are older or because they are the custodians of tradition, others are subject to this authority.

By contrast, society is *cooperation* when it implies relations among individuals who are equal, or are considered as such, and relations founded on freedom. In effect, when individuals cooperate without being circum-scribed by the authority of the elders or by tradition, they themselves elaborate social realities and then submit to them in complete willingness.[7] This is not to say, incidentally, that all social ties originate from cooperation, nor that constraint presupposes that society is already formed, because individuals, and perhaps even social groups themselves, are subject to maximal constraint when they are young. So cooperation, at least in its pure or refined state, appears as a progressive victory of the social spirit,[8] and not as a primary given: equality is not natural to individuals, but is mastered little by little. More precisely, it is only once social relations are globally organized (through a mixture of constraint and cooperation) that cooperation becomes dissociated in the guise of society so created, in opposition to constraint, which itself then assumes the guise of a crystallized society that imposes the weight of its traditions on the individual. Likewise, while cooperation marks the internalization of the social in the individual, this internality, while not resulting from it directly, is akin to the social only in the innate and psycho-biological sense of the word. In fact, the rules of reciprocity that constitute cooperation (on both the intellectual and the moral level) are 'external' to individuals, as is all acquired social behaviour, and, if they better suit the psychological nature of the individual than do rules imposed by constraint, that, as we have seen, is because they allow the personality to flourish instead of remaining crystallized and 'heteronomous'.

This last point allows us to understand a double relation essential from the point of view of the relations between individuality and the development of reason: [p. 247] egocentrism goes hand in hand with constraint, and personality with cooperation. It is easy to understand that egocentrism is correlative to constraint, even though at first sight the self and social authority seem to be contradictory. On the one hand, indeed, egocentric individuals can only be led by external constraint: which explains the generality of this process at the earlier stages of social life. On the other hand, and in return, the constraint exercised over an individual reinforces his egocentrism: far from leading him to the state of personality, as does cooperation, constraint only socializes him on the surface and leaves intact the deep habits specific to egocentrism. In short, constraint and egocentrism constitute the initial and correlative forms of sociality and individuality. As for personality and cooperation, they are simply two sides of one and the same phenomenon: the social ties in which individuality engages cease to be coercive and become cooperative to the extent that individuality renounces its egocentrism so as to become personality, and personality becomes possible to the extent that cooperation prevails over constraint.

One final remark. A common objection is that every social fact combines cooperation and constraint, and one might add that every individual is always simultaneously a self and a personality. Granted, but one need only admit a possible proportioning of the two elements in each pair, or more precisely between the forces of attraction specific to the two poles of each system, for it to be legitimate to dissociate in principle these two elements or these poles. Evidently, then, cooperation is in fact indissociable from constraint but their respective actions remain no less opposite. In the same way personality obviously overlays the self, but it exists only on condition of its meaning being inverted.

With these distinctions in mind, we are now in a position to deal with the relations between individuality and the development of reason. A few examples selected from the area of child psychology will show how reason eludes both the egocentric individual and coercive society, and is based instead on the twofold constitution of personal consciousness and cooperative social relations. [p. 248]

II. THE SELF AND THE INDIVIDUAL INTELLECT

Is the individual as such, as equipped by heredity and as capable of enrichment through contact with the physical environment, able to accede to reason independently of progressively acquired external social relations? We believe not: the individual so defined fulfils the conditions necessary for this ascension, but not the conditions sufficient actually to make him do it.

Three examples will illustrate both his richness and his impotence: practical intelligence, immediate experience, and symbolic thought.

The individual in himself possesses a *practical* or *sensory-motor intelligence*. For example, show a small opening from which a watch chain has just been seen falling to a one-year-old child and he immediately tries to put the chain back in the box. In order to do so, he places one end of the chain in the aperture, which escapes and falls. He tries the same operation with the other end and sees his failure. After several attempts he stops, examines the situation, and abruptly places the chain on the ground, gathers it into a ball, and triumphantly introduces it into the required opening. Here is an act characterized by intelligence and yet society had nothing to do with it. Of course, imitation may have had something to do with the prior use of his hands, in various manipulations implicating the grasping schema,[9] etc., and perhaps social stimulation is often needed to revive the baby's interest. But one easily imagines an individual putting in a greater number of months, or years, to solve these sorts of problems and solving them without such adjuncts. So this is definitely the case of behaviour patterns that the social factor may accompany, perhaps always accompanies, but which do not result from it.

Now, can we possibly compare this practical intelligence, operating just as much in the first months of life as throughout childhood, to the reflected and certainly socialized intelligence that makes use of language as an indispensable instrument? From a purely functional point of view, this is undoubtedly so. The sensory-motor schemes,[9] coordinated and differentiated by the subject as their application requires, are analogous to concepts. [p. 249] The practical assimilation of objects to these schemes prefigures judgment and incorporation of means to ends, reasoning itself. But, from a structural point of view, an essential difference appears to differentiate these operations from those of reflected intelligence. It must be understood that, in effect, they tend toward success and not toward truth: they seek to attain a goal, and not to note the existence of relations for their own sake, which condition the means appropriate to attaining that end. Consequently, practical intelligence is not accompanied by reflection: consciousness is oriented outwards, with no attention toward the method followed, that is, toward the operations themselves.

A quite typical case of this opposition between practice and reflection is that of the logic of relations. '*Gestalt psychology*' has shown the importance of relativity right from the perception of colour in higher animals. A chicken trained to peck its grain on a clear grey background, when faced with this grey on a white background, will pick at dark grey when it no longer sees that this new colour is actually that to which it is habituated: this is proof that it perceives relations and not absolute colours. So a use of relations enters into all acts of practical intelligence and, particularly, into the example of the chain just mentioned. And yet, when presented with three similar boxes and told that 'Box A is heavier than box B, and it is lighter than this other box C', children between 5 and 7 years old are still unable to determine which box is heavier: they answer that B is heavy, C is light and A is half-light, half-heavy! In other words, reflection on relations is something quite different from perception of relations, and what may occur first in practical construction, may occur last in reflection. It so happens that, on the verbal plane, the child reasons with absolute qualities (this box is heavy, the other light, etc.), at the very places where, in his sensory-motor activity, he begins with relations. This is because reflection, being a 'conscious realization', presupposes the formulation, or the concourse of points of view, and of any number of operations implying a reversal of values, in which the role of social life is apparent.

A second characteristic of the individual intellect will allow us to carry this analysis further. The individual, by possessing practical intelligence, [p. 250] is certainly likely to profit from his experienced contact with physical reality. Except that individual experience is what we call *immediate experience*, as opposed to scientific or corrected experience which presupposes a concourse between different points of view, and consequently, cooperation. Immediate experience is empiricism, which takes sensible reality such as it appears for objective fact. In many cases, and precisely when practical needs are at work, this experience suffices to lead to truth. In this way, direct observation allows the child to acquire some fairly subtle knowledge, for example, the correct explanation of how a bicycle works (this explanation can be discovered as early as 5 or 6 by gifted children and it is available by 8, on average, in normal boys). Only two sorts of circumstance can cause complications, and this is where the inadequacy of purely individual experience becomes noticeable. In the first place, appearance continuously demands correction and this correction presupposes relating various points of view. This is the case, for example, when slightly complicated 'displacement groups' must be constructed: i.e. to understand that the mountain does not move as we approach it, that the stars are not small balls situated at rooftop height that only move when we walk, that the shores do not move as the boat advances, etc. No doubt the infant already elaborates similar 'groups', during his first two years, when he constructs his space and his notion of object permanence. But these groups remain limited, and one wonders if the act of imitating others, thereby objectifying his own self in various people, right at the start, is not an important factor for the child in the objectification of his universe. In general, in all cases, by the age of verbal thought, one can easily see how much individual experience still remains 'realist': without a system of reference constituted by the points of view of other individuals, the child is continuously led to consider his own as absolute. So he does not dissociate subjective appearance from objective reality, because of the lack of reciprocity between perspectives. Such is the first characteristic of 'immediate experience'. No doubt one can conceive of an individual who lives long enough, and is gifted enough, to compare his own successive points of view among themselves: [p. 251] then he could criticize them and would constitute a society unto himself. But, in fact, this sort of operation always results psychologically from socially acquired habits of putting things into relation.

A second characteristic of 'immediate experience' follows from the first: it is 'adualistic', that is, it projects subjective adherences into things that emanate from the self alone. This is how the child attributes intentionality to the movements in the universe as long as these movements remain conceived of as they appear, and are not ordered into objective displacement groups. He is an animist to the extent that he is a realist: he can only conceive of the quaking mountain or the moving moon as endowed with life and will. Here again, one might imagine an individual who perseveres enough in his self-criticism slowly to dissociate the self from external reality and to detach it from all subjective adherence. But, in fact, social contact is what brings about consciousness of the self, and that conscious realization is what leads to the progressive delimitation of the psychical and the physical.

Up until now, the individual as such has appeared to us as being essentially oriented toward practical intelligence and immediate experience, thus as resisting reflection, and the implied corrections to the representation of things. This is not to say, however, that the individual is incapable of thought. But we observe a new dissociation between the social pole and the individual pole of the mind once thinking in the small child becomes superimposed on the act, that is, once the systematic evocation of absent objects completes the perception of an immediate fact. The individual orients himself quite as spontaneously toward *symbolic thought*, proceeding through concrete and motivated symbols, that the group elaborates into a 'semic' thought proceeding through abstract and arbitrary signs.

All thought is a system of meanings.[10] Granted, this can and must be said of perception and of sensory-motor intelligence: perceived qualities are nothing other than the signs of concrete objects constructed by the intellect, or actions inherent in this construction; the most elementary practical schemes thus confer a complex set of meanings on all sensory data. Except that, on the purely active plane, the signifier is unified with the signified, that is, the sign is an objective aspect of the thing itself. One might call this concrete sign the 'index',[11] and, even when the index is arbitrary from the experimenter's point of view [p. 252] (as is the case with a 'signal' triggering an act in animal training experiments), for the individual it can never be more than an extension of the thing itself. (If the subject comes to suspect its artificial character, from his point of view, the signal becomes a conventional, and thus social, sign between the experimenter and himself.) By contrast, whenever there is thought (and this is precisely what we believe distinguishes thought, properly so called, from purely practical intelligence), the signifier dissociates itself from the signified and the system of signs takes on a life of its own.

Now these signs, once differentiated from concrete 'indexes', can be of two sorts. According to a classic distinction of Saussurian linguistics, there are two types of signs: symbols, which are 'justified' signs (for example, a blindfolded woman who symbolizes justice) and signs properly so called, which are 'arbitrary' symbols (for example, words or mathematical symbols, whose structure is unrelated to what is signified). This apparently insignificant difference greatly advances the opposition between socialized and individual thought. Indeed, being arbitrary, the 'sign' is essentially social. Not only is such-and-such a sign attributed a signification so-and-so in virtue of an explicit convention or tacit agreement, but the system of signs is even coextensive with the system of concepts, that is, with a system of schemes whose generality, abstraction, and fixedness of definition presuppose thought in common. In this respect, the agreement between Saussurian linguistics and Durkheim's sociology is too striking to leave any remaining doubt on condition, naturally, that one does not consider this social aspect of 'semic' meanings[10] as exclusive of the psychological activity of a personal intelligence.

But if the 'sign' necessarily presupposes the social, the constitution of the 'symbol', on the contrary, while able to present every degree of socialization, requires nothing more than individual thought having attained a certain level of development. On the one hand, being 'justified', the symbol is always an image: a concrete object acting as an image, or a mental image. On the other hand, the 'signified' is in no way required to assume even a relative fixity or systematization in the symbol, as it must in the sign. While the symbol can designate a concept (as in the case of socialized symbols), it can also connote any individual scheme at all, whether practical or affective, [p. 253] relative to a specifically determined concrete object or to a more or less globally classified group of objects. In this way, the symbol merely extends sensory-motor intelligence. When an infant pretends to be asleep, mimicking his habitual gestures with a smile (closing his eyes, sucking his thumb, holding a cloth in his hand that simulates the pillow), he plays out a symbol before thinking it, and this symbol is nothing other than an action scheme taken out of its context and thus promoted to the rank of image. When this same infant says 'Meow' while sliding a pebble down a box, the symbol will be entirely created, by assimilating an absent object to present data by endowing it with some link of resemblance to it.

The symbol is thus the instrument of individual thought *par excellence*. Here are two examples of the manifestation of this symbolic thought, both essential to the individual's psychological development: child's play and affective thought.

There are numerous types of games of which the three principal types are: games involving sensory-motor exercise, symbolic games, and rule games. Rule games are social and are of no interest to us here. Exercise games appear in the first months of life; they are common to young animals and to children, and correspond pretty well to the conception of K. Groos: the functional exercise of the principal psycho-biological activities. That leaves symbolic games, which appear to be specifically childlike and which pose a problem that is not entirely resolved. Indeed, one notices, from the second year of life until the end of early childhood, that in most cases, when left to himself, the child uses reality and the objects entering into his sphere of activity, not necessarily to adapt himself to them, but rather to assimilate them to himself so as to have them represent internal realities, scenes from prior experience, or the world as he wants to make it. So pebbles, sticks, or blades of grass, become symbols of anything at all, and fiction systematically prevails over reality. Why is this so?

While almost all theories of play have tried to account for the functional aspect of this symbolism (pre-exercise, compensation, catharsis, etc.)[2] very few (besides the outmoded conception of Stanley Hall) [p.254] have raised the structural problem of why there are symbolic games and not games of some other sort. K. Groos, who actually started with the question of fiction, considers that his hypothesis of pre-exercise resolved it: the child insists on playing at activities fictitiously which he cannot yet seriously apply himself to. But explaining the symbol by its subject matter, in other words the filiation of content established between the fictional symbol and simple exercise, seems insufficient to resolve the problem. Indeed, on the one hand, pre-exercise in no way implicates the symbol: sensory-motor exercise, curiosity, etc. are all typical cases in which pre-exercise does without fictions.[3] Why should not everything be this way? For example, if playing at eating dinner was a preparatory exercise for a little girl, one fails to see why she does not spend all of her time observing and questioning the cook, rather than spending hours placing blades of grass over pebbles to play out dinner scenes fictitiously. On the other hand, and above all, symbolism extends infinitely beyond any preparatory exercise. Here are two or three examples observed in my own daughters. I found one stretched out on the sofa with her eyes closed, her arms wrapped around her, and her legs tucked up under her chin, 'I'm a dead duck', she then explains, alluding to a duck she had seen in the kitchen that had greatly impressed her. The second came close to me, in my office, and, straight and motionless, began to make an intolerable racket vaguely resembling 'ding, dong, etc.'. I turned around and jokingly placed my hand against her mouth. Reply: 'Don't do that, I'm a church.' Or again the first one, whom I told to be careful of slippery rocks while we were out walking in the mountains, immediately invented a story-game involving what happened to an imaginary friend of hers who slipped and fell to the bottom of a ravine, into a river, etc. So what is the meaning of these symbols or fictions?

There is no question here of pre-exercise, except to say with Claparède[4] that the child simply exercises her faculties of observation, imagination, etc. But, if so, why is the game symbolic? [p. 255] For us the answer to this problem involves structural and not only functional considerations: fictional games extend exercise games, not, as Groos believes, because of their content, but because of the structure of the child's thought. The symbol is nothing other than the spontaneous instrument of individual thought, one that extends the sensory-motor scheme specific to action on a representational plane; it plays the same role in individual thought that words and concepts play in socialized thought. So, in order for this thought to become symbolic, it need only pursue individual ends, i.e. it needs to satisfy desires, compensate for or purge a painful reality, imagine the unachievable, etc., in sum, it must assimilate reality to the self rather than accommodate the self to reality: this is the source of children's games, which are the affirmation of all forms of the self, and which thus fulfil all of the functions insisted upon by different authors. Moreover, for the child's thought to be translated symbolically, she need only be preoccupied by some practical or intellectual subject or some lively interest (that she sees a dead duck, or the village church, or that she might have slipped): where inner thoughts permit us to return to subjects that have impressed us, children's thoughts, because they are less socialized, less conceptual and less discursive than our own, need symbolic representation and play.

Such, then, is symbolic play: thought that, on the one hand, is doubly individual, in its function which is to assimilate reality to the self and not the self to a collective and common truth and, on the other, in its structure which is based on concrete symbols and not on conceptual and collective signs.

The second example which must now be discussed, that of dreams, is a more specifically affective thought, what Freudians call 'the unconscious', or what Bleuler calls 'autistic' thought. But let us restrict ourselves to two remarks. First, this thought is simply the extension of symbolic thought itself: the child's first dreams realize desires whose symbolism is hardly more complex than that of their waking games. Second, the 'symbol', in the most relaxed forms of individual thought whose existence psychoanalysis has the merit of having demonstrated, as opposed to logical and collective 'signs', is 'symbolic' in precisely the Saussurian sense of the word, which again demonstrates the unity of these phenomena. [p. 256]

In conclusion, the individual pole of thought now appears to be characterized by three principal traits: practical intelligence, immediate experience, and symbolism. This is why in recently studying the logic of the child and his representation of the world we were principally struck by two circumstances. The first is that the logic of the child, because it is less socialized, is less rational than our own: in fact, it remains intermediate between symbolic thought and rigorous and deductive thought. Children's concepts with their syncretism, juxtapositions, difficulty in handling logical operations (the logic of relations, the addition and multiplication of classes, etc.) are all examples of this situation. On the other hand, in its representation of things and of causality, the egocentrism specific to immediate experience and the irreflection specific to practical intelligence explain a multitude of notions that are animist, artificial, or possessing a bimorphic dynamism, about which it would take too long to elaborate here.

No doubt over the course of the preceding pages we have considered the young child in some extreme aspects of his psychology. In order to grasp the individual as such, we have, so to speak, dissociated children's intelligence by isolating the individual pole from its complementary social pole. Play and its symbolism in particular, while constituting the most characteristic aspect of this individual pole, are far from covering the totality of a child's thought. But this dissociation is legitimate if one seeks to attain what is individual in us. The individual never presents himself in a pure state, and the child is dual, even more so than we ourselves, oscillating endlessly between the social and egocentrism. But we understand the meaning of this artificial dissociation: what we have attempted to emphasize in children's egocentrism is its deep epistemic attitude. In this respect, there is certainly an individual pole to the mind: it is that of naive, immediate, and pre-critical, thought.

III. SOCIAL CONSTRAINT

It is now important to show how the individual escapes from this egocentrism in order to become a rational personality. Here one must resist the temptation to bring up the social as both a unique and simple explanation. [p. 257] Society no more knows how to create reason than does the individual himself. Reason is an ideal immanent in all acts of thought as in all practical operations. As such, it is pointless to try to exclude it from sensory-motor intelligence, even from immediate experience, or from symbolic thought: no matter how rudimentary they remain, the systems of schemes and meanings specific to these activities implicate reason in full, just as all living organisms, whether they be primitive or aberrations, presuppose life in terms of its most general laws. If we maintain that the individual as such is not rational, it is simply in the following sense. Although never entirely realized as an ideal, reason is a form of equilibrium toward which all cognitive systems aim, no matter how little equilibrium they may have. Note that there is nothing mystical in this way of speaking: biological phenomena themselves, such as assimilation, accommodation, organization, etc., imply forms of equilibrium that remain ideal, since no assimilation is ever absolute, and yet all organization aims to accomplish it. With this in mind, one might say that individual thought is a system that aims toward equilibrium (in this it is rational), but never attains it (in this it is not rational). So the problem, then, is not to know what creative causality will make reason penetrate the individual from the outside, but simply what circumstances will permit the rational equilibrium immanent in the individual to further realize itself. In this respect, it is a play on words to make society a cause: individual interaction can only result in bringing each consciously to realize the conditions of rational equilibrium better, but, strictly speaking, neither society nor the individual creates the laws of this equilibrium. As we saw at the beginning of this discussion, reason is elaborated through reflection, and so the only problem is to know how the individual, in order to attain a rational equilibrium, comes to 'reflect' what is immanent in all acts of thought.

These indications suffice to demonstrate why it is careless to speak of 'society' globally, as if any kind of social contact could enrich individuals by making them more reasonable. So the moment has come to return to our distinction between constraint and cooperation, and to see how both of these processes transform individuality.

Regarding social constraint, it seems to us that one can argue that it makes no deep changes to individual thought. [p. 258] True, egocentrism is limited by the group, even when this group simply imposes its authority on individuals from the outside, but then the egomorphism specific to sponta- neous thought is simply transformed into sociomorphism. This sort of modification certainly changes the content of representations, but it in no way transforms their structure. The 'self' remains unconverted.[5]

In this light, let us return to the principal aspects of individual thought. First, practical intelligence, on the social plane, gives rise to *technique*. Now, it is customary to present technique not only as an essential product of the collective consciousness (tools in and of themselves crystallizing an implicit knowledge, spread through tradition), but as one of the starting points of rational knowledge. Two distinctions must be made concerning the first of these assertions. Doubtless collaboration between individuals is indispensable in promoting practical intelligence into true technique. In this respect, technical progress can be assimilated to that of science: both presuppose free research conducted in common. But this is true only as long as technique is the work of cooperation, as long, then, as technical work can be done in complete autonomy. Now the history of technology shows well enough that such cooperation has interacted adversely and endlessly with the coercive currents of tradition and that technique in the process of being formed is endlessly grappling with 'sanctioned technique'. In such areas, the authority of the group is nothing but a hindrance: constraint is only a factor of immobilization and even of incomprehension, as compared to cooperation which alone can be considered a source of progress.

As for the second question, it may be strongly tied to the first. For some, from Bergson to certain sociologists such as Malinowski, technique is a source of rationality. For others, such as Essertier, it in no way leads to science on its own, unless a scientific outlook issuing from other sources comes to reflect upon its results. As this author so clearly states, man has long been 'a mechanic ignorant of mechanics'. [p. 259] This last thesis corresponds to what child development has taught us: sensory-motor intelligence alone does not lead to reflection, and a 'conscious realization' is needed to transfer what is already acquired on the plane of action onto the plane of thought. Furthermore, when thought arises, it spontaneously aims toward symbolic satisfaction as well as toward the egocentric representations of objects and causes. This is why, at the beginning of his development, the child seems more intelligent in his action than in his thought (he resolves subtle geometrical and mechanical problems practically at the same age at which his representation of the world is still animist and anthropomorphic), and by the same token, this is why technical skill contrasts so strongly in non-civilized peoples with the set of their other collective representations. Except that, when one compares the child to the life of social groups, one might ask why scientific reflection was not more precocious in humanity's development. If an initial hiatus exists between egocentric thought and practical intelligence, their continuity is soon seen re-established in the individual: eventually the child translates the results of his practical research into exact and adapted causal connections. It is here that the first thesis reclaims its rights, and that technique, once freed, seems to extend itself into what is properly called science.

Perhaps the truth is to be found in the following considerations. Practice remains sterile from the point of view of reflection as long as social constraint comes not only to slow technical progress, but also and especially to consolidate egocentric attitudes of thought. But practical intelligence extends into reflected intelligence as soon as constraint is broken through the play of cooperation and, simultaneously, egocentrism is reduced. We will examine this last point when considering cooperation in what follows. On the other hand, let us take up the first point, by studying what now becomes of immediate experience and symbolic thought under the influence of collective constraint.

Immediate experience is in no way transformed or affected by social constraint: there is only a change of aspect in the content of representations, and egocentrism becomes *sociomorphic*. First of all, one observes the effects of this sort of transformation in children themselves under the effects of adult constraint. To the extent that the child learns to respect and obey his parents, he comes to attribute many powers to them that he first attributes to himself. In consequence, artificialism is replaced by an initial magico-phenominist causality. [p. 260] But if one compares children's representations with the quantity of collective representations in lower societies, one cannot help but be struck by their resemblance, even though the former are egocentric and the latter are entirely permeated with sociality. This is because the passage from one to the other is explained in the same way as that just mentioned: instead of placing himself, or more modestly his parents, at the centre of everything, as does the young child, the 'primitive' adult places his social group there instead. Is this really such a great advance? Is there really such a difference as to preclude all comparison, at the scientific level, between the child who controls the motion of the sun or the moon by running through a field, and the Son of Heaven who controls the motion of the stars while making the rounds of his kingdom or his palace? Many other analogies could be drawn, but this is not the place to examine them closely. Let me simply mention the idea of a world order (of a moral causality imposing an anthropocentric rationale on all things), the idea of 'mana' that is both spiritual and physical, the union of phenomenalism with magical dynamism, not classification relative to the objective nature of things, but to their relationship to man, etc. Despite the numerous psychological differences that separate the beliefs of adults who are socially and mystically organized from the fragile and fuzzy beliefs of the individual child, from the point of view of the development of reason, they share a common epistemic attitude. This attitude consists in taking the world as it appears in immediate experience, instead of elaborating it through rational construction; and, in both cases, this immediate experience involves a non-differentiation between the subjective and the objective, whether the subjective be individual or collective humanity. Clearly, some rationality already enters into this global and immediate experience: this is seen through identification in 'participation',[6] and in the notions of conservation in 'mystical causality'.[7] The reason is that, in the most basic contacts of the mind with reality, the mind assimilates things according to its own functional drives. But the problem remains of knowing why this assimilation sometimes results in impersonal science and sometimes in an anthropomorphic vision of reality. This is because, in the first case, [p. 261] it is precisely an assimilation to the mind as such, stripped of all that comes from the 'self', whereas in the second case, the assimilation of the 'self' covers over and clouds the assimilation to the mind. So, whether the 'self' is the individual child or the individual submerged due to constraint in the social group itself is of no concern: in both cases, rational assimilation is distorted, and the experience of reality remains immediate because it is ego- or anthropocentric.

As to the third point, *symbolism*, this is exactly the same: social constraint in no way abolishes symbolic thought, instead it crystallizes and consolidates it. Indeed, it is a remarkable thing when one analyses this fluctuation of symbolism in the life of 'civilized' just as much as 'lower' social groups, from the point of view of the alternation between constraint and cooperation. In a general way, one might indeed say that the social symbol is instrumental in fusing egocentric thought and collective representations. Although collective symbols are externally imposed on everyone and thus realize the most complete communion (i.e. are common to all members of a group), whether one take for example a myth, a religious rite, a dogma, or even a political symbol (tribal, patriotic, etc.), the vitality of such symbols comes from the fact that each person can incorporate them into his intimate affectivity and so can fill them with the most personal contents. So the consensus permitted by symbols is at antipodes of what science calls 'the agreement between minds'.[12] The agreement between minds, such as it occurs in pure science, or following a moral, social, technical, or similar discussion, involves the acceptance, after discussion and confrontation of diverse points of view, of a specific truth whether experimental or simply logical. Thus it presupposes both the conscious realization of personal differences, and the coordination of these perspectives into an invariant or a covariant which is capable of verifying them. In contrast, the consensus specific to social constraint is unity achieved by authority, and, in the most basic cases, unity achieved alone without a conscious realization of individual perspectives or reasoned elaboration due to free personalities. This is why the consensus of authority is almost necessarily symbolic: whenever it appears conceptual, as in theological and almost all political ideology, it still participates closely in symbolic logic.

Having said this, one cannot help but be struck by the overall diminution of symbolism when one compares the elite of civilized societies, [p. 262] in which at least some small amount of cooperation reigns, to the elite of so-called lower societies, in which social constraint is certainly much more considerable, at least from a purely intellectual point of view. Wherever mystical representation is the only reflection, where magic takes the place of science, where judicial and commercial relationships are accompanied by obligatory religious ceremonies, where technique is imbued with traditional coercions, then symbolism constitutes the essence of social communication. In contrast, wherever cooperation between autonomous personalities seeks to constitute a science, a technique, and a morality independent of authority as such, symbolism declines to the benefit of the communion of ideas themselves.

Now, here again, it is difficult not to seek the explanation of such facts in individual psychology. As we have seen, the symbol is a concrete and 'justified' sign, or an image, to the extent that image connotes its content by pure subjective analogy, whether the image is plastic, mental, or consists in mythical and pseudo-conceptual allegories. This is why anything is permitted in play and in the affective thinking of the individual, and even on the plane of logical thinking, to the extent that the individual remains egocentric. In this respect, children's verbal and notional syncretism shows us how many subjective assimilations specific to symbolism can be extended at the very heart of socially imposed concepts.[8] Collective representations elaborated within a regime of constraint are nothing other than this collective crystallization of a basic way of thinking and partially escape rational elaboration.

In sum, however opposed the 'mechanical' interdependence of thought saturated in sociality, peculiar to gerontocratic societies, and the egocentric thought of the child might at first seem, upon analysis one notices that they share important mechanisms in common. The place of technique in relation to science is comparable to that of sensory-motor intelligence in relation to reflected thought; representation of the world peculiar to the sociomorphic thought of the 'primitive' and that of the child both present an identical central attitude, [p. 263] that of immediate and non-corrected experience; finally the opposition of the symbolic pole and the notional pole of thought is found as much in little evolved collective representations as in an individual who is becoming socialized.

One final remark, unfortunately even more schematic than the preceding ones, seems of a nature to clarify this parallelism by illuminating the nature of social constraint. If there are certain analogies between the so-called primitive and the child, it is certainly not due to some 'biogenetic' law, the use of which has proven dangerous in biology and completely hazardous in psycho-sociology. There is a simpler explanation: gerontocratic constraint retards the intellectual development of those who are subject to it. Now one might argue that the individual in lower societies experiences an increasing constraint from tradition: he is almost less free as an adult than as a child. Indeed, the education of children is very liberal in the least evolved societies that we know. At adolescence, however, a severe educational constraint begins that ends in an initiation. And the young men must follow the Elders and the Elders themselves must follow tradition in a way that subjugates them like the dogmas of a Church obligate its highest dignitaries. With us, on the contrary, childhood marks the *maximum* of intellectual and moral constraint. Adolescence is a liberation, as much by the primacy of exchange with peers, over obedience to adults, as by a sort of intellectual revolt on the part of each new generation with regard to the preceding ones. Finally the typical adult is autonomous, at least in the sort of professional zone of his intellectual consciousness and moral conscience.[6] These diverging lines of individual development seem sufficient to explain why there remains something somewhat childlike about gerontocratic societies: social constraint crystallizes the mentality of the child, whereas cooperation and the development of autonomous personalities are required to reduce it. As for understanding why lower societies are more gerontocratic and coercive than our own, is it not precisely because the mentality of their individuals remains childlike, that is, both egocentric and dominated by an intellectual and moral respect for the adult? Indeed, this sort of circle between the structure of the group and the mental attitude of its individuals is in no way vicious: it is what observation constantly shows us. [p. 264] But, since all individuals are children before attaining virility, it is natural that human societies began by this sort of crystallization of the childlike.

Permit us to remind you, concerning these different remarks relative to social constraint, and in particular concerning these final ones, that these are conjectures of a child psychologist concerning subjects that he knows nothing about. Only the training due to a week of synthesis excuses such licence ...

IV. COOPERATION

It is now time to analyse the role of cooperation. This other sort of social rapport can be defined as reciprocity between autonomous individuals. Its intervention seems able to explain the transition from 'self' to personality, and, consequently, the advent of rational values. Recall that cooperation is only one of two poles in any social process, certainly the pole opposed to constraint, but perhaps in fact indissociable from it. In principle, if we judge cooperation by the ideal that it implies and not uniquely by how it is put into practice, it acts in the opposite way to constraint. Now, this distinction between principle and fact is legitimate precisely in the case of cooperation, whereas it is devoid of meaning for authority as such. Indeed, constraint imposes ready-made beliefs or rules, in whose elaboration the individual bound by them plays no part. By contrast, cooperation proposes only a method – the method of mutual coordination and verification – and the complete application of this method remains an ideal that is never attained (even in science where questions of prestige and authority play at least a secondary role).

So cooperation exists from the beginning of social life, or from the most basic of social interactions, but at first it occurs only as fused with constraint and dominated by it. Afterwards, however, it partially dissociates itself and hence can manifest its opposite action, even forming a special technique of intellectual cooperation, such as tends to reign in positive science. How can this dissociation be explained? [p. 265] In the social realm, Durkheim has superbly shown how the individual manages to deliver himself from the gerontocracy, when social density accumulates and the effects of mutual interpenetration neutralize the constraints specific to various groups. In this respect, the strange mixture of civilizations, or of social currents, that permitted the Presocratics to free themselves from theological authority so as to establish free reflection, illustrates the Durkheimian thesis. But to this interpretation of the transformation of the collective context, psychological observation must be added. In children, cooperation appears as a spontaneous drive from the first years onwards. At the beginning of childhood this drive is only hindered by the illusions of viewpoint characteristic of egocentrism, and is thwarted by all authoritative education, as when adult constraint prevails over cooperation between children, or between children and adults. The opposition of gerontocracy to cooperative drives seems to explain the mentality of individuals in sparsely populated and segmentary societies, in which constraint predominates. But as soon as social density increases, this opposition turns into victory for the new generation. This is the case for us, when the adolescent escapes from adult authority, at least interiorly, to find the raw source of his future activity in his relations with his peers. This situation has struck teachers to the point where all new pedagogy is oriented toward using cooperation between children or adolescents in the school itself, and is conceived as an essential factor in intellectual and moral education.

What then are the effects of this cooperation? With this in mind, and with the sole aim of simplifying this discussion by making it more schematic, let us return to the three groups of questions raised regarding individual thought and social constraint.

First, sensory-motor intelligence extends itself into *reflected intelligence* under the effects of a free interaction between individuals. In this respect, it is worth insisting once again on the fact that reflection is not spontaneous to individuals. Elementary consciousness is turned toward things, and, as long as a sensory-motor operation achieves its goal, this goal alone mobilizes the subject's attention. When the operation fails, then a conscious realization of the difficulties occurs, and the individual comes to reflect upon his methods and not simply on their point of application. [p. 266] In the example cited above, when the watch chain had to be put into the box, the child discovers that his first method is futile and then invents the procedure of making the chain into a ball before placing it inside all at once. Except that this conscious realization of the methods and procedures could not be very fruitful when an individual's action is not reflected in that of others, that is, when cooperation does not complete pure individuality. Indeed, left to himself, the individual begins to conceive of his own operations as external data, situated on the same plane as that of material things: he does not discover himself as subject. This is why Koehler, by neglecting intellectual activity in his elegant experiments with apes, was able to interpret the invention of a new procedure as a sort of spontaneous reorganization of the perceptual field. And this is why 'technique' does not simply extend into science when it is not met by reflection. Indeed, without knowing one's self as a thinking subject and without consciously realizing his own intellectual activity, the individual is limited to watching his own operations and even goes so far as to correct them, but he cannot return to the source of these operations, that is, to the very relations that his mind implicates or elaborates. This is why, to recall the example discussed earlier, perception and sensory-motor intelligence can make use of a system of relations and of combinations of relations that verbal thought is long unable to master. Similarly, the use of spatial relations does not necessarily lead to a knowledge of geometry.

With this in mind, how does reflection develop? By means of a conscious realization which simply extends that provoked by the very contact with things, a conscious realization that is only enriched through contact with other individuals. Consider the infant who manages to place a chain into a narrow opening. Independently of all society, his attempts and failures have directed his attention, not only toward the goal to be attained but toward the operations required and their corrections: consequently, in one sense, he has begun to become aware of his own activity, except that he does not yet know how to abstract the relations at work in these operations (relations of size, volume, etc.), nor how to combine them mentally. He does not think his action. Will he succeed by refining this action, that is, by differentiating the procedures under the influence of new experiences, to the point of always gaining a greater grasping of his activity as such? [p. 267] Theoretically, it would seem so, except if 'systematic errors' or illusions of perspective due to the absence of a system of references flaw his vision of things. Unfortunately, this is what always happens in 'immediate experience', and one fails to see how the individual can avoid this danger if all he ever does is to make comparisons between his own operations. But what actually happens is that an individual reflects himself in others and eventually compares his operations to those of others. This is the point on which we must now focus.

In asking how the individual comes consciously to realize his own self, J. M. Baldwin had already very clearly noted that the essential motor of development is reciprocal imitation, or specifically, reflection (properly speaking) of one's self in others and of others in one's self. The infant only discovers his body through examining it by means of a never-ending comparison with others' bodies: through imitating the facial movements of others he becomes able to attribute a visually[9] representable face to himself, etc. Similarly, by simultaneously opposing and assimilating ourselves to others, we discover our psychism, our intellectual and moral qualities, in a word, our self to the extent that it is distinct from others' selves and in what measure it is the same. This everyday observation is of a nature to show us precisely how others play a useful role, and in what consists the 'systematic error' specific to egocentrism: everyone knows how difficult it is to judge ourselves, and of our propensity to erect our own particular perspective as absolute.

Now, there is no doubt that this process is equally at work in the domain of intelligence itself. In other words, we reflect the operations of our mind by comparing them, not only amongst themselves, but also to those of others' minds. Not only does the formulation necessary for this exchange then become an instrument of reflection, not only does the discussion born of these oppositions become internalized in each of us in the form of internal dialogues or dialectics, but moreover, and above all, each operation and each assertion is situated in a whole set, such that they acquire their proper value in relation to those of others. [p. 268] So reciprocity becomes both the source of lucidity and a factor in rational coordination.

Having chosen the case of the logic of relations to illustrate the non-reflection of sensory-motor intelligence, let us use the same example to show how reciprocity can be a source of regulation. Heavy and light, which an individual initially considers as absolutes become relative, when he attempts to reflect upon his actions, only to the extent that the same objects being evaluated are simultaneously placed in different frames of reference: an essential discovery is thus made by the child when he realizes that a big boat, while heavy from his point of view, floats because it is light, 'because it isn't heavy for the lake'. Now, how does the child come to make such distinctions, if not because his evaluations are gradually contrasted with those of others, because what is heavy for a small person is light for a big one[10], etc.? The relativity of a notion is thus reflected upon only as a function of cooperation.

This last point itself naturally leads us to examine the notion of experience. Thanks to cooperative reflection, 'immediate' experience specific to the individual as such undergoes an essential transformation: it is extended and corrected into *objective*, or if you will *scientific, experience*. Immediate experience is not erroneous in and of itself, no more than sensory-motor intelligence is fallacious. It is perfectly true that the moon follows us, that mountains get bigger, smaller and change shape according to our movements, that I am the centre of the world and that the universe revolves around me. Only such experiences, no matter how incontestable they might be, present the inconvenience that they fail to satisfy intelligence: the 'self'-centred world is incoherent, and, although it seems subject to that 'self's' activity, it offers no support to it. Intelligence, by contrast, demands a certain permanence, and concurrently, a universe that endures. This permanence and objectivity are precisely what characterize scientific experience. To assert with science that the moon is not a small ball that vanishes and reforms itself periodically in the atmosphere and is under the control of our movements, but that it constitutes an object with permanent dimensions whose trajectory can be explained in terms of an over-arching system, is doubly satisfying to the mind: [p. 269] first, it assures the rational conservation of things and, by the same token, it allows each one of us to leave himself by situating his perspective in a coherent and enduring totality. The transition from immediate experience to scientific experience thus consists, not in the abolition of the first, but simply in relating it to other systems of reference, and this relating consists not in an accumulation of immediate experiences, but in a coordination that transforms their meaning. In this way scientific experience is the construction of a reality deeper than appearance, and yet which accounts for the latter by interconnecting these various 'phenomena'. The work of science, then, is both critical and constructive, critical because it dissociates subjective appearance from reality, and constructive because the reality that is thus apprehended relies upon an intellectual elaboration and not simply upon an accumulation of passive experiences.

So how does the transition from egocentric phenomenalism to objectivity operate? Here again, one has to guard against seeing something other than the extension of coordinating intelligence itself in the work of cooperation. As we saw earlier regarding reflection, contact with others transforms sensory-motor intelligence, but only by allowing each individual better to see himself by comparing himself with others: rather than simply comparing his own operations among themselves, and thus remaining prisoner to a systematic illusion, he now confronts them with those of others and becomes able to 'reflect' them.

Likewise, the individual begins by comparing his immediate experiences amongst themselves, and this coordination is sufficient to begin elaborating space, the notion of an object, causality, and all of the instruments for solidifying the universe; then, by comparing his experiences with those of others, he simply extends the coordination thus undertaken. Only, here again, this extension marks an inversion in meaning to the extent that the growing correction of immediate experience necessitates a return to one's self and a reconstruction *ab ovo*.[13] Here again, the progress made is of a reflexive order, and this is why objectivity is something completely other than a simple addition of disparate experiences.

To understand this opposition between the point of departure and the point of arrival, let us not be afraid to compare the development of the child to the most significant stages in the evolution of science. [p. 270] Clearly, if Newton was able to elevate space and time relative to our human perspective into absolutes manifesting without reserve the *sensorium Dei*,[14] it was because he remained victim of that 'immediate experience' to which each of us spontaneously adheres from childhood on, and which it requires an endlessly renewed effort to correct and to coordinate with knowledge as a whole. How then did Einstein come to that precise point of rationality? Was it by reconciling different accumulated experiences amongst themselves in a way that left them all absolute? This, however, is what might conceivably have been done by renouncing the rational principle of relativity of speed to reconcile Michelson and Morley's experiment with absolute space and time: that would have been the triumph of quality over mathematical coherence. Or was it by initially renouncing the immediate point of view to situate himself within the set of all other possible perspectives? This second method gives the result best suited to bringing us to understand the nature of science, and one of the greatest services that Brunschvicg made to philosophical reflection will remain his having drawn out this 'lesson': on the one hand, the most rigorous objectivity is born from this coordination, and relativity, far from implying that phenomena are subject to man, has become synonymous with rationality; on the other hand, the thinking subject, rather than deify his self and project it into an illusory absolute, external to phenomena, is attributed real activity once he replaces his body and measuring instruments into their own particular perspective, and situates his mind in the immanence of the coordinating principles themselves.

Now, *si parva licet componere magnis*,[15] this surge[16] for coordination is what characterizes science from the time when the Presocratics tried to correct the errors of the senses to the greatest triumphs of modern analytical mathematics. This is precisely the surge that animates the child when he tries to coordinate his individual experience with that of others, that is, his particular perspective with that of all possible viewpoints. When five and half years old, one of my daughters who was having fun spinning around, so as to see the trees and the house dance in her dizziness, asked me if I also saw them move. The simple fact that she asked me that question led her to decide in the negative, and, to account for the difference between us she elaborated the following theory: there are two sorts of 'byhand'[17] [p. 271] (this is how she called the air produced by moving one's hands, fans, branches, etc.) white 'byhand', which is transparent and low to the ground, remaining at children's height and continuously moving according to their movements, and blue 'byhand' , which is higher up and motionless: now, she added in substance, 'when I turn I make white byhand, and you are in the blue byhand, so I see (or I make) [*sic*] everything turn, and you don't see anything'. It would be hard to find a clearer example of the transition from an immediate and egocentric concept ('byhand' as a phenomenon that illusorily depends on our own movement), and a coordination, that, as naive as it may be, is no less scientific in structure (if the child lived in water and not in air the explanation given would be pretty much correct). Indeed, whether it is this child, or those who give up believing in the apparent movement of the moon and the sun because they ask themselves whether the stars follow everybody; or those who refuse to put any stock in dreams when they come to realize that each person dreams differently; or again, those that discover the correct explanation for why boats float by supposing that a big boat, while heavy, is light for the lake; in all these cases – that is, wherever there occurs a particular spatial perspective, a specific individual's sensory evaluation or, generally speaking, the limitations of the self – the transition from immediate experience to corrected or scientific experience, presupposes the coordination of points of view, i.e. in effect, cooperation.

This is also true of the second aspect of immediate experience, which is in fact inseparable from the first: its dualism. How does one dissociate the psychical from the physical, the intentional from the mechanical, or the living from the inert, when the universe remains relative to the self? Social constraint, as we saw earlier, is of no help here: on the contrary, it consolidates the animism and the participation between the cosmic and the human. But as soon as there occurs both the critical and coordinating reflection specific to intellectual reciprocity between individuals, the subjective withdraws inside the mind and the external world organizes itself into a totality independent of us.

There is a third and final aspect of cooperation that it is now worth recalling to mind: the elaboration of a *system of signs*. But there is hardly a question on which it is easier to reach an agreement, thanks to the very suggestive encounter between Durkheim's sociology and the linguistics of de Saussure and Bally. [p. 272] The latter shows us that the system of signs is built at the same time as that of meanings,[10] and Delacroix has highlighted in depth what this double construction consists of from the point of view of the intelligence of things in themselves. Now Durkheim, independently of the linguists, has shown through a classic analysis that this double universe of words and of concepts itself presupposes the collaboration between individuals. It is impossible, it seems to us, to account for a child's psychology without using this set of notions. The opposite pole to the individual symbol, with its contents made of mobile and affectively charged subjective facts, is that of socialized concepts designated by words. Now, by their evolution, children's most primitive concepts, or pseudo-concepts intermediate between indefinable symbol and defined notion, show precisely how pure individuality remains unthinkable, and how cooperation organizes thought. A pseudo-concept,[18] such as what one of my daughters symbolized by the onomatopoeia 'vouvou' (which happened to be one of her first words), successively connoted dogs, cats, the designs in a carpet, people working in the garden (and like the dogs, seen from up on her balcony), and finally anything seen from that balcony. This pseudo-concept was thus halfway between an individual symbol and a true concept. By contrast, the concept of 'dog' used in socialized thought, both in intension and in extension, connotes only a well-defined class of objects, and a class for which the sign used to designate it receives a specific and relatively fixed meaning from individuals in the linguistic group.

Today, these are just banalities, but we recall them only to show the differences in value of Durkheim's numerous arguments in favour of a sociological theory of reason. In fact these arguments are of two sorts, some functional and structural, others genetic. Now, the first are entirely well founded: the definition or delimitation of concepts is correctly seen as a social product; homogeneous time and space are due to the interaction of individuals, thereby eliminating subjective length of time and qualitative space; in short, the major categories, and scientific notions in particular, presuppose common thought. But notice that such arguments always appeal to cooperation, and this is why the social products mentioned here are rational kinds. [p. 273] On the other hand, Durkheim's reasons for the so-called genesis of categories are extremely fragile: that general ideas are born of the sociomorphic classification into tribes and clans, that causality originated from the idea of 'mana', time from periodic celebrations, and space from the topography of the first villages, such things might be true if there were no children. But since children do exist, and since formative processes of notions clearly analogous to those described by Durkheim are easily observed in them, we see that the group's intellectual constraint on its individuals, relied upon for this second sort of argumentation, is actually uncreative and merely crystallizes children's mentality. Moreover, it happens that these latter notions, crystallized through the original group's constraint, remain mythical and anthropomorphic, whereas ideas that are simply cooperative are, on the contrary, rational: here we find a new indication favouring the opposition between constraint and cooperation.

In conclusion, cooperation is the source of three sorts of transformation in individual thinking, all three of which are of a nature to permit individuals to have a greater consciousness of reason immanent in all intellectual activity.

In the first place, cooperation is a source of reflection and of self-consciousness. On this point, it marks an inversion of meaning, not only in relation to specifically individual sensory-motor intelligence, but also in relation to social authority, which engenders coercive belief and not true deliberation.

In the second place, cooperation dissociates the subjective from the objective. It is thus a source of objectivity, and rectifies immediate experience into scientific experience, whereas constraint is limited to consolidating the former by simply promoting egocentrism to the rank of sociomorphism.

In the third place, cooperation is a source of regulation. Over and above simple regularity perceived by the individual and heteronomous rule imposed by constraint in the areas of both knowledge and morality, it installs autonomous rule, or the rule of pure reciprocity, a factor in logical thought and the principle behind notional systems and signs.

By its triple nature, reflective, critical and regulatory, cooperation thus seems more truly social than does constraint. [p. 274] Social constraint is only the external appearance of society. True intellectual socialization is due to cooperation: we are more social than the 'non-civilized'. Triumph of collective thought is to be found in science, and not in 'primitive' sociomorphic thought due to group constraint, which is nothing other than a transposition and a solidification of the egocentric thought common to all still poorly socialized individuals.

So cooperation alone is creative. But this is not to say, as bears repeating, that it confers upon individuals a rational power that emerges *ex nihilo*.[19] The true creation of cooperation is the rule of reciprocity that permits individuals to correct what remains disequilibrated in themselves and to show the equilibrium immanent in all conscious activity. Indeed, it is this reciprocity that illuminates the personality, which is precisely the ideal lacking in constraint and which is unknown to the individual self.

V. CONCLUSION: PERSONALITY

It now remains to show how personality is formed as a function of cooperation and thereby reintroduce the individual in the elaboration of reason.

But the demonstration will be brief, because cooperation and personality are one and the same, not antagonistic poles of a heterogeneous system. So it is pointless to ask whether cooperation produces personality or vice versa: one might just as well seek to discover whether the terms of a relation are the source of the relation or whether it is the relation itself that makes the terms relative to one another! What needs to be analysed, on the other hand, is how the initial 'self' blossoms as personality thanks to cooperation, and how the social thus joins, rather than opposes, what is innermost in an individual. Perhaps the creation of a rational equilibrium is to be found in the secret of this agreement.

The individual is endowed with a certain number of hereditary drives from birth, some of which entail his future intelligence and others his social capabilities. [p. 275] So, in one sense, he is intelligent and social from the first day of his life. However, as we have just seen, a double constraint is immediately exerted upon him, and exerted from the outside: on the one hand, the material universe impinges upon his mind and so engenders a sort of immediate experience, prior to rational assimilation; on the other hand, the social group toward which the child gravitates in virtue of his instincts, just as he gravitates toward experience in virtue of his hereditary organization, applies pressure on his individuality and imprints him with a certain number of 'external' characteristics. Now, this situation in itself engenders a double antagonism: an antagonism between a still non-assimilable universe and thought as yet insufficiently formed, and an antagonism between social constraint that extends beyond the self and a self not yet sufficiently socialized. From this, there emerges an initial state of compromise or of 'false equilibrium': intellectual phenomenalism and egocentrism, on the one hand, collective constraint and social egocentrism, on the other, combine into an non-differentiated state in which neither society nor the individual entirely finds their merit, any more than does reason. This situation of latent disequilibrium is ended by cooperation, by replacing the false equilibrium of constraint with a true equilibrium.

How does this occur? By making the individual and society interdependent, while intellectual activity and experience become correlated thanks to the same processes. In other words, cooperation in a certain sense is the product of internalization of 'external' society, just as knowledge is an internalization of experience: indeed, it suppresses the self (as self-centred) to the benefit of reciprocity, just as reason suppresses subjectivity to the benefit of forming an objective reality. Only one cannot conclude, as does Durkheimism, that it simply extends constraint without inverting its meaning, just as one cannot conclude, as does empiricism, that reason simply results from experience without a perpetual reorganization of its data. This is the irreducible hallmark of the existence of the individual personality, just as it concurrently asserts the irreducible value of intellectual activity. In effect, the internalization of the social, realized through cooperation, is not a simple automatization of rules and beliefs imposed by constraint, through individual habit: it is, on the contrary, the elimination of all heteronomy because individuals, by differentiating themselves from one another, forego considering their own point of view as absolute, [p. 276] submit to the method of reciprocity, and thereby reject the common and non-differentiated rules that constrain them from without. The 'social' exterior is thus reduced to pure reciprocity: it meets the inner social and the individual in a new synthesis that surpasses both egocentrism and coercion.

One sees how cooperation marks the birth of the personality. The difference between constraint and cooperation, from the viewpoint of theoretical reason as well as of practical or moral reason, is that which opposes a simple general or common law to a system of relations or laws of perspective (or again, as they say in physics, of combined 'covariants' and 'invariants'). What constraint imposes is a common law, or a set of beliefs, symbols, rules, etc., fixed in content: the individual need only accept them, hence making him submit to others, or resist them, hence reinforcing his egocentrism. In practice, submission and resistance combine into a compromise in which the strictest rules evolve and the individual becomes able to reconcile his own self with the law. But such a system has no room for personality, that is, for an individual's autonomous regulation. In contrast, cooperation implies only a set of rules and relations such that each person becomes aware of his own particular point of view while still situating it in a coherent whole: the individual becomes interdependent with the social, that is, the individual, by submitting himself in all autonomy to the method of reciprocity, creates an agreement between the originality specific to the self and the discipline of rule. This agreement is precisely what constitutes personality. So from the point of view of reason, the difference is essential: constraint is falsely generalized verbal logic that hampers the interaction between intelligence and experience, cooperation is the logic of relations that assures this interaction by the very fact that it coordinates the perspectives that characterize each person's point of view.

So, once again, we find an opposition between constraint and cooperation, although, actually, the two processes are always blended in every society, just as dogmatic assertion and attempts at rational verification are always blended in our individual minds. But – and we insist on this – recognition of this sort of distinction leads, on the one hand, to the impossibility of accounting for the role of personality and, on the other, to the confusion of subjective values with rational values. [p. 277] This is what the example of Durkheimism shows on both points.

All of Charles Blondel's subtlety, the fruits of which are admired in so many special studies, was not enough to overcome the difficulties of orthodox sociology in dealing with personality. In his analysis of *conscience morbide*,[20] the 'self' is naturally charged with original sin: by merely identifying the rational with the collectivity, the self finds itself reduced to the expression of a coenæsthesia that consciousness normally 'settles' into, and which remains pathological when poorly settled. But, when discussing the will in the treatise by Dumas,[11] Blondel tries to explain why there exist strong personalities, as far removed from the conformist and the sheep spirit of individuals in whom social constraint meets no resistance as from the anarchy of those whose self resists all discipline, forcing him to invoke a crystallization of this same coenæsthesia around collective imperatives. But how can one represent the 'self' if it must simultaneously fulfil the two conditions of being repressed and of being 'crystallized around an ideal'? The antagonism that Blondel has deeply felt between 'self' and 'personality' is certainly real, but it seems to us that it can only be explained if one attributes the self its own activity from the beginning, by interpreting its limitations as a simple illusion of point of view, and not as an original and irremediable inadequacy: so the limitations of self are due to its egocentrism, and as soon as this is surpassed, the self, thus 'converted', becomes a personality. Now, if the sacrifice of egocentrism means[10] precisely the constitution of such an ideal state, that the self crystallizes around a collective ideal, then there is no mystery if this ideal, instead of coming to the self from the outside, results from the simple coordination of individual perspectives.

But this sort of solution presupposes an opposition in nature between two fundamental processes of social life, an opposition that Durkheimism was never able to bring itself to accept. Yet better than anyone, Durkheim, at the beginning of his career, distinguished a mechanical interdependence, the source of constraint, and an organic interdependence, involving cooperation. [p. 278] Also, with great clarity, he opposed the different repetitions of society, crystallized as opinion, with regard to an already finished and outmoded society. Now this distinction, without necessarily overlapping that of cooperation and constraint, does however lead to them, at least as concerns the intellectual and moral aspects of civilized societies. However, despite these intimations, Durkheim bent all of his efforts toward the reconciliation and the very identification of two groups of drives. And whether in questions of morality or of purely theoretical rationality, he was led to bring together the heteronomy specific to the group's authority and the autonomy of personal consciousness specific to cooperative reciprocity. What is the result of such an assimilation? We have glimpsed it throughout these pages. A disciple of the master went so far as to say: 'The character of necessity attached to Pythagoras' theorem is not essentially different from that which is endowed the mystical beliefs of the Bantu or the Arunta'.[12] The seriousness of this text, more than any of the arguments used so far, can make us understand the necessity of our distinction. Sadly, it is often true that a student subjected to the spiritual constraint of his teacher accepts the truth of the Pythagorean theorem in the same way that the young Bantu, upon his initiation, accepts the collective representations of his tribe, and this is what frightens modern pedagogy, enemy of verbalism and educative constraint. But the mathematician, of any age, if he limits his appeal to the autonomous reason immanent in his personal consciousness, will find himself internally obligated by this conclusion in a way that mocks any authority: this is what the child will soon discover, if he is raised according to cooperation between minds and not in respect of the verbal.

The conclusion we arrive at, then, is that reason is neither individual nor social in and of itself, but requires personality and cooperation for its elaboration. Reason is an ideal equilibrium, immanent in all conscious activity. So it is rightly called to realize itself as much in individual thought as in communal thought. Only individuals, like societies, are liable to disequilibrium, [p. 279] individuals by remaining prisoners of their own point of view, and societies by replacing free coordination with purely *de facto* authority. However, these two somewhat contrary sorts of disequilibrium entail one another, and arrive at the same result from the point of view of the development of reason: this is to substitute anomy or heteronomy, two parallel forms of irrationality, for autonomy. However, any disequilibrium tends to be eliminated if the individual corrects himself by converting to reciprocity, or if the group organizes itself while respecting individual autonomy, and consciousness will renew its search for a rational equilibrium: in this way personality makes itself at one with cooperation, and both become apt to reflect the ideal.

DISCUSSION

BERR: I would like to thank Piaget for his paper. It's a remarkable presentation by its clarity, its logical structure, and its richness of ideas and facts. I myself am entirely in agreement with Piaget's thesis.

BLONDEL: I too was keenly interested in Piaget's discussion; I admire his lucidity. My book entitled *La Conscience morbide*, to which Piaget alluded, tackled a rather different subject: it dealt with how the alienated individual loses his adaptation to his social context, how he becomes desocialized. Because of the physiological cerebral trouble with which he is afflicted, he loses his security in the most fundamental concepts, those that allow us to think of ourselves in relation to our social group. He cannot think of himself as he thinks of the world.

Piaget sees a parallelism between children's thoughts and primitive mentality. He finds in both the three traits of egocentrism, symbolism, and participation. The parallel continues between adult thought and the formation of more evolved societies. But the question remains as to whether it is individual progress that makes society progress or inversely, whether it is social evolution which develops the individual. Which of these two terms comes first?

There is an important difference between children's thought and the conception of primitives. The systems that children construct, when they talk to themselves in a sort of waking dream, are not collective representations; they cannot use them with their friends, amongst whom these representations are inoperative. By contrast, the representations that we notice in the primitive are collective; [p. 280] they are imposed on all of the members of the group. According to Piaget, when society progresses, cooperation replaces constraint. But cooperation is simply another form of constraint; it is illusory to believe that, through cooperation, the individual ceases to be constrained. He is simply constrained in another way.

PIAGET: To ask which of the two terms, individual or society, precedes the other, is like asking whether the chicken came before the egg or the egg before the chicken. We find a correlation with no assignable precedence. There is covariance and parallelism between society and the individual; the phenomenon must be studied by the methods of both psychology and sociology, without placing them in irreconcilable opposition. When I show analogies between the children's thoughts and that of the primitive, I by no means pretend that one can establish a point by point correspondence between them; only there are undeniable general resemblances. As for the objection that autistic conceptions are individual in the child and collective in primitive societies, it is guilty of begging the question.

MAUSS: Piaget's terminology does not match my own; that makes it difficult to compare our ideas. I am currently teaching a course on the observational method in the collective psychology of archaic populations; for I believe that systematization in collective psychology is not yet possible; we know too few things for certain and data collection is paramount. But the research method for collecting these facts is of essential importance. This leads me to observations which are other than, and in opposition to, those of Piaget. In my opinion, Piaget has studied not the psychology of children in general, but that of the most civilized children. It is important to consider other psychologies, those of children raised in very different milieux. In Morocco I saw very poor native children, from the age of 5, plying a trade with astonishing dexterity. It involved making braids and sewing them; it is delicate work that presupposes a very clear grasp of geometry and arithmetic. The Moroccan child is a technician and starts work much younger than children here do. So, in some things he reasons younger and sooner and differently – manually – than do children from our good bourgeois families. Even in our kindergartens, pupils do not do 'manual work' as such, but simply play games. It is apparent, then, that we need to conduct rigorous and extended ethnographic observations, for example in North Africa, before drawing any sort of general conclusion.

There is another divergence between Piaget's method and our own. Durkheimians in general, myself included, centre our research on the elements of reason taken separately, category by category. Piaget believes that it is possible to grasp the entire system of experience in general; this is why our results are necessarily different. [p. 281] Furthermore, we attribute an importance to the notion of symbol that Piaget attributes to it in neither collective psychology nor child psychology.

The French psychologists, notably Dumas and Meyerson, insist upon the distinction between sign and symbol. I admit that I cannot understand it. Humanity always finds itself faced with the same problems; it must invent something, fabricate it, and communicate the procedure. The means of invention are always experience, and those of communication, the sign or the symbol (they are the same thing). The place of society in this process is to supply the tool to be modelled, and the tradition by which to use it, but it is also to recognize, or refuse to recognize, the invention supplied by an individual. Even today the *Service technique de l'air* discourages almost all inventors (for example, the aerodynamicist Constantin). The invention often ends up being adopted elsewhere. In this respect, I remember the definition given by Henri Lévy-Bruhl (Centre de Synthèse): 'We call a historical phenomenon a phenomenon that has become social.'

The same reserves apply from the moral point of view. The difference between primitives and ourselves is not as great as Piaget believes. He makes the notion of reciprocity the privilege of an individual who is no longer a child, or of a society that is already civilized. But the Fuegians, the Australian aborigines, the other primitives or so-called primitives such as the great Neolithic civilizations, possess the notion of reciprocity; except that reciprocity does not always mean equality. From the first generation to the second, as from the second generation to the third, there is reciprocity but not equality; likewise between men and women. In this regard, I recommend the studies by the French sociologists on forms of settlement.

We will perhaps be able to agree on a uniform notion of man. But, about the question of the role of the individual in the forming of reason in general, we do not know if we can reach an agreement; let's wait for the observational data.

PIAGET: If I understand Mauss correctly, we are in agreement concerning the possibility of drawing a parallel between the individual as studied by psychological observation and society as studied by statistical methods. Except that sociologists see in society only a statistical and historical phenomenon. Whereas I believe that we must use psychological methods to study one of the essential facets of social life: the pressure of one generation on another.

MAUSS: Agreed, but we can use statistics and comparative history to study the opposition between the sexes, between different ages, and between the generations in a society. It's a balance that remains to be determined. In sum, you start from the individual, we start from the social, but we still examine the same object from the two opposite ends of the telescope.

BERR: The ideal is precisely to unite psychologists and sociologists while letting each pursue his work with his own particular methods. [p. 282]

MAUSS: What is more, we exaggerate our opposition to the procedure of psychology. Durkheim himself took two courses in psychology, even though he did not carry it very far. We have all continued in that tradition.

PIAGET: Here is a question that was raised in a recent article by René Hubert: Do you think that Pythagoras' theorem is necessary in our representations in the same way as it was for the first men who thought of it?

MAUSS: No. There is a great difference, and it is easy to describe. Human thought has gone from a completely symbolic and empirical representation to demonstration, geometry, and reasoned experience. All knowledge at first rests only on the authority of the symbol; when the authority of reason comes to be added, it is a great stride forward.

AUTHOR'S NOTES

[1] Fondation 'Pour la Science'. Centre international de la synthèse ('For Science' Foundation. International Synthesis Centre), third international synthesis week: Individuality. Talks by M. Caullery, P. Janet, C. Bouglé, J. Piaget and L. Febvre, Discussions, Paris, Alcan, 1933, pp. 67–121 (Michel Ferrari, translator).
[2] On this subject, see the excellent chapter devoted to play in Claparède, *Psychologie de l'enfant*, 8th ed., (Geneva: Kundig). For an English translation, see E. Claparède (1911), *Experimental pedagogy and the psychology of the child*, trans. from the fourth edition by M. Louch & H. Holman, (London: E. Arnold; New York: Longman, Green & Co.).
[3] Notice, in this regard, how animal awareness of the 'as if' is problematic: kittens that run after moving objects and children who symbolize have nothing in common.
[4] Op. cit.
[5] What difference is there, for example, between the 'cult of the self' in Barrès' first period of romanticism and the nationalist romanticism in his second period and that of all defenders of order and tradition?
[6] E. Meyerson, *Le Cheminement de la pensée*, (Paris, Alcan, 1931).
[7] I. Meyerson, 'La Mentalité primitive, étude critique', in *Année psychologique*, vol. XXIII.
[8] J. Piaget, *Le Langage et la pensée de l'enfant* (Neuchâtel: Delachaux et Niestlé, 2nd edition, (1931), Chapter IV). For an English translation, see J. Piaget, (1955). *The language and thought of the child*. 3rd ed. (London: Routledge & Kegan Paul, 1959).
[9] See Guillaume, *L'Imitation chez l'enfant* (Paris, Alcan, 1926). For an English translation, see P. Guillaume, *Imitation in children* (E. P. Halperin, trans, Chicago: University of Chicago Press, 1971).
[10] See Piaget, *La Causalité physique chez l'enfant* (Paris, Alcan, 1927). For an English translation, see J. Piaget, *The child's conception of physical causality*, trans.

M. Gabain, (London: Routledge & Kegan Paul, 1928).
[11] *Traité de psychologie*, by G. Dumas, 1st edition, vol. II, p. 395 (Paris: Alcan, 1923–1924).
[12] R. Hubert, 'La Psychosociologie et le problème de la conscience', in *Revue Philosophique*, 1928, I, p. 233.

TRANSLATION NOTES

1　Synthesis week.
2　French, *savoir*, i.e. formal knowledge or expertise.
3　French, *connaissance*, i.e. active knowledge or understanding.
4　in and of itself.
5　French, *l'esprit de système*.
6　French *conscience* has two meanings, corresponding to *consciousness* and *conscience* in English. Although these meanings are distinct, Piaget claims that there is an underlying connection between epistemic (consciousness) and deontic (conscience) modalities: 'logic is a morality of thought just as morality is a logic of action' (*The moral judgment of the child*, London: Routledge & Kegan Paul, 1932). For discussion of this commonality, see L. Smith, *Necessary knowledge* (Hove: Erlbaum, 1993, sections [21] and [25.2]).
7　French, *autonomie*.
8　French, *l'esprit social*.
9　French, *schéma* (English *schema*). In a footnote to his paper reprinted in P. Mussen (ed.), *Handbook of child psychology*, vol. 1. (New York: Wiley, 1983), Piaget reserves the term *scheme* (plural, *schemes*) for operational activities, and the term *schema* (plural, *schemata*) for the figurative aspects of thought, i.e. attempts to represent reality without trying to transform it (e.g. imagery, perception, memory). The difference is evident in Piaget's well-known texts on infancy, originally published in the 1930s.
10　French, *significations*
11　French, *indice*. The term index is used following Piaget (1970), op. cit, see note 9.
12　French, *l'accord des esprits*.
13　from the beginning.
14　God's sense organ.
15　From Virgil, *Georgics*, Book iv, 'if one may compare small things with great'. Thanks to Uta Frith for this reference.
16　French, *élan*.
17　French, *amains*.
18　Piaget uses the term 'pseudo-concept' in his early papers ('Essai sur la multiplication logique et les débuts de la pensée formelle chez l'enfant', *Journal de psychologie normale et pathologique*, 19, 222–261, 1922). See R. van de Veer and J. Valsiner, *The Vygotsky reader* (Oxford: Blackwell, 1994, p. 263) for antecedents in the work of the Sterns.
19　out of nothing.
20　Literally, morbid consciousness.

7 The development in the child of the idea of homeland[1] and of foreign relationships

[p. 283] The study of tensions from a psychological and sociological perspective presupposes the knowledge of certain facts of child psychology. The first question to address is whether, because of their unique mode of formation, the intellectual and affective behaviours that characterize the attachment toward one's country and the first relations with foreign countries contain the initial traces of subsequent international non-adaptations. Then one should examine, even if the preceding point seems at first to be contradicted by the facts, why the child does not acquire during development a sufficient sense of objectivity and reciprocity enabling later resistance to tensions and non-adaptations that will influence him as an adolescent or an adult.

We based the following analysis on a dual perspective. From the beginning of our study, we have been struck by the fact that the child did not seem to manifest, during the initial phases of development, any particular tendency toward nationalism; rather, the gradual discovery of one's own nation and those of others presupposes the laborious construction of an instrument of coordination, both intellectual and affective, more complex than it might appear at first sight, and therefore fragile and vulnerable to subsequent deviations. In studying social and international tensions in general, it is therefore useful to attempt to give a detailed description and track down closely how the elaboration of this instrument of coordination takes place, because subsequent deviations depend ultimately upon its solidity or its least resistance. [p. 284]

We acknowledge that our study was limited to children, both foreigners and Swiss, who lived in Geneva and that one can always take into consideration the contribution of the adult context in the interpretation of our findings. But, with these qualifications in mind and pending confirmation from studies conducted in other settings, we discovered a paradox that, although particular to a specific region of Europe, is no less instructive.

This paradox consists of the following: far from constituting a primary, or even precocious starting point, the feeling as well as the notion of homeland appear relatively late in the normally developing child, and without any necessary tendency toward patriotic sociocentrism. To the contrary, in order to attain the intellectual and affective awareness of one's homeland, the child has to go through a process of decentration (with respect to his city, his canton,[2] etc., where the child lives) and coordination (with perspectives other than his own) – a process that brings the child closer to the understanding of other countries and of points of view different from his own. To explain the ease with which the different forms of nationalistic sociocentrism appeared later, one has to admit either that influences exterior to the drives manifested during the child's development intervene at a certain moment in time (but then, why are these influences accepted?) or that the same obstacles to the early decentrations and coordinations (from the very beginning of the formation of the concept of homeland) reappeared at subsequent levels and constitute the general cause of all deviations and tensions.

Our interpretation follows the second line of thought. At first, the child considers as solely possible only the points of view directly tied to his own situation and activities: this state of mind, that we will call the unconscious egocentrism (both intellectual and affective) of the child, initially opposes itself to both the understanding of the concept of homeland, as well as to objective relationships with foreign countries. On the other hand, the victory over egocentrism requires the elaboration of an instrument of coordination, both intellectual and affective, difficult and slow to master, which consists essentially of operations of 'reciprocity'. At each new step of this construction egocentrism reappears under new forms more and more detached from the early context[3] of infancy. These are the diverse forms of sociocentrism, originating from primary egocentrism and causes of subsequent deviations or [p. 285] tensions, but whose understanding requires a detailed analysis of the initial stages and early conflicts between egocentrism and reciprocity.

We will present under three successive headings the information we have been able to collect: in the first part, we will study the intellectual and affective elaboration of the concept of homeland (between 4–5 and 12 years of age); in the second part, we will analyse the child's reactions to nations other than his own; and in the third part, the problem posed by intellectual and affective reciprocity.

Two hundred children were interviewed aged between 4–5 and 14–15 years.

I. THE DEVELOPMENT OF THE IDEA OF HOMELAND

The gradual discovery that the child makes of belonging to a particular homeland rests on a close parallel between intellectual elaboration and affective construction. This fact is of no surprise, because all mental behaviour is always both cognitive and affective (cognitive functions determine the 'structure' of behaviour patterns, while affective functions ensure the 'dynamic' or energetic quality, that is their finality and elements of 'value'). But, in this case, we do not only find interdependence: the two aspects, cognitive and affective, form some sort of isomorphic parallel, because the intellectual understanding of reciprocity is, at first, just as difficult for the child as is affective reciprocity as soon as he goes beyond directly experienced relationships.

Intellectual aspect

We have found that normally developing children aged up to 7–8 years lacked the prior knowledge for the understanding of the concept of country.[4] For example, a 7-year-old boy told us that Paris is in Switzerland because French is spoken there, while Berne is not in Switzerland. The younger children, mostly until 5–6 years of age on average, do not seem to know that Geneva is in Switzerland. At first, therefore, children have a simple notion of the territory in which they live, their town for example, [p. 286] consisting in a few aspects experienced more or less directly (approximate size, dominant language, etc.), but which are combined together with verbal expressions not yet understood such as 'canton', 'Switzerland', etc., without an over-arching systematic integration. Of these verbal assertions due to the influences of older peers and adults, one in particular predominates around 5–6 years of age: that 'Geneva is in Switzerland'. The question is, however, whether the acquisition of this knowledge has an immediate influence on the subject's attitude.

Although the child affirms that Geneva belongs to Switzerland, until 7–8 years of age on average, the child continues to think in a mode of juxtaposition: when asked to draw circles or closed figures representing the relationships between Geneva and Switzerland, the child cannot represent a relationship between the parts and the whole, but draws a series of juxtaposed units:

ARLETTE C., 7;6.[1]
   Have you heard of Switzerland?
   Yes, it's a country.
   Where is this country?
   I don't know, it's very big.
   Is it near or far from here?
   It's near, I think.
   What's Geneva?[2]
   It's a city.
   Where's Geneva?
   In Switzerland. (The child draws Geneva and Switzerland as two juxtaposed circles.)

MATHILDE B., 6;8.
   Have you heard of Switzerland?
   Yes.
   What is it?
   A canton.

And what is Geneva?
A city.
Where is Geneva?
In Switzerland. (The child draws the two circles juxtaposed.)
Are you Swiss?
No, I'm Genevan.[5]

CLAUDE M., 6;9.
   What is Switzerland?
   It's a country.
   And Geneva?
   It's a city.
   Where is Geneva?
   In Switzerland. (The child draws the two circles juxtaposed, but the circle
   representing Geneva is smaller.)
   *I'm drawing the circle of Geneva smaller, Geneva is smaller. Switzerland
   is very big.*
   Very good, but where is Geneva?
   In Switzerland.
   Are you Swiss?
   Yes.
   And are you Genevan?
   Oh no, I'm already Swiss.

It is evident that these subjects consider Switzerland on the same level as
Geneva, but situated outside of it. No doubt, Switzerland is 'near' to Geneva
and 'bigger'. But the assertion that Geneva is in Switzerland is understood
from neither a spatial nor a logical point of view. Spatially, Geneva is next to
Switzerland. Logically, one is Genevan but not Swiss, or 'already Swiss' (as
Claude puts it) [p. 287] but no longer Genevan, which in both cases shows a
lack of understanding of the inclusion of parts in the whole.
   During a second stage (7–8 to 10–11 years), children understand the spatial
nesting of Geneva in Switzerland, that is, their drawings represent not a
simple juxtaposition but a true embedding. But this spatial and temporal
nesting does not yet correspond to a relationship of inclusion between logical
classes,[2] because, while the class of Genevans is relatively concrete, that of
the Swiss remains more detached and abstract: one still cannot be Swiss and
Genevan 'at the same time':

FLORENCE N., 7;3.
   What is Switzerland?
   It's a country.
   And Geneva?
   It's a city.
   Where is Geneva?

In Switzerland. (The drawing is correct.)
What is your nationality?
I'm from Vaud.[2,5]
Where is the canton of Vaud?
Not very far from here, in Switzerland. (We ask her to redo a drawing with Switzerland and the canton of Vaud: the result is correct.)
Are you Swiss also?
No.
How come, you said that the canton of Vaud is in Switzerland?
You can't be both at the same time, you have to choose. You can be from Vaud like me, but not both at the same time.

PIERRE G., 9;0. (The child responded correctly to our first questions. His drawing is correct.)
What is your nationality?
I am Swiss.
How come?
Because I live in Switzerland.
Are you also Genevan?
No, that's not possible.
Why?
I'm already Swiss, I can't also be Genevan.
But if you are Swiss because you live in Switzerland, can't you also be Genevan because you live in Geneva? . . .

JEAN-CLAUDE B., 9;3.
Have you heard of Switzerland?
Yes, it's a country.
And what is Geneva?
A city.
Where is this city?
In Switzerland. (The drawing is correct.)
What's your nationality?
I'm from Berne.[2,5]
Are you Swiss?
Yes.
How come?
Because Berne is in Switzerland.
So one can be from Berne and Swiss at the same time?
No, that's not possible.
Why?
Well, because one is already from Berne.

The hesitations of these subjects are evident: some, like Florence, deny that one can be 'both two things at the same time', just after having affirmed and represented in their drawing that Geneva and Vaud are in Switzerland; others, under the influence[6] of assertions continually heard at home or in school, hesitate to admit [p. 288] dual membership of the city (or canton) and of the country, and, ultimately do not believe it is possible:[7] Jean-Claude, who admits it for a brief instant, rapidly declares that it is not possible as soon as one mentions the words 'at the same time', and Pierre, who says he is Swiss and not Genevan, to justify his assertion, can only find a reason that is also applicable to Geneva itself ('because I live in Switzerland'). Can one say that the real patriotism of these children is to the canton but not national? But there are as many subjects not living in or unaware of their canton, as there are Genevans who know themselves at home. We know children who know little about their canton of origin, but declare themselves resolutely to belong to it because of family attachments. In reality, the country at this stage is still only an abstraction: the only things that count are the family, the city, etc. Assertions are made about them, but the synthesis of these received assertions does not yet give place to a coherent system.

But, around 10–11 years of age, begins a third stage, during which systematization of thought occurs correctly:

MICHELINE P., 10;3. (The child responds correctly to the first questions. The drawing is also correct.)
  What is your nationality?
  I am Swiss.
  How come?
  Because my parents are Swiss.
  Are you also Genevan?
  Of course, Geneva is in Switzerland.
  So, you can be two things at the same time?
  Yes, because Geneva is in Switzerland.
  What if I ask a person from Vaud if he is also Swiss?
  Of course he is, the canton of Vaud is in Switzerland. A person from Vaud is Swiss just like us. All the people who live in Switzerland are Swiss and also belong to a canton.

JEAN-LUC L., 11;1. (The child responds correctly to the first questions and draws without errors.)
  What's your nationality?
  I am from St. Gallen.[2,5]
  How come?
  My father is from St. Gallen.
  Are you also Swiss?
  Yes, St. Gallen is in Switzerland, even though German is spoken there.
  So, you are both at the same time?
  Yes, it's the same thing because St. Gallen is in Switzerland. All the people who are from Swiss cantons are Swiss. I am from St. Gallen and Swiss; there are others who are Genevan and Swiss or from Berne and Swiss.

Only at this stage does the notion of country become a reality and correspond to an idea of homeland for the child. The problem then becomes one of determining whether this achievement is merely conditioned by intellectual relationships (inclusion of parts in the whole), whether the more or less late or early understanding of these relationships is subordinated to affective factors or whether these two factors evolve in close parallel. [p. 289]

Affective aspect

It is evident that just by conversing with a child one cannot analyse feelings in the same manner one can identify the logical structures that characterize intelligent thought. But without attributing an absolute meaning to the content *per se* of the value judgments that the child will bring along[8] or, above all, forgetting the importance of affective reactions that the child cannot express, it is, however, possible to gain some indications of the form itself of motivation, of the real motives[9] unexpressed, by comparing responses according to ages to even entirely trivial questions ('What country do you prefer?', etc.). It is therefore striking to see that to the three stages that we have just briefly described, there corresponds, with regard to affective judgments, three stages characterized by a clear decentration away from motives that are essentially relative to subjective or individual impressions (the most momentary or even fortuitous) toward a submission to the common values of the group, first the family, then the larger social group.

In fact, during the first stage, when we ask for value judgments, the child does not even think about showing a preference toward Switzerland. The child likes any country, as a function of momentary interests, and if Switzerland is chosen it is for similar reasons. Here are the preferences of three young authentic Swiss children:

EVELYNE M., 5;9.
> *I like Italy. It's more beautiful than Switzerland.*
> Why?
> *I was there this time during the holidays. They have very good cakes, not like in Switzerland where there are things inside that make you cry.*

DENISE S., 6;0.
> *I like Switzerland because it has pretty houses. I saw them in the mountains, there were lots of chalets. It's pretty and you get milk.*

JACQUES G., 6;3.
> *I like Germany more because my mother is coming back from there tonight. It's very far and very big and my mother lives there.*

These childish affective reactions can be compared to the intellectual difficulty, characteristic of this first stage, in coordinating one's country or canton or city into one and the same concept. The question becomes that of knowing whether this is because the country does not yet constitute [p. 290] an affective reality since it is merely juxtaposed to canton or the city, instead of containing them as a whole does with the parts, or whether it is because of the lack of logical inclusion that the country does not yet constitute a true object of affectivity. A third solution is evidently possible: because they centre reality around their own actions and immediate interests, children during this first stage are not yet capable of decentring intellectually enough to include their city or the territory of their canton within the larger whole that contains them, nor can they decentre enough affectively to attribute a value to collective realities beyond their tight individual or inter-individual circle: these insufficient intellectual and affective elaborations regarding the concepts of country or homeland are, in this respect, two interdependent and parallel aspects of a same spontaneous and unconscious egocentrism, which constitutes a primitive and concurrent obstacle to any coordination between logical relations and affective values.

Here are the reactions characteristic of the second stage, in response to the same questions of preference or choice:

DENIS K., 8;3.
  I like Switzerland because I was born in Switzerland.

PIERRETTE J., 8;9.
  I like Switzerland because it's my country. My father, my mother are Swiss, so we like Switzerland.

JACQUELINE M., 9;3.
  I like Switzerland. It's the most beautiful country to me. It's my country.

One feels immediately that, while conserving the same egocentric verbal expression as during the first stage, these motivations[10] assume quite a different tone: family attachment and paternal tradition predominate over strictly individual motives. The country becomes the homeland,[11] and little does it matter that the child still has difficulty in constructing an exact hierarchy between city, canton and nation: their common affective, and thus non-differentiated, value, derives from family values. We find a close parallel between logical non-differentiation (that already allows for spatial or spatial-temporal inclusion, but still opposes conceptual inclusion) and affective non-differentiation, which reduces the different terms to one and the same value of family tradition. More precisely, in both cases, two major achievements are accomplished simultaneously: a beginning of intellectual decentration, allowing the subject to subordinate spatially his territory (urban or regional) to a larger reality that contains it, [p. 291] and a beginning of affective decentration, allowing the subordination of egocentric motivations to broader collective values. But, in both cases, this decentration is still in its initial phases and is limited by the non-differentiation we mentioned earlier (and which is due to the expansion of a residue of egocentrism to the new level recently attained).

Finally, during the third stage, motivations change and adapt more or less to some of the collective ideals of the social and national group:

JULIETTE N., 10;3.
I like Switzerland because there are never any wars.

LUCIEN O., 11;2.
I like Switzerland because it's a free country.

MICHELLE G., 11;5.
I like Switzerland because it's the country of the Red Cross. In Switzerland we have an obligation to be charitable because of our neutrality.

Neutrality, freedom, the country that was spared from the war, the Red Cross, official charity, etc.: one would think one is reading a naive summary of popular patriotic speeches. But the trivial quality of these motivations is in itself revealing: it is to the more general collective ideals that the child becomes sensitive. Limiting oneself to observing that the child repeats what he is told at school does not sufficiently explain what pushes the child to repeat it and above all, why he understands it: the child gives us these reasons because, beyond personal feelings and motives of family piety, he discovers finally that a broader collective exists that has its own values distinct from those of the self, of the family, the city and visible and concrete realities. In brief, the child attains a hierarchy whose summit has values which are relatively abstract. At the same time, he becomes able to coordinate spatial-temporal and logical relationships within the framework[12] of the invisible totality constituted by the nation or country. Here, again, we find a close parallel between cognitive and affective or moral decentrations or coordinations.

II. OTHER NATIONS

We will briefly present the results of the second part of our study from two perspectives. The first purpose of our study is to identify whether the notions or feelings [p. 292] about other countries or people of other nationalities (assuming that the child knows of any) develop according to the same schemas[13] as those discussed in the first part of our study, or if there is a noticeable difference between these two kinds of mental constructions. More importantly, our second purpose is to prepare the analysis of the third part of the study which focuses on reciprocity: regardless of whether the child's ideas and affective reactions toward his own country and foreign countries develop in a similar or different manner, it will be instructive to examine how the child attains, as a function of these very attitudes, the intellectual and moral reciprocity that constitute the instrument *par excellence* of social and international understanding. In fact, during the three stages, the decentration just described with respect to the child's initial egocentrism may result partly from active relationships established by the subject, and will in such case result necessarily in a certain reciprocity: more precisely, decentration will become one with this reciprocity, of which it is a result as much as a cause.[14] But this decentration may also result partly from the pressures of the social surroundings: in this case it will not then develop automatically into an attitude of reciprocity, but may transform egocentrism into sociocentrism, as well as actual comprehension. For this reason, it is necessary to conduct another preliminary investigation using interview procedures similar to those of the first studies, of children's reactions to countries other than their own before asking questions specifically about reciprocity. But, because of the similarity observed from an intellectual point of view between the new reactions and those just described, there is no need to examine separately the aspects of logical structuration of the responses from the affective aspects, the latter only presenting a new focus of interest.

During the first stage, we find in the child the same intellectual difficulties with respect to the inclusion of parts in the whole for countries other than his own, as well as the same value judgments based on subjective and temporary motives.[3]

ARLETTE, 7;6. (Genevan).
Do you know other countries, foreign countries?
Yes, Lausanne.[2]
Where is Lausanne?
In Geneva. (juxtaposed circles) [p. 293]

PIERRE G., 9;10. (see part I, second stage).
Do you know any foreign countries?
Yes, France, Africa, America.
Do you know what the capital of France is?
It's Lyon, I think, I went there with my father, it's in France. (Juxtaposed drawings, Lyon touching France *'because the city of Lyon borders France'*.)
The people who live in Lyon, what are they?
French.
Are they also from Lyon?[5]
Yes ... No, that's not possible. They can't be two nationalities at the same time.

MONIQUE C., 5;5.
Are there people who don't live in Geneva?
Yes, they live in Les Diablerets.[2]
How do you know?
I was there on holiday.
Are there people who live neither in Geneva nor in Les Diablerets?
Yes, in Lausanne. My aunt lives there.
Are there differences between the people who live in Geneva and the others?

Yes, the other people are nicer.
Why? The people who don't live in Geneva are nicer than the people who live in Geneva?
Oh yes, in Les Diablerets I always get chocolate.

BERNARD D., 6;3.

Have you heard of people who aren't Swiss?
Yes, the people from Valais.[2,5] (The Valais is, as everyone knows, one of the twenty-two Swiss cantons[2] and the child himself is from Valais.)
And have you heard about other countries? Are there differences between countries?
Oh yes, the lake[2] *isn't everywhere.*
And the people, are they the same?
No, not everyone has the same voice. And they don't have the same pullovers. In Nax[2] *I saw some beautiful pullovers all embroidered on the front.*

HERBERT S., 7;2.

Are there differences between the different countries that you know and between the different people who live in these countries?
Oh! Yes.
Can you give me an example?
Yes, well, Americans are stupid. If I ask them where the rue du Mont-Blanc[2] *is, well, they can't tell me.*

There is no need to highlight the similarities between the present reactions of this stage and those described in part I: their convergence is even less surprising as the children in general have no awareness of belonging even to their own country (see Bernard again).

The reactions during the second stage highlight instead that while there is identity in the formation of notions of foreign countries and the child's own country, there is also frequent antagonism of content between two types of ideas or affective reactions. First, identity in formation: in both instances we find a decentration from an initial egocentric perspective toward a subordination to the notions or traditions of the child's immediate context, and especially of that of the family. But then – and here begins the possible antagonism – according to whether the child's social context is tolerant, critical or even [p. 294] hostile toward foreigners, the subject's reactions toward other nationalities can vary in many ways. Here are some examples of these acquired attitudes, the last example allowing the determination of their level of logical structure:

MURIELLE D., 8;2.

Have you heard of foreigners?
Yes, the Germans, the French.
Are there differences between these foreigners?
Yes, the Germans are nasty, they are always fighting wars. The French are

poor and everything is dirty over there. Oh! and, I've heard of the Russians, they are not kind.

Do you know any French, Germans or Russians personally, or have you read anything about them?

No.

So how do you know these things?

Everyone says so.

FRANCOIS D., 9;0.

Have you heard of foreigners?

Yes, the Italians, from Germany, from France, from England.

Are there differences among all these people from all these different countries?

Oh! yes.

What differences?

The language, and in England everyone is ill.

How do you know?

Daddy told Mummy.

What do you think of the French?

They had a war, they don't have much to eat, only bread.

What do you think of the Germans?

They are nasty. They fight all the time with everybody.

But, how do you know that? Have you ever been to France or Germany?

Yes, I've been to the Salève.[2]

And that's where you saw that the French have hardly anything to eat?

No, we took our lunch with us.

But then how do you know all these things you told us?

I don't know.

MICHEL M., 9;6.

Have you heard of foreigners?

Yes, the French, the Americans, the Russians, the English ...

Very good. Are there differences among all these people?

Oh! yes. They don't all speak the same language.

What else?

I don't know.

What do you think of the French, for example? Are they kind or not? Try to tell me all you can.

The French aren't very serious, they don't care, and it's dirty in their country.

And what do you think about the Americans?

They are very rich and very intelligent. They found the atomic bomb.

And the Russians, what do you think of them?

They are nasty, they always want to fight wars.

And what do you think of the English?

I don't know ... They are kind ...

Tell me, how did you find out about all the things you told me?
I don't know ... I just heard them ... people say these things.

CLAUDINE B., 9:11.
Do you know about any countries other than Switzerland?
Yes, Italy, France, England. I know Italy well, I was there during the holidays with my father and mother.
Where were you, in which city?
In Florence (correct drawing).
A child who lives in Florence, what's his nationality?
He's Italian.
Is he also Florentine?
Oh! yes, Florence is in Italy ...
Do you know a city that is in France?
Yes, Paris, Lyon ... (correct drawing).
People who live in Paris, what are they? [p. 295]
French.
Parisians also?
Yes; oh! no, you can't belong to two countries at the same time.
Is Paris a country?
No, a city.
So you can be Parisian and French at the same time?
No, I don't think so, you can't have two names ... ah! but yes, Paris is in France.

It is not difficult to understand the mechanism underlying these reactions. While the decentration of the attitudes centred around family traditions can develop into an initial form of healthy patriotism, it can also result in the sort of tribal thinking characterized by values based upon the devaluation of other social groups. By renouncing his own subjective and momentary judgments in favour of the opinions in his environment, the child progresses, in a sense, as long as his thought is integrated in a system of relationships that enable expansion and flexibility. But this opens two possible directions: that of submission (with its positive and negative aspects) and that of reciprocity, which requires autonomy in the judgments of partners. Now nothing yet in the arguments presented above announces this autonomy or reciprocity; everything is as if, by discovering the values tied to the immediate context, the subject begins by imposing on himself a duty to accept these opinions about other national groups.

It is also clear that harsh judgments are not the rule and that favourable opinions are also accepted. In this case, though, one must raise the psychological problem posed by every action of a social group, even by all education in general: is the spirit of understanding the result of the content of ideas instilled or of the process of exchange itself? That is, does the child who receives judgments ready made, even the best, learn to make judgments himself and does he develop the instrument of coordination that will enable him, in case of failure, to redress deviations and master tensions?

Let us also examine the reactions typical of the third stage, during which intellectual and affective progress appear to bring the child closer to an autonomy of logical judgment and evaluation, as well as to an attitude of reciprocity inseparable from this autonomy:

JEAN LUC L., 11;1 (see part I, third stage).
> Do you know about any foreign countries?
> *Yes, a lot, France, Germany . . .*
> A foreign city?
> *Paris.*
> Where is this city?
> *In France, it's the capital of France* (correct drawing).
> People who live in Paris, what's their nationality?
> *They are French.*
> And what else?
> *They are also Parisians because Paris is in France.* [p. 296]

MARTIN A., 11;9. (He lists a large number of foreign countries.)
> Are there differences among all these people?
> *Yes, they don't all speak the same language.*
> Are there other differences? Are some better, more intelligent, kinder?
> *I don't know. They are a little similar, but each has its own mentality.*
> What do you mean by mentality?
> *Some like war, others want to remain neutral. It depends on each country.*
> How do you know?
> *I've heard people say so and I've heard it on the radio and at school the teacher explained that Switzerland is a neutral country.*

JACQUES W., 13;9. (He lists a large number of foreign countries.)
> Are there differences among all these people?
> *Yes, there are different races, different languages. And they don't have everywhere the same faces, the same characteristics, the same morality and the same religion.*
> So do all these differences have an influence on people?
> *Oh! yes, they don't think alike. They each have their own memories.*

JEAN B., 13;3. (He lists a large number of foreign countries.)
> Are there differences among all these people?
> *Among all these countries the only difference is that of size and location. It's not the country that makes a difference, but the people. And also there are all kinds of people everywhere.*

But here we have the same problem encountered with regard to the second stage. Is the progress due to the increasing conformity of judgments between the subject and his surroundings, with a tendency toward the elimination of extreme opinions in favour of the mean and of moderation, or is it the result of a sort of new detachment from the immediate context in favour of a broader perspective? We described above (part I), with regard to this third stage, how the subject's thought attains simultaneously a logical structuration of totalities and an affective discovery of the broader totality consisting in the national group in relation to the various immediate communities such as the family and the city. Contrary to the reactions of the second stage, easily engaged in opposing the homeland to foreign countries, these reactions appear to go toward an attitude of reciprocity. But how far can it be stretched?

Compared to the first part of the study, the general concusions of this second part are:

The mastery of the idea of homeland can be interpreted as the achievement of a gradual process of decentration, correlative of a broadening of coordinations to include increasingly larger totalities. But [p. 297] the study of the reactions toward other nations shows that this decentration oscillates between two possibilities: either the egocentrism, although mastered at one level, reappears at another level in the form of a sociocentrism that is more or less naive or sophisticated, or, to the contrary, the mastery of egocentrism indicates progress in the development of reciprocity. It is now time to examine whether it is possible to evaluate the importance of the latter.

III. RECIPROCITY

In order to study the understanding of reciprocity itself, while remaining on the topic of relationships between one's homeland and other countries, we put two types of questions to the same children aged from 4–5 years to 11–12 years. From the perspective of the construction of logical relations, which we saw were good indicators of the child's elaboration of the idea of homeland, we asked each subject to define what a foreigner is and if the subject himself could become a foreigner in certain situations (travel, etc.). From the perspective of motivations and affective attitudes we asked the two following questions, which, when compared, yielded fruitful results: 'If you didn't have a nationality, which country would you choose, and why?' and 'If I asked the same question to a little French boy, which country would he choose and why?'

As for the aspects studied above, for this crucial aspect of reciprocity, a full parallel was found between intellectual elaboration and affective under-standing. From the point of view of logical structuration, the answers during the first stage reveal the notion of foreigner to be absolute, without any understanding of reciprocity, that is of the relativity of this relationship: foreigners are people from other countries whereas the Swiss (or the Genevans, etc.) cannot become foreigners even outside of their own country. From the point of view of affective motivations, the subjects at this same stage think that if they were without nationality they would choose the one they already have, but they do not understand that French or English children would do the same with respect to their own country. During the second stage, these two questions yield intermediate responses that demonstrate a beginning of reciprocity and residues of egocentrism, and at the third stage reciprocity predominates for both questions. [p. 298]

Intellectual aspects: the notion of foreigner

As in part I, with respect to the same stage and to the notion of country, certain forms of acquired knowledge are indispensable for the subject to understand the question posed to him. Before the subject understands the exact meaning of 'foreigner', it is useless to ask questions about reciprocity; otherwise one obtains answers such as the following:

GEORGES G., 6;10.
> What is a foreigner?
> *I don't know?*
> Have you seen any?
> *Oh! yes.*
> How did you know they were foreigners?
> *From their clothes mainly. They have old clothes and always go to the countryside.*

CORINNE M., 6;11.
> Do you know what foreigners are?
> *I don't know, but I've seen some. They are soldiers.*

Once the word is understood, however, the question about reciprocity may be asked and at this first stage, we find generally negative results.

GEORGES B., 7;5.

> What's your nationality?
> *I'm Swiss.*
> Are you a foreigner?
> *No.*
> Do you know any foreigners?
> *Yes.*
> Who, for example?
> *Those who live far away.*
> For example, if you travel to France, could you also become a foreigner in certain situations?
> *No, I'm Swiss.*
> A Frenchman, could he be a foreigner?
> *Oh! yes, a Frenchman is a foreigner.*
> And in France, is a Frenchman a foreigner?
> *Oh yes.*

IVAN M., 8;9.
> What is your nationality?

I'm Swiss.
Are you a foreigner in Switzerland?
No, I'm Swiss.
And if you go to France?
I remain Swiss, the same[15] as before.
Do you know any foreigners?
Yes, the French.
A Frenchman who comes to Switzerland, is he a foreigner?
Yes, he's a foreigner.
And a Frenchman who stays in France?
It's the same as before, he remains a foreigner.

MARIE B., 8;10.
What's your nationality?
I'm Genevan.
Are you a foreigner?
No.
Do you know any foreigners?
Yes, the people from Lausanne.[5]
If you go to Lausanne, do you become a foreigner?
No, I'm Genevan.
And a person from Lausanne, is he a foreigner?
Yes, he lives in Lausanne.
And if he came to to Geneva, would he still be a foreigner or not?
He's still[15] from Lausanne, he's a foreigner.

Before reaching the conclusion that these reactions are due to a lack of understanding of reciprocity, one must address two possible objections. [p. 299] First, one could argue that there is simply a verbal misunderstanding: in this case, the lack of understanding of the verbal expression itself of 'foreigner' and not of the idea would be the cause of confusion. That is, the word 'foreigner' takes on an erroneous meaning, such as 'foreigner = not Swiss' or = 'not Genevan', etc., which would entail a non-reciprocity, even though the subject would be capable of true reciprocity. Our observations allow us to respond easily to this objection. The responses presented above belong to a group of reactions which are very common before 7–8 years of age, the duration of which varies more or less according to different domains. For example, at this stage the child often says that he himself has a brother, but that his brother does not have one; he shows correctly his left hand and his right hand, but he cannot do the same for the interviewer sitting across from him;[4] he has neighbours, but is not a neighbour for them[5] etc. It is not therefore a matter of chance if relative names are transformed into absolutes; it is because the child lacks logical relativity or operational reciprocity.[16]

A second objection could then be raised; could there not be just a simple default of logic, affecting the direction of the relativity itself, and not at all of reciprocity, in terms of mental attitude? This objection can be answered with two points. First, relativity (in this particular case the 'symmetric' aspect of the relations involved) results from an operational activity: to convert $A = B$ into $B = A$ amounts to carrying out an operation of conversion and, from a psychological perspective, the operation is the cause and the relations constructed are the effect. If there is a lack of understanding of the relativity of a notion, it is because of inadequate operational mechanisms. The operations responsible for relativity consist precisely in a system of reciprocity. Second, the main argument in favour of a fundamental mental attitude rather than a simple question of logic is that, as described below, there is correspondence between the lack of intellectual understanding of reciprocity and an egocentric motivation in the values themselves.

During the second stage, we find a series of intermediary reactions situated between the ones of the preceding stage and reciprocity. Here are some examples: [p. 300]

JACQUES D., 8;3.
Do you know what foreigners are?
Yes, it's people from Valais. My aunt is from Valais and when she comes to Geneva, she's a foreigner.

ELIANE K., 8;9.
What's your nationality?
I'm Swiss.
In Switzerland, what are you?
Swiss.
Are you a foreigner?
No.
Is a Frenchman a foreigner?
Yes.
What is a Frenchman in Switzerland?
French, but also a little Swiss if he's here.
And a Frenchman in France?
He's French.

JEAN-JACQUES R., 8;8.
What's your nationality?
I'm Swiss.
What is a Swiss person who is in Switzerland?
Swiss.
Is he a foreigner?
No.
What is a Swiss person who goes to France?
He's a foreigner and a Swiss person because he's Swiss.
What's a Frenchman?
A foreigner.
If a Frenchman came to Switzerland, what would he be?

He'd be Swiss because he came to Geneva.
And if he stayed in France?
He'd be French.
Would he also be a foreigner?
Yes.
When the Frenchman is in Switzerland, is he also a foreigner?
No, he's in Switzerland.

JULES M., 8;9.

Do you know what a foreigner is?
Yes, it's people who come from other countries. There's a foreigner in my class, he comes from France.
Can a Swiss person become a foreigner?
Oh! no.

MONIQUE B., 9;4.

What's your nationality?
I'm from Vaud.
What is a Swiss person who is in Switzerland?
Swiss.
Is he a foreigner?
No.
If a Swiss person goes to France, what is he?
Both a foreigner and a person from Vaud.
Why?
Because the French don't know us very well and they see us as foreigners to them.
What's a Frenchman?
A foreigner.
What's a Frenchman who comes to Switzerland?
He's French but also a little Swiss.
Why?
Well, because he came to Switzerland.
What's a Frenchman who stays in France?
A Frenchman and a foreigner.
And if I asked the same question to a French child, how would he answer?
He's French.
Would he tell me that he is also a foreigner?
No, he's French.

These reactions are interesting when compared to those described for the second stage in parts I and II. With respect to judgments about their own country, we saw that these same subjects manifested a somewhat bipolar, if not equivocal attitude: a certain logical activity, on one hand, demonstrating progress with respect to the egocentrism of the first stage in the direction of decentration and coordination; but also a certain lack of autonomy, on the other hand, manifested by a submission to family opinions, and thus resulting in the transformation of the initial egocentrism into sociocentrism, as opposed to decentration. Here we find [p. 301] the same bipolarity but with respect to reciprocity, and it is at this new level that we must look for an explanation of the findings presented above. On one hand, the child does, in fact, free himself sufficiently from his immediate point of view, to be able no longer to affirm that a Swiss person who lives in another country never is a foreigner, etc., demonstrating progress toward reciprocity. This reciprocity, however, incessantly stops halfway, so to say, because a trace of sociocentrism still remains, an example of which is the affirmation that a Swiss person (or a Genevan), etc. is not on an equal footing with the others. One should, no doubt, refer to a sort of fragility of the developing instrument of coordination to explain these types of oscillations.

During the third stage, however, the question seems to be completely mastered:

MURIELLE F., 10;6.
Do you know what a foreigner is?
It's someone who is in a country other than his own.
Could you be a foreigner?
Not for the Swiss, but for other people if I'm not in my country.

ROBERT N., 11;0.
Do you know what a foreigner is?
Yes, all the people who do not belong to the same country as us.
And could you become a foreigner?
Yes, for everyone who is not Swiss, I was born in a country other than theirs, so I'm a foreigner.

MARION B., 12;4.
What's your nationality?
I'm Swiss.[5]
What's a Swiss person who lives in Switzerland?
Swiss.
Is he a foreigner?
No, not for the Swiss.
If he goes to France, what is he?
He is still a Swiss person, but he becomes a foreigner for the French.
And what's a Frenchman in France?
French.
And if he comes to Switzerland, what is he?
French, but he's a foreigner for us.

PIERRE J., 12;6.
What's your nationality?
I'm Swiss.
What nationality is a Swiss person who lives in Switzerland?
Swiss.

Is he a foreigner?
No: maybe for foreigners, he's a foreigner.
What do you mean?
For the French, the Germans, for example, a Swiss person is a foreigner.
Very good. If a Swiss person went to France, what would he be?
For the French, he's a foreigner, but not for us, he's still[15] *Swiss.*
What's a Frenchman who lives in France?
He's French and not a foreigner for other French. He's a foreigner for us.
If a Frenchman came to Switzerland, what would he be?
A foreigner.
Why?
Because he's not Swiss; for us, all those who are not Swiss are foreigners.
[p. 302]

At this level there appear to be no obstacles to reciprocity from the point of view of intellectual structuration. Is the case the same from an affective perspective?

Affective motivation

Although there appears to be no direct relation between the question of knowing how to choose a country in the case of a loss of nationality and that of knowing whether one is always oneself a foreigner for others for the same reason that foreigners exist for oneself, we found a striking similarity between corresponding reactions during the three stages examined.

During the first stage, not only does the child choose his own country, but also he imagines that a national of another country would also choose Switzerland, as if one could not but acknowledge this objective superiority! Here are some examples selected from toward the end of the first stage (the question has no meaning before this for younger children as they are not yet aware of their own nationality).

CHRISTIAN K., 6;5.
If you were born without a country, which one would you choose?
I'd want to be Swiss. (The child is Swiss.)
Why?
Because!
If you could choose between France and Switzerland, would you choose Switzerland?
Yes.
Why?
Because the French are nasty. The Swiss are nicer.
Why?
Because the Swiss didn't go to war.
If I asked the same question to someone who is French, if I said: 'Tell me, imagine that you were born without a country and that you could now

choose any country you wanted', what do you think this child would choose?

He wants to be Swiss.

Why?

Because he wants to be Swiss.

And if I asked him who were nicer, the Swiss or the French or if they are both the same, what would he say?

He would say, the Swiss are nicer than the French.

Why would he say that?

Because ... they know the Swiss are nicer.

CHARLES K., 6:11.

If you were born without a nationality and you could choose any one you wanted, which one would you choose?

I would become Swiss.

Why?

Because there's more food.

What do you think, are the French nicer, the same or less nice than the Swiss?

The Swiss are nicer.

Why?

I don't know.

If I asked a German child, for example: 'Tell me, you were born without nationality, you can choose any one you want', which one do you think he would choose?

He'd say: 'I want to be Swiss.'

Why? [p. 303]

Because it's better in Switzerland.

And if I asked him who is nicer?

He'd say the Swiss.

Why?

Because they didn't go to war.

BRIAN S., 6;2 (English).

If you were born without a nationality and now you could choose any one you wanted, which country would you choose?

English, because there are lots of people I know there.

What do think, are the English nicer, less nice, the same as the Swiss?

The English are nicer.

Why?

The Swiss fight all the time.

If we asked a Swiss child to have a free choice in nationality what would he choose? What do you think?

He'd choose English.

Why?

Because I was born there.

Couldn't he choose another country?
Yes, maybe France.
Why France?
It's a beautiful country. I spent the holidays there at the seaside.
And for a Swiss child, who is nicer? The Swiss or the English?
The English.
Why?
Because.
Why?
Because that's the way it is.

One is surprised to observe that, once the child understands the question, he displays a chauvinism that the subjects in part I (first stage) do not appear to have. But, beyond the fact that toward the end of the first stage the subject begins to rely on statements he has heard (as he will do increasingly during the second stage), one must take into consideration a factor directly related to the interview itself. The interview in fact begins with a question about the nationality of the child, which creates an intentional bias, whereas in part I, at the beginning, no attention is drawn to this point.

During the second stage, reciprocity appears in the form of a symmetrical choice attributed by the subject to children of other nationalities:

MARINA T., 7;9 (Italian).[5]

If you were born without a nationality and now you were free to choose, which would you choose?
Italian.
Why?
Well, it's my country. I like it more than Argentina where my father works, because Argentina isn't my country.
Are Italians just as, more or less intelligent than Argentinians? What do you think?
Italians are more intelligent.
Why?
I see the people with whom I live, they are Italian.
If I asked an Argentinian child to have a free choice in nationality, what do you think he would choose?
He'd want to remain Argentinian.
Why?
Because it's his country.
And if I asked him who was more intelligent, Argentinians or Italians, what do you think he would answer?
He'd say the Argentinians.
Why?
Because they didn't go to war.
Fair enough. In reality, who is right in his choice and in what he says, the Argentinian child or you or both of you?

I'm the one who is right.
Why?
Because I chose Italy. [p. 304]

JEANNOT P., 8;0. (Welsh,[2] gifted child).
  If you didn't have a nationality and you were free to choose any nationality
  you wanted, which one would you choose?
  I'd choose Welsh.
  Why?
  I don't know.
  Who is nicer, an Italian or a Welshman, or are they the same? What do you
  think?
  The Welsh are nicer.
  Why?
  Because I know.
  And who are more or less intelligent?
  The Welsh are more intelligent.
  Why?
  Because my father is Welsh.
  If I asked an Italian to have a free choice in nationality, what do you think
  he would choose?
  Italy.
  Why?
  Because I know an Italian boy at school and he wants to be Italian.
  And if we asked this boy who was nicer, the Welsh or the Italians, what
  would he say?
  I don't know what he would think. But maybe he would say Italian.
  Why?
  I don't know.
  And if I asked him who was more intelligent?
  He'd say Italian.
  Why?
  Because he has a father also.
  What do you really think? Who is right, you or the Italian boy? You didn't
  give the same answer, so who do you think gave the best answer?
  I did.
  Why you?
  Because the Welsh are more intelligent.

MAURICE D. 8;3 (Swiss).
  If you didn't have a nationality and you were free to choose any nationality
  you wanted, which one would you choose?
  Swiss nationality.
  Why?
  Because I was born in Switzerland.
  Tell me, considering the French and the Swiss, do you think that they are

just as nice, nicer or less nice than each other?
The Swiss are nicer.
Why?
The French are always nasty.
Who is more intelligent, the Swiss or the French? Or do you think they are the same?
The Swiss are more intelligent.
Why?
Because they learn French quickly.
If I asked a French child to have a free choice in nationality, which country do you think he'd choose?
He'd choose France.
Why?
Because he lives in France.
And what would he say about being nice? Would he find the Swiss as nice as the French or would he find one nicer than the other?
He'd say the French were nicer.
Why?
Because he was born in France.
And who would he find more intelligent?
The French.
Why?
He'd say that the French want to learn quicker than the Swiss.
Really, you and the French boy are not giving the same answers. So who do you think gave the best answer?
I did.
Why?
Because Switzerland is always better.

We observe that having elicited a choice of home country from the subject (as in the first stage), his perspective is easily reversed in favour of the children who are foreign to him. A relative parallel exists with what we have observed with respect to the intellectual structuration of the second stage. But (and this strengthens the parallel even more) all one needs to do is to add [p. 305] at the end of the conversation 'But really, who is right?' to shatter this emergent reciprocity and to bring the subject back to an attitude similar to that of the first stage.

The third stage, finally, is characterized by a true understanding of the reciprocity of points of view, and a resistance to the final suggestion.

ARLETTE R., 12;6 (Swiss).
If you didn't have a nationality and you had a free choice in nationality, which one would you choose?
Swiss nationality.
Why?
Because I was born in Switzerland and I'm from here.

Fair enough. Who do you think is nicer, the French or the Swiss, or do you think they are the same?

Oh! In general, they are the same. Some Swiss are very nice and some French are very nice, it doesn't depend on the country.

Who is more intelligent, a Swiss person or a French person?

They all have qualities. The Swiss sing quite well, the French have great composers.

If I asked a Frenchman to choose freely any nationality he wanted, which one do you think he'd choose?

French.

Why?

Because he was born in France and it's his country.

And for a Frenchwoman, who would seem nicer, a Frenchman or a man who is Swiss?

I don't know. Maybe for her the French, but I'm not sure.

Between the two of you, who would be right?

You can't tell. Everyone is right from her own point of view. Each person has her own opinion.

JANINE C., 13;4.

Choice of nationality: *I would choose Swiss.*

Why?

Because it's my country and I like it.

Who is nicer in your opinion, the Swiss or the French?

They're the same. It's doesn't depend on the country, but on the people.

And who is more intelligent, the Swiss or the French?

It's also the same. France is bigger, so there are more people who think, but in Switzerland we also have scientists and professors.

What would a Frenchman choose?

He'd choose France.

Why?

It's his homeland and he's attached to it.

For him, who is more intelligent, the Swiss or the French?

It's hard to tell. Maybe he'd say that they're the same or maybe he'd say that it's the French because he'd believe that there are more people in France who think.

Really, who is right? Who do you think gave the best answer?

You can't tell, it depends on the way each person thinks. Everywhere you can find all kinds of people, some more intelligent, others less intelligent, some nicer and others not as nice.

Despite the superficiality of the questions that could not be avoided, we see how the general directions of development remain clear. Our conclusions can be summarized by two major points. One is that both the discovery of one's own homeland and the understanding of other people develop in the child according to a process characterized by the passage from egocentrism to the [p. 306] establishment of reciprocal relationships. But the second point is that this gradual development is constantly exposed to deviations of which the common schema is the reappearance of egocentrism in broader or socio-centric forms at each new level of his evolution or as a result of each new conflict. Consequently, the main problem is not to determine what one must or must not instil into the child; the problem lies in the mode of formation of this indispensable instrument of objective thought and affective under-standing, namely reciprocity in thought and in real life.

AUTHOR'S NOTES

[1]   These two numbers indicate the age of the child: 7 years and 6 months.
[2]   Geneva is represented by a small circle inside the large circle that is Switzerland, but Switzerland is often conceived as the part between the large circle and the small circle.
[3]   We met some new students, 7 year olds, who in Geneva had never heard of France ('No, I don't know what that is') but only of Savoy,[2] etc.
[4]   J. Piaget, *Le Jugement et le raisonnement chez l'enfant* (Delachaux et Niestlé, 1924) [in English, *Judgment and reasoning in the child* (London: Routledge & Kegan Paul, 1928)].
[5]   Nicolescu, *Les Idées des enfants sur la famille et le village (étude sur les enfants roumains)*. Thèse de Genève, (1936) [Nicolescu, *Children's ideas about the family and the village (a study of Rumanian children)*, Thesis, Geneva (1936)].

TRANSLATION NOTES

1   French, *patrie*.
2   A canton is a semi-autonomous political region of Switzerland. Switzerland is a federation comprised of 23 cantons. In 1977, when this chapter was published, Switzerland had only 22 cantons. The 23rd canton, the Jura, was created in 1978. Each canton speaks one of the four Swiss national languages: German, French, Italian or Romansch (a Latin-based language spoken by a small minority living in South-Eastern Switzerland).

   Throughout the chapter, particularly in the dialogues with children there are a number of references to various cantons, towns and other geographical land-marks in Switzerland, as well as surrounding areas and other countries. Five Swiss cantons are mentioned: Geneva, Valais, and Vaud, which are French-speaking; and Berne and St. Gallen, which are German-speaking.

   Geneva is the name of both the city and the canton in which the city is situated. The city of Geneva is situated on Lac Léman (Lake Geneva), and one of its main streets is the Rue du Mont Blanc. The Salève is a mountain in France, situated on the border with Switzerland and overlooking Geneva.

   Vaud is a canton which borders Geneva. Lausanne and Les Diablerets are towns situated in Vaud. Nax is a small town in the canton of Valais.

   Lyon is a city in France, not far from Geneva. Savoy (see Author's Note 3) is a region in France that borders Geneva.

   Wales is one of three countries (England, Scotland, Wales) included in Great Britain.
3   French, *cercle*.
4   French, *pays*.
5   Adjectives are frequently used in French to designate the canton or city of origin.

Equivalent terms (e.g. Genevan for *Genevois*) are not always available in English. In these cases, the expression 'from' is used to translate the French (e.g. *Vaudois* is translated 'from Vaud').

In French, markers are used with adjectives to indicate gender (e.g. *Vaudois* indicates a male and *Vaudoise* indicates a female inhabitant of the canton of Vaud; *Suisse* and *Suissesse* indicate male and female nationals of Switzerland, respectively). The English translation does not differentiate the child's gender.

6 French, *pression*.
7 Sociocentric thought is as much a constraint as egocentric thought, manifest in this case as a modal error whose removal is necessary for the construction of true knowledge of national and international relationships.
8 The child will bring along (*portera*) norms, but these are not used coherently, i.e. the norms do not intervene autonomously in the child's thinking.
9 French, *mobiles*.
10 French, *motivations*.
11 Piaget uses the Latin expression *terra patria*.
12 French, *cadre*.
13 French, *schémas*.
14 French, *ne fera qu'un avec cette réciprocité, dont elle résultera autant qu'elle la provoquera*.
15 French, *toujours*.
16 Note that Piaget's *Judgment and reasoning in the child* (London: Routledge & Kegan Paul, 1928) includes both a study of children's understanding of nationality as well of kinship relations. For a re-analysis of the latter, see J. Piaget, G. Henriques and E. Ascher, *Morphisms and categories* (Hillsdale, NJ: Erlbaum, 1992) for a recent study of children's understanding of the logical aspects of kinship relationships.

8　Egocentric thought and sociocentric thought

[p. 307] The potential interest of studies of the child's mental development for sociology resides in more than the fact that this development is at every level a socialization of the individual as much as it is a matter of the individual's adaptation to the physical world. It derives primarily from the fact that this socialization in no way constitutes the result of a unidirectional cause such as the pressure of the adult community upon the child through such means as education in the family and subsequently in the school. Rather, as the analysis demonstrates, it involves the intervention of a multiplicity of interactions of different types and with sometimes opposed effects. In contrast to the somewhat academic sociology of the Durkheim school which reduces society to a single whole, collective consciousness, and its action to a unidirectional process of physical or spiritual constraint, the more concrete sociology which the personal and social development of the child obliges us to construct must be wary of sweeping generalities if it is to make sense of the systems of relations and interdependencies actually involved.

I

With respect to the development of intelligence and thought (which, in the interests of simplicity, will be the only area we consider here), it is essential to remember – for this fact dominates all discussion of the socialization of these functions – that cognitive mechanisms in children involve not two but three distinct systems. It is not simply a matter of distinguishing on the one hand the development of sensory-motor processes determined primarily by nervous and mental factors and, on the other, verbal and conceptual thought which will incorporate materials derived from social life once it reaches a certain level of maturation. On the contrary, it is necessary to distinguish: [p. 308]

1　Sensory-motor functions (perception and various perceptual activities, sensory-motor learning, sensory-motor and practical intelligence), the constitution of which precedes the appearance of language but whose action remains essential throughout the entire course of development, providing substructures or the roots of actions.

2 Intellectual operations strictly limited to internalized, reversible, coordinated actions in well-defined structures such as the 'groupements' of concrete logic (classes, relations, and numbers, bearing from 7–8 years upon manipulable objects) or the lattices and groups of formal logic (second-order operations bearing from 11–12 years on operations that were initially concrete).

3 Representational thought consisting of the evocation of tableaux or of the provision of accounts by means of symbols (representational images, game-like symbols) or signs (language) but without such evocations or representations necessarily requiring the intervention of transformational operations.

This representational thought appears with the symbolic function between the age of 1½ and 2 years and functions in a 'pre-operational' state until about 7–8 years, subsisting at the margins of operations but with a gradual subordination with respect to the latter from this age and a more complete subordination from 11–12 years.

Now the clearest proof that three and not merely two distinct systems are involved is that the third system to be constituted, the operational system, is in certain respects closer to the sensory-motor system (the first) than to the representational system (the second), even accepting that this last intervenes as an intermediary between the two. In effect, an operation is an action properly so called and consequently the coordination of operations extends coordinations sketched out at the sensory-motor level in various ways: the various operational forms of conservation are thereby already prepared as early as the sensory-motor level by the conservation of object permanence, and the operational coordinations of Euclidean geometry are grafted onto the sensory-motor coordination of displacements (the empirical 'group' of displacements acquired by the second year already, one might say, anticipates the later reversibility of geometrical operations). [p. 309]

From such a point of view, representational thought constitutes by turns a necessary preparation for, and an obstacle to, the formation of operations. It is a necessary preparation because in order to pass from effective or sensory-motor action to internalized or purely mental action, it is necessary for a system of symbols or signs to intervene. However, the role of verbal signs as such should not be exaggerated. Research in progress involving deaf-mutes seems to indicate that concrete operations of seriation, classification and so forth develop normally in individuals in whom the symbolic function is intact[1] (in contrast to the case of aphasics), and despite the absence of language as such. But representational thought becomes an obstacle to the degree that it entails centration on (static) situations rather than transformations, and thus on configurations more than on the movement from any one of them to any other. This is because representational thought inhibits the achievement by thought of the mobility and reversibility (or reciprocity) necessary to its functioning, to the advantage of privileged representations which become distorting precisely to the degree that they are privileged: such are the false absolutes to which representation sooner or later clings, in contrast to the relativity characteristic of operations. It is thus that large and small, heavy and light, left and right, etc. acquire an illegitimate meaning to the degree that notions give rise to pre-operational representations and do not become adequate instruments of thought until the point at which logical relations are constituted as a function of over-arching structures of seriation, correspondences or reciprocities, etc.

II

With this in mind, the sociological interest of the three levels which we have distinguished is that all three give rise to socialization processes but to processes which are clearly distinct from one another.

Let us first emphasize the fact that all three are occasions for the socialization of intelligence or thought, for human intelligence is subject to the action of social life at all levels of development from the first to the last day of life. It should be emphasized at this [p. 310] point that we have never thought otherwise, and to accuse us of individualism, as, for example, Wallon has done, on the grounds that we attribute the same role both to egocentrism in thought and to 'autism' (according to meanings which are specified below), is to credit us with an opinion exactly contrary to our own. We refuse only to accept that 'society' or 'social life' are sufficiently precise concepts to be employed in psychology. To hold that social life acts at every level of development is to say something as obvious, but also just as vague, as to attribute a continuing influence to the external physical environment. In effect, in the same way that the physical milieu acts in quite different fashions on the newborn, on the child of 2 to 5 years, on the adolescent and on adults familiar with scientific method, so also does 'social life' exercise entirely different influences at these various levels, and if genetic psychology offers anything to sociology it is precisely in aiding the latter to differentiate between types of social interactions acting on the individual, this differentiation being facilitated by the analysis of processes of socialization and by examination of the order of appearance of each type as a function of such development.

In this respect sensory-motor intelligence, more or less during the period when it alone is at work and when it precedes the appearance of language and conceptual thought, corresponds to an elementary type of socialization resting entirely upon the interdependence of actions. The socialization of thought as such is not yet involved (because thought is not separated from action and does not yet exist as thought) and the adults surrounding the infant can only be regarded as particularly active bodies, especially intense sources of pleasure and pain, and in particular as bodies whose manifestations correspond in a remarkable fashion with those of its own body. The principal instrument of this cumulative socialization is thus imitation, Baldwin having revealed in some depth the role it plays simultaneously in the conquest of other people and the discovery of one's own body and the self to which the body is attached.

At the other extreme, which is to say at the level of concrete and, in particular, formal operations, the socialization of thought rests essentially upon exchange and cooperation, which is to say upon instruments implying the reciprocity and equality of partners. All [p. 311] argument based on authority is, in effect, a contradiction of rational thought, and at this level at which the distinctive constraints of logical necessity intervene, thought ceases to be properly operational insofar as it deviates in directions which prove sooner or later to be of a sociocentric nature (and to which we will return later).

But, between the two, purely representational thought gives rise to far more complex socialization processes. Together with the symbolic function, in effect it institutes an entire range of signifiers oscillating between the individual symbol (such as the beginnings of playful symbols, or gestures with a meaning intermediate between exercise and fiction; such as mental images or internalized imitation of shapes, etc.) and the collective sign (language). The result is that in the beginning thought finds itself in an intermediate state between individual representation (imaged representations, symbolic thoughts,[2] etc.) and collective representations (concepts, etc.). Furthermore, as no operational cooperation is yet possible and as the only instruments of socialization remain the imitation of those close to the infant and the educational constraints imposed by adults, this intermediate state cannot yet attain the level of socialization characteristic of logical thought, which is to say a level implying simultaneously the autonomy proper to operational thought and the cooperation proper to exchanges bearing upon operations.

We have proposed that this intermediate state be designated by the term 'egocentrism', in the absence of a better word, but seeking to remedy the shortcomings of this equivocal term by a restrictive definition: early childhood egocentrism is the unconscious confusion of one's own point of view with that of the other. In effect, the child between 2 and 7–8 years, who is already subjected to external social influences without being capable of assimilating them by the means of a controlling operational mechanism of his own, has not yet achieved either personal autonomy or the reciprocity appropriate to exchanges between autonomous individuals; he thus simply assimilates to his own activity whatever he acquires from without, failing to distinguish in each of his thoughts that which comes from himself and that which emanates from the other. In its most individualized form, egocentric thought merges into symbolic play or games of the imagination which are in fact transpositions of reality as a function of the child's own desires or interests. In its most socialized form, [p. 312] egocentric thought is a kind of copy of adult thought but a copy which is itself also a transposition in the absence of any equality between the models taken over and the limited intellectual structure of the child who assimilates these to the structure.

In brief, the socialization of thought occurs in steps. It is achieved at the level at which individual intellectual operations are constituted as a function of inter-individual cooperation and, reciprocally, at which cooperation appears as a simple correspondence between the operations effected by individuals: at this level of socialization it becomes impossible to dissociate the individual and the social in the heart of thinking, not because these are confounded by the individual himself but because these constitute the two indissociable aspects of the same individual and inter-individual instrument of coordination. But, before arriving at this state of operational equilibrium, thought is dominated by contrary tendencies due to the child's own spontaneous activity and to group constraints (family, scholastic, etc.). Here the socialization of thought takes the form of a compromise involving overt manifestations of submission to these constraints, but which in reality remains determined by the unconscious intellectual egocentrism that characterizes all representational production at the pre-operational level. The social and the individual are thus not indissociable but simply non-differentiated in the consciousness of the individual who confounds them.

III

Such an analysis could seem complicated and flimsy if it was destined only to be capable of explaining the thought of the child on the path to socialization. But the warrant for its objectivity seems to us also to derive from the fundamental fact that the study of the various forms of collective thought at the heart of societies in evolution requires the reintroduction of a tripartite analysis in place of, if one may put it this way, the sociological common sense which only envisages conflicts between 'the individual' and 'society' or between individual and collective consciousness.

In effect, a consideration of the principal manifestations of collective thought reveals three forms which are at once irreducible to one another and reflections of heterogeneous processes of socialization, which is to say that they reflect different relations between the activities of individuals and the coordination of the group. The three are techniques, scientific thought and sociocentric ideologies. [p. 313]

Techniques cannot be reduced to scientific thought, being of a very primitive historic and pre-historic origin while scientific thought is a relatively recent development. The use of rudimentary tools is even available to anthropoids for whom thought is unknown and who know no other intellectual socialization than that of the sensory-motor level.

In contrast, all human societies we know of have elaborated multiple forms of ideology: religious, mythological,[1] political, etc. Now all ideologies are to varying degrees sociocentric. In contrast, the characteristic of scientific thought is to achieve a liberation from this sociocentrism and to pursue this liberation by means of an operational coordination as a guarantee of objectivity and connected to actions on a reality already ensured by techniques.

Thus one sees the triple analogy between these three forms of socialized intelligence or thought and the three structures described with respect to the socialization of the individual. In the first place, ideologies come to be inserted between techniques and scientific thought as does representational thought between practical or sensory-motor intelligence and operational intelligence. In the second place, scientific thought is linked to techniques, after it is formed, just as operational thought, after it is constituted, feeds some of its roots right back into sensory-motor intelligence. In the third place, ideologies, like representational thought in relation to operational thought, function both as preparation but also as obstacles in relation to scientific thought: on the one hand, in certain respects they herald its appearance, in the sense that ideological thought leads to the elaboration of general notions (causality, legality, matter, etc.) which are reproduced in other forms in scientific thinking; but on the other hand, ideological thought is sociocentric, just as pre-operational representational thought is egocentric, and this distorted centration impedes the scientific thought which is called to overcome these effects, just as egocentrism creates an obstacle to the constitution of operations which themselves gradually eliminate these by virtue of their mechanisms of reciprocity and decentration.

From the point of view of the theory of collective representations, this third analogy, which is illuminated by the first two, is undoubtedly the most important because, beside its general interest, it allows a separation of the part due to the objective truth and the part due to [p. 314] collective subjectivity in common or socialized thought.

Let it be granted that all ideology is sociocentric, as the school of Durkheim had foreseen with respect to primitive collective representations by demonstrating their 'sociomorphic' character. But Durkheim's desire to safeguard the unity of collective consciousness and to derive scientific thought from religious thought prevented him from recognizing the fundamental duality that exists between these 'sociomorphic' forms of social thought and objective or scientific forms of communal thought, and above all prevented him from appreciating that this duality can be found even in the collective consciousness of the most evolved and civilized societies. In Durkheim as in Comte there was, beside the sociological man of science, a kind of idealistic theologian of the collective consciousness which concealed from the scientist the oppositions and struggles in favour of a unity determined more by the system than by the facts. In the case of Marx, in contrast, a clear appreciation of struggles and conflicts prevented the concealment of these oppositions and this lesson remains instructive independently of any opinion one might have of the political views of this author. Between techniques, or the productive actions of man on nature, and the sciences, or systems of intellectual relations allowing an objective understanding of man and nature while reinforcing techniques, are inserted ideologies which essentially constitute a reflection, not of society as a whole – because this, from the beginnings of the stage of the first social differentiations is divided into unequal and antagonistic classes – but of particular sub-groups with their interests, conflicts and aspirations. Contemporary neo-Marxists have revealed in particular how literature, metaphysics and even the philosophical aura which more or less intimately surrounded the sciences in their early stages, unconsciously reflect social or, more precisely, sociocentric preoccupations. Ideology is thus to society what symbolic thought is to the individual:[2] more precisely it is a form of symbolic thought but one which is more conceptual than the mythical thinking characteristic of primitive sociomorphism.

One may therefore conclude that, *mutatis mutandis*,[3] certain general structures can be found as readily in the processes of collective ideation on a historical scale as in the processes of socialization which takes place on a psychogenetic scale. It is always and everywhere the case that [p. 315] elementary forms of intelligence originate from action, first in sensory-motor action and then practical and technical intelligence, while advanced forms of thought rediscover this active nature in the constitution of operations which between them form efficacious and objective structures. But equally it is always and everywhere the case that between the act and the real operation is inserted the verb, on the one hand, a source of independent representation, but equally a source of deviations in the sense of a subordination to the thinking subject: between the egocentrism of the small child, imagining things from the point of view of its own momentary interests without comprehending the reciprocity of possible points of view, and tribal sociomorphism or the refined sociocentrism characteristic of class consciousness, or national consciousness, there are considerable differences of scale and content but one finds again, in respect of logical norms of reason, the same factor of distortion which is the centration of thought on the individual subject or collective subject, in contrast to the decentration characterizing objective or operational thought.

IV

Following this sketch of the broad outlines of an interpretive framework which we have described in more detail elsewhere,[3] let us now examine one or two of the criticisms to which it has been subjected, and at the same time the merits of certain contrasting conceptions. We can begin without moving beyond the context of this work by considering the published critique due to Wallon together with the ideas this author introduces as alternatives to our own.[4]

The eminent adversary whom we intend to answer here manifests a distinctive characteristic which encourages us to make a different choice. As we have already remarked on other occasions, we have never gained the impression from reading his friendly critiques of being well understood by him, to the extent that we are frequently in agreement with his proposals (for example, on the role of nervous maturation), even if we do not entirely manage to understand why he claims that we disagree. [p. 316] But if Wallon, who is a great child psychologist, does not seem to understand me entirely, this doubtless has some deeper cause and it is this which urges me to explain myself more precisely.

The essential contradiction which Wallon perceives between us in the paper cited, if I have understood correctly, is that according to him the child will start from the social (in the sense of non-differentiation between the group and the self) in the process of progressively individualizing himself, while according to me (which is to say according to Piaget interpreted by Wallon, with the reservations which we have just made), the child starts from the self in the process of becoming gradually socialized (this is what Wallon refers to as the 'individualism of Piaget').

There is a major divergence, to be sure, if one does not carefully ponder the meaning of the words used. But the seriousness of this little argument seems to me to relate precisely and perhaps solely to the fact that in the middle of the twentieth century, two psychologists enamoured with concrete reality fail to use the same words with the same meanings and do not even succeed temporarily, and in the interests of an objective and efficacious exchange of views, in adopting the meanings attributed to the incriminating words by their adversaries.

Even so, let us try and understand. Wallon considers that the child begins with the social, in the sense that the child does not manage to differentiate his ego from actions exercised upon it by its surroundings. It thus proceeds from a kind of 'confusionism' (p. 22). For my part I believe that thought begins in a state of egocentrism but expressly define this state as a lack of differentiation of one's own point of view and the point of view of the other, or in other terms as the absence of any clear consciousness of self. Is Wallon's social 'confusionism' truly so incompatible with Piaget's egocentrism? In the second place, Wallon shows how the child individualizes himself by progressive 'differentiation': this differentiation, which is initially affective, 'is pursued over several years. All progress in the consciousness of self brings with it a concomitant progress in the capacity to imagine society' (p. 22). As for intelligence (where the differentiation clearly comes later), I have sought on my side to show that the conquest of personal autonomy is a function of reciprocity which implies simultaneously both differentiation and coordination of points of view. Is Wallon's self, acquired through differentiation, [p. 317] really so incompatible with Piaget's personality and reciprocity? I would not wish to be the judge and jury in this.

On the other hand, there are two points on which Wallon seems to me to be mistaken. In refusing to adopt my definition of egocentrism, finding in it only 'individualism', Wallon refers to a comparison which I have attempted between the initial thought of the child and Bleuler's 'autism'. Regarding autism as a state specific to the pathology of schizophrenics he rather peremptorily rejects this comparison as 'inadmissible' (p. 46). But if one moves from Wallon to Bleuler, the creator of this notion of autism (and whose pupil I was at Zurich), one realizes that Bleuler includes within autism Freud's symbolic thought; he added to it only the fundamental idea that if symbolic thought obeys the *Lustprinzip*,[4] this is precisely because it ignores the rules of reality and of social life, and does so because it is 'autistic'. From Bleuler's perspective there was thus nothing inadmissible in considering the symbolic play of the small child as a part of this category of thought which he called 'undirected and autistic'. To avoid any equivocation, I have ever since then renounced the term 'autism' and talked only of symbolic thought. But whatever the term employed, it seems to me once again that to consider playful and symbolic thought to be unsuited to all logic, precisely for want of adequate socialization (due to cooperation and reciprocity, and thus to the differentiation and coordination of viewpoints) is the very opposite of 'individualism'.

Finally, there is the crucial point on which Wallon insists (after already having made allusion to it in *Les Origines du caractère*): the passage from egocentrism to cooperation is the counter-argument to Rousseau's individualism; it takes us from *Emile* to *The social contract*! An anti-Rousseauist who is an expert on this, Ernest Seillère, had written at the time my first book appeared an entire article showing how this individualism of Rousseau was utterly contradicted by current work at the 'Institute J-J. Rousseau'.[5] Wallon, in contrast, rediscovers Rousseau in Piaget and sees in such a conjunction 'the force of highly persistent ideological attitudes' (p. 19). One may appreciate my embarrassment. As I have supposed, like Marx, that ideologies produce an unconscious deviation in the thought of individuals, I can only venture to affirm that I have not deviated and, given that all my beliefs are the very opposite of Rousseau's sociology, nor do I remain an adherent to this despite myself. But the ideological argument is reversible. One could also [p. 318] ask under the influence of which ideologies was Wallon led to identify my views with those of Rousseau. And when one discovers how readily certain Polish reviews adopt the same interpretation, one comes to believe that a solution to the problem is still a long way off.

But let us return from imaginary contrasts to real ones. The true differences which exist between Wallon and myself – and such differences do exist – concern the relations between sensory-motor intelligence and operational thought. According to Wallon, sensory-motor intelligence, which he calls the intelligence of situations, has no direct relationship with thought itself. The latter appears with representation which is to say with imitation (but without a relation between this and sensory-motor imitation), and above all appears with language. Thought, which begins with a syncretic phase (already a kinship between what we have called egocentrism and egocentric syncretism!), only becomes articulated gradually (by 'couples', 'molecules', etc.) and is finally organized in operations. This last point is without doubt the only one on which Wallon declares himself explicitly in agreement with me.

Here, therefore, we have not three but two systems without any relationship with one another: the 'intelligence of situations', and thought. Consequently, in the absence of any recognition of egocentrism, operational thought derives entirely from representational thought and, in the absence of any relation between sensory-motor functions and thought, the operational function is constituted without any recourse to movement or action as such.

Now, two difficulties occur to us with respect to such a thesis. We will not make much of the first for its interest to sociology is only indirect: how are operations to be explained which are (and let us stress this one more time) internalized actions and not representations without reference to movement in some form or another? There is thus no continuity between verbal thinking and operations but rather the necessity for an essential reorganization, the roots of which go back to sensory-motor mechanisms. In contrast, the second difficulty seems to us more important from the perspective of the sociology of thought.

Persuaded of the verbal origins of thought, Wallon has written a quite beautiful work, *Les Origines de la pensée chez l'enfant*, without going beyond 4 years and in which he is content to make extracts from natural verbal [p. 319] conversations and without recourse to any material apparatus on which the action of subjects could be exercised before questioning them.[6] What kind of thought is therefore involved here, and how can the passage from this initially incoherent verbalism to structured logical operations be explained without artificial means?

It is here that the absence of a third factor, which would be egocentric thought (a compromise between the verbal constraint of the surrounding human environment and its own activity), makes itself felt in the clearest way and is not compensated by appeal to just one of the products of this egocentrism, namely the syncretism of prelogical thought. It has just been asked whether Wallon has not been, on this point, in some degree the victim of Durkheimian sociology which regards social life as a single entity, explaining without distinction the constitution of logic and sociomorphic or sociocentric forms of thought. If on the contrary, inspired by the Marxist distinctions between techniques, ideology and science, concrete thought is reunited with action (which is to say, rational operations with movement), then verbal or purely representational thought would be incapable of playing the role which Wallon seems to attribute to it. Inserted between sensory-motor action and operational action, verbal thought certainly partly prepares the latter, but only partly; in other respects it constitutes an obstacle, diverting thought in the direction of the imaginary and the optative, in a word, to the subjective in contrast to active objectivity; it is precisely in this respect that purely verbal or representational thought is egocentric, as by analogy are sociocentric ideologies with respect to collective scientific thinking.

AUTHOR'S NOTES

[1] Representational imitation, gestural language, symbolic play, etc.
[2] In the strict sense of the word, which is to say in retaining the distinction between the motivated symbol and the arbitrary or conventional sign.
[3] See 'Explanation in sociology', Chapter 1, this volume.
[4] H. Wallon, 'L'Etude psychologique et sociologique de l'enfant', in *Cahiers internationaux de sociologie*, vol. III (1947), pp. 3–23.

TRANSLATION NOTES

1   Piaget uses the term *cosmogoniques*, for which there is no direct English equivalent. The French word embraces both scientific and mythological theories of the origins of the universe, but as Piaget is emphasizing here the non-scientific the latter mythological emphasis is retained.
2   Note that egocentrism during infancy is stated by Piaget to be as unconscious as it is complete (*The child's construction of reality*, London: Routledge & Kegan Paul, 1954, p. 92) and that fully logical thinking is never attained even in adulthood due to ineliminable forms of egocentrism (*The language and thought of the child*, London: Routledge & Kegan Paul, 1959). By parity of argument, socially shared forms of knowledge are marked by similar features with sociocentrism during the earliest stages of any society as latently embedded as it is complete and with fully rational knowledge never attained even in science.
3   This Latin expression means *with necessary changes*.
4   Piaget uses the German term, which may be translated as the 'pleasure principle'.
5   Piaget's first post was at the Institut J-J. Rousseau in Geneva and his first book *The language and thought of the child* (Third edition. London: Routledge & Kegan Paul, 1959) was published in 1923.
6   For criticism of verbal methods, see Piaget's 'Autobiography', (in E. Boring (ed.) *A history of psychology in autobiography*, vol. 4. Worcester, MA: Clark University Press, 1952). For Piaget's 'critical method', see 'Avant-Propos de la Troisième Edition', *Le Jugement et la raisonnement chez l'enfant*, Neuchâtel: Delachaux et Niestlé, 1947, or L. Smith, *Necessary knowledge: Piagetian perspectives on constructivism* (Hove: Erlbaum, 1993, Section 11).

9   Problems of the social psychology of childhood[1]

[p. 320] The sociological problems raised by childhood fall into two main categories: the problems of social relationships between children and adults, and the problems of social relationships among children themselves. Before approaching these questions, however, it is necessary to situate them within the framework of sociology in general. This must be done because, if from a certain point of view they are a matter of two particular sociological problems among innumerable others, from another point of view they involve questions that are more general than one might think. The latter stems from the fact that education is one of the fundamental factors in social cohesion and that it arises precisely from social relationships between children and adults.

I. THE PROBLEM OF GENERATIONS AND THE SOCIALIZATION PROCESS

It has often been contended that, contrary to animal societies where the transmission of social traits through biological inheritance preponderates, human societies depend almost exclusively on educational transmission and development.[2] In other words, transmission of social traits in human societies is held to be effected through 'external' action of individuals on one another. Our role here is not to discuss this assertion with respect to animal societies (where the role of heredity has, perhaps, been exaggerated) but to examine it from the point of view of childhood.

Social instincts and 'external' transmission

From birth the child is plunged into a social atmosphere. From the first smiles at the end of the second month and from the beginning of elementary forms of imitation, it is thus possible to speak [p. 321] of active exchanges with the surroundings. There are those (e.g. Charlotte Bühler) who maintain that the smile is selective with respect to other people and that it therefore constitutes evidence for the existence of a social instinct. People speak, as well, of an instinct for imitation. The problem of internal social transmission (social instinct) versus external social transmission (education in the broad sense of the term) must, then, be posed in terms of early childhood before children begin to speak.

The term instinct can be taken in two senses, i.e. in the sense of a hereditary 'drive' (the German *Trieb* as opposed to *Instinkt*) and in the sense of an inherited action (for example, a reflex or group of reflexes). With this distinction in mind, it has been well known (since P. Guillaume) that imitation is learned (albeit in the sense of a spontaneous 'learning' and not of an education, even though the latter often plays a non-negligible role in such learning).[3] The idea of a hereditary action structure does not, therefore, imply a hereditary technique. Thus, if one wishes to speak of an instinct for imitation (or, as Claparède did, of an 'instinct for conformity'), it would only be a matter of an instinctual drive. We believe, however, that when the word instinct is used to designate nothing but a simple drive, it is debased. This is because nothing proves that drives are inherited as isolable tendencies. What is inherited is a whole system of primary structures present (before learning takes place). A particular drive can only emerge on the occasion of and through the effect of interactions between those structures and the environment.[4] It appears to us, therefore, that the notion of an instinct for imitation is devoid of meaning.

The question is more complex in regard to whether the smile is a manifestation of a social instinct. Today, as a result of the works of Tinbergen and K. Lorenz, we know that instinctive reactions are generally linked to very specific and well-characterized perceptual stimuli to which animals are sensitive during a short period of their lives and that these stimuli release specific reactions. In such cases, one can speak of an instinct in unequivocal terms because there is a hereditary 'structure' (and not just a 'drive'). The question is then to establish whether the baby's smile is associated with such releasers relative to people. If that were so, it would reveal the existence of a social instinct properly so called. The works of R. Spitz and K. Wolf, of Ahrens, or of Kaila have definitely shown the existence of certain configurative indices or sign gestalts[5] (associated particularly with the upper part of the face, with the eyes and nose without any significant influence of the mouth). Such indices, for example, come into play if more or less schematized masks are substituted for living faces. These releasers only provoke a smile, however. Subsequently, the smile is also triggered by moving objects and not by more complex reactions. One cannot, therefore, find in this a manifestation of a social instinct in the full sense of the term. In other words, even if the smile as such included an instinctual component, that instinct would only transmit an instrument of affective contact from one generation to the next and not an already realized social trait. [p. 322]

Another very eloquent example of this is furnished by the acquisition of that eminently social trait, language. It is fundamental that there is hereditary transmission of the mechanisms making such acquisition possible.[1] However, language itself is learned through external transmission. Ever since humans began speaking, there has never been an example of the hereditary appearance of a ready-made linguistic structure.

In addition, certain poorly defined instincts such as 'the gregarious instinct', drives of sub- and super-ordination, or 'educative instincts' have been generously attributed to human parents by analogy with the care that certain animal species take of their offspring. These, however, involve pure drives without hereditary structures, and consequently, drives that, despite their generality, in no way ensure transmission of social traits by biological means.

In short, it is true that in human society the transmission of social traits is effected in an essentially external manner, which is to say through direct action of previous generations on those that follow by means of a mechanism that can, in a broad sense, be called the educational process. This process brings up a first problem central to the sociology of childhood because, in education, the actions of the educator and even more (which is of interest here) the reactions of the educated must be considered.

Generations

Hypothetically speaking, if human societies did not have differences between generations and were composed only of contemporaries who had never known their parents and who were endowed with indefinite longevity, it is clear that a set of intellectual, affective (even religious), and moral traits would be fundamentally different from what they are in actual societies. And if the average lifespan or the average age difference between generations were to change appreciably, considerable change would become evident in the whole of our 'collective representations'.

To take only one example, recall that there exists among children a predominant attitude that what parents or the adults who educate them say is true and that [p. 323] their orders are just (even if the child does not obey them).[6] No doubt, such internal subordination also occurs with regard to leaders (e.g. people's attraction to heroes). In such cases, however, it remains to be determined what part transferences stemming from more elementary familial attitudes play. No less importantly, it remains to be determined what the role of reactions against these primitive attitudes is, which would again testify to the influence of such attitudes. The initial spontaneous submission of new generations to preceding ones is pregnant with both positive and negative consequences. As we shall see, it leads to specific results in intellectual, affective, and moral areas; and where, intensively maintained, it leads to singularly rigid social conformity. This latter effect is seen in the initiations of adolescents that constitute the essence of the education that certain primitive societies give their children. By contrast, in those societies where the child is subject to maximum spiritual constraint (in the form of familial and scholastic discipline) whereas the adolescent tends to be freed from such constraint, spontaneous submission at the start eventually provokes conflicts between generations. This is another indication of its importance. In every case, however, the existence of generations introduces into social evolution a set of traits that do not simply condition the transmission of beliefs and values as such, but that themselves also constitute beliefs and practices whose role is considerable. Moreover, it goes without saying that conflicts between generations are often the source of social progress.

The essentially educational character of human societies (I say essentially because it is educational transmission that, lacking sufficient instincts or hereditary transmissions, is charged with socializing individuals) leads to a set of specific epiformations in contradistinction to hereditary processes in the biological sense which are limited to transmitting rather than creating anything except by hybridization. It is not at all certain whether genetic sociology has yet extracted all that is included in such facts. It appears probable that there is and that there always will be more to be drawn from child psychology for the study of diachronic sociology. If A. Comte was right in emphasizing the importance of the problem of generations, it is psychogenetic experiment alone that can lead to the source of their interactions. [p. 324]

The socialization of individuals

If the preceding considerations are correct, it follows that the individual is not born but progressively becomes social. To understand this assertion, however, two misunderstandings have to be discarded. The first misunderstanding has to do with the preformist illusion. From the moment that the adult, the adolescent, or even children 7 to 12 years old are highly socialized, one is led to believe in 'potential' social traits in the newborn. That would be correct if there existed solid social instincts. Since, however, we have just established the limits of such instincts in the human species, preformation, here as elsewhere, is only an illusion of common sense consolidated by the Aristotelian theory of power and action. The other possible misunderstanding is more subtle. Babies are born into a social environment and are, therefore, from the first nursing and the first diapering, subject to familial discipline and regularity. As Wallon would say, babies grow in symbiosis with their mothers. From the beginning, their behaviour is conditioned by social factors. One might, therefore, maintain (and people have maintained) that the human being is, from the first day, socialized in the same way that human adults are socialized and that development ends in a kind of recapturing of individuality and distancing from collective imperatives. There exists, however, not the least contradiction between this assertion and our own unless it is in the semantics of the words used. Are they used to describe the external situation from the point of view of an observer, or are they used to describe genetic and formative interactions from the point of view of the subject observed?

To the observer, from the external point of view, an infant in the cradle is a social being to whom one may, if one wishes, assign a social class according to the part of the city where he was born, etc. From the point of view of the subject, the question is simply to know whether the structure of his reflexes, conditionings, perceptions, etc., will be modified by social life in the same way that, later, his intelligence will be modified by language and acquired notions. As it happens, it is possible to answer this question exhaustively and precisely for each of the mental functions. At birth, nothing has been modified by society and the structures of the newborn's behaviour will be the same whether he is nursed by a robot or by a human being. As time goes on, however, these initial structures are more and more transformed through interactions with the surroundings. Interactions begin on the sensory-motor level (smiling, playing with the voice and face, imitation, etc.) and are consolidated as a function of mental evolution as a whole. For example, at the same level of development where we find the scheme of the permanent object (i.e. behaviours that [p. 325] lead to finding an object that has left the perceptual field) one witnesses, from the affective point of view, what psychoanalysts have called 'object choice'. In other words, one sees a fixation of affectivity onto people, especially the mother. (People are, moreover, rapidly distinguished from physical objects because they, in turn, react and adapt to the child.) With development, such social interactions increasingly multiply, although it is necessary in each case to distinguish carefully what is authentically social interaction from what is not. For example, a conditioning is not a social product even if it is the mother who, by opening the door in a certain way, triggers an empty sucking reflex in anticipation of nursing, whereas some concept interlinked with language and with a certain collective education is a result of socialization in the sense that the individual would in no way have succeeded in constructing it without the cooperation of the group or even simple social transmission.

In this regard, the sociology of childhood occupies once again a key position in studying the steps in socialization and is even found to be the best way to respond to certain vexing questions concerning individual and societal contributions to mental structuration. (In the discussion between Tarde and Durkheim, the answers to such questions remained simply verbal.) Or if one prefers more precise language, childhood sociology is the best way to distinguish biological from social contributions to the construction of structures. This does not mean that the psychological factor is negligible, however, because the existence of a synthesizing factor cannot be denied, although its necessity cannot be demonstrated here.

Socialization, which is confused with what we just called an educational process in the broad sense, takes many forms. The action of previous generations on those that follow is just one aspect of it, although it presents itself in indefinitely varied ways. The child is socialized and 'educated' through interactions with his contemporaries as well. This, too, is an authentic source of development whose importance is not always sufficiently appreciated even though it leads to specific and fundamental results. The child can even be 'educated' by his relationships with younger children. More than one socially maladapted youngster has recovered his equilibrium by assuming responsibility for children younger than himself (not to mention the formative role played by functioning as leader in social groups during the years from 9 or 10 to 15 years or so). In short, although the programme of child sociology is to study the many varieties of social relationships in which the child is involved, [p. 326] we must not lose sight of the more general perspective that such study is also a study of the socialization of the individual, i.e. of the formative processes central to human societies.

II. RELATIONSHIPS BETWEEN CHILDREN AND ADULTS

Social relationships between children and adults can be divided into three distinct categories even though the majority of the time they are inseparable. These categories are (a) intellectual relationships having to do with the transmission (and eventually with the formation) of 'collective representations', (b) affective relationships in general, and (c) moral relationships.

A. Intellectual relationships

The sociological importance of intellectual relationships between children and adults obviously arises from the simple fact that, first of all, such relationships ensure the transmission of language (the acquisition of which begins as early as the second year), with all that language, as a system of signs and consequently as a system of meanings, implies. Specifically, language involves a set of ideas (e.g. classes, relations, and numbers), a set of operations (e.g. logical connectives *and, or, if . . . then*) and a set of norms of thought. A first problem arising in this regard concerns the social nature (in whole or in part) of logic as a system of transmitted operations and norms that is more or less imposed on the child by the adult in the course of their intellectual exchanges. By the latter we mean the cognitive aspect of exchanges in general, whatever they may be.

Logic

From the presociological perspectives of rationalism and classical empiricism, logic was considered to be either innate or acquired through individual experience, and the educative actions of adults upon children were supposed only to involve exercise or consolidation of these structures independent of social life.

Under the double influence of analytical sociology and the reflective work of certain schools of logic, a second hypothesis was formulated. Among sociologists, for example, Durkheim considered logic as being completely social in nature. It was, he thought, a system of norms regulating communication and exchanges of thought. By its very nature, it proceeded from collective life [p. 327] and was inscribed in language. The individual, himself, remained incapable of normative regulation of this sort. In the course of his training and education and under the pressure of the group, logic was transmitted to him. All of this amounts to saying that the child acquires logic as a function of adult transmission, first of the language system and then of family and school education in general. From a completely different point of view, the logicians of the Vienna Circle, principally Carnap, came to consider logic first as a general syntax and then as completed by a theory semantics. (The recent tendency has been to complete further the system through a pragmatics. This does not interest us here, but it definitely attenuates the rigour of the system.) Detached as much as possible from the psychology of the subject, logic rests on nothing more than language itself. From this it results that the child's acquisition of logic does not proceed from his spontaneous activities but from educative and, above all, from linguistic transmission. (This does not interest logicians, although some of them privately concern themselves with the question and conclude how it will be shown.) There is, therefore, a partial meeting point between the Durkheimian point of view and that of the 'logical empiricists'.

If, now, we consult the facts, we see immediately that logic is in no way innate in children. Although this does not prove the necessity of social influences, it does give the hypothesis some legitimacy. Certain general characteristics of logical operations, e.g. reversibility, transitivity, conservation of sets, etc., are acquired only around 7 or 8 years of age on the level of concrete operations (with manipulation of the objects on which reasoning bears) and around 13 to 15 years of age on the plane of formal or hypothetico-deductive operations. Similarly, the large operative systems (e.g. hierarchical classifications based on inclusions, seriation of asymmetrical transitive relations, double entry tables, biunivocal (two-way) correspondences with conservation of equivalences, etc.) are progressively constructed and are only completed around 7 or 8 on the concrete plane. There is, therefore, a very progressive construction of logical structures and not an *a priori* necessity or emergence ruled by simple internal maturation.

As for the role of language, which we shall discuss before going on to social factors in general, it is far from being as simple as one might suppose according to the second hypothesis. In the first place, we just recalled that the child who speaks (from 2 to 3 years onward) does not for all that succeed in mastering logic. In fact, the operations linked to verbal structures (formal operations or propositional logic) are precisely the last to arrive (12 to 15 years). They are preceded by concrete operations which are closer to the coordination of action than to structures properly called linguistic. Subsequently (and this in no way contradicts what has just been said), this construction, so progressive and so slow, of logic by the child begins before language. The sensory-motor structures in play [p. 328] in the preverbal intelligence of the infant already indicate a significant advance in the direction of operations that will be restructured on the plane of language. There is, therefore, a logic of action, and the roots of logic are to be sought in the coordination of action, not in language. And that is so even though language is necessary for the completion of logical structures, particularly in their formal aspect. These interpretations suggested by the study of the development of normal children are, moreover, confirmed by examination of deaf-mute children, as shown by P. Oléron. None of this in any way excludes the intervention of social factors in general, but it does decrease the importance of that special and well-defined factor constituted by adult linguistic constraints on the child. If language represents only a clearly necessary condition for completing logical structures but not a condition sufficient for their formation, and if logical structures are not innate, there remain only two solutions. Either logic is drawn solely from the activity of the individual subject or it results from interactions between individual activities as well as from the internal coordinations belonging to these activities. Interestingly enough, the first of these solutions seems to lead back to classical empiricism. It must, however, be carefully noted that, in his logical or logico-mathematical experiences, the child abstracts logic not from the properties of objects but, rather, from the coordination of his actions upon those objects which is not the same thing at all.

Two facts, however, appear to impose the second solution. In the first place, it is quite clear that the child's action becomes more and more socialized with development. As early as the sensory-motor level, imitation, first of gestures known by the subject then, starting about one year, of new models, already creates a commonality of acts. And this commonality only increases when action comes to be accompanied by words. In the second place, communication and exchange presuppose operations.[7] If we analyse these operations from the logical point of view, paying close attention to their genetic development (see below Section III A), we become aware that they are exactly the same operations at play on the intra-personal plane of the coordination of actions, e.g. correspondences, grouping or dissociating objects, intersections, etc. The term 'cooperation' must, therefore, be taken in its precise etymological sense of co-operations. At that level, to wonder whether it is intra-personal operations that engender interpersonal co-operations or vice versa is analogous to wondering what came first, the chicken or the egg.

The transmission of ideas

Logic thus corresponds to the most general structures of the coordination of action, interpersonal coordination as well as intra-personal. It is therefore obvious that it is encouraged and practised in the degree that there are actual exchanges between the child and his surroundings, including exchanges between himself and adults. It is equally [p. 329] obvious, however, that the exercise of logic presupposes cooperative exchange, properly so-called, even though intellectual relations between children and adults include many other kinds of exchanges varying from simple coercive transmission to exchange. (The latter, therefore, only constitutes one of the two poles of a spectrum.)

This distinction is important from the theoretical point of view and is also fundamental as far as educational practice is concerned. Considering things from the global viewpoint of molar sociology and ignoring the concrete microsociology dear to G. Gurvitch, from the moment there are relations between adult and child, one generation begins to transmit the whole of acquired knowledge to the following generation. This includes both conceptual structures and methods and leads, subsequently, to an accrual of knowledge such that all of humanity may be compared to a single man who learns indefinitely. Since, however, transmissions can give rise to deviations, reality differs considerably from this ideal picture. One can even go as far as to say that pure transmission is always distorting and that for a notion to be adequately communicated, it must be reconstructed by the person to whom it is transmitted. In effect, a truth that is not recreated is no longer a truth but (since logic presupposes coordination of exchanges) is simply an opinion stabilized by extralogical factors.

The whole history of 'collective representations' is no doubt dominated by microsociological facts having to do with the relationships between adults and children. One of the poles of these common systems of representation is constituted by techniques and scientific thought, specific areas of intellectual cooperation where it is evident that transmission implies reconstruction. One does not learn a technique merely by watching it done any more than one acquires a scientific mind by passing examinations. In this regard, it is quite remarkable that from the most elementary grades, the child only assimilates ideas corresponding to the operatory structures that he has mastered elsewhere and is impermeable to notions that are not linked in some way to his 'spontaneous' structures (in the double sense of interpersonal and intrapersonal stressed with respect to logic).

The other pole of 'collective representations' is comprised of the whole set of uncontrolled opinions, obligatory beliefs, myths, and ideologies whose formation one supposes to be linked to their very mode of transmission. That is, [p. 330] the prestige of older children and adults plays a role in the conceptions provoked in younger children to whom notions are transmitted. The product of such transmission constitutes, then, a form of thought more symbolic than objective.

Now every intermediary exists between the extremes. The result is that, all too often, schools organized in such a way that the authority of the teacher and verbal transmission are primary end up deflecting the scientific spirit in the direction of simple collective obligatory beliefs. When a Durkheimian sociologist wrote that the truth schoolchildren attributed to the Pythagorean theorem did not differ essentially from the kind of truth attributed by 'primitive' youths to the beliefs with which they had been inculcated at the time of their initiation into the adult life of the clan and tribe, he expressed a state of affairs that is, unfortunately, relatively frequent. He also formulated, without wishing to do so, the most severe condemnation that could be voiced against certain teaching practices or against transmission of knowledge from the adult to the child.

In brief, if one could reconstitute in detail the sociogenesis of a certain number of 'collective representations' in the manner in which psychoanalysts have been able to interpret certain myths (and without justifying, by doing so, the generality of this mode of interpretation), one would no doubt rediscover an important nucleus that depends on the intellectual relationship between adult and child that corresponds, in so far as the mechanisms of thought are concerned, to what ends in the formation of the 'superego' on the affective plane.

B. Affective relations

Affectivity corresponds to the energetics of action and cognitive functions correspond to their structure in such a way that these two aspects of action are of necessity linked to one another. The fact that we begin our analysis with one rather than the other only has to do with what is easier and not with hierarchical rank. There are both an intra-personal affectivity (need, interest, effort, etc.) and an interpersonal one (attractions, etc.). It is the latter that is of interest to sociology.

The stages of development and the social environment

First of all, let us note that there exist stages of affective development. They are less well characterized than the stages of intelligence, but from the point of view of the major developmental periods, there is correspondence [p. 331] between the two evolutions because they are in part interdependent with one another. Thus, at the sensory-motor level, affectivity, even interpersonal affectivity, is linked to the perceived present just as cognitive structures are. There is, then, progressive and synchronic constitution of the affective 'object' and the cognitive scheme of the permanent object.

At the pre-operational level, just as representation is more lasting than perception alone, pre-operational values in the form of spontaneous likes and dislikes are more enduring, but they are still unstable. As we shall see in Section II C, when the concrete operations are organized (around 7 or 8 in our society), values become structured into autonomous normative systems. One finds, therefore, reversible operations upon values and the energetic regulation of action (acts of will) which correspond to operations upon propositions.[2] Finally, the affective transformations of adolescence correspond to the formal operations.

If we recall these facts of psychogenesis, it is because they are obviously connected to sociology in the sense that the stages of development are far from being just a manifestation of internal organic maturation. Equally, they depend in large measure on the child's social environment, in particular, on his relationships (familial, scholastic, etc.) with adult surroundings. The stages involve a constant order of succession (otherwise one would not have the right to speak of stages), and under this aspect they do depend in part on the individual's biological maturation. They do not, however, involve a fixed chronology, since the average age of appearance of a stage varies, frequently considerably, according to the immediate social environment and the education that the child receives.

Thus, in the area of cognitive structures, certain notions, having no direct relationship with what is taught in school, are acquired at different ages according to his environment. For example, notions like conservation of the substance or the volume of a ball of clay whose form is modified are acquired sooner in the city than in the country. (These notions are not taught in school because adults think that they are obvious and incapable of occasioning any sort of measurement by the child.) As for formal operations (i.e. those that rest on the structure of the group of four transformations and on the lattice[8] of the propositional logic) [p. 332] they start around 11 or 12 in our society and attain equilibrium around 14 or 15. There exist, however, social environments and, doubtless, even whole societies where they do not develop at all. A considerable amount of specific psycho-sociological research still needs to be done from this comparative point of view.

With regard to the stages of affectivity, exactly the same problems arise as to the relationship between endogenous factors and the actions of the family and social environments. This is because, as everyone knows, the structure of the family depends on the whole structure of society as it is viewed synchronically even more than on its biological roots, whose importance is hardly more than historical. Freud and his disciples did, however, furnish an interesting picture of the evolution of familial feelings starting with oral reactions and primitive 'narcissism', passing through oedipal phases, and ending with the formation of the superego. On this view, it is as if this development were a matter of a series of internal metamorphoses of instinct and, consequently, of universal psycho-biological mechanisms influencing social phenomena but not dependent on them (cf. Freud's *Totem and taboo*). A curious thing (which, moreover, stems more from sociology than from psychology) is that the continental European schools of psychoanalysis have in large part remained completely faithful to this conception of orthodox Freudianism while American schools, the so-called culturalists, have rightly insisted on the considerable variations in the ages corresponding to these stages and in their importance (particularly in so far as Oedipal reactions are concerned) according to family structure and culture. In this regard, the works of Fromm, Erikson, Sullivan, etc., on the variation of elementary affective reactions according to *cultural patterns* of the parents are familiar, as are the works of Whiting on the distinct results of different types of education in various societies. In addition, ethnologists like Malinowski, Ruth Benedict, or Margaret Mead insist on the considerable variation in sexual repression in these cultures.

The child's and the adolescent's superegos

From the sociological point of view, affective relationships between child and adult present two especially interesting aspects: the formation of the 'superego' (using Freud's language) and the crisis of adolescence. The constitution of the superego marks the affective subordination of the child to the adult; the crisis of adolescence reflects the insertion of the individual into adult life with [p. 333] either momentary or lasting upheaval of the superego or, again, with its reintegration during the final construction of the personality.[9]

Freud has two precursors insofar as the 'superego' is concerned: J. M. Baldwin, with his 'ideal self', and especially P. Bovet with his analysis of the child's respect for his parents. (We shall take this up again under Section II C.) With regard to the special question of the superego, the founder of psychoanalysis simply contributed a demonstration of how, after the crises of the Oedipal phase, the child comes to incorporate the will and personality[10] of his parents through a system of unconscious identifications and in this way to submit himself to a discipline (at times going so far as to punish himself) which he believes to be of endogenous origin even though it stems from the external family situation. This process constitutes, therefore, a powerful factor in conformity and social consolidation that exactly parallels the consolidation of beliefs resulting from coercive intellectual transmissions (see above, Section II A). The parallel is, in fact, so strong that one might even at times speak of a superego that is intellectual as well as affective, giving as the prime example the way in which orthodox Freudians have remained faithful to Freud's doctrines!

The affective subordination attested to by superego formation passes, however, either through a momentary or a definitive crisis beginning as early as pre-adolescence but especially evident during adolescence itself. In this regard, one must insist on the fact that for a long time most studies of adolescence confused two phenomena that are sometimes linked to one another, but that often are also independent. These phenomena are the biological phenomenon of puberty and the phenomenon, more social than anything else, of the insertion of the individual into the collective life of adults.

From the point of view of integration into society (the psycho-sociological importance of which greatly predominates over its biological importance), adolescence is essentially characterized by the fact that the individual no longer considers himself a child. He ceases to see himself as inferior to adults and, in fact, begins to feel that he is their equal, that he is one member among others of the Society in which he expects to play a role and make a career. One, therefore, sees immediately that adolescence conceived in this way does not necessarily correspond with puberty. Essentially, its average age will depend on the ambient social structure. In gerontocratic societies where young adults are, like children, submissive to the elders, infantile mentality lasts much longer and the processes of adolescence are strongly blurred.[3] [p. 334]

The adolescent crisis, as do all developmental phenomena, involves factors at once intellectual and affective. Intellectually, it is the advent of formal or hypothetico-deductive operations that permits the individual to detach himself from the immediate and local perceptual situation to which the child is more or less confined, and permits him to move into what is possible and does not yet exist. In consequence, he becomes capable of conceiving projects, of building a life plan, and of constructing theories that make it possible for him to judge or to perfect the society around him. Affectively, the child constructs a scale of values that also goes beyond the restricted circle of his immediate surroundings and that constitutes the central axis of his 'personality'. The latter is to be conceived as a late-occurring synthesis quite different from the 'self' and characterized, above all else, by submission of the self to the role that the child assigns himself in society. Thanks to these two instruments, i.e. the formal operations and a 'personal' hierarchy of values, the adolescent plays a fundamental role in our societies of liberating coming generations from older ones. This leads the individual to elaborate further the new things that he acquired during his development as a child at the same time that it frees him, at least in part, from the obstacles issuing from adult constraints.

Extrafamily feelings

The affective relationship between children and adults leads to the formation or consolidation of feelings that are, from adolescence onward, destined to transcend the framework of the family but that were subordinated to it during childhood. Because the problem is of interest to sociology, two examples must be cited.

In the first place, one should mention (and lacking space as well as competence, we can only limit ourseves to this brief mention) the great problem of the formation of religious feelings.[11] A number of authors have tried to connect such feelings to the affective bonds between children and adults, but it is not clear whether such bonds constitute the source of religious feeling or simply a tool for their consolidation. Everyone is familiar with Freud's essay, *Totem and taboo*, where he traces totemism to Oedipal reactions. Fewer people are acquainted with the small and penetrating work of Pierre Bovet devoted to this subject. In that work, Bovet teases out the ancestry between filial and religious feelings. Bovet's argument consists in demonstrating how, before discovering his parents' imperfections, [p. 335] the young child attributes moral and intellectual qualities to them (omniscience, all-powerfulness, authority to regulate what is good and just, etc.) that, classically, are divine qualities. From this it follows that when he is disappointed by reality, the child will then project this paternal ideal onto other planes going beyond the family circle.

Patriotic feelings (the name of which alone evokes kinship with familial feelings) occasions less difficult analyses, which long ago motivated us to conduct a small survey with A. M. Weil (1951).[12] Struck one day by the fact that the youngest schoolchildren in Geneva generally say that they are 'Genevan' but 'not Swiss' because 'one cannot be two things at the same time' (even while admitting that Geneva is in Switzerland), we sought to establish whether this was due to verbal incomprehension or whether it was a matter of an evolutionary stage presenting some general interest. We established that an evolution of this sort does exist. From the cognitive point of view, the remark just cited testifies to difficulties the child has with class inclusions. For the child, it does not follow from the fact that class *A* (Genevans) is included in class *B* (Swiss) that a person can belong to both classes at the same time. Added to this are difficulties with reciprocity. For a young Genevan, the French are 'foreigners' everywhere, even to themselves and even in France, whereas the child himself is never a foreigner, even to other people. From the affective point of view, the child initially shows no preference for his own country over others (his feelings remain attached to his immediate environment). This changes as soon as he realizes that he belongs to his own country. Then he imagines that any individual born elsewhere would also like to belong to his country if he had the choice. It is only barely at the level of formal (hypothetico-deductive) operations, that the child, become pre-adolescent, begins to feel truly patriotic feelings motivated both by his birth and family. Only then does he understand that everyone in every country prefers his own homeland for the same reasons. In this case, then, a simultaneously cognitive and affective reciprocity completes conscious realization proper.

C. Moral relationships

We shall consider moral reactions separately even though they are, naturally, both intellectual and affective. We do so because this is a domain where, from a sociological point of view, one sees most clearly that educational transmissions from one generation to the next or from the adult to the child in no way consist [p. 336] of simple transmissions but are, instead, creative of new social realities that doubtless would not exist in a society of pure contemporaries.

The origins of duty

In his studies of imitation in children, J. M. Baldwin was forced to admit that once children begin to imitate adult conduct, they discover that all models are not immediately imitable. This is because the adult is superior and is the source of various kinds of orders. On the other hand, knowledge or consciousness of the self (which is to say its very formation) is not innate but results specifically from social or imitative exchanges through simultaneous construction of the *alter* and the *ego*. That being so, the child does not come to attribute to himself a self that is in every way identical with his parents' selves since there remains a higher zone corresponding to this lacuna in imitation. There follows, therefore, in direct continuity with the imitative process that generates the self, a kind of incorporation (but without reciprocity) of this higher zone. This results in what Baldwin called the 'ideal self' and that Freud would later call the 'superego'.

In his investigations of the origins of obligations of conscience, Bovet formulated the problem in much more concrete terms. K. Abraham, a disciple of Freud, had wanted to know why children obeyed their parents. Bovet responded that two conditions were necessary to account for obedience, but that these were sufficient only in combination. He claimed, moreover, that the process he described explained the formation of all obligations of conscience. The first of Bovet's conditions is that there be an order of undetermined duration that one individual gives the other. The second condition is that the person receiving the order accepts it and, in doing so, feels a specific feeling, i.e. 'respect', toward the person who gives the order that determines this acceptance. In effect, the child will not accept just any order. For example, he does not accept orders from his juniors. For commands to be accepted, the child must be affectively tied to whoever gives them. The problem, then, has to do with the nature of the link.

Respect

Regarding this link, Bovet takes an original position both vis-à-vis Kant and vis-à-vis Durkheim (who on many points, as one knows, [p. 337] restated the Kantian *a priori* in terms of collective consciousness). Kant did not consider respect to be an interpersonal feeling like affection or fear. Rather, he considered it to be a feeling resulting from a direct action of moral law on affectivity. (Kant himself said that this result was incomprehensible since it obviously contradicted the absolute discrepancy he saw between 'categorical imperatives' and 'sensibility'.) 'In respecting a person,' Kant said, 'I respect him insofar as he applies or embodies moral law, not as an individual as such.' Bovet squarely reverses this position. On the one hand, respect is an interpersonal feeling like any other. It is, however, a feeling composed of an element of affection (one does not respect someone to whom one is not drawn in any way, except to respect a person's function only – we shall come back to this) and an element of fear (stemming from the superiority of the respected individual – fear of displeasing, etc.). Both elements are necessary; neither is sufficient by itself. On the other hand, respect conceived in this way is genetically the source, not the result, of moral law. This is because the small child agrees to obey insofar as he respects his parents. He does not begin with a consciousness of moral law detached from them and then come to respect them because they embody and impose that moral law.

For both Durkheim and Kant, respect is not an interpersonal feeling but the feeling *sui generis* that collective imperatives produce in the affective consciousness. One, therefore, only respects an individual insofar as he represents a collective discipline, at the limit respecting the function and no longer the man (as, for example, might be the case with a magistrate). In the case of the young child, this amounts to saying that he respects his father or mother as heads of the household and not as people. Such a distinction might be established at a certain age, but it is implausible at a year and a half or two years when, with the beginning of language, the first instructions are accepted. Considering the beginning phases, it appears, therefore, that Bovet was right. Neither Kant nor Durkheim account for the spontaneous respect that very young children show toward adults before there is any notion of moral law or collective discipline.

As for other possible factors, Bovet examines them one by one showing either that they are insufficient or that, implicitly, they reduce to respect. For example, imitation might play a role; but [p. 338] then the question is to know who the child imitates and why. He does not imitate his juniors but, rather, his seniors and adults. Moreover, when imitation appears to be the source of duty, it is because the model chosen is respected and was chosen precisely for that reason. In the same vein, it is possible to compare duty to habit (Simmel), whose characteristics of regularity and coercion it shares. There is an important difference, however. A 'bad habit' (e.g. smoking too much or biting one's nails) is regular and coercive without involving any feeling of obligation whereas a 'good habit' (e.g. getting up early in the morning) may involve consciousness of obligation. Such awareness arises under the influence of forgotten instructions, from respected examples, or because it is unconsciously assimilated into analogous schemes that have been constructed under the double action of instruction and respect. In particular, such unconscious assimilation comes into play in the case of a third possible factor, i.e. the orders one gives oneself and the decisions one takes that obligate oneself without the apparent intervention of an outside party.

The limits of unilateral respect

Bovet's interpretations appear to have definitively established the sources of the morality of obedience and heteronomous duty that characterize childhood, that play such a considerable role in adults in all societies, and that play a quasi-exclusive role in those particular societies based on age and gerontocracy. Bovet himself does not, however, claim to have explained the feeling of 'good'. We do not think that the process of simply internalizing orders and then, as interfering influences multiply with age, of choosing between contradictory orders, can account for the autonomy of the moral consciousness that develops between 7 or 8 and adolescence.

We do not think that it is necessary to modify Bovet's schema in any way but simply to fill it out. This is because he only analysed one type of respect and, in reality, there are two possible varieties (or two poles) of respect. The type not analysed by Bovet is what everyone calls 'mutual respect'. The type he did analyse might, therefore, be called 'unilateral', in the sense that the child respects his parents but they do not respect him, or at least they do not respect him in exactly the same way that he respects them. This is clear from the fact that they do not feel [p. 339] 'obligated' to follow the orders that the child eventually gives them. By contrast, mutual respect involves reciprocity.

In order to bring out the distinction between the nature and results of these two types of respect, we sought to analyse the various modes of obedience to rules and, especially, consciousness of them in the case of a system of collective discipline currently exempt from adult control. The system of rules we studied was the game of marbles played by boys in French-speaking Switzerland where children do not play marbles after primary school. It might be objected that this example does not involve moral relationships existing between adults and children and that it should be reserved for a later section (Section III). We shall see, however, that this is not the case. With regard to obeying rules, we observed, naturally, that obedience to rules increases with age. Small children of 5 to 7 years play marbles without caring a great deal about exact application of the rules while at the same time imagining that they are imitating how older boys play. With regard to consciousness of rules, however, we found a completely different picture. We limited ourselves to asking whether the rules could be changed and whether individual initiative could constitute the starting point for a new valid and legitimate rule. Older children are, in practice, very respectful of the law and morality belonging to this collective game. They consider rules as emanating from the communal will and accept any change so long as it is ratified by a collective decision of the players themselves. By contrast, small children play according to their understanding but consider the rules as intangible and 'sacred'. In a way correlative to and leading back to adult influence, they attribute to rules a higher origin than the society of players. For example, it was the Good Lord who inspired parents with the rules of marbles that they impose on their children, or it was the government. Generally, it is the parents themselves who are supposed to be the originators of the rules. A new rule proposed by a child, even if unanimously accepted by the players, is therefore not a 'true rule'.

Such facts lead one to the view that there are two poles to the child's morality and also to adult morality insofar as it is derived from the formative mechanisms and not the content of child morality. (We say this because society's action on the individual passes in large part through the intermediary of childhood socialization.) One of these poles is mutual respect. We shall see below (Section III C) how, because of the effect of reciprocity, such respect leads to a morality of autonomy and to the elaboration of norms. [p. 340] The other pole is unilateral respect leading to a heteronomous morality. We suspect, examining the preceding reactions, that this morality involves a more literal obedience, having less to do with the whole person because that person in no way contributes to the elaboration of the norms to which he is obligated. It remains for us to briefly demonstrate this point.

Heteronomy, moral realism, and objective responsibility

By reason of the very structure that generates the morality of obedience (i.e. unilateral respect leading to acceptance of orders), the value of imperatives will owe less to what they impose than to their imperative character and to the authority of those from whom they emanate. From this it follows, for example, that if distributive justice is brought into conflict with adult authority (in little stories presented to children with the idea of analysing their moral judgments), the youngest subjects will believe authority right and justice wrong. Likewise, when it is a matter of retributive justice, young subjects accept any sanction and, in theory, are inclined to choose the most severe punishment without considering context or equity.

The fundamental phenomenon resulting from these initial attitudes is what might be called 'moral realism'. In other words, what results is a tendency to attribute to rules a value in themselves without regard for circumstances or for psychological context. The most obvious manifestation of this moral realism is the objective responsibility that one encounters in children as well as in all primitive forms in the evolution of law. In contradistinction to subjective responsibility, which consists in evaluating the act according to the intention behind it, so-called objective responsibility consists in judging the act from the point of view of its material consequences. In particular, objective responsibility consists in judging action from the point of view of the magnitude of deviations observed between its execution and the rules prescribed. Precisely because of moral realism, the latter are considered as existing in themselves. Thus, in the case of the child, it happens that someone prescribes a rule of truth before the child has a clear idea of what a lie is, because he lacks the social experience needed to understand that truth is necessary for mutual trust. Because of unilateral respect, he accepts the idea that lying is a punishable fault and sticks to this rule detached from any context by moral realism. The result is that lies are considered all the more 'naughty' when they deviate from reality. For example, telling someone that you received a good grade at school even though [p. 341] you were never examined is considered only a small lie 'because mummy believes it'. This is the proof that it was plausible. But to tell someone, simply by exaggerating, that you were frightened by a dog as 'big as a cow' is a naughty lie because no one has ever seen dogs of that size and no one will believe it. Objective responsibility arises, therefore, as a function of the way in which the rule under consideration is acquired.

III. RELATIONSHIPS AMONG CHILDREN

In proportion to a child's development, his relationships with his con-temporaries (first within the family, but especially at school) become more and more numerous and acquire a growing genetic importance quite distinct from his relationships with adults, a schematic table of which we have just provided. Now let us take up the same three subdivisions again, but this time connecting intellectual relationships to social relationships in general.

A. General and intellectual relationships

In Section I above, we asserted that the socialization of the child is progressive and is effected in steps. We based that assertion solely on the fact that social traits are acquired from the outside and not through hereditary or internal transmission. From this it follows that if the hypothesis of a slow progression is correct, in studying the social relationships of children among themselves (a situation where the child is left to his own devices and is not confined and guided as he is with adults), one should find beginning phases where collaboration among children is not yet possible since children lack the instruments necessary for coordination.

The social and intellectual egocentrism of the first years

In studies of inter-child relationships, three possibilities have to be distinguished and observation and experiment must impose a choice among them. The first possibility consists in considering the child as a kind of *tabula rasa* upon which the social environment deposits its contributions bit by bit. This hypothesis is difficult to maintain once one establishes the intricate sensory-motor elaboration [p. 342] of conduct already in place when verbal exchanges and representation begin. By contrast, the second hypothesis consists in considering the child as an independent individual whose formation is regulated by internal maturation and particular experience and who, after making contact subsequently with his contemporaries, elaborates a certain number of new links superimposed on his individual traits and constituting his social life. This is the interpretation of common sense and, as well, of Rousseau codified in the doctrine of *Emile* and in his *Social contract*. But it disregards what sociology has taught us about the role of collective influence in the formation of mental functions. The third solution is that mental life is constructed in conjunction with the group. Because, on this view, instruments of exchange as well as internal representative connections must be constructed starting from what is given or acquired sensory-motorically, there would at first be non-differentiation of social and individual contributions. Only later would there be coordination. This means that points of view would at first be confused and that only later would they be differentiated and connected in orderly fashion.

How, then, shall we designate the level where points of view are confused? To call it subjectivism would evoke the idea of a previously constructed individual subject who is only socialized after the fact. To stress his absorption into the group would evoke the opposite interpretation. We have, therefore, spoken of egocentrism, defining this term as a lack of differentiation of the self from its surroundings. More precisely, from the perspective of epistemology, progress in coordinating points of view always involves decentration with respect to the initial point of view. We have, therefore, stressed more than anything else the deforming centration present at the start and have spoken of egocentrism by analogy with anthro-pocentrism, etc. Unfortunately, words being stronger than definitions in psychology, people have often taken what we have said about egocentrism in the everyday and affective sense of the term which makes everything we said false. Whence a certain number of futile discussions. That is of little consequence if one agrees on the facts, however. What Wallon called the syncretism of early childhood (after a term borrowed from Claparède), is, for example, very close to egocentrism as we used the term; and a number of authors who opposed our conception accept decentration which amounts to the same thing.

With this in mind, let us examine the facts with regard to the three hypotheses. Three categories of data may be mentioned. These are data relative to notions implying reciprocity, data relative to behaviour itself, and finally data relative to language. [p. 343]

As far as notions implying reciprocity are concerned, it is striking that in every case where such notions imply a coordination of viewpoints, the subject's own point of view initially holds sway. Let us take as an example a young child who is presented with a scale model representing three mountains or three buildings (fashioned in such a way that there is an obvious change in the relative positions of the objects when they are viewed from the four different sides of the model). The child occupies perspective 1; the experimenter occupies perspective 3; and the child is asked to select drawings that best depict what the experimenter sees. In this situation, young children respond by showing drawings from perspective 1 because they see things from that perspective. If the child and the experimenter now trade positions so that the child occupies perspective 3 and the experimenter occupies 1, the child will show drawings from perspective 3 as the drawing corresponding to what the experimenter sees. To take another spatial example, usually a child of 4 years (on average) can show you his right and left hands when asked to do so. It is, however, necessary to wait until he is 7 for him to be able to point to the right and left hands of a person facing him. Again, this is because he remains fixed on his own point of view and considers it absolute. A further example is provided by the fact that a young subject who has a brother will say that his brother does not have a brother because there are only two in the family. From these different situations, it is obvious that intellectual or cognitive egocentrism has nothing to do with a hypertrophy of the self. In the case of brothers, the subject even forgets himself! Rather, it has merely to do with the unconscious primacy of the subject's own point of view, lacking discovery of the diversity of viewpoints and, even more, lacking the ability to coordinate them.[4]

It will perhaps be said that this coordination is not brought about for want of the necessary intellectual operations, since it occurs at the level between

7 and 12 years in concert with the constitution of 'concrete' logical operations. But we have already seen that these operations, although (or because!) they are prepared by the coordination of actions (starting as early as the sensory-motor level), are in no way independent of social life. The internal operations of the individual and the interpersonal coordination of points of view constitute a single and same reality, at once intellectual and social. And it is the same for the intellectual egocentrism of the pre-operatory level and social egocentrism. [p. 344]

In effect, the epistemic egocentrism of which we just gave examples is only the expression of corresponding processes on the behavioural plane. In this regard, one can either cite facts derived from direct observations or from experiments. Among the former, the easiest to study is the behaviour of youngsters in collective games, especially in games with rules such as the previously cited game of marbles. After 7 years of age, players correctly coordinate their games and make an effort to follow the same rules (albeit variable) throughout a single game. By contrast, younger children each play for themselves without concern for the rules of their neighbours. When one asks who won, they are, therefore, generally astonished, as if everyone won at the same time (meaning that everyone succeeded according to his own idea, not that he submitted to a regulated competition).

With regard to experiments, one can, as Ruth Nielsen did, study children's behaviour in situations where they can either act alone or in collaboration (constructions, drawings, etc.) and elicit occasions that should, in principle, favour collaboration. For example, one might use a table too small to allow each member of a group to construct something individually or use a blackboard too small for each one to draw on or, especially, use a table where there is room enough for two to draw but with their pencils tied to one another by a string that passes through a ring fastened to the table. Each of these techniques ends in the same results. In every case, there is a gradual transition from egocentric non-coordination to gradual collaboration, generally with relatively more rapid modification between 6½ and 8 years. ('Solitary' constructions were seen 70 per cent of the time in children aged between 5½ and 6½, but only 1.7 to 3.2 per cent of the time in children aged 6½ to 8½ years old; solitary drawings were seen 63 per cent of the time in children aged 6½ to 7½ years and 26 per cent of the time in 7½ to 8½ year olds.)

Language

If such is the evolution of spontaneous and elicited behaviour, one can expect to find an analogous development on the plane of language. Long ago, we did three studies on this. In those studies we divided children's statements into socialized language (questions and answers, information, etc.) and egocentric language (monologues and 'collective monologues' where everyone speaks for himself without bothering with others' responses although stimulated by others' presence). First, in a single scholastic environment (Maison des Petits in Geneva), we found a quite clear progression in socialized language with age. Second, [p. 345] the study of conversations among children led to an analogous conclusion. Specifically, we saw a transition from so-called primitive discussions (contradictory affirmations without justification) to true discussions (with justifications and the beginning of proofs). Third, the analysis of explanations given by one child to another (concerning making a mechanism understood by means of a drawing) demonstrates the initial difficulty the child has in placing himself at the point of view of the partner who does not yet understand; adapted communication progresses only gradually. The first of these studies gave rise to numerous verifications in many other countries. It also gave rise to many opposing findings from which today it is easy to draw two lessons.

The first lesson, which is not of any interest, is that frequently the term 'egocentrism' is taken in a sense different from ours, i.e. in the sense of simply speaking about oneself (which can be done in a socialized fashion!).[5]

The second lesson, and the only one of interest, is that the simple division of statements into egocentric and socialized language varies considerably with the environment according to the degree to which the adult intervenes, etc. Naturally, egocentric statements increase with symbolic play (which is an assimilation of objects to momentary subjective interests); they decrease with work, etc. In the USSR, Vygotsky[13] and Luria have taken the egocentric monologue of the child as the starting point for the adult's internal language. This seems quite correct but does not explain primitive social non-coordination. The most important thing, however, is that even if the percentage of egocentric statements does not provide as stable an index as we had hoped, the analysis of discussions as well as explanations among children yields much more certain results. The verifications proposed by Ruth Nielsen on the plane of action itself in order to verify our hypotheses on language demonstrate a much more significant convergence than the comparison of language alone in different environments. [p. 346]

The steps in socialization and their relationship to operatory reversibility

In a series of previous prefigurations (partially socialized behaviours are found at all levels from the moment language begins) but especially starting around 7 or 8 years on average, one witnesses systematic progress in the direction of cooperation. This is demonstrated by the spontaneous evolution of games with rules, psychological experiments using tasks to be accomplished in groups, and pedagogical experiments on work done by teams at school.

A question that has frequently occupied researchers from Varendonck's very early work on children's societies up to recent investigations is the question of 'leaders' (we shall return to this in Section III B). Recent unpublished research by B. Inhelder and G. Noelting shows that if the individual temperaments of leaders surely play a role, that role becomes more and more subordinated to a function. In fact, by about 11 or 12 years of age a person with a dominating character is only fully employed by the group if he serves a specialized function that, in fact, is subordinated to over-arching organization.

From the sociological viewpoint, one of the most interesting aspects of the development of cooperation among children is its interdependence with the progressive emergence of logical operations. These operations consist of the concrete and the formal operations. The former begin about 7 to 8 years of age (and bear on objects that the child manipulates or can manipulate). The latter appear around 11 or 12 and correspond to the propositional logic. That logic is based on lattice structures and, therefore, on combinations, in addition to the group of inversions and reciprocities. Intellectual operations constitute internalized actions that are reversible. (On the concrete level, this reversibility is accomplished either by inversion or by reciprocity; on the formal level, it is accomplished by both at once.) In addition, operations are coordinated into over-arching structures. (These are the elementary *groupements* seen between 7 and 12 years and the lattice and group of four transformations seen from 11 or 12 onward.) With all of this in mind, it easy to understand that there must be a close kinship between cooperation or interpersonal actions and the intra-personal coordination of actions and operations.

From this point of view, intellectual egocentrism characterized by difficulties of decentration can, in a general way, be considered as the expression of the young child's pre-operative structures of thought. In particular, decentration manifests [p. 347] the irreversibility of that form of thought (which we have noted since 1923),[14] while progress in cooperation, along with the decentration and the reciprocity that it implies, would be correlative to operatory reversibility and, therefore, to the very constitution of these operations.

This raises the question already mentioned under Section II A of whether it is the intellectual development of operations that makes possible and explains the social development of cooperation or whether the opposite is true. Now, cooperation, in itself, constitutes a system of co-operations, i.e. of putting the operations of one partner into correspondence with those of others (which is itself an operation), of forming a union (which is another operation) of one partner's intellectual acquisitions with those of others, etc. Moreover, in the case of conflict, it includes removing contradictions (which presupposes another operatory process) and, most importantly, of differentiating distinct points of view and introducing reciprocity among them (which is an operatory transformation).

The question reduces, therefore, to knowing whether it is the interpersonal operations of cooperation that engender the intra-personal operations proper to the coordination of actions (and, therefore, to logic) or whether it is the inverse, it being understood that it is a matter of the same operations. This identity, then, makes the problem disappear. It is one and the same evolutionary process, both social and individual; it is one and the same general coordination of actions with external exchanges between individuals as well as internal exchanges in the course of trial and error and the unfolding of action that simultaneously takes account of both the interpersonal and the intra-personal aspects, because such aspects are inseparable. If one poses the problems of the relationship between logic and society by, on the one hand, only considering the coercive 'collective consciousness' and, on the other, by only considering the child as a *tabula rasa* to be socialized without any connection between sensory-motor and logical structures, the problem remains indefinitely complex. If, however, one examines the developing child from dual aspects of the sensory-motor and the social (in the sense of cooperation and not only of coercive transmissions from adults to children), the problem is simplified to the point of disappearing.

B. Affective relationships

In the last several years, affective relationships among children have been studied a great deal, first under the inspiration of K. Lewin and then [p. 348] in the wake of studies by J. L. Moreno. In the context of curiously confused general ideas, Moreno provided techniques responsive to experimental verification or, in other words, utilizable independently of all prior inter-pretation (all precautions taken and disengaging oneself *a priori* from the author himself). Another important source of information relevant to the relationship between hereditary structure and social acquisition are the twin studies, a notable model of which has been provided by R. Zazzo.

As everyone knows, K. Lewin was influenced by gestalt theory from which he borrowed the notion of 'field' but by broadening it to include affective phenomena. Thus, the 'total field' includes objects whose desirable charac-ter[6] depends as much on the field itself as it does on the subject. The total field also includes the subject whose positive drives are determined by the desirability of the objects in the field and whose negative ones are determined by various psychic barriers interposed between the subject and objects by the group through its imperatives and prohibitions. Lewin, who was passionate about mathematics, sought to describe the structure of the field in topological terms, but a subjective topology remote from pure geometry. What was perhaps more productive was his attempt to analyse the total field in the language of the theory of graphs. This attempt is without doubt the origin of the 'sociograms' subsequently utilized by sociometry. In Section III C below, we shall give an example of the research of the Lewinian school done by R. Lippitt which is especially concerned with moral structures.

Of Rumanian origin, Moreno studied medicine in Vienna before establishing himself in the United States. Moreno was inspired by metaphysical considerations having to do with spontaneous creativity. (Comparing small matters to great, just as one can retain Kepler's laws and forget his mystical beliefs, one can easily abstract out Moreno's metaphysical considerations.) In any case, Moreno furnished two techniques that have had increasing success. They are applicable to the study of social relationships among children (as well as to relationships between adults and children). These techniques are psychodrama or collective symbolic play and sociometric tests intended to measure group cohesion.

Beginning with the latter, Moreno set himself to forge a new measuring instrument for social psychology, the statistics used in individual psychology being unusable in the latter area. In addition, he proposed to study groups even in their spontaneity, [p. 349] or in other words, in the course of their development without limiting hindrances or instructions imposed by the investigator. The method, then, essentially consists in learning from every subject who are the members of the group with whom that subject would like to associate in one or another situation. This establishes a hierarchy of attractions as a function of situational criteria. One also learns those members with whom the subject would not like to associate, which establishes a hierarchy of repulsions as a function of the same criteria. In general, three or four different criteria are freely chosen in function of the life of the group (lived knowledge) and, as far as possible, independent of cultural influences foreign to group life. The results are then transcribed into a sociogram. Each individual is represented by a circle that has positive or unreciprocal connections associating it with each of the other circles according to the choices indicated. These connections constitute the 'lattice' that attaches one of the individual 'social atoms' to another. They therefore express the positive and negative feelings at play in the group (feelings Moreno called the *tele*). It is understood that they can be real or can remain potential until the moment of actual encounter.

Thus conceived, the sociometric test can, of course, be broadly developed by, on the one hand, multiplying the problems to be resolved and making them more specific (choice of criteria and modes of connection). On the other hand, such tests can be extended by perfecting the logico-mathematical analysis of sociograms (by qualitative methods based on general algebra[7] and topology and by quantitative methods, both kinds of methods being used in the theory of graphs). This is why a large number of research projects are currently oriented in this direction. Happily, these studies carefully set aside the surprising mass of pseudo-theoretical notions that Moreno hoped to impose as a necessary adjunct to his sociometrical intuition.

As things now stand and while awaiting the reconstruction of its theoretical foundations, sociometric tests have given rise to two sorts of criticism. One sort derives from general sociology (Gurvitch, Znaniecki, von Wiese, etc.); the other sort derives from experimental analysis (Zazzo and B. Reymond-Rivier). In general, people have rightly reproached Moreno for considering individuals only (as if their attractions and repulsions had an exclusively endogenous origin) and for disregarding the group as such with its [p. 350] laws of totality. In this regard, it is striking to establish how Moreno seems to disregard 'group dynamics', i.e. the set of polarizations and tendencies born of group life and not of individual 'instincts'. Examples would be establishment of a head or leader, resistance to the leader, canalization of temperaments into specific functions of the group, etc., or in other words, reactions determined by the group as much as by individual temperaments. On the other hand, Moreno has been reproached for only recognizing attractions and repulsions, although social reactions are much more differentiated, and for sticking to feelings when he speaks ceaselessly of actions. The latter considered in their respective totalities as real unities give rise to many other types of bonds between the so-called social 'atoms'. Neither can one, as Zazzo remarked, dissociate the spontaneity due to culture. One must also ask in what sense the choices subjects make in sociometric tests are actually 'spontaneous' and in which sense they are inspired by scales of values at play in the child's environment.

In an experimental study, H. H. Jennings gave sociometric tests to 493 young girls every eight weeks for two years and seven months. He observed numerous variations with permutations among the leaders and the lonely. Especially important also was the work of B. Reymond-Rivier who did controlled studies using individual tests and analysing the motivations that led to choices. Her work demonstrated that choices are not always dependent on attractions. Certain subjects chosen for some group activity as a function of particular values remained little-liked by their comrades. Moreover, Madame Reymond observed a law of evolution in motivations proceeding from heteronomy to autonomy and increasing internalization.

Psychodrama and sociodrama are therapeutic techniques and do not interest us as such. However, as group improvisations of scenes having to do with affective 'complexes' or of interpersonal conflicts of any sort, they do provide a new and instructive instrument of analysis in an area that could be very productive. In effect, we know that the symbolic thought used in the child's imaginative play and dreams initially serves the function of expressing subjective assimilations and satisfying interests by transposing reality.[15] Individual symbolism first appears in the symbolic games of children at the end of the sensory-motor period and is manifested purely through gestures before being accompanied by words.[8] Between such symbolism and the system of meanings connected with the collective signs of language, [p. 351] there are many intermediaries, the steps of which are found in the evolution of play. Although symbolic play initially owes nothing to the social group while games with rules are, by contrast, socially transmitted, there do exist symbolic games played by two or more people. In such games, roles become differentiated in the course of play and often involve minute spontaneous and momentary adjustments. These are the collective symbolic games that Moreno observed in the parks of Vienna and that inspired his first attempts at psychodrama. They are interesting because they constitute a socialization of affective aspects that are often the most intimate aspects of a subject's life. At the same time, they also constitute a socialization of symbolic thought that could lead to numerous investigations on a frontier as yet little explored.

Moreover, the therapeutic aspect of psychodrama may perhaps teach us something sociological. For those who are interested in psychoanalysis without being Freudian, the question brought up by the improvement seen in treatment is, in effect, to know whether the benefits of 'catharsis' are not due to the socialization of hidden affectivity. This is because conscious realization of the so-called unconscious domain is necessarily accompanied by and no doubt results from its 'communication'. Moreno's psychodrama gives invaluable data in this regard, and it does so, in a way, precisely because of the poverty of his theoretical apparatus (simple pleas in favour of 'spontaneity'). The therapeutic role of the socialization of individual conflicts constitutes, in effect, a weighty argument in favour of a social and cooperative interpretation of the personality.

Personality was for a long time considered to depend only on psychobiological factors. In reality, it involves multiple social factors as well and undergoes a complex evolution that is only completed during adolescence. Charles Blondel, in particular, has insisted upon the social components of the personality. He showed to what extent personality traits are linked to the role the individual plays in society or to the role that he assigns himself and that he desires to play. (Recall in this respect that *persona* designates a mask used in Greek drama.) It is at least certain that personality does not constitute a simple endpoint of the development of the 'ego' and that, in a certain sense, it is oriented in the opposite direction: it presupposes decentration of the ego which is subordinated to some social function or social hierarchy of values.[16] The formation of the 'person' raises, therefore, a problem that is far from being understood. Among possible methods of analysis that might help in teasing out the parts played by biology and by social experience, the study of monozygotic twins is of special interest. One must, however, lay aside the current prejudice that such twins are 'identical' in all respects. In the wake of rare studies putting the identity of such twins in doubt [p. 352] (that of J. von Allesch, in particular), R. Zazzo proposed a 'twin method' consisting in studying their differences and not just their similarities in order to find the roots of the personality. Now these roots are obviously social in the sense that one witness very early a polarization of the twin couple (dominances, etc.) at the same time that one sees an opposition or differentiation of that couple with respect to its surroundings.

C. Moral relationships

These remarks lead to the issue of the moral life among children (cf. above Section II C) that we shall now, again and separately, examine because of the remarkable originality of its consequences.

The mere fact that social institutions specific to childhood exist demonstrates the degree to which collective discipline can be imposed through exclusively child-to-child transmission. An example of such an institution is the game of marbles that, in certain countries, ceases at the end of primary school and does not involve the least amount of control on the part of adults or of children past the ages of 12 or 13. Now, collective discipline naturally involves a morality insofar as it concerns respect for rules, the condemnation of cheating, etc. At the same time, the sociologist Timacheff[9] has rightly reproached us for not having drawn from this game an analysis of sociology of law. It would, however, be easy to fill in this lacuna.

Mutual respect

Sticking to the moral life, the specific source of morality among children is the affective and cognitive reciprocity or 'mutual respect' that bit by bit disengages itself from unilateral respect. This starts as early as the level of concrete intellectual operations and cooperation (see above Section III A).

Mutual respect grows out of exchanges among individuals who consider one another as equals. It presupposes, first of all, an acceptance of common values, particularly with respect to exchange itself. Each of the partners appraises the others from the point of view of these values and sticks to their appraisal, so that one again finds in mutual respect [p. 353] the combination of sympathy and fear belonging to all respect. In this case, however, fear is not fear of a greater power but is reduced to fear of losing the esteem of those whom the subject, himself, esteems.

Two questions nevertheless arise with respect to such relationships. First, are they reducible to unilateral respect? And second, in what way do they differ from simple mutualism or from a reciprocity that consists in paying back evil with evil or good with good? To begin with, one might see in mutual respect a double unilateral respect, each partner estimating the other to be superior in a particular domain without having the domains overlap. However, even if this were the origin of mutual respect, the fact of reciprocity alone brings with it new values and, especially, new conduct that is quite distinct from double obedience of partners to each other. Obedience disappears and is, in fact, replaced by the autonomous observation of norms. On the other hand, the difference between our mutual respect and mutual-ism[10] is precisely that there are norms in the sense of new obligations, of which we shall speak later, and not simply complementary interests or tendencies toward non-normative reciprocity (treat others as they treat you).

Normative reciprocity and autonomous obligation

The preceding problems centre on understanding why and how mutual respect leads to obligation. The reason is that, since they accept the values of exchange upon which their reciprocal esteem is based, partners in an exchange cannot fail to apply them without contradiction. This leads to normative reciprocity. Obligation thus engendered is, therefore, quite differ-ent from unilateral submission to other people's orders and is closer to, but on affective rather than cognitive terrain, that special obligation called logical necessity or the obligation to be coherent and non-contradictory. Such obligation is distinct in essence from intellectual submission to authority or to coercive beliefs.

The principal character of moral obligation of this sort, as is the case with logical obligation as well, is its autonomy. This is meant in the sense that the subject participates in the elaboration of the norms that obligate him instead of receiving them ready-made as happens in the case of the norms of unilateral respect that lie behind heteronomous morality. The development of this autonomy is [p. 354] particularly clear in the case of the evolution of the rules of social games. Whereas young children consider rules as sacred and intangible, older children modify them without difficulty, provided there is mutual agreement. This latter is a respect for democratic norms of the common will as well as for procedure.

It is not, however, only in the very restricted area of exclusively juvenile social life that the growing autonomy of obligations is manifested. The duties and obligations imposed by adults during earlier developmental phases are also reinterpreted from the point of view of normative reciprocity and autonomy. We have seen (see above Section II C) how rules of truth are accepted by little children even before being understood. This was due to the effect of unilateral respect. During this initial stage, the child concludes, therefore, that lying is a moral fault but only with regard to adults since the order not to lie comes from them. Lying to a friend is, therefore, inoffensive. At the level of mutual respect, by contrast, children asked about this point all told us that to lie to a friend is 'much naughtier' because circumstances never force one to lie to friends whereas with big people . . .

From this reinterpretation of the rules of truth as a function of reciprocity and mutual trust flows naturally, then, a transformation of the form of responsibility. Objective responsibility, the most direct product of the heteronomy engendered by unilateral respect, will give way to subjective responsibility based on intentions alone. A lie will, therefore, no longer be evaluated except in terms of the motivation behind it. That, we say, is a natural consequence of the autonomy acquired by the moral conscience.

Justice

The most authentic products of reciprocal morality are the construction of distributive justice and the tendency to moderate retributive justice in the name of fairness.

Very early on, fair parents can impose an example of distributive justice on their children and enforce it by adequate commands. It nevertheless remains that there is latent conflict between justice based on the idea of equality and the very authority that eventually represents it. We are not referring to the injustices every parent involuntarily commits and to which the child is particularly sensitive. Authority leads to obedience without leading to correlative rights, whereas justice leads to a balance of obligations and rights [p. 355] that is all the more exact because the right of one of the partners is identically equal to the other's obligation. From this, it results that it is, before all else, in relationships among equals that the child discovers the sense of justice. Moreover, when he is the victim of or witness to injustice, he quite often discovers it at the expense of the adult rather than under adult pressure.

It is as easy to verify this hypothesis by observing the spontaneous social life of children as it is by a direct analysis of moral judgments relative to the idea of justice. The first of these methods demonstrates up to what point the feeling of justice extends in play groups: equality before the rules with special provisions for small children playing with older ones, e.g. different distances marbles must be 'shot', rules dividing winnings, arbitration in case of conflicts, etc. The second method demonstrates that in cases of conflict between distributive justice and adult authority, the former always has precedence after 7 or 8, even though the child may externally obey. Furthermore, judgments in regard to retributive justice are more and more nuanced, frequently placing in doubt the very value of punishment and in all cases subordinating literal observations to considerations of fairness.

Cooperation and authority

These diverse facts lead to the conclusion that cooperation among children constitutes a relatively rich source of moral realities and that adult authority is far from representing the only factor generating values and norms in this domain.

One can cite two types of experiments verifying these conclusions. One sort of experiment was conducted by R. Lippitt, among many others, who spent a year at our institute in Geneva before becoming the disciple of K. Lewin. Lippitt organized a study comparing three groups of schoolchildren of 11 years old. One group was organized 'autocratically' where discipline was imposed by the teacher. Another was organized 'democratically', with organization effected by the children in free consultation with the teacher. And a third group was purely 'laisser-faire'. Subjects in the second group surpassed the others, particularly in the decrease of aggressivity and maintenance of habits of collaboration long after the experiment was over.

A second type of experiment attempted by a number of educators in different countries and under diverse conditions (normal situations, re-education of young delinquents in reform schools, refugee camps, or war orphans, etc.) had to do with attempts at [p. 356] self-government[17] bearing either on certain aspects of or on the whole of the students' collective life. These applications, whose pedagogical significance has been closely studied, cannot be discussed here. They are, however, of great psychosociological interest because they demonstrate the possibilities as well as the limitations of childhood social life and morality.

AUTHOR'S NOTES

[1] This acquisition appears to be linked to certain optimal ages.

[2] See Piaget, *Intelligence and afectivity: their relationship during child development*, trans. T. Brown and E. Kaegi (eds) (Palo Alto: Annual Review of Psychology Monograph, 1981) for this parallelism and an analysis of the will as a reversible affective operation.

[3] To the point, for example, that there is almost no adolescence in Samoa, according to Margaret Mead.

[4] One might well cite examples of intellectual egocentrism other than those involving non-coordination of points of view. Infantile animism and artificialism as well as 'moral causality' (confusion of physical law and obligation), etc., also constitute examples of confusion of points of view. They arise through assimilation of external data to schemes of action.

[5] On the other hand, R. Zazzo, *Les Jumeaux, le couple, et la personne* (Paris, 1960, p. 399) refuses to bring together the two meanings of egocentric language, i.e. language without rational reciprocity and language not intended for others. His argument is that one must distinguish the case where the child 'speaks for (*pour*)' himself' from the case where he 'speaks according to (*selon*) himself'. According to our definitions, an orator who forgets to place himself at the point of view of his public is, precisely, speaking for himself.

[6] 'Desirable character' is our translation of *Aufforderungscharakter* or 'character of solicitation'.

[7] In particular, the theory of networks in the algebraic sense of the term (cf. Glivenko, G. Birkhoff, etc.).

[8] For example, the first symbolic play seen in one of our children was to pretend to be sleeping (while smiling and amusing herself) and then to put her teddy bear to sleep, etc.

[9] Timacheff appears to know our work only through the control experiments of I. Caruso and for that reason is not aware that Caruso's data confirmed ours on all points except for some negligible chronological details (the order of the succession of stages constituting their only essential characteristic).

[10] In his chapter on moral feelings in Dumas' *Traité de psychologie*, M. Davy maintains that our interpretation of mutual respect reduces it to simple mutualism because it lacks any insertion into a framework of 'social constraints'. Internalization of such a framework would, Davy believes in accordance with Durkheimian tradition, suffice to explain the formation of autonomy.

TRANSLATION NOTES

1 This work first appeared under the title 'Problèmes de la psycho-sociologie de l'enfance' in G. Gurvitch (ed.), *Traité de sociologie* (Paris: Presses Universitaires de France, 1960, pp. 229–254), not in 1963 as stated in the French text.

2 The French text reads (p. 320): '*les sociétés humaines reposent presque exclusivement sur une transmission et une formation éducatives*'.

3 The French text is defective at this point and so is amended in this translation using Piaget's original paper: '*Le terme d'instinct peut être pris en deux sens: celui d'une 'tendance' héréditaire (en allemand* Trieb *opposé à* Instinkt*) et celui d'une structure d'action héréditaire (par P. Guillaume) que l'imitation s'apprend (au sens d'ailleurs d'un 'apprentissage' spontané et non pas d'une éducation, encore que celle-ci joue souvent un rôle non négligeable dans cet apprentissage)*'.

4 A maturational interpretation of Piaget's constructivism is effectively under-

mined by this claim.

5   In the French text (p. 321): *'signegestalts'*.

6   The French text reads (p. 323): *'Pour ne prendre qu'un exemple, il existe chez l'enfant une attitude dominante à l'égard de ses parents ou des adults qui l'éduquent, et qui consiste à considérer comme vrai ce qu'ils disent ainsi que comme juste ce qu'ils prescrivent (même s'il n'y a pas obéissance effective).'* Piaget has in mind the problem stated at the outset of Chapter 5, this volume, about the child's understanding of truth.

7   See Chapters 2 and 3 for a structural model of communicative exchange.

8   French, *réseau*. This term, whose standard meaning is *network*, has been translated as *lattice*. In discussions of his logical models, Piaget usually characterizes concrete operations in terms of *groupements* and *semi-treillis* (*lattice*) structures. Since *treillis* are a special form of *réseau*, *lattice* is appropriate. However, Piaget sometimes refers to the *réseau* of kinship relations, where *lattice* may be less appropriate than *network*. See also J. Piaget *et al.*, *Morphisms and categories* (Hillsdale, NJ: Erlbaum, 1992).

9   See Chapter 6, this volume.

10 See J. Piaget, *Intelligence and affectivity* (Palo Alto, CA: Annual Reviews, 1980).

11 See J. Piaget, *Recherche* (Lausanne: Édition La Concorde, 1918).

12 See Chapter 7, this volume.

13 For Piaget's reaction to Vygotsky's interpretation of his work, see J. Piaget, 1962, 'Comments on Vygotsky's critical remarks concerning "The language and thought of the child" and "Judgment and reasoning in the child"' (Cambridge, MA: MIT Press). Partially reprinted in L. S. Vygotsky, *Thought and language*, trans. E. Hanfmann and G. Vakar (eds), (Cambridge MA: MIT Press).

14 Piaget provides no reference. No doubt he is referring to *Le Langage et la pensée chez l'enfant* (Neuchâtel: Delachaux et Niestlé, 1923). In English, *The language and thought of the child*, trans. M. Gabain (New York: World Publishing, 1955).

15 Piaget uses the word *'réel'* in re-addressing the problem which is stated in the first paragraph of Chapter 1 of his book – originally published in 1923 – *The language and thought of the child* (London: Routledge & Kegan Paul, 1959).

16 See Chapters 2 and 3, this volume.

17 Piaget uses the English term.

Select bibliography

Études sociologiques includes Piaget's references to specific texts: (JP) has been added in the list below at the end of the citation of all such references. Piaget also made many references to authors without indicating a corresponding text. It is in consequence not entirely clear which texts Piaget had in mind in such cases. In *Sociological studies*, a selective list of supporting references is included, subject to the limitation noted in the previous sentence. These supporting references are typically confined to one text per author and to an English edition. Even though in some cases the reference has a date of publication later than the date of original publication of Piaget's paper, the anachronism is more apparent than real.

ABRAHAM, K. (1913) *Dreams and myths*, New York: Journal of Nervous and Mental Diseases.

AHRENS, R. (1954) 'Beitrage zur Entwicklung des Physiognomie und Mimikerkenntnix', *Zeitschrift für experimentelle und angewandte Psychologie*, 2, 414–454, 599–633.

ALLESCH, G. J. von (1953) *Die Bedeutung der Psychologie im öffentlichen Leben*, Cologne: Westdeutscher Verlag.

BACHELARD, G. (1941) *Le Nouvel esprit scientifique*, Paris: Presses Universitaires de France.

BALDWIN, J. M. (1895) *Mental development in the child and race*, New York: Macmillan.

BALDWIN, J. M. (1902) *Development and evolution*, London: Macmillan.

BALDWIN, J. M. (1911a) *The individual and society, or psychology and sociology*, Boston: Badger.

BALDWIN, J. M. (1911b) *Thought and things, or genetic logic*, 3 vols, London: Sonnenschein, Lowrey & Co.

BALLY, C. (1935) *La Langage et la vie*, Zurich: Niehans.

BARRES, M. (1905) *Le Culte du moi*, Paris: Fontemoing.

BENEDICT, R. (1935) *Patterns of culture*, London: Routledge & Kegan Paul.

BERGSON, H. (1911) *Creative evolution*, London: Macmillan [original publication in 1907].

BIRKHOFF, G. and MacLANE, S. (1953) *A survey of modern algebra*, New York: Macmillan.

BLONDEL, C. (1914) *La Conscience morbide, essai de psychologie générale*, Paris: Alcan.

BOSSARD, H. S. and BOLL, E. S. (1960) *The sociology of child development*, 3rd edition. New York. (JP)

BOVET, P. (1912) 'Les Conditions de l'obligation', *Année psychologique*.

BOVET, P. (1927) *Le Sentiment religieux et la psychologie de l'enfant*, Paris.

BROOKOVER, N. B. (1955) *A sociology of education*, New York. (JP)

BUHLER, C. (1930) *The first year of life*, New York: John Day & Co.

CARNAP, R. (1937) *The logical syntax of language*, London: Routledge & Kegan Paul.

CARUSO, I. A. (1952) *Psychoanalyse und Synthese der Existenz*, Vienna: Herder Verlag.

CHILD, I. L. (1954) 'Socialisation', in G. Lindzey (ed.) *Handbook of social psychology*, Cambridge. (JP)

CLAPAREDE, E. (1913) *Experimental pedagogy and the psychology of the child*, London: Arnold [original publication in 1905].

CLAPAREDE, E. (1931) *L'Éducation fonctionnelle*, Neuchâtel: Delachaux et Niestlé.

COMTE, A. (1857) *The positive philosophy of Auguste Comte*, 6 vols, New York: Chapman [original publication 1830–1842].

DAVIS, A. (1948) *Social class influence upon learning*, Cambridge. (JP)

DEBESSE, M. (1948) *La Crise d'originalité juvénile*, 3rd edition, Paris. (JP)

DELACROIX, H. (1934) *Les Grandes Formes de la vie mentale*. Paris: Alcan.

DESCARTES, R. (1931) *Philosophical works*, 2 vols, New York: Dover.

DUGUIT, L. (1901) *L'État, le droit objectif et la loi positive*, Paris: Fontemoing.

DUMAS, G. (1924) *Traité de psychologie*, 2 vols, Paris.

DURKHEIM, E. (1915) *The elementary forms of the religious life*, London: Allen & Unwin.

DURKHEIM, E. (1956) *Sociology and philosophy*, New York: Free Press [original publication in 1938].

DURKHEIM, E. (1961) *Moral education*, New York: Free Press [original publication in 1925].

EINSTEIN, A. (1956) *The meaning of relativity*, Princeton: Princeton University Press.

ELIASBERG, W. (1925) 'Psychologie und Pathologie der Abstraktion', *Zeitschrift für angewandte Psychologie*, Beiheft 35, Leipzig: Barth.

ELIASBERG, W. (1959) *Psychotherapy and sociology*, New York: Philosophical Library.

ERIKSON, E. H. (1950) *Childhood and society*, New York, French translation, Neuchâtel, 1959. (JP)

ESPINAS, A. (1935) *Des Sociétés animales: étude de psychologie comparée*, Paris: Alcan.

ESSERTIER, D. (1927) *Psychologie et sociologie*, Paris: Alcan.

FAUCONNET, P. (1920) *La Responsabilité*, Paris: Alcan.

FREUD, S. (1950) *Totem and taboo*, London: Routledge & Kegan Paul [original publication in 1917].

FREUD, S. (1962) *The ego and the id*, London: The Hogarth Press [original publication in 1923].

von FRISCH, K. (1967) *The dance language and orientation of bees*, Cambridge, MA: Harvard University Press.

FROMM, E. (1951) *The forgotten language: an introduction to the understanding of dreams*, New York: Holt.

GIROD, R. (1953) *Attitudes collectives et relations humaines: tendances actuelles des sciences sociales américaines*, Paris: Presses Universitaires de France.

GLIVENKO, V. (1938) *Théorie générale des structures*, Paris: Hermann.

GOBLOT, E. (1918) *Traité de logique*, Paris: Colin.

GOETHE, J. W. von (1882–85) *Goethe Werke*, 4 vols, Stuttgart: Deutsche Verlagsanstalt.

GOLDMANN, L. (1947) *La Communauté humaine et l'universe de Kant*, Paris: Presses Universitaires de France.

GOLDMANN, L. (1966) *Jean Piaget et les sciences sociales*, Geneva: Droz.

GOLDMANN, L. (1969) *The human sciences and philosophy*, London: Cape [original publication in 1966].
GRANET, M. (1987) *Il linguaggio dei sentimenti*, Milano: Adelphi.
GROOS, K. (1896) *Die Spiele der Tiere*, Jena: Fischer.
GROOS, K. (1904) *Das Seelenleben des Kindes*, Berlin: Reuther.
GROTIUS, H. (1814) *The right of war and peace*, London: Boothroyd [original publication between 1583–1645].
GUILLAUME, E. (1944) *L'Importance économique de l'assurance sur la vie, la prévoyance économique et familiale à travers les ages*, Neuchâtel: La Baconnière.
GUILLAUME, P. (1927a) *L'Imitation chez l'enfant*, Paris: Presses Universitaires de France.
GUILLAUME, P. (1927b) *La Psychologie de la forme*, Paris: Flammarion.
GUISAN, F. (1931) *Le Danger des fictions juridiques*. Lausanne: F. Rouge.
GURVITCH, G. (1960) *Traité de sociologie*, 3 vols, Paris: Presses Universitaires de France.
HALL, S. (1921) *Aspects of child life and education*, New York: Appleton & Co.
HAVIGHURST, R. J. and TABA, H. (1949) *Adolescent character and personality*, New York. (JP)
HEGEL, G. W. F. (1949) *The phenomenology of mind*, London: George Allen & Unwin [original publication in 1807].
HÖLDERLIN, F. (1946–85) *Sämtliche Werke*, 8 vols, Stuttgart: Kohlhammen.
HUBERT, R. and MAUSS, M. (1909) *Mélanges d'histoire des religions*, Paris: Alcan.
HUSSERL, E. (1970) *Logical investigations*, 2 vols, London: Routledge & Kegan Paul [second edition original publication in 1913].
IZOULET, J. (1896) *La Cité moderne: métaphysique de la sociologie*, Paris: Alcan.
JENNINGS, H. (1962) *Behaviour of lower organisms*, Bloomington, Indiana: Indiana University Press [original publication in 1906].
JERUSALEM, W. (1924) 'Die soziologische Bedingtheit des Denkens und der Denkformen', in M. Scheler (ed.) *Versuche zu einer Soziologie des Wissens*, Muenchen.
KAILA, E. (1932) 'Die Reaktionen des Sauglings auf das menschliche Gesicht', *Annales Universitatis Abönsis*, 17, 1–114.
KANT, I. (1933) *Critique of pure reason*, 2nd edition. London: Macmillan [original publication in 1787].
KANT, I. (1948) *Groundwork of the metaphysics of morals*, in H. Paton (ed.) *The moral law*, London: Hutchinson [original publication in 1791].
KELSEN, H. (1991) *Pure theory of law*, in B. Paulson and S. Paulson (1991) *Introduction to the problems of legal theory*, Oxford: Oxford University Press [original publication in 1934].
KEPLER, J. (1965) Kepler's conversations with Galileo's sidereal messenger, New York: Johnson Reprint Corp [original publication in 17th century].
KIRK, G. and RAVEN, J. (1960) *The pre-Socratic philosophers*, Cambridge: Cambridge University Press.
KOEHLER, W. (1924) *Gestalt psychology*, New York: Liveright.
KOEHLER, W. (1927) *The mentality of apes*, London: Routledge & Kegan Paul [original publication in 1925].
KUO, Z. (1967) *The dynamics of behaviour development: an epigenetic view*, New York: Random House.
LALANDE, A. (1913) *Lectures sur la philosophie des sciences*, Paris: Hachette.
LALANDE, A. (1963) *La Psychologie des jugements de valeur*, 2nd edition. Paris: Hachette.
LEVI-STRAUSS, C. (1970) *Introduction to a science of mythology* 4 vols., London: Cape [original publication in 1964–1968].

LEVY-BRUHL, L. (1905) *Ethics and moral science*, London: Constable [original publication in 1903].
LEVY-BRUHL, L. (1923) *Primitive mentality*, New York: Macmillan [original publication in 1922].
LEWIN, K. (1964) *Field theory in social science*, New York: Harper & Row.
LIPPITT, R. and WHITE, R. (1960) *Autocracy and democracy: an experimental inquiry*, New York: Harper & Row.
LORENZ, K. (1959) *King Solomon's ring*, London: Pan.
LORENZ, K. (1959) *Methods of approach to the problems of behaviour*, New York: Academic Press.
LUKÁCS, G. (1971) *History and class consciousness*, London: Merlin Press.
LUKÁCS, G. (1972) *Political writings 1919–29*, London: NLB.
LURIA, A. R. (1959) *Speech: the development of mental powers in the child*, London: Staples.
LURIA, A. R. (1976) *Language and cognition: its cultural and social foundations*, Cambridge, MA: Harvard University Press.
MAISTRE, J. de (1965) *The works of Joseph de Maistre*, London: Allen & Unwin.
MALINOWSKI, B. (1926) *Myth in primitive psychology*, New York: Norton.
MALINOWSKI, B. (1948) *Magic, science and religion*, New York: Free Press.
MANNOURY, G. (1947) *Les Fondements psycho-linguistiques des mathématiques*, Neuchâtel: Editions du Griffon.
MARX, K. (1970) *Theses on Feuerbach*, Reprinted in *Karl Marx: collected works*, volume 5, London: Lawrence & Wishart [original publication in 1845].
MARX, K. *Capital: a critique of political economy*, 3 vols., London: Lawrence & Wishart [original publication in 1867–1879].
MAUSS, M. (1960) *Sociologie et anthropologie*, Paris: Presses Universitaires de France.
MEAD, M. (1943) *Coming of age in Samoa*, Harmondsworth: Penguin Books.
MERLEAU-PONTY, M. (1962) *Phenomenology of perception*, London: Routledge & Kegan Paul.
MEYERSON, E. (1930) *Identity and reality*, London: Allen & Unwin [original publication in 1907].
MEYERSON, E. (1931) *Du Cheminement de la pensée*, 3 vols., Paris: Alcan.
MICHELSON, A. A. and MORLEY, E. W. (1887) *American Journal of Science*, 34, 333.
MOORE, C. B. and COLE, W. E. (1952) *Sociology in educational practice*, Cambridge. (JP)
MORENO, J. L. (1943) *Sociometry and the social order*, New York: Beacon House.
NIELSEN, R. F. (1951) *Le Développement de la socialité chez l'enfant*, Neuchâtel. (JP)
NOELTING, G. (1958) 'Combinations of colourless and coloured chemical bodies', in Inhelder, B. and Piaget, J. *The growth of logical thinking*, London: Routledge & Kegan Paul.
OLERON, P. (1969) 'Intellectual activities', in P. Fraisse and J. Piaget (eds) *Experimental psychology: its scope and method*, London: Routledge & Kegan Paul.
PARETO, V. (1963) *A treatise of general sociology*, 4 vols., New York: Dover [original publication in 1916–1923].
PARMENIDES in G. Kirk and J. Raven (eds) (1960) *The pre-Socratic philosophers*, Cambridge: Cambridge University Press.
PASCAL, B. (1989) *Pascal: selections*, New York: Collier Macmillan.
PASCAL, B. (1961) *Pensées*, Harmondsworth: Penguin [original publication in 1670].
PERELMAN, C. (1963) *Cours de logique*, Bruxelles: Presses Universitaires de Bruxelles.

PETRAZYCKI, L. (1955) *Law and morality*, in H. Babb (1955) *Law and morality: Leon Petrazycki*, Cambridge, MA [original publication in 1909].

PIAGET, J. (1930) *Le Langage et la pensée chez l'enfant*, 2nd edition, Neuchâtel & Paris: Delachaux et Niestlé. In English, (1959) *The language and thought of the child*, third edition, trans. M. Gabain, New York: World. (JP)

PIAGET, J. (1932) *Le Jugement moral chez l'enfant*, Paris: Alcan. In English, (1965) *The moral judgment of the child*, trans. M. Gabain, New York: Free Press. (JP)

PIAGET, J. (1951) 'La Pensée égocentrique et la pensée sociocentrique', *Cahiers internationaux de sociologie*, vol. X, Paris. (See translation, this volume.) (JP)

PIAGET, J. (1959) *La naissance de l'intelligence chez l'enfant*, 3rd edition, Neuchâtel & Paris: Delachaux et Niestlé. In English, (1952) *Origins of intelligence in children*, trans. M. Cook, New York: International Universities Press. (JP)

PUFENDORF, S. (1698) *De Jure naturae et gentium*, 8 vols, Amsterdam: Wolters.

RAUH, F. (1903) *L'Expérience morale*, Paris: Alcan.

REYMOND, A. (1932) *Les Principes de la logique et la critique de la connaissance*, Paris: Boivin.

REYMOND-RIVIER, B. (1960) *Choix sociométriques et motivation*, Neuchâtel. (JP)

RIPERT, G. (1927) *Droit civil*, Paris: Cours de Droit.

de ROBERTY, G. (1904) *Etudes sur la philosophie morale*, Paris: Alcan.

ROGUIN, E. (1923) *La Science juridique pure*, Paris: Librairie générale de droit et de juridique.

ROUSSEAU, J-J. (1911) *Emile*, London: Dent [original publication in 1762].

ROUSSEAU, J-J. (1913) *The social contract*, London: Dent [original publication in 1762].

RUBBINS, F. C. (1953) *Educational sociology*. New York. (JP)

SAGERET, E. (1928) *Essais de philosophie synthétique*, Paris: Alcan.

SARTRE, J-P. (1958) *Being and nothingness*, London: Methuen, 1958 [originally published in 1943].

SARTRE, J-P. (1976) *Critique of dialectical reason*, vol. 1. London: New Left Books [original publication in 1960].

SAUSSURE, F. de (1960) *Course in general linguistics*, London: Peter Owen [original publication in 1916].

SEILLERE, E. (1927) 'L'Enfance de l'homme et du genre humain', in E. Seillère (ed.) *Pour le centenaire du romantisme: un examen du conscience*, Paris: Librairie Ancienne Edouard Champion.

SIMMEL, G. (1980) *Essays on interpretation in social science*. Ottawa: N. Rowman & Littlefield.

SPENCER, H. (1885) *Principles of sociology*, London: Williams & Norgate.

SPENCER, H. (1929) *Education*, London: Watts & Co.

SPITZ, R. (1965) *The first year of life*, New York: International Universities Press.

SULLIVAN, H.S. (1953) *The interpersonal theory of psychiatry*. New York: Norton.

TARDE, G. (1911) *Les Lois de l'imitation*, Paris: Alcan.

THALES in G. Kirk and J. Raven (eds) (1960) *The pre-Socratic philosophers*, Cambridge: Cambridge University Press.

THURNWALD, R. (nd) *Psychologie des primitiven Menschen*, Muenchen.

THURNWALD, R. (1932) *Economics in primitive communities*, Oxford: Oxford University Press.

TIMACHEFF, N. (1967) *Sociological theory*, New York: Random House.

TINBERGEN, N. (1951) *The study of instinct*, Oxford: Oxford University Press.

TINBERGEN, N. (1953) *Social behaviour in animals*, London: Methuen.

VARENDONCK, R. (1912) *Recherches sur les sociétés des enfants*, Bruxelles: Misch & Thron.

VARENDONCK, R. (1921) *The psychology of day-dreams*, London: George Allen & Unwin.

VYGOTSKY, L. (1978) *Mind in society*, Cambridge, MA: Harvard University Press.

VYGOTSKY, L. (1986) *Thought and language*, Cambridge, MA: MIT Press [original publication in 1934].

WALLON, H. (1942) *De l'acte à la pensée*, Paris: Flammarion.

WALLON, H. (1947) *Les Origines de la pensée chez l'enfant*, vol. I and II, Paris. (JP)

WALLON, H. (1949a) *Les Origines du caractère chez l'enfant*, 2nd edition, Paris. (JP)

WALLON, H. (1949b) *Etude psychologique et sociologique de l'enfant*, Paris: Presses Universitaires de France.

WALLON, H. (1951) 'Sociologie et éducation', *Cahiers internationaux de sociologie*, vol. X, Paris. (JP)

WALLON, H. (1954) 'Les Milieux, les groupes et la psychologie de l'enfant', *Cahiers internationaux de sociologie*, vol. XVI, Paris. (JP)

WALLON, H. (1959) 'Psychologie et éducation de l'enfance', special edition of *Enfance*, Paris. (JP)

WALRAS, L. (1954) *Elements of pure economics*, London: Allen & Unwin [original publication in 1926].

WEISMANN, A. (1882) *Studies in the theory of descent*. New York: Marston, Searle & Livington [original publication in 1875–76].

WEISMANN, A. (1891–92) *Essays upon heredity and kindred biological problems*. Oxford: Oxford University Press [original publication in 1889].

WHITING, J. W. (1953) *Child training and personality: a cross-cultural study*, New Haven: Yale University Press.

von WIESE, L. (1950) *Systematic sociology, on the basis of the Beziehungslehre and Gebildelehre of Leopold von Wiese*, London: Wiley.

WOLF, K. M. and SPITZ, R. A. (1946) 'The smiling response: a contribution to the ontogenesis of social relations', *Genetic psychology monographs*, 34, 57–125.

ZAZZO, R. (1960) *Les Jumeaux, le couple et la personne*, Paris. (JP)

ZNANIECKI, F. (1900) *The laws of social psychology*, Chicago: University of Chicago Press.

Name index

Subject index

psychogenesis 35–6, 95
psychological explanation 32–8
psychologism 2–3, 18, 212
psychology's relation to sociology 23–9, 97
public opinion 59–60, 73
punishment 162, 164, 179

qualitative values 97–133; circulation and social equilibrium 110–13; inter-individual (and collective 108–10; exchange 100–5); laws of equilibrium of exchange 105–8; normative coordination 113–28 (legal 121–8; moral 113–21); normative equilibrium and social equilibrium 128–9; scales of values 98–100

rationality/reasoning 1–3, 139, 159; constituted and constituting 197; ideal 188; individuality and 215–16, 221–47; orthogenesis 193–4; social life 185–6, 186–9; sociocentric thought 72–3
real explanation 64–70
reciprocal imitation 234–5
reciprocity 306; genetic logic 199, 209–10; idea of homeland 249, 256–7, 260–2, 262–74, 300; individuality 220, 235, 241, 245; logical operations and social life 148–53; morality of 120–1, 127–8 (*see also* mutual respect); normative 114–18, 314–15; substitution of scales/means and ends 116, 118–19; *see also* cooperation
recognition of rights 170–3, 180
reflection 195–6; individuality 221–2, 227–9, 233–5, 239
regulation 235, 239; explanation 56–64, 65, 66; *see also* rules
relativity 221–2, 235, 264–5
religion 109, 180, 299
representational thought *see* symbolic thought
'representative particles' 193
repulsions 311–12
'residues' 50–1, 55, 77–8, 96, 110–11, 160, 184
respect 118–21, 170, 205, 298, 301, 302–3; adult–child relationships 301–3; for the aged *see* gerontocracy; morality and law 169–70, 172–3, 180; mutual *see* mutual respect; spontaneous 289–90, 302; unilateral *see* unilateral respect
restitutive sanctions 162

reversibility 139, 142, 154, 156
rhythms 56–64
rights 164–5; normative coordination of values 116–17, 121–2, 123, 129; recognition of 170–3, 180
rule systems 162, 182
rules 3, 97; children's obedience 303; constraint 208–9, 241; explanation 52–3, 61, 66; morality and law 162, 166; social games 206–7, 315; totality 42–3, 44, 45–7; *see also* obligation, norms

sacred, the 192
sanctions 162, 164
scales of values 98–100; common 108–10, 111–13, 146–53
science: collective thought 71–80; evolution 236–8
scientific experience 235–6
scientific thought 71, 280–2, 284–5, 295
self 15, 217, 218, 230, 234, 242, 298, 300–1; and individual intellect 221–7
sensory-motor period 83, 84, 139–40, 143, 276–7, 293; individuality 221–2, 228–9, 233–5; and operational thought 284–5; socialization 278–9
services 173–4
signs 52–3, 97, 202, 238; symbols and 223–4, 245; totality 42, 44–7
smiles 287, 288
social class 60, 78–9
social/educative constraint 60, 76, 200, 217; autism and 201; and cooperation 136–7, 138–9, 208–9, 219–20, 241, 244; and egocentrism 202–6; genetic logic 200; individuality 227–32, 239–40; personality 240, 241–2, 242–3
social equilibrium 110–13, 131; normative equilibrium and 128–9
social experience 6, 11; empirical under-determination 7–8
social facts 42–7
'social logic' 75–7, 137–9
social transmission *see* external transmission
socialization 217–19, 290–2; genetic logic and 184–214; language 307–8; operational development 84–5, 143–5, 276–7, 279, 284–5, 308–10; processes 278–80, 281
society, individual and 199, 210, 217–20